Formations of European Modernit

Formations of European Modernity

A Historical and Political Sociology of Europe

Gerard Delanty
University of Sussex, UK

First published 2013 by
PALGRAVE MACMILLAN

Palgrave Macmillan in the UK is an imprint of Macmillan Publishers Limited, registered in England, company number 785998, of Houndmills, Basingstoke, Hampshire RG21 6XS.

Palgrave Macmillan in the US is a division of St Martin's Press LLC, 175 Fifth Avenue, New York, NY 10010.

Palgrave Macmillan is the global academic imprint of the above companies and has companies and representatives throughout the world.

Palgrave® and Macmillan® are registered trademarks in the United States, the United Kingdom, Europe and other countries

ISBN: 978-1-137-28790-8 hardback
ISBN: 978-1-137-28791-5 paperback

This book is printed on paper suitable for recycling and made from fully managed and sustained forest sources. Logging, pulping and manufacturing processes are expected to conform to the environmental regulations of the country of origin.

A catalogue record for this book is available from the British Library.

A catalog record for this book is available from the Library of Congress.

For Aurea

Contents

Preface and Acknowledgements   ix

Introduction: A Theoretical Framework   1

Part I   Sources of the European Heritage   31

1   The European Inter-Civilizational Constellation   33

2   The Greco-Roman and Judaic Legacies   50

3   Christianity in the Making of Europe   67

4   Between East and West: The Byzantine Legacy and Russia   83

5   The Islamic World and Islam in Europe   97

Part II   The Emergence of Modernity   111

6   The Renaissance and the Rise of the West Revisited   113

7   Unity and Divisions in Early Modern European History: 130
    The Emergence of a Westernized Europe

8   The Enlightenment and European Modernity: 147
    The Rise of the Idea of Europe

9   The Rise of the Nation-State and the Allure of Empire: 169
    Between Nationalism and Cosmopolitanism

10   The Historical Regions of Europe: Civilizational   195
     Backgrounds and Multiple Routes to Modernity

11   Europe in the Short Twentieth Century: 215
     Conflicting Projects of Modernity

Part III   The Present and its Discontents   243

12   Europe since 1989: Nationalism, Cosmopolitanism and   245
     Globalization

13   Age of Austerity: Contradictions of Capitalism and   273
     Democracy

14   The European Heritage as a Conflict of Interpretations   287

Conclusion: Europe – A Defence   302

Notes   307

Bibliography   311

Index   332

Map of Europe   338

Preface and Acknowledgements

This book emerged out of an attempt to write a new edition of my earlier book, *Inventing Europe: Idea, Identity, Reality* (1995). The relative success of the book, which was translated into seven languages and widely cited, and the need to take account of significant developments within Europe and the wider world that occurred since the early 1990s seem to make a compelling case for a new edition. However, this soon became an impossible task as the direction of my own work had changed and the considerable amount of scholarship over the past two decades or so presented a challenge to some of the conceptual foundations of the book, which were primarily driven by a critique of the instrumentalization of history. So it was not simply a case of updating and revising an older work in light of changing times and new research. The result is an entirely new and longer book that offers a more comprehensive perspective on the course of European history and society than one confined to a critical history of the idea of Europe. In a more specific sense it seeks to answer the question: what is the fundamental structure of Europe? In more normative terms, I pose the questions, what are the limits and possibility of the idea of Europe in the present day?; or, how should we evaluate the European heritage today?

The following, in brief, is where I have felt it is necessary to offer a new interpretation on the question of Europe and its history.

First, it is now essential to look at Europe in both a historical and contemporary perspective from a global angle and to see it as one among many world historical regions. My earlier book, while certainly considering the global context in the historical analysis, was primarily focused on the internal dynamics of European integration as far as the present day was concerned. In this book the global perspective is more strongly emphasized both in historical and contemporary context and a greater place is given to the possibility of cosmopolitanism. In doing so, it builds on what is now a very considerable body of literature in global history that puts in new perspective the rise of the West and the relation of Europe to the so-called non-western world, a theme I explored in several publications and in particular concerning the relation between Europe and Asia. However, recourse to the global context – which needs to be more than a northern hemisphere perspective – alone is inadequate. The theoretical challenge is to combine a consideration of the global context with internal processes of development, since without such a macro-sociological account it is not possible to explain how long-term structures are formed: endogenous factors alone rarely account for societal or cultural formations, but neither do purely external accounts.

Second, following from the previous point, I am less inclined to emphasize the over-riding importance of the transnationalization of the nation-state by the EU and the coming of a new post-national community within Europe. Although there is no doubt that the Europeanization of the nation-state has been one of the most important developments of the past five decades, it cannot be regarded as the central focus for research on Europe, which is now in the throes of a crisis that calls into question some of the most important assumptions of the post-Second World War project of European integration. From a critical and normative perspective, one of the most important contributions of the project of European integration has been in the sphere of rights. This has tended to neglect the question of social justice and the problem of solidarity. The present work places a stronger emphasis on the social question in the analysis of European transformation and the need to take full account of not only the transformation of the state, but also of major economic change in the nature of capitalism, all of which have implications for democracy, social justice and solidarity.

Third, I am more sceptical today than I was in *Inventing Europe* of a constructionist approach that primarily seeks to show how notions of identity, Europe, nations etc are invented discourses; this includes the argument I made in that earlier work that Europe has always been produced out of a relation of hostility to the East and that without an external other the self had no identity. Such a position is useful for the critical purpose of unmasking the 'Grand Narratives' of history, but once this is done, and it has been done extensively, there are other and more important objectives, which cannot be easily achieved by recourse to what are fairly simplistic arguments and often polemical positions. How to take account of a more complex set of considerations, which suggest that Europe is not a single entity, has been one of the challenges in the writing of this book.

Moreover, it seems to me, that the target of a critical approach must now not only be the older Eurocentric conceptions of the European heritage, but questionable claims made in the name of the critique of Eurocentrism as well as the arrival of pernicious interpretations of history, such as the clash of civilization thesis. So a corrective measure is needed not only against the illusions that the older approaches pro-

duced, where these are still influential, but also the self-serving proclamations of relativism or of western triumphalism.

Fourth, my work over the past two decades has become more firmly
embedded in two bodies of theoretical literature, namely the social
theory of modernity and cosmopolitanism, which inevitably led to a
shift in emphasis. This book, as is suggested by the title, postulates the
centrality of modernity as the context in which to understand the
making of Europe and for making sense of its unity and diversity. As is
much discussed in recent and extensive literature, modernity is now
conceived as historically variable and is not specific to Europe, which
represents only one variant. This serves not only as a useful framework
in which to address global questions, but also as a way to understand
the internal processes and dynamics that led to the formation of
Europe as a structural reality and not only as a discourse or idea.
Moreover, it also suggests a way out of the impasse of constructionist
approaches that confine the analysis to identity and cultural constructions and makes for a firmer macro-analysis of long-term change and
continuity. An analysis that is confined to the level of an account of
the idea of Europe will provide only a limited perspective. The cosmopolitan perspective, as developed in my book *The Cosmopolitan
Imagination: The Renewal of Critical Social Theory* (2009), is also strongly
present in this book as a critical and normative position that complements the perspective on modernity.

Twenty years ago political scientists and legal scholars dominated
the study of Europe, but today the social sciences have a good deal
more to offer to the study of Europe as a world historical region. The
present work is primarily a contribution to the historical and political
sociology of Europe. The macro-sociological perspective it offers is
guided by the critical theory framework to provide a reconstruction of
historical structures of consciousness and societal formations. The aim
of such a 'critique' is to render intelligible that which is opaque in
order to reveal alternative readings of the social world and the possibilities inherent in the present. Such a work is obviously extensively
based on the work of numerous historians. Historians are concerned
largely with the particular and are sceptical of accounting for phenomena by reference to broader constructions. Where they offer wider
interpretations they do so for the non-specialized reader and rely on
the narrative structure for a unity that is otherwise not possible. The
sociological approach I have adopted seeks to place historical phenomena in wider frameworks of analysis without necessarily relying on the
form of a narrative. This is perhaps to do less justice to approaches in

historical research, since the tradition of comparative history does offer a broader framework for the interpretation of specific phenomena. However, this has been predominantly confined to specific topics and is generally understood to be methodologically restricted to comparing different societies or phenomena within a shared time frame, thus making long-run analysis of Europe difficult except in comparative terms. The rise of transnational and global history offers scope for innovation in seeing societies as interconnected. However, it does not tell us much about the emergence and transformation of the moral and political self-understandings of societies and how they engage with their past and imagine their futures. This is where sociology and history meet.

This book, inevitably given its coverage, owes a great deal to the work of others. I have been particularly influenced by the work of Johann Arnason in regard to the conception of civilizations. Peter Wagner's work on the social theory of modernity has been a considerable influence in my own thinking. Piet Strydom's cognitive approach to social theory has been hugely important. I am also very grateful to Paul Blokker, Patrick O'Mahony, Chris Rumford and Monica Sassatelli with whom I have co-authored variously on papers and books for their insights, which have both directly and indirectly helped me in developing the arguments in this book. For comments on an earlier version, I am much indebted to William Outhwaite, Monica Sassatelli and, for extensive comments on the theoretical approach, Piet Strydom.

The work has benefited greatly from discussions with Aurea Mota over the past three years of writing the book and it is to her that it is dedicated.

Gerard Delanty
Brighton and Barcelona

Introduction: A Theoretical Framework

This book seeks to provide an interpretation of the idea of Europe through an analysis of the course of European history. In order to undertake this formidable task it is necessary to clarify some of the theoretical questions that are at stake and to place the question of Europe in a broader framework of analysis. The starting point in any such study is the recognition that the facts of European history alone do not answer the question of how we should understand the shape of Europe as it formed in the course of its history and still less how we should evaluate the significance of Europe in the present day. The significance of specific events can undoubtedly be understood by reference to a shorter time-scale, but the long-term analysis that such a task requires is beset with many difficulties, leading most historians to avoid such ventures which often are sustained only by polemics or a selective reading of history. This is in part because the historian generally does not begin from the perspective of the present day, which we are forced to do so in addressing the question of the contemporary significance of the idea of Europe. But it is also because the historian is not concerned with making sense of the unintended consequences of specific events for later periods or with the developmental dynamics of societies for which a broader framework of analysis is required.

There are of course many works on the history of Europe. However, these are generally expanded national histories and often are encyclopaedic in scope, for instance Norman Davis's (1996) *Europe – A History*. Works on shorter periods generally also rely on the form of the narrative and are potentially limitless in terms of possible coverage. Major recent ones on the twentieth century are Tony Judt's *PostWar*, E. J. Hobsbawm's *The Age of Extremes* and Mark Mazower's *Dark Continent* (Judt 2005; Hobsbawm 1994; Mazower 2000). However all of these rely on narrative history and are sceptical of the usefulness of theoretical categories. The chronological form of the narrative does not offer an answer to important conceptual or normative questions, such as questions about the rise of modernity, the formation of a political heritage, the formation of a structural pattern, or the causal relation between cultural orientations and power. The solution for the historian who strays into such domains, as Tony Judt acknowledged, was the expression of the historian's own point of view on what is important. The result may have been exemplary works on modern Europe, and *PostWar* is indeed one of the finest works on Europe, but we do not get an organizing framework that renders history meaningful or a conceptual language for making sense of the past, which can only be described and recounted in chronological terms. The danger, on the other hand, with theoretically driven approaches to history is simplification and over-generalization, if not distortion. But it seems to me to be essential to distinguish between narrative or chronological history and reconstructive history, which seeks to understand how the present should relate to the past, a question that Adorno (1998) famously posed in 1959, in an essay entitled 'The Meaning of Working Through the Past?'.

The book does not offer a chronological history of Europe; nor does it attempt to provide a complete narrative account of European history. I have also resisted the temptation of polemics as a luxury that the social scientist can ill afford. The aim is rather an attempt to account for the formation of Europe through the lens of a theory of modernity and from the perspective of the present day. The guiding question is how should the European heritage be assessed today and what is at stake in such a question? This is both a normative question as well as a theoretical one, for the object of inquiry must be theoretically constituted. It is not possible to know what questions to ask if one does not have a theoretical framework in which to pose questions. Europe, when viewed in historical and geographical perspective, is not a self-defined entity, but was shaped through a process of construction out of which cultural and social forms were produced. So in speaking about Europe we are also taking up a position in relation to history and to possibilities within the present. My objective, formulated in the terms of a critical theory of society, is a critical reconstruction of the significance of Europe for the present day.

Since the foundation of the European Union there has been considerable interest in the question of the meaning or identity of Europe. This has been predominantly confined to the internal construction of

Europe through the transnationalization of the nation-state, though with an increasing interest in the implications of Europe for the individual – in the sense of European identities – as opposed to the state. While encompassing much of what has been regarded as Europe, clearly Europe is not something that is defined only by the EU. Inevitably such questions as to the definition of Europe involve an interpretation of the history of Europe and of the place of Europe in the world. The number of publications on issues around the identity of Europe, the European heritage, Europeanization as a social and political transformation has grown enormously in the past decade or so and reflects, too, a Europeanization of the social and human sciences. There are now sophisticated theoretical works on European integration many of which are inspired by sociological theory (Zimmermann and Favell 2011; Favell and Guiraudon 2011; Wiener and Diez 2004), European identity (Risse 2010; Checkel and Katzenstein 2009; Sassatelli 2009), European citizenship (Eder and Giesen 2001) and the European public sphere (Eder 2006a; Fossum and Schlesinger 2007; Trenz and Eder 2004). Despite the appearance in recent years of sociological works addressed specifically to the relatively new notion of European society (Fligstein 2008; Outhwaite 2008, 2012) there is as yet no systematic theoretically grounded work that offers an interpretation of the course of European history in which historical and sociological analysis is combined.[1] Various authors have provided insightful accounts of specific historical and philosophical questions, but have not undertaken a systematic analysis of European history and the formation of modern European society.[2] The writings of historians such as Tony Judt (2005, 2010, 2012) and older ones, such as George Lichtheim, author of *Europe in the Twentieth Century* (1999[1972]), are still among the most important interpretations we have of European history, though in the case of Judt these are not strictly historiographical books, but works of interpretation. Lichtheim appealed to the 'category of totality' and based his work on the view that there are 'certain definable trends shaping the totality of events during a given period' (1972: xiv). The very notion of a history of Europe as such is itself a relatively recent idea, with the first works appearing only in the 1930s, H. A. L. Fisher's three-volume *History of Europe* in 1935 being one of the first (Fisher 1935).

This book is a contribution to the debate on the idea of Europe and offers an interdisciplinary approach drawing especially from history, sociology and political theory, but also from geography and anthropology. The central theoretical arguments derive largely from social theory and historical sociology. Two additional reasons for the use of concepts in social theory are that they suggest a way to avoid theorizing Europe by using notions derived from the institutions of the EU's own discourse of its history as well as from common-sense notions of history, which at best are a poor guide to history.[3] Concepts and theoretical frameworks offer a means of understanding a historically and culturally variable phenomenon such as Europe without reducing it to the meanings people ascribe to it, thus making possible its explication even when it is not a consciously existing phenomenon. The now relatively advanced field of historical sociology offers a promising foundation on which to approach such questions.[4] The sociological task is always to place a particular event or phenomena in a broader context, both historical and global. This modest aim is perhaps all that can be attained when it comes to the interrogation of the course of European history. The challenges in any such account of the course of European history are formidable, not least due to the impossibility of establishing clear variables, let alone independent ones, for virtually every conceptual reference point has varied over the course of history – for instance the borders of countries as well as Europe itself – and concepts used to make sense of later events cannot be retrospectively applied in many cases to earlier ones.

In this Introduction I outline the central theoretical framework that informs the work and the critical debates in which it is grounded. Some of the key arguments are returned to in later chapters, but are outlined in what follows in a necessarily concise manner and without extensive bibliographical referencing.

Some myths about Europe

The older accounts of the idea of Europe attributed to Europe a foundational origin and an oppositional 'Other' that gave it form and meaning. These Eurocentric interpretations are now mostly discredited, though they still have considerable influence in shaping what many people regard as the natural reality of Europe. This attitude can be summed up as the view that Europe originated in Greece and Rome, it is Christian, but became secular, western, and more or less coincides with the European Union. The 'Other' of Europe has generally been taken to Asia, or Islam, communism, the obscure category of the 'Orient', as the shifting signifiers of the East. The traditional account, which in this book is referred to as a 'Grand Narrative', postulates an underlying essence or spirit which progressively (and inexplicably) unfolds in history making possible progress and, in some accounts, the European Union. In the historiography of the European Union this history is often presented as a story of the overcoming of internal divisions in the movement towards political unity. In such teleological accounts unity and diversity become gradually reconciled to the progress of the European project and the overcoming of obstacles, which roughly summarized include the catastrophes of history.

In opposition to these Grand Narratives alternative interpretations of history have now come to the fore and offer more critical accounts. The problem of Eurocentrism is also much more at the heart of any analysis of history (Amin 1989; Blaut 1993; Dainotto 2007). There are also works on the 'idea of Latin America' (Mignolo 2006) and the 'idea of Africa' (Mudimbe 1994) that need to be brought into the debate about the idea of Europe. This book is largely a response to the new myths of European history that such alternative accounts have generated, since not much methodological progress has been made.[5] Against the Eurocentric inclined Grand Narratives, the dominant tendency is to emphasize the 'dark side' of Europe. Even in standard histories of Europe in the previous century, the emphasis has been on the negative side of history (e.g. Mazower 2000; Meier 2005) or what Walter Mignolo (1995, 2011) has referred to in two books as the 'dark side' side of history. Clearly such correctives are needed to counter-act the rosy picture of the rise of Europe and the uncritical celebration of its achievements. Under the influence of post-colonialism stronger critiques of Europe argue that Europe is a product of a globally connected world and that its history is inseparable from colonialism and world domination. Unmasking the illusions of Europe's own narrative of its history is clearly important, but this will not answer the question, no matter how darkly it is painted, as to the specificity of Europe. But a corrective is not an alternative and the critique of orientalism has not led to new methodological shifts. Many such accounts end up in the contradictory position of using historiographical research to refute long-discarded conceptions of the European past while also claiming historical research is limited by a Eurocentric lens; others are seemingly unaware of important historical research to begin with and offer only thinly veiled polemics aimed against obscure or non-existent targets.[6] A favourite target is Max Weber's much misunderstood, albeit enigmatic, opening statement of the *Protestant Ethic and Spirit of Capitalism*.[7] Critiques of Europe inspired by Edward Said's path-breaking *Orientalism* in 1978 offer a limited and often myopic account of the European heritage as one of the domination of the non-European world. Said's book was important in drawing attention to the role of cultural representations and in particular the representations that colonial Europeans constructed of the Orient (Said 1979). However, it offers a limited perspective on the entire course of European history, for which it was never intended (see Malette 2010). Most conceptions of the European heritage confine their scope to a limited range of questions and are cautious about universalistic claims, which are now more likely to be a critique of Europe. So the target of Eurocentrism is often unclear and an academic construction that has exaggerated the global significance and historical power of Europe.

One theme in the literature on the making of the idea of Europe is that its identity was forged against an external and often abstract Other – generally taken to be Islam, with later incarnations being variously the Orient, Russia and communism – that gave to it an identity that it otherwise did not have. This notion was implicit in the older literature, as in Henri Pirenne's (2001) thesis in the 1930s that 'without Mohammed there would not have been Charlemagne', by which he meant the rise of Islam gave to Europe in the Middle Ages a notion of an Other. In the orientalist critique this becomes a stronger thesis to the effect that the only unity possible in Europe was one created against an external enemy who had to be fabricated and imagined in ways that presaged the path to empire. Although I am sympathetic to the argument, it needs to be relativized for the following reasons. The relation between Europe and the East, especially Islam, included both positive as well as negative images, especially prior to the colonial period. Relations between East and West were not entirely based on ignorance or conflict, but included considerable exchange, borrowing and dialogue. Moreover images and relations changed and were often so variable that it is difficult to postulate a continuous Other. The radical and cosmopolitan vision of figures such as the Renaissance philosophers of the Spanish Salamanca school or Enlightenment thinkers such as the geographer Alexander von Humboldt need to be incorporated into assessments of the European heritage, which also had a critical side to it.

A relational approach requires a multi-dimensional account of relations, in particular with respect to long periods in history when a dichotomous relation rarely predominated for long. It must also be considered that Europe was not sufficiently well defined to articulate an identity until at least the nineteenth century; internal differences always undermined the articulation of a collective European identity. It is not logically possible for a Self to construct an Other if there is no

Self in existence to begin with. Finally, the thesis assumes the existence of Europe and Asia as essentially separated and self-contained worlds, when for every example of a clash or conflict one can find an example that illustrates peaceful co-existence and negotiation, if not mutual acceptance and commonality.[8] The implausibility of the orientalist argument ultimately runs into the objections that have been voiced against the 'clash of civilizations' thesis, which similarly postulates hermetically sealed civilizations that can only collide. Orientalism thus ends up requiring Occidentalism. The result of polemical positions of the right (Huntington's clash of civilizations or the end of history scenario) or of the left (Said's orientalism or the liberal notion of a 'dialogue of civilizations') is a failure to uncover the complex pattern of encounters between Europe and the non-European world, including the unintended consequences of the earlier encounters and the reflexivity of modern culture.

This book is both a critique and a defence of the idea of Europe; it is a reconstructive critique in that it seeks to discover the structure of qualitative shifts in the relation between state, society and individual, how they occurred and what their consequences were for the formation of social and cultural structures for European history. The aim is to offer an account of the significance of Europe that divests Europe of its illusions and to see it as it is, namely a world historical region. As Dipesh Chakrabarty (2000) has argued in *Provincializing Europe*, Europe needs to be 'provincialized', that is, it should not be viewed as a normative or evaluative reference point for all parts of the world; in other words, it should be discovered as it is. 'Provincializing Europe' is a demonstration of the limits of the global relevance of Europe without denying the validity of many of its achievements or the possibility of internal logics of development.

So far, then, the polar opposites of Eurocentric and anti-Eurocentric accounts are a poor guide. What then is the solution? The tendency in current scholarship that moves beyond the orientalist versus occidentalist polarity is threefold. This will be briefly outlined before assessing the implications that follow. As a result of the global historical turn, there are now a larger number of studies that place Europe in the context of a more globally connected world. The emphasis on global connections in the analysis of major historical periods and episodes is one of the main historiographical alternatives to internalist accounts of the rise of Europe. The older approaches tended to see the global context as secondary or unimportant and to attribute primary causal weight to endogenous processes. As a result of many studies that build on the classic works of Braudel, McNeill, Hodgson, and Wallerstein the importance of the external context must now be seen as an essential part of the explanation of major social change in history.[9] The idea of Europe needs to be contextualized in a global context rather than, as is the mainstream tendency, to see Europe as emerging out of the internal relations between the nations of Europe. The concern with the global context also offers an alternative to post-colonial polemical positions on history as a history of domination. Entities such as nations, the European Union, social movements etc are not simply self-generating; they are shaped in a process of interaction with other social forms. The result is that the social world – whether contextualized as national, European, global – must be seen as a product of cross-cultural fertilization, encounters, dialogue and mediation rather than as self-contained and impermeable (see also Delanty 2011a).[10] This suggests the importance of a relational approach, which is the theoretical assumption, though not always evident, underlying such insights.

A second development in the literature is what can be termed constructionism or the critique of representations approach that sees Europe as a socially constructed discourse (Delanty 1995a). This was already signalled in Said's work and is much influenced by the pioneering work of Foucault. It is commonplace nowadays to say that Europe is invented, that it is a historically variable construction and has no objectivity other than in the discourses that construct it. An account of the idea of Europe will therefore have to consider the process by which Europe became a reality in terms of politics and culture. That entails a consideration of how such discourses were constituted and underwent change. This is where sociology meets history, for the sociological aim is in part to account for the formation of entities that appear to have a natural form and to demonstrate the connections that link the individual with history and with the wider global context.[11]

Thirdly, closely related to the constructionist emphasis on Europe in terms of a model of discourses, there is increasingly a position emerging that emphasizes multiplicity as opposed to unity. In this latter account, there is not a single conception of Europe, but multiple Europes (Biebuyck and Rumford 2012). No longer is Europe seen as a singular entity akin to the West or Western Europe, but takes a plurality of historical forms. Such arguments have been influenced by perspectives on history from Central and Eastern Europe as well as the revival of some older accounts of Europe in terms of multiple logics of history. While none of the accounts deny the existence of Europe as such, there is a notable departure from western centric interpretations.

Instead Europe is portrayed as polycentric or de-centred and shaped more like a borderland than by bordered space or a relation determined by core and periphery (see Balibar 2003).[12] In the work of scholars such as Balibar it is more than a matter of multiplicity: the plurality of forms of Europe point to a hybrid conception of Europe as a borderland.

While I am broadly sympathetic to the constructionist approach and claims that Europe takes a plurality of forms, this in itself is insufficient. The problem with such approaches is that they are not able to address questions that go beyond a cultural level of analysis to account for societal structures, such as capitalism, state formation, demography and ultimately lack explanatory power. The aim of such exercises is generally, following Foucault, to demonstrate how something – an identity for instance – was created and thus to de-naturalize the object in question so that what appears as 'essentialist' or natural to its bearers is from the theoretical perspective constructed. To say something is invented is only to recognize its constructed nature and that it was constituted in a formative process, as opposed to being natural.

The problem with this is that it can lead to the view that identities should be perceived by social actors as constructed. This is to conflate an explanatory category – constructionism – with an empirical category. Social actors may still view their identities as essentialist, that is as natural, and thus produce effects that create reality. The objectivity of such realities can easily escape constructionist approaches unless complemented by a deeper macro analysis of long-term societal trends and the formation of cultural structures. In other words, discourses and other such notions of social constructions produce structure – that is reality – forming effects. Constructionism alone does not adequately demonstrate how a structure is formed. Without such a perspective on structure formation, it is impossible to make sense of the formation of a historical pattern or a heritage that takes shape over the course of centuries.

The emphasis on multiplicity brings in an important added dimension, but any account that considers only the fact of numerical difference ultimately fails to account for the phenomenon – in this case the idea of Europe – that exists in multiple forms. The argument for multiplicity, 'multiple Europes', is essentially an argument for variation and needs to be supplemented with a perspective on what variation produces. So it is not enough to identify different European traditions or varieties of modernity without showing how they are linked and how the linkages produce structure forming effects in terms of cultural models and societal forms. Appeal to the notion of hybridity does not solve the problem, for if people believe their societies are based on primordial and unique characteristics, the academic view that every society or culture is hybrid does not explain such beliefs nor account for the consequences that follow from such beliefs.[13] For similar reasons, an exclusive preoccupation with the global context is inadequate if it is not accompanied with an account of the internal formation of the object under investigation. This book takes seriously the formative influence of the global context for Europe and asserts the more general relevance of an interactionist or relational account for the analysis of historical and sociological phenomena. However, the relational perspective is in danger of over-emphasizing process at the expense of structure. Structure formation is the other half of the process of the making of history. Structure is a form that is produced by processes and while being constantly re-worked by social actors, it gives shape to social life.[14] In other words, the new directions – with their emphasis on global connections, discourses, multiplicity, hybridity – lack a clear grasp of how a social and cultural structure forms. The result is a relativization of Europe to a point that the objective reality disappears or is explained away by process and discourse. With the demise of the Eurocentric Grand Narratives with their singular and universalistic conceptions of history, the critical function of such exercises in relativization have lost much of their purpose. The danger is now that new pernicious myths will take their place. This book is in part an attempt to counteract such new myths, including the myth of Europe as borderless, hybrid, cosmopolitan and inclusive. It is both a critique of Eurocentrism and of the myths of history that have been produced in the de-masking of Eurocentrism.

Problems in conceptualizing unity and diversity

One of the central questions that arises from the above considerations is how can similarity and difference be understood for a large-scale unit of analysis such as Europe. In conceptual terms, this is one of the key questions to be addressed in this book. The relation between unity and diversity can be posed in a number of ways and the solution resides in addressing each level separately and, above all, in avoiding to conflate them. The result of conflation is the production of meaningless analytical concepts, such as 'unity in diversity', which may have an appealing political function, but do not provide a methodological direction for scholarly inquiry. Unity and diversity should be theoretically conceived of as different expressions of the same phenomenon rather than two different realities. Thus unity is something that emerges from the differences by reflection on them and thus allows making sense of the difference. Luhmann (1995: 240 and 273) thus speaks of the 'unity of the difference'. In this view, unity resides in the reflexive idea of Europe and can be found at the level of a cultural model that influences social structures. The work of Castoriadis is also interesting in conceptualizing unity and diversity. His work, as Klooger points out, suggests a model of unity as coherence as the mutual intelligibility and meaningfulness of signifying structures (Klooger 2013: 492). Notions of unity must be understood in relation to a social ontology, which in Castoriadis's thought does not require the absence of contradictions, tensions or disunity for it is always partial.[15]

The following is a brief summary of six considerations in unpacking the question of unity and diversity.

Political unity versus cultural diversity

One way to approach the problem of unity and diversity is to see unity as political and diversity as cultural. In this view, the political traditions of Europe provide a basic source of unity while each country has a unique cultural tradition. From an EU perspective, the thesis can be formulated to posit political unity in the framework of the EU, at least as a limited political unity, and to relegate culture to the regional and national levels. This is more or less the official position as far as the EU is concerned and has been the basis of such well-known philosophical positions as Habermas's (2001b) conception of a post-national Europe that has overcome the divisions that nations engendered as a result of their different cultural traditions. The problem with this approach is that political unity is not quite so evident and, on the other side of the coin, the unity implied by cultural identity and tradition is not so easily reduced to group differences. More generally the separation of culture from the political produces more problems than it solves. For instance, it is possible to find examples of cultural unity (in lifestyles, consumption, education) and political diversity. Yet, on the whole in normative terms political bonds of commonality are easier to achieve than common cultural worlds.

Homogeneity versus diversification/heterogeneity

Explaining unity is one of the most challenging tasks for sociological and historical inquiry. If the notion of a continent is no longer accepted as a meaningful analytical or historical category, what then is the alternative designation of commonality?[16] Unity can be understood in terms of a homogenizing process whereby Europe is formed out of increasingly common structures or institutions that become adopted in a long-term historical process. But explaining how these structures arose is by no means self-evident. Narrative accounts of history simply declare their arrival or assume their existence. Is the development of individualism, religious dissent, trade unionism or the emergence of the charted town in medieval Europe to be attributed to a common structure that produces such outcomes, separate logics of development or – to follow Ragan (1987: 25) – the intersection of a set of conditions that produces large-scale qualitative shifts? Unity is now best seen as evolving through various mechanisms and processes, which include conquest of the periphery by the core as well as through piecemeal diffusion and borrowing. In other words, the notion of unity points to the formation of a structural pattern that solidifies over a long historical period. To grasp it is by no means easy and without a wider theoretical framework it is probably impossible.

Homogenization does not eliminate heterogeneity, which can result from local variations of common structures. Borrowing from a common source – e.g. Christianity – can produce regional and national variations. The idea of Europe is also one such common cultural structure. From a long-term historical perspective, homogenizing and diversifying trends may variously be more in evidence. Long periods of homogenization may precede periods in which diversifying trends unfold, challenging the dominant codes, centres, elites and institutions. Both processes can be understood in terms of a model of conflict, for homogenizing forces can provoke the resistance of the periphery and thus undermine the possibility of commonality. However understood, commonality cannot be separated from conflict, which is always present since commonality is a product of power and, as argued by Foucault, where there is power, there is resistance. But commonality is also more fundamentally a product of reflexivity, in the sense of the appropriation of normative and cognitive ideas which in turn give rise to difference since there are always different interpretations of such ideas. Perspectives on homogenization and heterogeneity require sociological analysis and cannot simply take sameness and difference for granted as somehow self-positing as cultural givens. So unity is a structure forming process that is produced as opposed to being a fixed starting point.

Commonality versus divisions

A version of the previous discussion is to abandon any notion of unity and diversity as somehow reconcilable, due to internal divisions. According to this argument, which has been variously espoused, the history of Europe is characterized by major divisions and that these divisions have undermined the possibility of unity. Thus, for instance, no single empire ever succeeded in dominating the continent and since the Peace of Westphalia in 1648 the European political order was based on sovereign nation-states who opted for a shaky normative system based on a balance of power. In the same way, Christianity fragmented into rival traditions – Latin versus Orthodox and the internal divisions within the former as well as subsequent splits within the Protestant tradition – leading to a divided continent. Mainstream historiography, as noted above, is in effect premised on the basis of national histories and a general denial of something called European history. In this view, taken to the extreme, the only unity possible is that which has been forged against a common enemy. The position in this book is that while the divisions within European history were often more important than unity, it is essential to have an analytical notion of unity, unless the idea of Europe is entirely abandoned and replaced by national history. To speak of unity is to refer to the formation of a structure that shapes the space of action. It is not possible to reject this in favour of a view of history as without structure. The argument will be developed that the European heritage has been characterized by forms of commonality and that expressions of unity cannot be explained exclusively by reference to a common enemy since there is also a need to take account of reflexive relations with other actors and the demands and expectations of cultural values and normative principles.

The existence of 'enemies' of Europe has never been sufficiently constant to provide enduring reference points to overcome internal divisions. The differences that have tended to be more important are, as Freud argued, those of the 'narcissism of the minor difference' (see Blok 1998), which goes some way to explaining the prevalence of civil war in European history. The notion of the enemy within or outside must be complemented with a consideration of friends and of the ambivalence of the stranger.

Continuity versus rupture or change

To speak of Europe assumes in some sense continuity in history. Where that continuity begins is only one of the problems with any notion of continuity, which cannot be abandoned in favour of change or rupture. The emphasis in recent times has certainly shifted in the direction of rupture and a questioning of the older forms of periodization – historical epochs or, more recently, historical 'transitions' – which were invented to solve the problem of rupture and to retain a basic model of continuity. However, history cannot entirely be reduced to rupture since any such notion requires a concept of a prior state that has come to an end. Moreover, if everything is in continuous change, it is not possible to discern continuity.

The problem with a long-run analysis is compounded by the problem that there are no reliable independent variables – geographical, political, cultural – that have remained constant over long periods of time. Many of the supposedly enduring reference points – such as historical eras, continents, East and West – have in fact been products of later ages seeking to construct their history. Later attempts to postulate a three world system in which Europe is part of the first world have today been discarded following the disappearance of the second world in 1990 and the transformation of the third world into developing and underdeveloped countries. Other systems of world analysis such as core and periphery or North and South have not succeeded as viable alternatives. The recognition of this problem in defining world regions, which requires some notion of historical continuity, has led to the constructionist solution: entities such as Europe, Asia, Africa etc are discourses that exist only in the terms of the discourse. But this is an incomplete solution to the problem since it in effect abandons the possibility of a structuring process taking shape.

One way in which to reconcile continuity and rupture is to see continuity in terms of progressive variation, which may entail re-interpretations of older traditions, as in the notion of 'Renaissance'. This could also be conceived in terms of a working out of a problem, such as Weber's notion of the problem of rationality and the explanation of suffering, Eisenstadt's argument concerning the inherent problem of how the profane and the sacred might be overcome in the civilizations of the Axial Age, or the contradiction of capitalism and democracy in modernity. The approach adopted in this book is to see the continuity of the European heritage as a process of continuous translation, including both repudiation – rupture – and re-interpretations of that which has gone before. Thus, for instance, early Christianity emerged from the confluence of Greek and Judaic thought, while rejecting both; Renaissance humanism rejected the Gothic culture of the medieval age in favour of a new interpretation of pagan antiquity in order to reinvigorate Christianity; the post-modern came as a re-interpretation of the modern. The creative renewal of the past would thus appear to be a significant feature of the European heritage.

One of the difficulties with long-run historical analysis – such as the concern of this book with an interpretation of the entire course of European history – is that it runs the risk of path-dependency and 'exceptionalism', for instance the fallacy of attributing to early civiliza-tions or religion a determining power over the present. The aforemen-tioned notion of an elemental problematic is one way to avoid this, but it too runs the risk, as best exemplified by Weber or Marx,[17] of giving to it a determining power. This is one reason why most histor-ians[18] avoid long-run accounts of history or when they do so they offer only a circumscribed narrative account, which ultimately explains nothing for it offers only description and at best a limited causal expla-nation restricted to a short period (see Sewell 2005, Chapter 3). However, it is possible to offer a diachronic or long-run analysis of history if due consideration is given to the prevalence of rupture, the existence of developmental logics and the fact that historical outcomes are always contingent while producing structural patterns. To understand such con-tingencies, synchronic analysis is essential in order to explain how specific choices or courses of action are selected at specific points and how arising from these selections specific discourses are formed. Long-run structural variables become transformed in particular moments by the choices social actors make leading to social change and thus apparently historically embedded paths undergo radical transformation producing structural outcomes.[19] It is the analysis of these that are the focus for the sociologist.

Internal accounts versus external accounts

As noted above, accounts of Europe tend to be either endogenous – explaining the rise of Europe by reference exclusively to internal processes – or exogenous, where the emphasis is on the relation to the wider world. The former has constituted the dominant tradition in historical scholarship, but there is now a clear move in the direction of the latter. This is due in no small measure to the signal work of global historians such as Fernand Braudel, William McNeill, Marshall Hodgson and comparative historical sociologists such as S. N. Eisenstadt and Immanuel Wallerstein, who laid the foundations for much of contem-porary scholarship on global linkages and effectively brought an end to the older Eurocentric accounts of world history in which Europe, always narrowly defined, could somehow explain itself or that it was sufficient to invoke a 'European exceptionalism'. However, as argued above, the emphasis on the external context while being a necessary corrective to the Eurocentric inclined histories of the past, cannot in itself provide an alternative. For instance, it cannot explain the internal transformation of Christianity as a result of the various traditions of dissent since the fifteenth century, class conflict or, for instance, the institutional transformation of the European university system. The position taken in this book is that a stronger emphasis on the global context is needed rather than seeing Europe as somehow a world within itself and that the external and internal perspectives are both required. The upshot of this is that while the very notion of the unity of Europe must be considerably relativized, a perspective is still needed on internal logics of development. The unity of Europe is a reflexive awareness on the part of the participants and an analytical category for the social theorist seeking to make sense of European specificity.

Specificity versus relativity

While the trend in recent scholarship has been to relativize the idea of a unified and authentic European tradition, it is evident that a notion of European specificity is still needed, since it cannot be credibly argued that there is no difference between Europe and the rest of the world. The relativization of European specificity as reflected in some of the aforementioned points – generally concerning conflict, divisions and heterogeneity – has had value in bringing a much needed critical perspective to bear, but the danger is the loss of perspective and conceptual confusion. In this book a strong argument is given on European specificity, but which will require both a definition and a consideration of Europe in terms of a theoretical framework.

While we should be critical of naturalized conceptions of Europe as a geographically or culturally determined space, it is nonetheless possible to use the term in a meaningful sense. This will depend on the purpose to which it is put, for some objectives are better met by taking nations or regions or the global system as the point of reference. No concept can be used to explain everything and no category can be applied to every instance. It is therefore the case that Europe may be for some purposes an appropriate concept or category of reference. Instead of seeing Europe as a continent, the Occident or as a self-defining civilization, it should instead be seen as a world historical region shaped temporarily as well as spatially in a long-run historical process.

In this view, then, the question as to the specificity of Europe is above all a question of the nature of the structural pattern of European history, for to speak of unity and cultural specificity is to refer to the formation of cultural and social structures that establish such commonality as a result of contingent conditions and choices.

Towards a theoretical framework

On the basis of the above considerations, the presuppositions of this book are that unity is co-terminus with diversity and, conceived of in terms of a developmental model in the sense of a historical process, it makes possible diversity. Diversity may be logically prior to unity where the latter establishes an integrative framework, but diversity requires some kind of matrix to define its elements. Both terms make sense only in relation to a constitutive structure. In other words, the idea of Europe as a world historical region refers to a constitutive process of structuration that produces unifying trends – that is societal structures and cultural models – as well as variations of those trends. These variations make possible diversity. Europe is constructed in a historical process in which commonality is produced through on-going variation. Such commonality can be seen in terms of shared historical experiences as well as shared memories of those experiences. Historical memory is central to any notion of the continuity of a historical tradition. But structure forming effects go beyond memory and cultural traditions to include the reflexively developed application of cognitive and normative ideas, such as freedom, equality, democracy, personal and collective autonomy, the idea of the individual, all of which derive from the cognitive order of society (Strydom 2011b).

An important mechanism of change is adaptation, including appropriations from encounters with other cultural worlds. This results in hybrid cultural forms, which in time take on the solidity of fixed cultures that have lost their contact with their diverse backgrounds. It may also result in so-called hyphenated cultures, such as Greco-Roman or constructions that rediscovered a commonality that had been forgotten, as in the notion of a 'Judaeo-Christianity' tradition. In these instances, the hyphen indicates two different, but linked cultures or ones that have a shared but distant common origin, but have undergone separate paths of development.

This process does not exclude contradictions or require uniformity; it may also be multi-directional and uneven; and it may take the form of 'invented traditions', since the commonality produced may not have an authentic relation to its assumed past, but is a product of modern society seeking to define itself in relation to history (Hobsbawm and

Ranger 1983). Moreover, societal learning is also part of this as are regressions. Habermas's notion of history having a learning process is an important part of the argument in this book.[20] This does not mean that history moves by a cumulative logic towards ever greater progress, but that in the course of history societies evolve ways of problem-solving and living together that take communicative forms as opposed to recourse to violence to settle disputes or recourse to the received wisdom of the past. This is because human beings have the capacity for reflexivity, enabling them to articulate new relations to the world and new interpretations of established ideas and the development of knowledge.[21] Such forms of learning are the basis of the possibility of culture and make possible solidarity and egalitarianism at least as an aspiration and provide normative or counter-factual reference points for modern societies to reach beyond themselves. This can be seen as occurring in three highly contingent steps, for one does not necessarily lead to the next: generative processes, transformative processes, and institutional processes.[22] Generative processes involve the creation of new ideas, or new claim-making, which cannot be accommodated within the given order. Such processes are associated with social move-ments, which are generally the initiators of social change. Transformative processes follow from the selection of the variety gen-erated and occur typically when a dominant social movement brings about major societal change through the mobilization of large seg-ments of the population and the transformation of the political system.[23] Transformative processes occur typically when a dominant social movement brings about a major societal change through the mobilization of large segments of the population and the transforma-tion of the political system. Institutionalizing processes occur when a social movement succeeds in institutionalizing its project in a new societal framework, for example in the establishment of a new state or in new legislation and brings about the re-organization of state and society. These processes can be observed to be at work in all modern societies, making possible their creative renewal. Moreover, they have both pluralizing and unifying tendencies insofar as they engender structural patterns that become the basis of modernity.

The broad theoretical framework in this book is drawn from recent developments in social theory and historical sociology concerning the notion of modernity, and is influenced by Wagner's work on the theory of modernity (Wagner 1994, 2009, 2012). As used in this book modernity is a condition that involves the actualization of regulative ideas such as freedom, equality and autonomy and their realization in the modern world; it is an emancipatory condition that proclaims human autonomy, both individual and collective, as an aspiration for modern times and that this must be realized in the concrete institutional order of society. However, unlike Wagner, I see the social condition of modernity, which I refer to as a societal model, as a structure forming configuration shaped by the relationship between capitalism/market society, state formation, and civil society. Modernity thus entails ideas of freedom, liberty and autonomy, which derive not from modernity *per se*, but from the cognitive order of society and are, as such, trans-historical in that are not products of any single part of the world, despite the fact that they have become important parts of the cultural models of modern societies and took root at a fairly early stage in the formation of Europe. There is also not simply one transformative idea, as Wagner claims, such as autonomy, but many, and it is often the combination of these ideas that make possible the specific form of a particular variant of modernity (e.g. the liberal, socialist, republican variants of political modernity were products of different appropriations of the ideas of freedom, equality, autonomy, self-government, individualism, and social justice). These are part of what I call the cultural model of society[24] and take the form of what Charles Taylor has termed a 'social imaginary', namely a future-oriented projection of the possibilities within the present (see Taylor 2004).

Modernity is thus marked by the belief that human agency can transform the world in the image of a possible future. However, these ideas of modernity are in tension with the social order since, for either the existing societal model resists modernity or is incompletely realized in practice, leading to the feeling that modern society is fragmented, a theme central to social thought from Rousseau to Hegel and the classical sociologists. Thus, as many contemporary theorists – most notably, Arnason, Castoriadis, Habermas, Touraine, Honneth and Wagner – have argued that there is a central conflict at the heart of modernity, between communicative rationality and instrumental rationality, between democracy and capitalism, between autonomy and power, different orders of recognition etc. This dual face of modernity gives to modern societies a dynamism and a creative force, since modern societies try to resolve or overcome the contradiction between the ideas of modernity and the concrete form modern society takes. The result, to use Kolakowski's (1990) formulation, is that modernity is 'on endless trial'. However, this does not mean that everything is entirely open, for modern societies have created structural forms. The various forms modernity have taken are determined by the relationship between capitalism, the state and civil society, as there has never been one configuration. Such structural configurations reflect the interpretation of the transformative ideas associated with modernity. The idea of Europe is itself one of these transformative ideas, and the way its realization is pursued depends on the selection and combination of cognitive order ideas (e.g., freedom, equality, solidarity, social justice) with it. It is this process of selection and combination that separates liberals, republican, conservatives and socialists. For this reason, modernity cannot simply be reduced to one basic orientation.

Modernity thus needs to be defined to include cultural structures along with social, political and economic dimensions, which Stuart Hall (1992) considers to constitute the four main processes of modernity. Thus defined, modernity is not only a general theoretical framework, but a 'middle-range' theory with explanatory powers. In other words, the idea of modernity should not be confined only to the cultural dimension – as is the tendency in much of the literature, which tends towards an overtly philosophical conception of modernity – nor reduced to societal structures as in classical modernization theory, but involves cultural and social structures. This approach to modernity recognizes the plurality of historical forms, often referred to, following Eisenstadt (2003) as 'multiple modernities' but better considered, following Wagner (2012), as 'varieties of modernity', and that modernity is not necessarily European, but exists in numerous world settings. Moreover, modernity is not an historically path dependent order, but is historically contingent and variable, since, first, the ideas of modernity, that is the cultural model, can be differently interpreted and, second, will be realized in different institutional ways. However, the varieties of modernity approach is insufficient, since what needs to be accounted for in specific instances is the formation of enduring structures. These structures are produced by societal models and by the cultural models of societies in particular times and places. They are given form by social actors from specific selections and combinations of ideas.

This book concerns European modernity, which is itself a specific form that modernity took in Europe, roughly from the sixteenth century onwards, when the first consciousness of modernity arose around a new critical humanism, as Stephen Toulmin (1990) has argued in *Cosmopolis: The Hidden Agenda of Modernity*. While not reducible to an age as such, it makes sense to locate it as far as the European context is concerned as having its beginning in the early modern period. The argument is that Europe, while having civilizational antecedents, is largely a product of modernity. The term itself was rarely used before the early modern period and only with modernity did the idea of Europe acquire a meaning that was not purely geographical. Modernity is the constitutive matrix that gave to Europe a direction and meaning. It cannot be emphasized enough that this modernity was simply the form modernity took in Europe, which does not mean that this is the only or universal form. As far as Europe is concerned, it does not make much sense to project it backwards into early history, despite the obvious existence of antecedents, in the sense of 'early modernities' (Eisenstadt and Schluchter 1998). The project of autonomy crystallized only in the early modern period and did not take on an enhanced momentum until the age of revolution from the late eighteenth century. A feature of modernity is the accelerated momentum of global connections and flows of ideas, a movement that is multi-directional. So, for instance, as Bayly (2004: 471) has pointed out, the language of rights was variously appropriated throughout the world in the revolutionary period from the end of the eighteenth century (see also Hunt 2010). This illustrates the tendency that once something has been invented it does not simply go away, but remains as a resource and is taken up in different ways. The history of modern societies is thus characterized, for instance, by the tendency towards the amplification of democracy. Once the seeds of democracy were set they had often startling results that were never fully domesticated.

The upshot of this approach, then, is that European modernity unfolded around a specific societal model, the chief characteristic of which was that neither the state nor capitalism entirely dominated society since both had to be balanced and accommodate claim-making from civil society. So a particular model of modernity developed in Europe in which the ideas of modernity influenced the shape of society in a very specific way. A key aspect of the shape of European modernity was the prevalence of a strong politics of solidarity emanating from class struggle and a relation between state and capitalism that set limits to the capacity of either to dominate entirely the social order. Europe as a result became neither entirely ruled by capital nor by a hegemonic state. Europe modernity unfolded over the centuries through contestation over its societal model and was marked by various crises; it was also realized at different speeds and with national and regional variations.

This approach does not deny the pre-modern history of Europe as formative in the making of modern Europe, but rather places it in a wider context. The argument, outlined in the first section of the book, is that the formative process by which Europe was constituted was an inter-civilizational constellation of interacting civilizations rather than a primary western civilization. These were the Greek and Roman civilizations, the Judaic, Christian and Islamic religions, the Byzantine offspring of Rome and its Russian successor. Europe emerged from a formative process in which many cultures were involved and what was produced in the end was not a common civilization, but a matrix that was highly plural albeit with high levels of commonality and at times high levels of reflexivity. The ancient civilizations bequeathed to modernity certain orientations and values, but the form it took, however varied, cannot be reduced to the civilizational background. The civilizational background is presented in this book as the sources of the European heritage and its modernity, but due to the globalizing nature of modernity these sources became considerably diluted. This perspective draws attention to Latour's (1993) argument in his book, *We Have Never Been Modern*, that modernity produced forms of knowledge that purified themselves of their pre-modern past, which is a history of hybrid forms. Although Latour was writing about the sciences, the point is relevant to the historical formation of modernity. While the ancient civilizations have lost their determining power over the present, they have provided some of the most important orientations for modernity. This approach, as noted above, is influenced by 'civilizational analysis' as developed by Johann Arnason (2003). However, in departure from Arnason, my analysis of modern Europe and the predicament of the present requires a broader framework than one based on civilizational influences and encounters, for the closer we get to the present the more difficult it becomes to account for change by recourse to civilization logics.[25] The most powerful influences on the present derive from the reflexive appropriation of new ideas and the development of normative and cognitive horizons that have been opened up with modernity.

The framework of modernity offers the most promising way to make sense of Europe. It provides an interpretative paradigm capable of contextualizing the idea of Europe along with other discourses of Europe in institutional processes as well as generative and transformative ones and thus avoids the limits of purely constructionist approaches, which tend to see everything only in terms of discourses. It is also a way to make sense of long-term historical processes, which from the perspective of a theory of modernity can be seen as a variable configuration of state, capitalism and civil society relations. In these configurations, which define the societal model, the influence of civilizational legacies are also to be found shaping the specific form of society at a particular juncture. An additional advantage of this approach is that it builds into the very understanding of modernity an interpretative and reflexive dimension: modern society understands itself to be modern and, as part of this self-understanding, the normative consciousness of modernity – that is its cultural model – is built into the structure of society and its publics. This is why modernity is accompanied by a self-transformative condition for it involves the constant questioning of the world and the pursuit of different visions of how the social world should be organized. However, in departure from purely interpretative accounts of modernity, I am arguing for greater attention to the developmental dynamics arising from specific societal forms and also from the reflexive appropriation of cognitive ideas. Finally, the approach offers a way to understand the specificity of Europe from a global perspective as one version of the wider condition of modernity as a world historical region. A comparison of world historical regions and their forms of modernity can tell us more about the nature of European modernity than what can be discovered from an analysis confined to Europe (see also Domingues 2011; Therborn 2002, 2003; Wagner 2011).

Defining Europe

The account of modernity provided goes some way to defining Europe: There is neither a primary origin – geographical or cultural – that gives Europe its identity nor an external Other against which it formed its identity. Nor is there a historical centre that has remained constant, but shifting ones and which do not coincide with geography, though arguably the Carolingian kingdom constituted the most long-lasting historical core, as Jacques le Goff (2006) has argued. Europe was formed in a long historical process involving the interaction of many cultures and the subsequent transformation of the new forms by modernity. The referential basis of Europe is not only different cultures – within and beyond Europe – nor the social and material aspects of society, but also the sphere of ideas, in particular those that were reflexively engendered by modernity.

Modernity is not settled for once and for all, but is a continuous project and may entail rival projects, as was the case for much of the twentieth century with the collision of liberal democracy, fascism and communism (which, as argued in Chapter 11, can be considered to be rival projects of modernity). Several theorists – Bauman, Lefort, Heller, Eisenstadt, Wagner – have characterized modernity as a condition in which there is a loss of markers of certainty with the result that every-thing is open to interpretation. The pursuit of stability and certainty in a world in which everything is open and contingent defines the modern spirit.[26] What has remained relatively constant are the refer-ence points – the ideas of modernity – but which are differently inter-preted. While these are variously emphasized in social and political theory as autonomy (Wagner 2012) or freedom (Honneth 2011) or justice (Forst 2002), modernity entails not just one cognitive idea but several. These ideas themselves undergo change and re-configuration as well as different combinations emerging. Thus the idea of Europe was once associated with the idea of freedom, while in later times a shift occurred whereby it became associated with the idea of rights and justice. Once ideas become embodied in social and political forms, they inevitably undergo change in their meaning. Once the idea of Europe became embodied in the institutional form of the EU since 1958, its meaning unavoidably changed.

As noted, this characterization of modernity applies to any society that considers itself to be modern, which today includes more or less every part of the world. In this sense, modernity is a singular condition (Wagner 2012; Jameson 2003) while taking multiple forms. European modernity can be defined around three central dimensions, which can be seen as the concrete embodiment of the idea of Europe: a concep-tion of the public, a conception of the individual, and a conception of the world. These three dimensions crystallize the concept of modernity discussed above in terms of cultural and societal models, while also taking account of the relevant legacies of the inter-civilizational back-ground and degrees of reflexivity. But such models are not permanent and can take on new shapes.

The first concerns the basic form of the European social model, which can be seen in terms of a conception of the public defined in relation to solidarity. One of the characteristics of Europe is its concern with solidarity and social justice, as reflected in the history of social struggles over rights, conflicts between democracy and capitalism, and in modern times with the institutionalization of social citizenship (see Karangiannis 2007) and social democracy. The affirmation of solidarity and the constitution of the public has been the basis of a European tra-dition of political community that has often been neglected in accounts of the European heritage that have tended to over-emphasize other features.

Secondly, the European heritage has a strong relation to a concep-tion of the individual, in particular one that asserts the autonomy of the individual. The sources of this lie within Christianity and in Greek philosophy. It is not possible to conceive of Europe without a notion of Europeans, though the latter emerged only since about the sixteenth century and with the Renaissance and Enlightenment acquired an augmented meaning, which affirmed the concern with solidarity, for the autonomy of the individual and the autonomy of society are linked. The emphasis on the individual in European thought and in social practices had the paradoxical effect that it produced a certain tension between the individual and Europe, as it has between the pursuit of individual and collective liberty. In the past two decades there has been a new interest in the idea of Europeans as opposed to Europe and the possibility of European identities.

Thirdly, Europe entails a conception of the world. Along with the idea of Asia, the idea of Africa, the idea of Latin America, the idea of Europe reflects a consciousness that is defined in relation to rest of the world. All notions of Self and Other have been mediated through the wider category of the World. Europeans became reflexively conscious of themselves as the inhabitants of Europe as distinct from other parts of the world, Asia, Africa, the Americas, the definitions of which changed over the centuries. The world-projections of Europe included of course the equation of Europe with the world when Europe was a hegemonic order in the age of Empire. In the present day Europe is a post-hegemonic and, as argued in Chapter 12, a post-western power. Against the older notion of a continent, the idea of Europe is better conceived of as a world historical region.

All three dimensions entail a form of knowledge, for Europe is an object that must be reflexively known and in this respect, specific forms of knowledge gave to Europe the means of gaining knowledge of itself and its past. Such forms of knowledge include memories as embodied in literature and arts, public memories associated with political and military events, philosophy and the human and social sciences. It may have been a feature of Europe more than elsewhere that such memories and modes of knowledge were given a durable form in institutions such as academies and universities. As Foucault has shown, Europe devised elaborate 'technologies of the self' by which the individual can be known. It also devised geographical and historical forms of knowledge that constructed the world according to its own self-image and categories using such notions as continents, civilizations, historical periods, races. All of these forms of knowledge, for good and for bad, worked to produce a European cultural model.

The possibility of cosmopolitanism

In what sense can it be said that Europe might be cosmopolitan? I do not argue that Europe is cosmopolitan or that it is more cosmopolitan than other parts of the world. However, the question of the nature and extent of cosmopolitanism is highly relevant to the theme of this book for four reasons.

Firstly, there is a long tradition in European political thought that invokes the idea of cosmopolitanism from the Greek Stoics to Kant and developments in late twentieth century thought. The cosmopolitan idea exists to varying degrees of tension with the republican tradition and the idea of the nation. Social and political theorists have related cosmopolitanism to the politics of solidarity, in particular in the Kantian tradition taken up by Habermas of 'solidarity among strangers'. This is relevant to an understanding of political community in Europe and the extent to which it can be widened in an inclusive direction. It should be stated that this does not imply that cosmopolitanism is distinctively European, for despite the western genealogy of the word it is a condition that is present to varying degrees in any society. It may be the case that some non-western societies are more cosmopolitan than Europe. In addition to the Kantian tradition of cosmopolitanism, there is also the important tradition associated with Alexander von Humboldt and the notion of a world consciousness (Kozlarek 2011; Walls 2009).

Secondly, cosmopolitanism offers an alternative approach to history from Eurocentric ones or approaches that see the relation between Europe and the rest of the world in terms of an orientalist model of domination or one of an irreconcilable clash of civilizations. Cosmopolitanism is thus relevant to the concern with identifying the communicative relations between Europe and the world, without being reducible to the condition of dialogue, as in the notion of a dialogue of civilizations. It offers a perspective that challenges the Eurocentric assumptions concerning the uniqueness of Europe as well as the notion that the unity of Europe was formed only against an external enemy. While not all relations between Europe and the rest of world can be considered to be cosmopolitan any more than they can be regarded as based on domination or a response to an external enemy, it is important to identify those that are tendentially cosmopolitan. Moreover, many expressions of cosmopolitanism arose as the unintended consequences of non-cosmopolitan events. So it is possible that Europe through the reflexivity of modern culture became cosmopolitan in spite of a non-cosmopolitan past.

Thirdly, cosmopolitanism offers a critical perspective on the historical process and contemporary politics since the values and principles it is concerned with are largely counter-factual, in the sense of being opposed to the *status quo*. At the heart of cosmopolitan lies an imaginary, a way of imagining the world. Cosmopolitanism therefore tends to be in a relation of tension with social reality, but it is nonetheless part of social reality insofar as it concerns the raising of normative claims and the exploration of potentials contained within the present. From a cosmopolitan perspective, the question is not whether social reality is cosmopolitan, but to what extent it is or potentially might be. As such, it refers to an empirical condition that is present to varying degrees in terms of normative counter-factual ideas, in the projects of social actors seeking to bring about social change and in institutional forms. It is a misunderstanding of cosmopolitanism to see it as another term for the transnationalization of the state or to refer to a globalization. Cosmopolitan phenomena may be present more in social struggles than in institutional forms, which, as argued earlier, need to be in relation to generative and transformative processes. To uncover this logic is the task of a reconstructive critical theory of society and history.[27]

Finally, despite its origins in Greek thought, cosmopolitanism is largely a development that came with modernity and is therefore relevant to the analysis of modernity. With modernity came the sense of the global connectiveness of the world; indeed, the very notion of the world was produced with modernity as the extent of its domain was in principle limitless. Modernity gave to cosmopolitanism the sense of people being connected and thus set the stage for the enlargement of the scope of the project of human autonomy.

My approach is guided by a critical cosmopolitanism.[28] This involves an emphasis on (1) the identification of openness to the world in the sense of the broadening of the moral and political horizon of societies, (2) self and societal transformation in light of the encounter with the Other (3) the exploration of otherness within the self (4) critical responses to globality and (5) the identification of transformative potentials within the present. This conception of cosmopolitanism is post-universalistic in that it does not proclaim universal values, but concerns the reflexive appropriation of universalistic values and principles in specific cases. It therefore entails a degree of relativization and reflexivity.

From the perspective of critical cosmopolitanism the task is to assess processes of self-transformation in which spaces of discourse open up and cultural models take shape. A critical cosmopolitan theory proceeds on the assumption that the cultural models of society contain learning potential in terms of moral and political normative criteria. It operates on the assumption that culture is a site of conflicting interpretations of the world. As used in this book, cosmopolitanism is a condition that makes possible the widening of the cognitive horizons of societies and individuals. This dimension of cosmopolitanism ties it closely with the idea of modernity, which is a condition that is inextricably connected with globality.

Structure of the book

The structure of the book is a balance between chronologically and thematically organized topics. The first part of the book looks at the civilizational background to Europe. Chapter 1 discusses the notion of European civilization in terms of an 'inter-civilizational constellation'. This serves as a background for the following four chapters that comprise Part I on the main civilizational currents that provided the principal sources of the European heritage: The Greek and Roman civilizations along with the Judaic tradition; Christianity; Byzantium and the Orthodox tradition within Christianity as taken up by Russia; the Islamic world, including the Ottoman heritage and European Islam. Part II concerns the emergence of modernity. The six chapters cover the sixteenth century and generally the Renaissance, the early modern period, the eighteenth century, the nineteenth century to First World War, and so-called 'short twentieth century'. Part III deals with the post-1989 context. Chapter 12 is a wide-ranging one on Europe since 1989, especially on the significance of the EU; Chapter 13 is specially addressed to the contemporary crisis of capitalism since 2008; and Chapter 14 returns to the question of the European heritage from the perspective of recent debates.

In theoretical terms, to sum up, the book aims to make sense of the course of European history through an account, on the one hand, of the formation of a European cultural model that emerges out of the legacies of the inter-civilizational background and, on the other, how in relation to this cultural model a societal structure takes shape. The tension between both gives form to Europe's path to modernity and defines the specificity of its heritage. European modernity is characterized by the formation of a societal model that has been strongly shaped by the creative tension between capitalism and democracy and between republicanism and cosmopolitanism. The structuring process that has shaped Europe made possible a model of modernity that has placed a strong emphasis on the values of social justice and solidarity. These values have been reflectively appropriated in different periods to produce different interpretations, societal outcomes and a multiplicity of projects of modernity.

Part I
Sources of the European Heritage

1
The European Inter-Civilizational Constellation

Since the emergence of a European consciousness from about the sixteenth century the question has been frequently posed as to the meaning of Europe. This was bound to be a contested matter and since then many definitions of Europe have been controversial. For some it is a political project while for others it is a cultural heritage that has been principally realized in different national forms. There is also little agreement on the geographical limits of Europe and how geography relates to the cultural and political dimensions. It has often been noted that Europe is a peninsula of Asia, but where Europe ends and Asia begins cannot be answered by geography alone. The large expanse of land that lies between both was the way through which the peoples of Europe arrived in the great migrations from Asia over thousands of years. Geography unites more than it divides and thus does not offer a ready-made natural barrier than might be the basis of a definition. The narrow isthmus that separates Europe from Africa at the straits of Gibraltar once made possible an Islamic civilization that occupied the two sides of the Mediterranean Sea, but in later times was seen as a frontier between 'continents'. The notion of Europe as a continent is itself a construction that is not based on a geographical landmass that is self-defining.[1]

The overall geographical size of Europe including the western regions of the Russian speaking area such as the Ukraine is comparable to the size of China and is just a little smaller than Brazil, but arguably reveals a greater cultural diversity. Geographical factors do not define Europe, as they do not define most other large-scale countries or world regions. However geographical factors are not irrelevant, for instance the relatively temperate climate and low altitude influenced patterns of migration, settlement and agriculture, in particular prior to the industrial age. The continent is relatively accessible through land – lacking major natural barriers, such as impenetrable mountain regions – and has benefited from being relatively navigational by sea and by rivers. The Ural mountains that supposedly mark the boundary of Europe and Asia in fact presented throughout history a lesser obstacle than the Alps. The result was a relatively high degree of mutual knowledge of the existence of the different cultures and civilizations. This has prompted many geographers going back to Alexander von Humboldt to argue that there is no geographical distinction between Europe and Asia and that the former is a peninsula of Asia. Others have argued that these notions are redundant and should be replaced by the wider category of Eurasia. No point in Western Europe is more than 350 km from the sea, a distance that is doubled for much of Central Europe and reaches some 11,000 km for the Russian plains (Mollat du Jourdin 1993: 4–6). Moreover, the course of Europe's rivers facilitates links between the seas and the agriculturally rich hinterlands. It is possibly this factor that made possible a high degree of mobility within the region.

While these factors did not lead to a common culture due to the differences between north and south, east and west, they provided environmental conditions for the formation of the diverse cultures that emerged in Europe and gave to it the character of a world historical region.

More important than geography are the cultural and political definitions of Europe, which have changed over the course of history. The idea of Europe in the nineteenth century was very different from the early modern idea that arose with some of the first references to a European identity in the fifteenth and sixteenth century and all of these ideas of Europe were very different from the twentieth century notion of Europe that came with the Cold War and the emergence of the European Union. Underlying these conceptions of Europe is an ever-changing geopolitical configuration shaped in space and in time by many forces. The resulting geopolitical configurations cannot be simply explained as an 'idea' or as a cultural construction that exists only as a symbolic imaginary. The interplay of power and culture within a geopolitical arena has often been interpreted as civilizational. It has generally been an implicit assumption that a civilizational form can be discerned in a long-term analysis of the geographical, cultural and political dimensions of European history. This involves the production of imaginary projections, but also entails more than mental constructions, such as an institutional or societal order in which the material conditions of social life are produced and take on the character of a structure forming process.

It is by no means self-evident what the term civilization means and what European civilization means. The term civilization is fraught with ideological associations of western leadership, Eurocentricism and the notion of European civilization has often been associated with ideas of the superiority of the West and other Eurocentric notions that have now been mostly discarded. In the nineteenth century the notion of civilization, more or less equated with Europe, was generally defined in terms of distinction based on civilization versus barbarism. In this definition there could only be one civilization for the non-western world was deemed incapable of civilization save in the adoption of western civilization. It was a common notion in the eighteenth and nineteenth centuries that cultures were subordinate to civilization. Cultures were largely national and the diversity of culture, it was believed, reflected the diversity of nations and peoples while under-lying all these cultures was a unitary notion of civilization. Several cultures competed to be the true representative of civilization, which was a singular and universal condition. Since Hegel, it was often thought, too, that civilization first arose in the East, but due to the alleged decadence of oriental cultures, it declined and was resurrected by the cultures of the West. European civilization has generally been regarded as the equivalent of Western Civilization, which as a universal condition was more or less equated with modernity and hence the idea of what has been called 'Western Civilization' as the universal reference point for all cultures to be measured if not also judged. However, the notion of European civilization has generally been discussed since the early twentieth century in terms of a notion of decline, as in the work of Toynbee and Spengler. Indeed, the very notion of 'decline' seems now to be part of the idea of civilization.

Setting aside the now questionable equation of Europe with a singular notion of West, the idea of civilizations in the plural did not exist, for only culture could be plural – civilization was the universal dimension of culture.[2] This tension between the universality of civilization and uniqueness of cultures lay at the centre of European Enlightenment thought, which celebrated reason, progress, science as well as the romantic pursuit of culture and national uniqueness. Since not every nation could be the greatest, the idea of cultural diversity was born. When historical and sociological scholarship finally recognized the plurality of civilizations, as in the pioneering work of classical sociologists such as Max Weber and the anthropologist Marcel Mauss, there was generally an implicit assumption of the superiority of the civilization that emerged within Europe. These scholars recognized the plurality of civilizations, but tended to see them as self-forming and separate from each other and based on relatively uniform cultures. In addition, even in cases where Eurocentrism was much less prevalent, teleological notions of a civilizational logic tended to prevail in studies of the non-western world. In such accounts, influenced by modernization theory and the legacy of colonialism, it was generally assumed that the civilizations of the non-western world would eventually adopt the western model of modernity and in doing so would inherit the universalistic aspects of European civilization. Clearly such assumptions based on the distinction of 'traditional' and 'modern' societies can no longer be uncritically taken for granted. While much of the world has been influenced by European civilization, it is increasingly recognized that this undoubted fact has not led to the absolute universality of European civilization, which has itself been influenced by non-western civilizations. The contemporary world more than ever since the rise of the West from about the sixteenth century is a multi-civilizational order in which there are radically different projects of modernity, none of which are simply the adaptation of Europe's route to modernity. The historical experience as well as the circumstances of the present day suggest the importance of a plural notion of civilizations as overlapping and hyphenated. Thus the term civilization should be used in the plural rather than in the singular.

Some considerations in defining civilizations

A critical and reflexive view of the idea of civilization suggests a condition that is not underpinned by a specific cultural, political or geographical set of given facts that are somehow prior to history or provide a template for later experiments. Civilizations are on-going structure forming processes which create the very elements that define them. They are not immutable or predetermined, but broadly defined orientations that shape otherwise diverse societies and are continuously changed as a result of new interpretations. The upshot of this is an anti-essentialist notion of civilization as a transformative process in which various elements and dynamics shape a broad spectrum of societies in terms of their cultural orientations and institutional patterns. In this view, civilizations are not defined as closed systems locked in conflict with each other and based on primordial cultural codes. Civilizations have also been shaped in inter-civilizational encounters: they are not self-positing. Virtually every major world civilization has been influenced by another civilization. Any account of civilizational history will have to address the inter-civilizational dimension as much as the intra-civilizational. Civilizations develop in non-linear ways: there is no one simple path from barbarism to civilization and modernity; nor is there a general descent from civilization into barbarism. Accordingly, what is needed is a multi-dimensional concept of civilizational patterns and encounters.

In this account, the cosmopolitan logic of the encounter with the culture of the Other is a key dimension of civilizational history. Such encounters take a diversity of forms, ranging from adaptations and borrowings, large-scale institutional transfers, translations, migrations of elites or of whole populations, repudiations, re-interpretations, even violent clashes.[3] One of the most significant agents of such civilizational encounters were universities. Universities throughout the Middle Ages were one of the most important places where other civilizations and cultures were studied. The process at work here can be understood as neither a matter of a conflict of civilizations nor a dialogue: universities were sites where conflicting interpretations of the world became the subject of scholarly interest before they diffused in the wider society. But more generally, as will be argued in later chapters, much of the Renaissance and Enlightenment involved the interaction of civilizations and thus presupposed the possibility of dialogue and learning. The fact that the conflict between civilizations and their internal units was often more consequential than unity does not detract from the fact that civilizations were formed in part out of their mutual engagement with each other (see for example Arjomand and Tiryakian 2004; Weingrow 2010).

So what is a civilization?[4] Four broad features define a civilization: a geopolitical configuration, institutional structures in which material life and power are embedded, cultural orientations or worldviews, and diasporic movements of peoples. As a geopolitical configuration, a civilization has a territorial dimension, which may be a world historical region. This does not have to be a very specifically defined territory, such as the territory of a state, and can be quite open. Most of the civilizations of the world have had a territorial basis, however much undefined their frontiers have been, and have been associated with key cities. Indeed, most, if not all, the major civilizations of the world were at some point in their history shaped by an imperial power and had an expanding border. An exception is the Judaic civilization, which was a diasporic civilization. But even this, although lacking an imperial centre, had in one of its later traditions, namely Zionism, a special relation to a specific territory. Second, civilizations also have a basis in material life and entail institutional structures in which resources and power are organized. These institutional structures are broader than specific societies and include what has been called 'families of societies'. Thus, for example, the tradition of Roman law gave to European civilization an enduring institutional foundation as well as a tradition based on writing which made historical memory possible. Without the institution of writing, civilizations would not have had a means of reproducing themselves (see Assmann 2011; Goody 1986; Goody et al 1968). Third, civilizations have distinct cultural orientations or, what the historical sociologist Benjamin Nelson (1976, 1981) called 'structures of consciousness', which are also broader than national identities and more like worldviews. The cultural component of civilizations has often been related to the major world religions. Judaism, Islam, Confucianism, Buddhism, Hinduism, Christianity have been the most influential forces in shaping the world civilizations around worldviews based on written texts that provided the foundational reference points for the societies that they created. Finally, civilizations are related to the diasporic flows of peoples. Such diasporas do not in themselves constitute civilizations, but without the migrations of large populations and the resulting creation of large-scale human settlements no civilization is possible. The cultural sources of many of Europe's civilizations were formed in the early migrations of the peoples who migrated to present-day Europe.

According to one of the foremost civilizational scholars, S. N. Eisenstadt, the major civilizations of the world have been products of the 'Axial Age' civilizations, a term originally used by the philosopher Karl Jaspers (Eisenstadt 1986). These civilizations emerged in the second half of the last millennium BCE in ancient Greece, Israel, India, China and Iran where far-reaching breakthroughs occurred and which led to lasting revolutions in the relation of culture and power. The Axial Age saw the birth of the world religions, which provided enduring reference points for intellectual elites to articulate different visions of the world. According to Eisenstadt, the most significant development was that the Axial Civilizations led to different degrees of conflict and creativity and what was to become European civilization was the civilization that was based on the greatest degree of internal conflict as a result of its distinct civilizational imaginary. Developing this argument, Eisenstadt (2003) has stressed the multiple nature of modernity, which is not exclusively based on modern Europe, but is plural and a reflection of different civilizational paths. This tendency to relativize European modernity by stressing other models of modernity and diverse paths to modernity – some of which have not been directly connected to Europe – can be read in light of readings of history that aim to stress the internal pluralization of Europe. One aspect of this is the internal pluralization of European civilization into different models of modernity as a consequence of, for example, major doctrinal disputes, as in the Reformation and Counter-Reformation or different traditions of nation and statehood. This is not to neglect the possibility of pre-modern civilizational trajectories within the more general western European civilization. Significant in this context would be the interaction of the Greek and the Roman civilizations with earlier civilizations, such as the Celtic one, which was largely replaced by Romanization.

On the basis of these ideas, a few points of a general theoretical nature can be made. What unites a civilization is not necessarily a set of values and dispositions that provide it with a worldview that can serve as a 'Grand Narrative'. To follow Eisenstadt, the Axial Age civilizations were in fact all revolutionary developments in which radical and new creative visions of the world were introduced. What emerged out of these were new ways of interpreting the world leading to different visions of social and political order. It was inevitable that such interpretations would also produce conflicts, since there was often little agreement about such interpretations and their political implications. Nowhere were such disputes as great as in the Christian tradition, which arguably witnessed one of the greatest amounts of dispute over doctrine and political authority in the history of religion. It is possible that this internal contestation within religious worldviews gave to the European heritage its characteristic critical tendency, even if Christianity was also one of the chief sources of intolerance.

Cultural dynamics and interpretative systems alone will not determine the shape of a civilization. Important too is the geopolitical and institutional context in which cultural orientations impact upon the material and institutional organization of power. As specific configurations of power and culture, civilizations can be dynamic fields in which some of the most fundamental structures of the social world are shaped in an on-going historical process. In this the legacy of older traditions that have lost their power to shape the world often return in new forms, providing civilizational continuity through their fragments. As the history of modern European secularism demonstrates, this continuity may often consist in the repudiation or re- interpretation of tradition, if not its outright re-invention.

Civilizations come into focus only in the longer perspective of history when large-scale structures take on the character of a historical pattern. For this reason the term 'civilizational constellation'[5] can be used to refer to a pattern that becomes discernable only when a wider, transnational view is taken. Therefore civilizations cannot be reduced to short-lived political entities, whether nations or empires. Such political entities may be pivotal to the shaping of civilization, but civilizations are ultimately products of what Fernand Braudel called the *longue durée* – they are shaped in a long historical process of structure formation. This does not imply path-dependency, but that contemporary societies, including world historical regions, are influenced by civilizational backgrounds.

As a singular condition, a civilization is internally pluralized. Benjamin Nelson, who was instrumental in developing a comparative historical sociology of civilizations, used the term 'civilizational complexes' to capture the sense in which civilizations were both internally differentiated and at the same time integrative frameworks. Often the integrative dimension was not apparent until a longer historical perspective is taken. The historical sociologist Johann Arnason, following philosophers Maurice Merleau-Ponty and Cornelius Castoriadis, refers to the cultural dimension of civilizations as 'ways of articulating the world' (Arnason 2003). As such, civilizations have at their heart conflicting interpretations of world; they are not self-enclosed systems of meaning based on enduring ontological visions, but entail evaluative orders of meaning and also more radically creative impulses. In this sense, then, the civilizational thrust can be a source of societal transformation and should not be mistaken for that which is simply handed down unchanged. This gives to civilizations, according to Arnason, a radical reflexivity in that their worldviews offer reference points for the evaluation of the present and an orientation for the future.

Finally, it can be remarked that civilizations, and in particular encounters between civilizations, have been important carriers of globalization. It has been increasingly recognized that globalization is not a recent development, but goes back a long time and can be related to the rise and expansion of the early world civilizations (see Hopkins 2002; Robertson 1992). Civilizational encounters arising as a result of trade, diasporic movements, world religions, imperial expansion were early instances of globalization. The rise of global connections was a direct consequence of civilizational encounters. Such encounters, which cannot be all explained in terms of wars and violent clashes, were decisive in shaping the worldviews of those civilizations that came into contact with each other. It has very often been the case that arising out of these encounters new civilizational forms emerged or new orientations within existing civilization took place. Increasingly, the logic of the encounter – adaptations, direct borrowings, cultural translations, mutual learning – has shaped the civilizations of the world: a phenomenon now known as globalization. Whether or not this has now led to the end of civilizations and the coming of a new global age is a matter that cannot be discussed here beyond making the claim that for the purpose of the present study, civilizations are the sources of modernity and it is modernity that will become the primary reference point for the idea of Europe when it eventually emerged as a consciousness. However their legacies have left their structural mark on modernity and influenced its different directions.

The European inter-civilizational constellation

The previous arguments suggest a multiple view of European civilization. The received view is that European civilization is underpinned by fixed reference points, which are often associated with the Greek and Roman civilization, Christianity, the Renaissance and Enlightenment. Modernity, generally defined by reference to the Enlightenment, is held to be part of this heritage, which culminated in 'Western Civilization'. An alternative view, more in keeping with current philosophical thinking and research in comparative historical sociology, would suggest that the civilizational nature of Europe is far less tightly defined. The historical heritage, including the conventional reference points, can be interpreted in different ways. Before exploring this below, a few points of a general theoretical nature can be made with respect to the sources of the European heritage.

European civilization can be understood in plural terms in three related senses. First, it can be defined in a way that includes a multiplicity of civilizations within Europe, as an intra-civilizational constellation; secondly, it can be defined in a way that includes a wider trans-continental dimension to inter-civilizational encounters; thirdly, the specific civilizations under consideration should be seen as themselves highly plural. The upshot of this is a notion of a civilizational constellation, which is particularly pertinent to the European case, although by no means exclusively European.

Under the first heading would be a notion of an intra-European civilization including a broader spectrum of civilizations than the Greek and Roman civilizations or a unitary notion of the Judaeo-Christian civilization. An alternative and more inclusive civilizational approach would have to include the Byzantine tradition and its later renaissance in imperial Russia where it lent itself to Orthodox and Slavic appropriations. Included too in a broad notion of the European civilizational constellation would be the Jewish diasporic civilization and the Islamic civilization, including modern Turkey and contemporary European Islam. These different civilizations are not entirely separate but interact with each other. The Judaic civilization, for instance, is present in Islamic and Christian civilizations and the Byzantine civilization was related to both western and eastern traditions. Russian civilization includes both western and eastern civilizational currents. Modern Turkey is a combination of the Ottoman Islamic heritage and westernization (these points will be explored further in the next chapters in Part I).

Implied in this plural notion of the European civilizational constellation is a strong emphasis on civilizational encounters and, in particular, a relation to the wider Eurasia context. This points to a hyphenated notion of civilizations as opposed to a singular notion, as in the notions of Greco-Roman civilization, the Judaeo-Christian civilization, Byzantine-Russian civilization. The second aspect, the trans-continental dimension of inter-civilizational encounters, highlights the role the non-European world played in the making of Europe. This was a relation that itself took many forms, ranging from violent encounters to mutual learning. Europe variously borrowed, adapted, translated, the cultural, technological, scientific creations of other civilizations, in particular those of Asia. The reverse of course also happened. As a result of centuries of trade and later as a result of imperial ventures and colonization, the various European-Asian civilizations have become quite mixed. The important point is that any consideration of 'European Civilization' must include the non-European dimension, a relation that has not one but many dimensions.

With respect to the various civilizations that make up the wider civilizational constellation, the internal pluralization of those civilizations must be emphasized. This internal pluralization can, in part, be explained by the wider inter-civilizational context, but it is more than this. Indeed, the very notion of a civilization suggests a diversity of social and cultural worlds that also bear some common patterns. As mentioned earlier, it has been argued by some scholars that civilizations have at their core certain cultural orientations that are common to the various social worlds of which they are composed. These orientations by no means provide stable reference points that constitute a received body of traditions such as a heritage or a self-enclosed world that remains unchanged. In the case of Europe this is strikingly evident in the Christian tradition, often seen as the defining aspect of European civilization. From a civilizational perspective this tradition has been internally highly pluralized and whose core ideas have given rise to conflicting interpretations of the world. The same can be said for the Renaissance and the Enlightenment, which have been far from a common singular culture.

In sum, the sources of modern Europe lies in the plurality of civilizations that together constitute what can be termed the European inter-civilizational constellation. These sources constitute the basic orientation for the European heritage, which has been continuously re-interpreted in light of the movement of that constellation. It is inevitable that the resulting heritage that it made possible would be a contested one, for it never gave rise to a single interpretation.

Memory and conflicting interpretations of heritage

The question of the European heritage is inextricably connected with the problem of memory. In memory both experience and interpretation are played out. Since memory is always the memory of a subject, which can be a community, the interpretative dimension is unavoidable. Historical experience and historical interpretation provide a political community with a mode of historical self-knowledge that is more than a collective memory, which assumes a basic continuity in the history of the community. The kind of memory that a cultural heritage encapsulates is one that includes the ruptures as well as the continuities of history. It has been variously referred to as a cultural memory or historical memory, in contrast to a collective memory of a defined group. Viewed in such terms, the European heritage cannot be defined in straightforward terms as narrative history or by reference to a foundational civilizational origin of which it is the history.

As a history of ruptures, the European heritage includes a relation to such discontinuities as major revolutions and periods of rebirth and renewal as well as controversies over the nature of authority as in religious doctrine and political ideologies, examples of which are the Renaissance, the Reformation, the wars of religion of the early modern period, the French Revolution, the October Revolution. All the great historical moments and events have led to a new relation to the past. Since 1492 for the first time the connection between empire and European-based civilization was abandoned with an aspiration to an overseas empire, first in the Americas and later in other parts of the world. Earlier the Great Schism of 1054 effectively severed the unity of a Christian civilization, which was divided furthermore with the Reformation. In the twentieth century, the end of the two world wars marked the end of an age. The year 1918 marked the end of the nineteenth century and the *ancien regime*, when it was finally abolished; 1945 marked the emergence of an American-led western world and the end of the European age; and 1989 marked the final demise of the post-Second World War order, the 'short twentieth century', as Eric Hobsbawm (1994) termed it.

So major social transformations lead to new expressions of historical time consciousness in which historical experience is subject to new interpretations. This has implications not merely for collective memory – of groups, nations, Europe itself – but also has direct political implications when it comes to commemoration (Eder and Spohn 2005; Parker and Strath 2010). For how memory records the past is reflected in the ways in which the past is commemorated in the public sphere. In such cases we move from memory to the public recognition of a heritage. The cultural and political heritage of Europe is becoming increasingly difficult to commemorate in the ways nation-states have commemorated the past, ways which have mostly been connected with acts of liberation from an imperial power, wars against neighbouring countries or genocidal atrocities against minorities. Moreover, unlike most nation-states, which are based on a sense of peoplehood, there is no European people as such and consequently commemoration cannot be the remembrance of a given people. This is one of the main differences between Europe and its nations. So the question of a European heritage cannot be so easily related to a specific people. What then might be the reference point for the European heritage? One view is that the reference point is the vanquished or absent other. There is little doubt that Europe has been defined in this way at certain moments in its history, but this can lead to the dubious conclusion that a European self or identity has been the result. The idea of the individual, and the related idea of a collective subject or self, has been a feature of Europe, but the sources from which it emerged have been more complicated than a creation of alterity.

It is helpful to consider heritage not just only in terms of a collective memory of a given people. The memory that is established in a cultural heritage is both a matter of *what* memories and *whose* memories.[6] These do not translate into each other very easily: specific memories – what memories – often become not the memory of a collective actor but societal or historical memories and thus transcend a particular subject. In this respect an important aspect of heritage is a memory conceived of as a mode of interpretation. The memories that are encapsulated in a heritage allow a society to interpret history and the relation of the present to history. To speak of heritage in such terms is to see it as a cultural model of interpretation. While this is pertinent to national traditions of memory and identity, it is highly relevant to the wider European context for the idea of a European heritage cannot be reduced to collective memories of a given people as such. Memory is central to any notion of a European heritage, but the memories of which it is the expression suggest more a mode of relating to the past that emphasizes the cognitive primacy of the *what*. Included in this will often be the range of previous interpretations; it may be the case that a heritage consists only of the memory of interpretations of a past that does not exist as history.

The body of traditions and the historical legacy that constitutes the European heritage has been interpreted by every age in light of the concerns of contemporaries. The European heritage cannot be separated from these interpretations. It was not until the Renaissance that the consciousness emerged that there was a European heritage based on a relation to antiquity. With this came the view that there was a European heritage that was shaped in the relation of the present to the past. This relation could only be one of heritage rather than a direct history since the present age was seen as a new experience. Thus the Renaissance mind defined itself by reference to Antiquity in order to break from the Gothic era. The cultural logic that was at work in this had a cognitive dimension in the way history was organized into epochs, ancient, medieval and modern. These were seen as ruptures – caused by regular episodes of forgetting, out of which there can be no direct heritage – and history was discontinuous while at the same time constituting paradoxically an underlying narrative of unity that transcended the ruptures.

One of the problems that the very notion of a European heritage was faced with was that the principal voice of that tradition, Christianity, had repudiated the classical roots of Europe in the Greco-Roman civilizations. Periodization in effect amounted to the secularization of history, which was no longer seen as fulfilling a divine plan, and the separation of human history and natural history. In a classic work, the French historian Paul Hazard (1953) referred to this development, which occurred in the late seventeenth century, as 'the crisis of the European mind'. Since the Enlightenment this relation to the past constituted the basic dynamic of modernity which opened up new fields of interpretations. The European heritage itself constitutes the site of many of these interpretations. The European heritage was not just defined by reference to an archaic and classical past that was lost, but by reference to other worlds. In a sense the European self, the subjectivity of modern Europe, was defined by reference both to an Other – the non-European – and to its own self – classical culture – which was experienced as distant and often irrecoverable. The secularization of Christianity and the emergence of modernity added to this sense of 'crisis'. Modernity replaced Christianity in much the same way Christianity had replaced Antiquity. The resulting mood of uncertainty as to what Europe is as a political subjectivity translated into uncertainty as to what body of traditions constitute European culture and civilization. For these reasons it cannot be said that there is a singular or essential foundation to the European heritage.

By means of historicism – the view that each period in history and every expression of culture is historically unique – the European mind solved the problem of discontinuity. Historicism, which triumphed in Germany, did not challenge the basic assumption of a civilizational foundation: it rather postulated different cultural expressions of European civilization, the universality of which was guaranteed by the diversity of its particular forms. The historicist position has been very influential in accounting for the alleged worldwide validity of European categories and modernity while denying some of the consequences, such as self-government.

In the last two centuries or so there have been many attempts to define the European heritage; some of these have reflected the ambivalence of Europe's historical self-identity, but others have been more self-confident. In the nineteenth century the general preference was for a singular notion of civilization. But this very notion was itself in tension with heritage as culture: culture versus civilization offered two contrasting attitudes to the European heritage. Culture referred to the singularity of national culture, while civilization referred to a universal condition in which cultures participated. Since the Enlightenment the civilizational theme was often portrayed as the progress of the human mind or by reference to a notion of moral progress. There can be little doubt that it was often a racialized category (Goldberg 2006).

European civilization cannot be explained in racial terms. There is no European race. European civilization can be seen as a diaspora of diverse groups formed out of waves of migration and civilizational processes over many thousands of years. The Indo-European tribes who spread across Europe and Asia about 5,000 years did not leave a common culture or civilization, but a language which never became the basis of a common cultural or political system. The consensus appears to be that they were a late Neolithic linguistic group, not an ethnic or culturally defined group and migrated westwards from the Pontic-Caspian steppe (Renfrew 1987). In any case, this Eurasian or Indo-European linguistic population did not coincide with the general geographical area of Europe, which also incorporates the non-Indo-European linguistic group, which includes – of those who have survived – the Uralic family of languages, comprising the Finns, the Hungarians, and Estonians in addition to the Basques and Georgians and the latter arrival of the Turks, a non-Indo-European people from Central Asia. Aside from the Latin and Hellenic linguistic groups, the most important of the archaic cultures that stemmed from the Indo-European tribes, and which had civilizational tendencies, were the Celtic, Germanic and Slavic peoples. If any has a claim to be the early Europeans, it was the Celts who were the first of the major Indo-European tribes to settle in Central and Southern Europe. The Celts were not a racial or ethnically defined people than a diverse group who shared a common cultural heritage. However, they were later displaced by the Germanic tribes and many were later Romanized and, as with all of early settlers, they were eventually Christianized. There was more or less no civilizational commonality arising from their common origins in the Eurasian linguistic group.

For a time Latin was a common language for the elites, but since its vernacularization the European elites have never been consolidated by a common language. Language then is not a defining feature of European civilization. The notion of a civilizational constellation offers a way to comprehend the transformative processes that were involved in the numerous groups that were to make up the mosaic of Europe.

Civilizations are important vehicles through which historical memory is transmitted. European memory and the meaning of Europe is, in part, shaped by civilization. But what that civilization consists of is not self-evident. Many conceptions of European civilization are highly contestable, due to the assumptions they make about the nature of civilization and often have political implications. Yet, it is possible to understand European civilization in a way that is relevant for the present day. Europe cannot be defined in narrow political terms as a set of core western nation-states based on the Carolingian Empire of the early Middle Ages. Such definitions are often exercises in the political instrumentalization of history and culture. Europe can also be interpreted as being based on a wider and more cosmopolitan sense of civilization as post-universal and entailing a dialogue of cultures. As Brague (2002) and others have argued, the European self, the subjectivity of modern Europe, has been variously defined by reference both to an Other – the non-European – and to its own self – classical culture – which was experienced as distant and often irrecoverable. It would be beyond the scope of this chapter to develop this further, but it can be stated that it is impossible to reduce the vast plethora of texts, struggles, laws, institutions that constitute the field of history to a single narrative. Recent scholarship on the Renaissance, for instance, paints a very different picture of its constituent components. This, too, can be said of the Enlightenment.

Following the approach of Jürgen Habermas, it is possible to see history as a learning process. Societies learn in ways different from the ways individuals learn, but it is possible to speak of such collective learning processes. Viewed in terms of a developmental learning process, civilization can be seen as a constant re-working of the legacies of the past. The capacity to learn from history was, Habermas (1979, 1987a) has argued, particularly characteristic of modernity which produced a condition in which power – both state power but also class power – was constantly challenged by social movements and civil society. The great social movements of the modern age – the workers movement, the anti-slavery movement, anti-colonial movements, feminism, and the ecological movement – have been among the most important carriers of collective learning. This implies not a conception of learning as progress in the sense of the Enlightenment notion of a history as a single continuous story of progress, but rather a more discontinuous and multi-directional one in which regressions can also occur. History conceived of in terms of learning processes places the emphasis on the critical capacities of social actors to challenge power and, moreover, draws attention to the potentials within modern culture for social actors to reinterpret the present and create new possibilities.

Without the capacity to learn from history the present will be condemned to repeat the errors of the past. While there is much evidence of such failures to learn from history, there are also examples of how societies have learnt from history. Certain aspects of the European civilizational heritage such as the constitutional and democratic state, human rights and the integrity of the human person, social solidarities, civil society and the critical reason associated with modern thought represent a legacy that is of continued importance for the present. These are products of the European political and cultural heritage and have become of universal significance in what is now a globally connected world, albeit one in which Europe is only a small part. Although these are values that are no longer specifically European, they have had their origin in the great social struggles and movements in the European past. As a learning process, then, history also contains the possibility for societies to transcend the given and inherited. In the present day such considerations are of the utmost importance as the European Union has for the first time established a political framework that embraces much of the European continent. However, it should be noted that such currents are as likely to run counter to the *status quo* than affirm it and thus cannot easily be harnessed for the purpose of constructing an identity for the EU.

The following chapters offer an historical account of the main civilizational sources of the European heritage. In line with the theoretical argument outlined in the foregoing, the argument will emphasize the internal pluralization of the civilizations under discussion, their interrelations and the wider inter-civilizational context, both within and beyond 'Europe'. The political, cultural and diasporic flows within the main civilizational currents will provide the principal reference points for a conception of European modernity that draws attention to the idea of a European commonwealth based on the creative tension of the republican and cosmopolitan orientations within European history.

2
The Greco-Roman and Judaic Legacies

The legacy of classical antiquity is an obvious place to begin an account of the origins of the idea of Europe, which has often been traced back to Greek and Roman antiquity. But the nature of that relation is far from clear as is the question of the relation of the ancient civilizations to what later became known as Europe, a notion that was more or less unknown to the ancients. Any consideration of the legacy of antiquity needs to take account of the fact that the very notion of a classical age was a product of a later era and the relation to antiquity has not been constant. The Christian tradition commenced with a break with what it regarded as a pagan epoch, while the Renaissance looked to the recovery of certain elements of the classical age and the Enlightenment sought to distance the modern age from the ancient civilizations and their legacy, seeing as it did in Benjamin Constant's formulation in 1819, a fundamental discord between the 'liberty of the ancient and the moderns'.

In our own time we often hear claims that Europe derives its common culture from Greek and Roman civilization. It would appear that the legacy of antiquity has been marked by ruptures as well as continuities to the extent that the very notion of a 'Greco-Roman' civilization is questionable. A closer look at the civilizations of antiquity reveals less a picture of unity than one of diversity and of transnational movements. It is now increasingly recognized that the European heritage as it emerged out of these civilizations was formed not in isolation, but out of borrowing, re-appropriating and mixing from different societies.

This chapter presents the argument that rather than speak of a single European civilization we should instead see Europe as formed by a civilizational constellation whose classical roots were shaped by Athens,

Rome and Jerusalem. The argument is also sceptical of the alternative view that a clash of civilizations emerged in antiquity or the argument that these civilizations were inconsequential for modernity. While not denying the significance of early rivalry between Greece and Persia, to take the most well-known example, the Mediterranean world was one in which the different cultures were deeply intermeshed due to trade, migration and conquest. Conflicts belonged to this, but it is not possible to postulate a primordial conflict that provided the foundation for later ones. Ancient conflicts did not predetermine later ones; there was no path-dependency, but variation based on common origins and subsequent processes of homogenization and integration established structuring forming processes that gave to Europe its cultural and societal shape.

Greek civilization and hellenism

It has generally been considered that European civilization begins with classical Greek culture in the fifth century BCE, a century in which Socrates and Pericles lived. In rejecting sacred kinship at an early stage, the ancient Greeks made the most important breakthrough. The Greeks established the political community of the polis in which a uniquely political domain was institutionalized and which has often been regarded as the beginning of democracy and the republican tradition of the self-governing political community. The modern republican interpretation, as reflected in the writings of Hannah Arendt, saw the Greek polis based neither on the state nor on the private world of the household, but on the public domain of citizenship (Arendt 1958). Although its claims to be a democracy in the modern sense of the term must be greatly qualified, the Greek polis established the notion of the individual as a citizen defined as a status based on rights. It can be seen as having given birth to the conception of political community based on civic solidarity and opposition to despotism. These characteristics are probably more significant than a general notion of democracy, for the ancient Greek city states were highly exclusionary. However, since history – understood as the unfolding of a structure – is largely the accumulation of unintended consequences, the Greek political imagination was an important source of democratic ideas and political innovation (see Arnason et al 2013).

Greek culture and society was not a homogeneous world. The notion of a classical age was a later invention and while it is possible to speak of a Greek civilization, this was highly diverse and influenced by

encounters with Asia, encounters that became more intensified following the conquests of Alexander who brought Greek civilization as far as
India. It has been much documented how Greek culture was
influenced by the Near East.[1] A historian of ancient Greece, Walter
Burkert, has outlined how, for instance, Homer was a combination of
Greek and eastern traditions (Burkert 1995). Mesopotamian influences
are much in evidence in Greek poetry and philosophy and there are
also links between Greek thought and Zoroastrianism. But the classical
age of Greek civilization did not see a direct link with the heroic age of
Homer: this was already perceived as archaic, but nonetheless was a
reference point for Greek memory.

To speak of Greek civilization we need to refer more directly to
Hellenism, the spread of Greek culture from the period that followed
the end of the classical fifth century Athenian polis, when the alliance
of Greek states that was the basis of Greek victory against the Persians
collapsed and a new Greek power arose in Macedonia. In the fourth
century BCE the armies of Alexander the Great conquered much of the
Near East and brought Greek civilization as far as India. The encounter
with India, replaced Egypt in importance for later Greek civilization,
but the resulting influence of Buddhism did not have a lasting impact
on Greek consciousness (Arnason 2006). The new Hellenic civilization
was weak in political terms and was eventually defeated by Rome, but
it left an indelible mark on the cultural orientations of the civilizations
it encountered. The Greek language was a global lingua franca; it was
widely spoken for several centuries across a huge region; it was the language of trade, culture and diplomacy. In inheriting Greek culture,
Rome was also inheriting a cosmopolitan culture that was as much
Asian as European.

The significant feature of this culture for Europe was the fact that it
was based on writing, as opposed to recitations which had made possible the transmission of the Homeric tradition. The invention of
writing made possible the creative renewal of the Homeric past and the
construction of cultural memory that is the basis of identity. The Greek
alphabet was one of the first systems of writing to replace the spoken
word (Goody et al 1968; Goody 1986). It was a scribal culture that
incorporated the oral tradition and writing and thus made a breakthrough beyond pictorial cultures of writing. According to Jan
Assmann, the Greeks created a scribal culture based on texts which in
turn formed the basis of its cultural memory. The adoption of writing
as the basis of a culture makes possible cultural continuity and coherence. Unlike Judaism, which was an early civilization based on writing,

there was no sacred texts and, importantly, it formed part of a 'free space that was occupied neither by the commanding voice of a ruler nor by god. This power vacuum favoured orality's penetration of Greece's scribal culture' (Assmann 2011: 244). This was because the world of texts did not occupy an official place and their texts were not the basis of systems of political control or social organization. Thus there was no 'tyranny of the Book' in the Greek world, as there was in the Judaeo, Christian and Islamic cultures. The Greeks, moreover to follow Assmann, had numerous books, all of which were contradictory and constituted an inter-textual culture in which authority could never be fixed despite several texts achieving canonical status: 'Thus a culture was born whose cohesion and continuity rested entirely on texts and their interpretation. Institutions of interpretation ensured cultural continuity, from *philologoi* to monks to humanists' (Assmann 2011: 254). It is possible to see this aspect of Greek culture, known as philosophy, as constituting a core feature of the European heritage that gave to it a radical reflectivity and orientation towards critique.

In terms of its contribution to Europe it needs to be reiterated that Hellenism was not European, but a mix of Aegean, Greek, and Asian cultures. It did not include the Celts for instance, although the Celtic culture was greatly influenced by the Greeks. For the Greeks themselves, *Europa* was a name of a princess from Asia Minor, but was neither the name of a civilization nor of a continent. In the Greek myths Europa was a name of a Phoenician princess who, having been seduced by Zeus disguised as a white bull, abandoned her homeland in present-day Lebanon for Crete where she later married the King of Crete. Aristotle believed Hellas was somewhere between Europe and Asia. Etymologically, its origins are unclear; although clearly Greek, it is thought to have had Semitic roots and was a term for the setting sun. Arnold Toynbee has suggested that Europe and Asia may have been nautical terms for a seafaring people.

It is in cartography that the earliest traces are to be found. In Greek cartography, Europe became a name given to territory beyond the Greek world and was often taken to be the half-sister of Asia and Libya (Africa). The idea of Europe as a continental civilization was alien to the Greeks, who introduced the political distinction between Greeks and barbarians, Greeks and Persians or Asians. It appears that Europe and Asia as geographical regions were of little significance to the Greeks for whom everything non-Greek was simply 'barbarian'. This was the view of Aristotle who made a threefold distinction between Greeks, Europeans and Asians, and held that the latter two were barbarians. However the authors of antiquity in any case rarely if ever used Europe, which was a less defined term than Asia, and both were at most vague geographical terms. Herodotus referred to the area north of the Black Sea, not as Europe, but as *Scythia*. It is possible that the conflict between the Greeks and the Persians was more significant and probably provided terms of reference for later conflict between Europeans and Asia. However, this should not be exaggerated. The Persian Wars were not only a conflict between Greeks and Persians and more Greeks fought with the Persians than against it (Gallant 2006: 124). The Greek and Persian cultures overlapped to a considerable extent. When the notion of the barbarian was later reinterpreted to mean the opposite to civilization the term acquired a meaning that was somewhat different from the Greek notion, for whom it simply meant speakers of a non-Greek language or a language that could not be understood. For this reason, any claims of a continuous genealogy of Europeans versus barbarians must be qualified with a consideration of changing meanings (Gruen 2011).

According to Hay (1957: 3) in his authoritative study on the early history of the idea of Europe, Isocrates in the fourth century BCE constructed an identification of Europe with Greece and Asia with Persia. Ptolemy, in the second century AD, used the term Sarmatia and distinguished between *Sarmatia Europea* and *Sarmatia Asiatica* with the River Don separating them (Halecki 1950: 85). This was to prove an enduring distinction and still remains as one of the conventional geographical definitions of Europe. Hippocrates refers to the Sea of Azov as the boundary of Europe and Asia. At about this time the earlier division between Persia and Greece gave way to a threefold division between Europe, Asia and Africa. Africa has earlier been associated with Asia but later these regions were regarded as separate with the Nile as the main dividing line.

Such arbitrary distinctions should not disguise the cosmopolitanism of Greek civilization, especially in its Hellenistic phase when the relatively closed world of the classical polis was undermined by the Macedonian conquests. This was a time when the Greek world was looking eastwards, not westwards, and when a global consciousness began to manifest itself on the Greeks. There is an interesting paradox in this in that the origins of Europe – essentially Asia Minor – were in what later was regarded to be outside Europe. Indeed many of these fell under Byzantine rule. The idea of Europe as a geographical region began to emerge with the decline of classical Greek civilization. It should also be noted that the idea of Europe was often in tension with the notion of the Occident and was generally less important than the latter. The concept of the Occident first referred to the Eastern Mediterranean and was not identical with the idea of Europe. It was a Hellenistic Occident, though in another tradition the Occident was held to be the source of paradise and somewhere in the unknown western oceans. It is possible that the Greeks were more strongly aware of the world being structured on a north-south axis than a west and east polarity. Troy, the mythic cradle of the Occident was after all east of the Dardanelles. Indeed much of the Greek Occident was in what later became the Orient. For all these reasons caution must be exercised in the claim that there was always a fundamental divide between West and East and that this coincided with a civilizational clash between Europe and the non-Greek world.

The characteristic distinction between barbarians and Greeks became less sharp in the era of the Hellenistic Empire. The Greek language bequeathed a tradition of cultural translation by which the cultures of the Hellenic civilization communicated through a common culture, which was decisive not only for the emergence of the 'Axial Age', but for the nascent idea of Europe civilization. The kind of culture this represented was one that by its very nature was not tied to a particular territory. There was a fundamental rupture in Greek civilization with the transition from Greek to Hellenistic culture, for the latter was not exclusively Greek, but absorbed elements of the new cultures that became part of the Hellenistic world, much of which derived from Persia (Assmann 2011: 252).

It is possible to detect a shift from the polis to the cosmic order of, what the Greeks called, the *oikoumene*, that is the wider inhabited world. This enlarged conception of the world was reflected, for example, in the first ideas of cosmopolitanism as expressed in the political thought of the Cynics and Stoics for whom loyalty to the wider human community was more important than the community into which one was born. Another expression of this cosmopolitan worldview was the movement towards 'Universal History' as the attempt to find ways to narrate the whole world rather than just one aspect of it. The emergence of what Inglis and Robertson (2005) have termed an 'ecumenical sensibility' that came with these developments bequeathed to later ages a European civilizational imaginary that cannot be understood as a narrow Eurocentric conception of the world. At this time the relatively closed world of the republic and the open horizon of the cosmopolis established two visions of political community in Greek thought. The tension between these two visions of political community has been an enduring feature of modern political thought and in many ways reflects the two aspects of the idea of Europe that collide with each other in the present day: an open vision of Europe versus a closed one. The republican tradition of the Greek polis and the Hellenistic vision of a global order were to have a lasting impact on the European political heritage, which can be seen as a tradition that has continuously reconstructed and reinvented this tension between these two conceptions of political community, which were intertwined but provided a basic set of orientations for the republican and the cosmopolitan traditions.

The Greek sources of European civilization were characterized by both loss and recovery. The papyrus roll used by the Greeks for the written text was less durable than the culture they recorded. Consequently as a result of the decay of the papyrus rolls, many of the great works of classical Greek culture were lost by the sixth century, until Arab scholars of the twelfth and thirteenth centuries recovered and translated them using new methods of paper production. Greek civilization survived during the long period of Roman civilization not directly, but only through translations, appropriations and traces. The implication of this is that much of the ancient sources of the European heritage are known only indirectly. Yet, much of the later Hellenic civilization did survive well into Roman times and was especially present in the Byzantine tradition (see Chapter 4).

All societies and civilizations have a myth of their origins, which has generally been linked to an act of emancipation or a revolutionary event that had a foundational status. The Roman myth of its origins was to become a foundational myth for Europe: the city of Rome was believed to have been founded in 753 BCE by Romulus, a descendent of Aeneas, who fled from Troy after its sack in the twelfth century BCE and eventually reached Latium where a Greek colony was founded. According to this myth, the Trojans fled to other parts of Europe to found a series of imperial dynasties. This myth of Aeneas was later appropriated by European monarchies for it was held that the exiled Trojans founded a series of cities in the West and many of the western monarchies claimed to derive their genealogy from the exiles of Troy (Tanner 1993). The Tudor, Habsburg and Ottoman historical myths of legitimation all proclaimed the Trojans to be their ancestors.

There is little if any archaeological basis to this myth, which tells a story of how the civilization that arose in Rome was a Greco-Roman civilization. As with all narratives it tells us more about the conception of history of contemporaries than about historiographical knowledge.

Roman civilization emerged out of a long process by which Greek culture was reshaped into a new form. The civilizational continuity that Europe has with the Greeks has often been seen as very much a Roman creation. However, it should not be forgotten that much of the Greek culture survived independently and was not entirely absorbed into the nascent Roman civilization. Some of this remained outside mainstream Roman culture and can be seen as constituting a counter-narrative to the dominant tradition associated with the patrician Roman legacy.

In one of the most important interpretations of Greek thought for the idea Europe, the Czech philosopher Jan Patocka (2002) in *Plato and Europe*, first published in 1973, sought to redefine the spiritual essence of Europe as a philosophical quest. The foundations of Europe are in the mind, rather than in political reality. Europe was born out of the ruins of the polis, but destroyed itself in the twentieth century; its most important idea is to be found in the philosophy of Plato and in particular the notion of the 'care of the soul': 'The history of Europe is in large part, up until, let us say, the fifteenth century, the history of the attempt to realize the care of the soul' (Patocka 2002: 37). This later was in danger of disappearing 'under the weight of something, something that might be deemed a concern, or care about dominating the world' (2002: 88). Patocka identified the basic idea of the inner life of the individual as the core of the European tradition and which influenced the Christian tradition. He stressed as the Greek philosophical achievement to be the belief in the fundamental uncertainty of human existence, that the individual is not a slave to the state or to history and that everything is open to scrutiny. This conception of the individual, he believed, was in danger of getting lost in later periods of European history. He may have been overly pessimistic about this, but the basic idea of the conception of the autonomy of the self was clearly one of the significant legacies of ancient Greece and constituted the basis of a tradition of anti-despotism that was an important influence in European history.

In stark contrast to Patocka, Carl Schmitt (2006), writing in Berlin in the 1940s, saw the source of the unity of Europe neither in the polis not in the soul, but in the Greek notion of the *Nomos*, which the spatial and juridical basis of civilization in that it gives both 'order and an orientation'. What he called the *Nomos* of the earth was in essence a juridical model for 'land-appropriation', which for Schmitt was a more important legacy than that of the polis for it laid the basis of what he called the *Jus Publicum Europaeum* – the legal order that governed

Europe since the sixteenth to the twentieth century. The enigmatic suggestion in this work is that this world order is now finally coming to an end and a new and global one is coming and will herald the decline of Europe.

Roman civilization

Greek civilization as it emerged during the Hellenic era did not have the enduring significance of the Roman civilization, which was a civilization underpinned by an empire that established a lasting institutional framework for European civilization. Although the Greeks were partly colonized by the nascent Roman civilization, Greek culture has largely come to us today through the Roman tradition and the later Christian tradition which was formed out of the confluence of Greek and Jewish thought. Due to the overlapping nature of the two civilizations, it is only with some qualifications that we can speak of Greco-Roman civilization. However, this must be qualified for there was never entirely a fusion of Greek and Roman culture, for Rome never fully absorbed Greek culture and consequentially Greek culture was never entirely Romanized. This may call into question the notion of a Greco-Roman civilization when what existed were simply two interacting civilizations.

The Roman Empire emerged out of the Roman Republic, but was more than an empire; it was a civilization. It was formed out of a geopolitical territory that emerged out of the conquests of the Roman Republic and by the time of Augustus was declared emperor in 31 BCE, when the Roman Republic finally became an empire, it included much of what we today call Europe, but more as well in that much of it lay outside the later historical territories of Europe. This empire was as much eastern as European or western; it included a great diversity of cultures, Celts, Germans, Romans, Iberians, Berbers, Illyrians, and Libyans. The Chinese once believed Antioch was the capital rather than its third largest city (Dudley 1995: 243). It created an enduring institutional framework based on the rule of law, which served as an integrative framework for Europe, and a system of writing that provided a framework in which non-Romans, such as the Germanic tribes, used to construct their own history. Such ideological power was one way in which the identity of Europe was shaped. In this sense civilization comes with the power that writing brings with it since it is writing that made possible historical memories. The worldview of the Roman Empire embodied both a civilizational worldview and various cultural orientations that were decisive for the course of European civilization.

The civilizational worldview did not fully crystallize until the adoption of Christianity as the official state religion of the empire, but the cultural orientations were present from an early period and could be described as a nascent global culture, which like the European culture that was to follow in its wake was not based on a single native culture, but a plurality of competing ones.

As a geopolitical entity, the Roman Empire was itself a civilizational constellation embodying a vast array of cultures connected by transport networks of roads and seaways. The Roman Empire shifted the eastwardly Hellenic civilization westwards, though much of present-day Northern Europe lay outside it. The Roman Empire was above all a Mediterranean civilization. Its diversity reflected the multi-ethnic world of the Mediterranean as well as the wider European continent including much of Germany and England. The fault-lines in these two countries that shaped so much of their history can be related to the lines that marked the final advance of Romanization. Although we often see Europe divided between an East and a West, this distinction made no sense in Roman times when a conception of Europe did not exist. The empire was Asian, African and as much as it was European. It was culturally cosmopolitan in the sense of being mixed, but was politically centralized and the imperial centre dominated the periphery. The pre-Christian Roman religion adopted many pagan traditions from all over the Mediterranean world with which it came into contact in its continuous expansion. The Roman Empire, while expanding in many directions from Rome after the Punic Wars against Carthage and the conquest of the Hellenic territories, was in its time a world empire. In his studies of the Mediterranean, Fernand Braudel portrayed the interaction of a plurality of civilizations within the unity of the Mediterranean: Christian, Jewish, Islamic and Orthodox civilizations interacted and the cross-fertilization of their cultures produced the world of the Mediterranean, which he associates with the multi-ethnic Roman Empire. Braudel (1994) never developed his concept of civilization, which remained a vague, suggestive notion entailing both unity and pluralism within it and at the same time included an intra-civilizational dynamic that was creative and transformative. Cultural trade, diasporas, translations, cultural diffusions and cross-fertilizations, produced the world of the Mediterranean and its civilizations.

It is possible to see the Roman Empire as consolidating a vast web of cultures that had already been in contact. It imposed on this already connected world a central authority which was supported by superior military power, integrative systems of transport and communication across sea and land, technological innovations, trade networks, and a political and intellectual elite who were united by a common language. The Roman concept of empire is closer to a civilizational vision of an open world endlessly expanding than the Greek polis of the pre-Hellenic period; it was not confined to a specific territory, for empire and world were one and the same. While the Roman Empire was won by military conquest, the civilization that was created out of that process was a more universalistic one than the earlier Hellenistic civilization for all its cosmopolitanism. Hellenism was ultimately a cultural world based on the universality of the Greek language; the Roman Empire was a political and legal order in the first instance. Although the earlier Greek distinction between Hellas and barbarians, generally equated with Persians, was less apparent in the later Hellenic period, nothing like the Roman distinction of citizens and non-citizens existed. The Roman Empire was based on a principle of universal rule that had no territorial limits. As a geopolitical configuration as opposed to a linguistic world, the empire was defined not by territory, but by the limits of its political system and a vast social, cultural and economic world.

The Romans were conscious of peoples living beyond the frontiers of the empire, which in principle was limitless before it collapsed under its own weight. It is now recognized that it is not easy to speak of 'barbarians' beyond the frontiers in a very clear-cut way. Roman frontiers were porous and not fixed points of closure; many served as points of communication in what in fact were very often expansive borderland areas (see Whittaker 1994). The establishment and expansion of such borderlands was instrumental in creating the foundations of a European civilization in which inside and outside was not absolutely fixed. The Roman frontier might be seen as the site of European civilization and not the central imperial core as such. The frontier was shaped in a constant push and pull in which the imperial territory expanded in multiple directions. In this sense, then, the frontiers of the Roman Empire connected as much as divided people. The lines on a map which we today call borders did not exist in the same way in the ancient world where the *limes* were not always linear and fixed, but zones or borderlands. It was through this expanding system of borderlands that Europe was created from Roman times onwards.

It must not be forgotten than in a seafaring age the Alps represented a far greater geographical, and hence a cultural, divide than the Mediterranean. The sea served to unite people rather than divide them. The entire trading networks of the ancient world criss-crossed the Mediterranean linking Cadiz, Carthage, Alexandria and Constantinople. New interpretations of the Mediterranean influenced by Horden and Purcell's interactionist analysis have stressed a world of interconnections established by exchange and commerce made possible by the sea (Horden and Purcell 2000; Harris 2006; see also Abulafa 2000; Gallant 2006). But the Roman Empire was an empire and asserted the dominance of the centre over the periphery.

An important part of the Roman contribution to European civilization has been commented on by Rémi Brague, namely a specific relationship to culture as the transmission of what is received (Brague 2002). Roman civilization was based on a culture that was based on the reworking of those cultures it came into contact with, in particular Greek, Hebraic, Near Eastern and African. These cosmopolitan currents were of course often checked by the republican tendencies of the metropolitan centre. This dynamic tension at the heart of the Roman Empire gave to Europe one of its creative impulses, namely the constant reworking of all cultures, including the heritage of the past. The implication of this is that Europe is not primarily based on peoplehood, but on a civilizational process that included violence as the primary means of securing its conditions of existence. The simple reality of the Roman Empire was its more or less total militarization, necessitated by the need to keep large standing arms. The armies of the modern age were far smaller and subject to greater restrictions than was the case in the age of the Roman Empire where war was a permanent feature of the age.

While the Roman civilization laid the basic structures of a European civilization, it also created a deep division, which ultimately made impossible less a common European civilization than an interconnecting constellation of different societies. When the Roman Empire finally split into an eastern and a western half the unity of its civilization was undermined but not fragmented. With the relocation of its capital in Constantinople in 330 AD, the Roman Empire had ceased to be exclusively Roman, although for long the citizens of Byzantium called themselves Romans. The consequences of the final political split between eastern and western empires in 395 has undoubtedly been exaggerated, at least until the Ottoman conquest of the Byzantine capital in 1453 when the definitive break occurred. The early division, which is better located in the sixth century when a distinct Byzantine civilization crystallized, did not engender the later division between East and West (see Arnason and Raaflaub 2011). While the eastern half included Egypt, the western half included Africa, which meant for the Romans the western parts of North Africa, Greece and the Aegean and most of the south of the Balkans went to the eastern empire. The Italian peninsula remained a dividing line between the two halves of the empire (Herrin 1987: 22–3). Yet despite these shifts and divisions, the notion of the Roman tradition as such was not bound to Rome, and like Europe, it was transferrable to the parts of the world that it came into contact with. In this sense it constituted what Stephen Greenblatt (2010) has called a 'mobile culture'.

The Byzantine Empire provided continuity with the Greco-Roman tradition which continued links between West and East after the division of the empire. It was founded as the 'New Rome', or the 'Second Rome' and its citizens called themselves Romans. But the decline of the Roman Empire was irreversible and complete in the sixth century when the eastern empire failed to recover the western half. What survived was the empire's main creation, a civilizational heritage, to a large degree now based on Christianity and which was to provide a framework for the homogenization of Europe in the Medieval era. Of the many architects of this homogenization were the Normans whose conquests established unity that later laid the foundation of the idea of Europe. The institutional framework of feudalism they created was decisive in laying the structural foundations of a societal order in Europe. Significant, too, in particular in transmitting the Greek and Roman legacy, was the Irish monastic movement from the late sixth to early eight century. The Irish monks – such as Columbanus, John Scotus Eriugena – founded monasteries across Europe and were critical in the transcription and translation of the texts of antiquity, thus providing civilizational continuity in an era of major change following the break-up of the Roman Empire and the re-configuration of core and peripheries.

While the word 'Europe' did exist, albeit without much meaning, the term 'Europeans' was rarely used in Ancient times. The word Franks was more commonly used by those who encountered Europeans well into modern times. This was simply because there was no other word to describe the invading Franks from Normandy who arrived from the West in the twelfth century. The notion of Europeans was absent and Europe did not signify a cultural or political reality other than a vaguely defined geographical domain that only roughly coincided with the notion of the Occident.

The decline of the Roman Empire in the West may have been paradoxically the source of the eventual rise of the North Western region of Europe, where continuity with Rome was more an ideology of the

Franks than a reality; for the fragmentation of the empire led to the emergence of new and very different societal structures, associated with feudalism and the Latin western Church. In the East, the greater continuity of the Roman tradition under the Byzantines reached a point of major rupture in 1453 with the final end of the Eastern Empire (see Chapter 4).

Jewish civilization

Along with Athens and Rome, Jerusalem is an important reference point in the European civilizational constellation. Together these traditions have shaped the European heritage. The Greek, Roman, Christian, Islamic and Judaeo traditions gave a lasting orientation to European civilization, which was never based on one single source. It would not be inaccurate to say European civilization derived from a multiplicity of cultures. More to the point however it was formed through the fusion, interaction and transformation of cultures, since the cultures did not always remain separate. The tensions that have been a characteristic feature of Europe have reflected this process of continuous creation. The logic of this process can be described as the process of civilization to which belongs an integral cosmopolitanism and a questioning of the authority of political rule, which derives from an anti-despotic current in ancient thought.

As a civilization, Judaism is a complicated case since the Jews unlike the Romans are specifically a people in an ethnic or religious sense and cannot be defined in terms of an imperial territory or state. The ethnic definition is of course contested as is relation to a territory. The religious unity of the Jews distinguishes them from groups that are defined by membership of a political community, territory or a shared language. It is closer to a culture than to a civilization, but embodies some of the features of a civilization. However, one can speak of Jewish civilization as distinct from the notion of a Jewish people, religion, or national groups.

Jewish civilization exists in two senses, as a diasporic culture – Eisenstadt's (1992) argument – consisting of the entire historical experience of the Jews and, secondly, as the religious culture out of which the Jewish civilization was formed. It is difficult to separate these dimensions, but the distinction is an important one, since the Jewish contribution to Europe has been twofold; first, as a diasporic people whose historical experience has included an important European dimension since the medieval era when Jews migrated to various parts of Europe; secondly, as the cultural origin of the Roman and Christian civilization. In this latter sense what is important is the religious and cultural dimension, rather than the specific contributions of Jews, due to its formative influence on other civilizational currents.

Regarding the diasporic dimension of the Jewish contribution to Europe, once they migrated to Europe Jews played an important role in the translations of ancient texts into Latin, often through Arabic translations. However, the Jews are a diasporic people who moved to Europe relatively late and were not unified into an organized unit. Unlike Christianity, there was not a political order unifying the different Jewish traditions and there was not a territorial basis for Jewish civilization other than a myth of an original homeland. Of course, too, the Jews were excluded from much of the economic and political life of Europe until their political emancipation.

The role of Judaism in the making of European civilization is closer to the example of Ancient Greece in that Judaism lay at the origin of the Roman and Christian tradition. Both Christianity and Judaism are based on the idea of a personal redeemer God. It is possible to see European civilization as a synthesis of the civilizational traditions that stemmed from Athens, Jerusalem and Rome. Unlike the Greco-Roman tradition, Judaism was monotheistic and it was this that provided a cultural orientation for Christian Europe. Jan Assmann has argued that Jewish civilization was in part shaped by the rejection of Egyptian sacred kinship (Assmann 1987). Max Weber (1952[1911–20]) in his *Ancient Judaism* also stressed the rejection of magic in Judaism, which he saw as not having developed the rationalizing tendencies of Christianity. But unlike the Greeks, who also rejected sacred kinship, the notion of divine authority that the Jews created instead led to a civilizational form that was based on monotheism, which in turn was conducive to a spirit of individuality born of the struggle to gain salvation through redemption by a personal God. A particularly powerful influence emanating from Judaism was the experience of exile and with it the critique of domination. As Brunkhorst (2005: 28–30) has suggested in his reconstruction of European solidarity, the mythic story of the Exodus of the slaves from Egypt and the confrontation with foreign domination in the name of a higher law provided the sources for a European tradition of resistance to domination.

The Old Testament has exerted a lasting influence on Europe. Many of the basic cultural orientations of Christianity were expressed in it, most importantly the idea of a personal God and the notion of a higher order of justice. It established the belief in the incomprehensibility and utter otherness of the divine. With Christianity, human history and divine history were conceived in non-cyclical terms. The emphasis shifted to the contingency of providence, in which human beings play a role in bringing about the conditions of their salvation. Christianity itself began as a Jewish sect and the schism of the sect and the religion was one of the major events in the making of Europe, since the new religion became the official religion of the Roman Empire and later of Europe itself. Thus to speak of the 'Judaeo-Christian' tradition is to refer both to a common origin and a history of the rejection of that origin and its crystallization in new forms. It is possible to venture the claim that this contradiction has been at the core of the European consciousness, which has had to confront the reality of a civilization that has been formed from diverse cultures all of which had to be refashioned by a church that itself saw itself based on a higher order truth as opposed to worldly wisdom.

The history of the Jewish diaspora in Europe draws attention to an aspect of the European heritage that is best exemplified by the Jewish historical experience. The Jews were the most transnationalized group in Europe since they were forced to take on economic functions such as itinerant trade, money-lending and other pursuits that depended on networks of international contacts that could cross a variety of borders. These networks developed into a myriad of economic, personal and communal connections that often bound Jews across early modern Europe (Miller and Urry 2012). The Jewish experience is too a reminder of the spirit of rootlessness that has pervaded Europe from the earliest of times.

Since the destruction of the European Jews in the Holocaust, the relation of Europe to the Jews has been subject of considerable debate and one in which the line between civilization and barbarism has had to be reconsidered in light of the deep currents of anti-Semitism that have been a part of European civilization and which were endemic to Christianity at a number of points in its history. But from a civilizational perspective the Greek, Judaeo and Christian traditions were interlinked in the making of the European civilizational heritage, which cannot be reduced to one of these traditions. The Christian tradition was itself the result of the intersection of the Greek and Judaic traditions. Despite this confluence of traditions within the Christian tradition, the notion of a 'Judaeo-Christian' tradition should be treated with caution, since the two religions went their separate ways and the fact of a shared origin does not guarantee commonality. The very term 'Judaeo-Christian' was not in currency until the early twentieth century when it emerged along with the idea of a singular western civilization in opposition to the communist atheistic one in the East. This construction was at the cost of the neglect of the much more plural nature of the civilizational heritage of antiquity.

3
Christianity in the Making of Europe

Christianity was not originally European but Asiatic and its origins were in Judaism. The oldest known Christian church is in Jordan. Yet it was to become the most characteristically European feature of the civilization that followed in the wake of the Roman Empire. The Christian church did not see itself as European as such but universal. It was not until the separation of the Roman and Byzantine traditions of Christianity from 1054 that the equation of the former with Europe, understood as the Occident, became established. For centuries Europe was more or less equated with Christianity. Although based on a universalistic belief system that itself was not specific to Europe but global, Christianity was an integral part of European civilization. Even the secular and republican societies that were to develop in Europe maintained links with Christianity, which adapted in different ways to modernity and to the secularization that it brought.

It is often claimed that the defining feature of Europe is Christianity, which is what marks it off from the non-European world. But what does it mean to speak of Europe as Christian? Given the diverse forms of Christianity that developed in the western and eastern parts of the Roman Empire, the legacy of the Reformation, counter-Reformation, and modern secularism the Christian legacy is by no means a clearly defined one. Moreover, Christianity saw itself as a world religion, and not as a European one. Indeed, a considerable part of the European heritage has been a distancing from its Christian past. Much of modern Europe was shaped in a process of secularization in which church and state were gradually separated. The early medieval struggle between pope and emperor was one of the constitutive forces in the making of Europe. Before modern secularism the conflicts of the early modern period over the confessional identities of the European states

67

established long-lasting tensions and much of modernity emerged in opposition and renunciation of the Christian heritage. In view of this to claim that Europe is defined by Christianity is by no means straightforward, for it was in many ways a paradoxical heritage since the internal divisions with Christianity have been the source of much of the divisions within Europe. Yet there is no denying the tremendous impact of Christianity in the shaping of Europe. To appreciate this we need to go back to the emergence of the early church in the late Roman Empire.

The rise of Christianity

Originally a sect that emerged out of Judaism on the African and Asian margins of the empire, it eventually became during the reign of Constantine I in 331 the official religion of the Roman Empire. Christianity was to become the single most important influence in the making of Europe, but it was itself not European in origin. Christ spoke a Semitic language called Aramaic while St Paul along with several other followers of the sect's founder spoke Greek, which was the language of the earlier Christian movement and the language in which the New Testament was written, since this was the language used by Jewish scholars in the era. Several more centuries lapsed before the teachings of Christ, as interpreted by his followers, became the basis of an organized church and Latin as its language. With the decline of the Roman Empire, the Christian religion survived and preserved many of its features. Unlike many other of the world religions, Christianity was based on a written as opposed to an oral culture and a centrally organized administrative system, which endured for sufficiently long to become the defining feature of the religion of the empire. It thus came about that Christianity was Roman rather than anything else and adopted the Latin language and much of the imperial symbolism. Even with the relocation of the Roman Empire in Constantinople, the idea of a 'New Rome' was promulgated to provide continuity with the old Roman Empire. Although this invocation of Rome was to lose any real connection with the western capital, it revealed the symbolic power of the Roman past over the present.

Christianity developed in the geopolitical area we call Europe, originally the relatively small Carolingian Empire. Charlemagne who styled himself the 'father of Europe' established the first major association of Europe with Christianity. Since the Muslim conquests of North Africa and the Near and Middle East, Christianity became territorially consolidated only in those areas of the later Roman Empire. With the expansion of the Muslim world westwards across North Africa as far as the Iberian peninsula, Christianity did not gain much ground in the Southern and Eastern Mediterranean and increasingly lost its earlier cosmopolitanism in becoming the religion of a Carolingian Europe, with its centre in the Franco-Germanic lands west of the Rhine. The Christianization of the Scandinavians and later the Slavs from the eleventh century was the first major step in the identification of Europe with Christendom.

Christianity provided Europe with a certain continuity from the Roman Empire to the rise of national states from the seventeenth century. The idea of a universal empire was taken over by the Church, which cultivated a historical memory that linked Christendom with the Roman Empire, which was repudiated as pagan and taken over and translated into the new Christian culture: the universal empire became the universal church and the cult of emperor worship was transposed to the papacy. The Church had the organization, the ideological zeal, and political capacity to make this possible. Since the fourth century, when the Roman Empire embraced Christianity, a huge Christian material culture began leading to a major redefinition of space. Christians took an existing Roman architectural form, such as the basilica, and adopted it to their needs (O'Malley 2004: 186). The cathedrals that were built across Europe gave to it a certain uniformity. Whether the continuity that it established diminished the discontinuities of history is, and will probably remain, a controversial issue. The decisive matter in this may be the timing of major ruptures. There is considerable evidence to suggest that the basic value orientations and institutional structures were in place before the collapse of a unitary Christian worldview and the entity that is known as Christendom. While the general move to modernity from the seventeenth century onwards resulted in the gradual erosion of medieval Christianity, what remained was a civilizational framework that proved to be highly resilient. From the sixth century the basic institutional structures of European civilization were established in the legal and administrative systems of the medieval states and their cities and universities.

The Frankish kingdom was the crucible for the formation of medieval Christendom and reflected a northern shift in Christianity from the Mediterranean. The Franks, who can be regarded as one of the heirs of the Roman Empire, created also an embryonic Europe, with the later western understanding of Europe having its core the Carolingian kingdom, which extended as far eastwards only to the Elbe, the mountains of Bohemia and alpine districts of Austria. Indeed, one of the first uses of Europe was at Charlemagne's court at Aachen (Barraclough 1963: 12). Originating in North East Gaul, they can be seen as mix of French and German cultures. Ever since the crowning of Charlemagne, the Carolingian king, as Emperor of the Romans in 800, this association of imperial rule and Christianity was forged as a political and cultural identity for Europe for many centuries. The association with Rome was largely symbolic, as the Roman Empire had disintegrated. Gregory the Great associated the Church with Europe by making the papacy the centre of gravity in Europe (Ullmann 1969: 135). However it was not only Christianity that gave to Europe a certain civilizational unity, but also the system of feudalism that developed from the Carolingian Empire in the ninth and tenth century and was later adopted by much of Europe. Feudalism played a greater role than the Roman past in the making of modern Europe since it shaped the basic societal model of Europe. This has been referred to by Moore (2000) as the first European revolution due to its transformative impact on European history; it was a period in which the peasantry and elite were both transformed by a social and political system of control and production. One of the main beneficiaries of the new system of power that it produced was the Catholic Church.

Christianity enjoyed about 1,000 years of unchallenged continuity in most of Europe, letting aside the question of the Byzantine schism (which will be considered in the next chapter). Some qualification is necessary here, for there were challenges to its ascendancy, as is evidenced by the numerous sects and heresies. What stands out in all of this was the capacity of the Church not only to withstand such attacks, but to consolidate itself as the religion of the former Roman Empire and even to present its self as the heir of that empire. The medieval notion of a universal monarchy was the last and unsuccessful attempt to forge a synthesis of religion and the state. The notion of a universal monarch, which goes back to Dante's *De Monarchia*, was a legacy of the Roman Empire and was invoked by the Habsburg emperor Charles V in the sixteenth century (Yates 1975). But the Holy Roman Empire of the German Nation, which attempted to lay claim to the Roman legacy, was a German Empire and was challenged by France and the notion of a universal monarchy had become an anachronism when Napoleon invoked it.

The early Church established an institutional framework for Christianity to develop in close association with political authorities. For several centuries Latin was a common language for the elites until its gradual vernacularization. However, the relationship between the church and state was such that neither side ever fully controlled the other. Although European states recognized ecclesiastical authority, they were rarely subservient to it and never embraced it to the same degree as in the Byzantine and Muslim traditions where the autonomy of the political was never as strong as in Western Europe. A civilizational feature of Europe was that religion never entirely dominated the state and ultimately the state remained the source of power. A feature of European political modernity has been the continued contestation of political power between the Church, the state, and civil society. Political authority always remained relatively contested and the Church's authority had to compete with the authority of science, especially from the Renaissance period, and the authority of political elites. In the end it was the state that won the struggle. The principle of *cujus regio, ejus religio*, whereby the ruler decided the religion of the population effectively, allowed political authority to assert superiority over clerical authority. In later centuries state power had to compete with civil society, which further diminished the political power of ecclesiastical authorities. But in Europe the political neutralization of Christianity had already been accomplished by the sixteenth century.

The Middle Ages is the key to an understanding of the making of Europe since it was in this period that the idea of Europe became concretely embodied in symbolic forms and the notion of 'Europeans' first emerged, though this was a term that has limited use. In the fifteenth century the first images of Europe as a contrast to Asia appeared. The heritage of antiquity was of course important, but more significant was the use made of that inheritance. The great historians of Medieval Europe, Marc Bloch and Jacques Le Goff, are agreed that it was in the Middle Ages that Europe was created as a process of unity and diversity that emerged out of the mixing of populations and the consolidation of political and societal structures. As Le Goff (2006) has argued, the emergence of a common Christian culture was decisive as far as Western Europe was concerned. The eleventh century was critical in the emergence of a common culture, generally referred to until the wars of religion of the seventeenth century as Christendom. The fact that the civilizations of the East were vastly superior to Europe, which derived many of its achievements from adaptations of Eastern sources in technology and science, does not detract from the significance of the gradual rise of the West in this Middle Ages. But this was a process that occurred more through internal colonization than imperial conquest, which was a later development.

In his study of the making of Europe in the Middle Ages, the historian Robert Bartlett (1993) has described the formation of Europe in terms of a process of internal colonization that brought about transformation and rapid societal convergence. Medieval Christendom was an expanding world in which the edge of Europe was pushed in many directions through settlements and migratory movements: the Norman conquest of England, the English conquest of the Celtic world in the western and northern regions of the British Isles, German expansion in the Baltic region and in Eastern Europe, the Catalan conquest of the south of Italy, the Castilian 'reconquest' of the Iberian peninsula. The 'Europeanization of Europe' was largely a product of the conquest and the resulting homogenization brought about by the expanding Frankish kingdom with its centre west of the Elbe. Bartlett describes how from this part of Western Europe expansionary expeditions were launched in all directions and that by the fourteenth century a large part of Western, Northern and Southern Europe had a relatively high degree of cultural homogeneity. While the early Middle Ages was a world of diversity, this had all changed by 1300 due to the spread of Norman customs. The spread of the alphabet, the chartered town, monastic orders, the cults of the saints and the adoption of the names of the saints, coinage, the Latin language and universities were structuring forming blueprints for the fashioning of European societies.

In all these movements Christianity was implicated and Europe was as a result gradually consolidated. Europe was as much the product of conquest and colonization as, in later centuries, the initiator. The Europeans who later colonized much of the world were themselves products of societies that were themselves formed out of conquest and colonization over several centuries. In Bartlett's (1993: 314) words: 'The European Christians who sailed to the coasts of Americas, Asia and Africa in the fifteenth and sixteenth centuries came from a society that was already a colonializing society. Europe, the initiator of one of the world's major processes of conquest, colonization and cultural transformation, was also the product of one.' But medieval conquest was different from later forms, for in the process of conquest and colonization medieval Christendom became increasingly homogenized while its outer regions were often divided and fragmented until a point has been reached when the centre established its power of the periphery. European overseas colonialism took a different form since such colonialism was based on the separation of colony and imperial centre and frequently involved slavery, but always entailed the appropriation of the colony for the enrichment of the imperial centre. Yet any account of the formation of Europe cannot ignore the process by which the various centres of political and economic power extended their power of the periphery incorporating it into territorial units that were themselves subject to later conquest. Bartlett's characterization of the difference between medieval and modern colonization is worth noting: 'When Anglo-Norman settled in Ireland or Germans in Pomerania or Castilians in Andalusia, they were not engaged in the creation of a pattern of regional subordination. What they were doing was reproducing units similar to those in their homelands. The towns, churches and estates they established simply replicated the social frameworks they knew back home. The net result of this colonialism was not the creation of "colonies", in the sense of dependencies, but the spread, by a kind of cellular multiplication, of the cultural and social forms found in the western Christian core. The new lands were closely integrated with the old. Travellers in the Middle Ages going from Magdeburg to Berlin and onto Wroclaw, or from Burgos to Toledo and on to Seville, would not be aware of crossing any decisive social or cultural frontier' (Bartlett 1993: 306).

It does appear to be the case that despite the narrowing of the geo-political base of Christianity and the exclusion of the Byzantine Empire, Christianity from about the sixth century to the fifteenth century had established itself as the common religion of Europe. It was more than a religion. Christianity provided the medieval European powers with a cultural model based on shared values. When that world was finally challenged from within by the Protestant reformers, the civilization it had shaped for more than a millennium entered into a new phase, which has generally been referred to as one of secularization.

The Christian worldview

Christianity provided some of the most important cultural orientations to Europe, including too a civilizational worldview. At the core of Christianity lies the belief in redemption, which cultivated modern individualism and the belief that the profane world can be mastered by the individual. It is often argued that democracy, equality in the eyes of the law and the idea of the liberty of the individual derives from the belief that all people stand equal before the eyes of God. It can also be argued that the values of solidarity and individual responsibility have a certain resonance in Christian ideas, although this should not be exaggerated since many of these values of 'the gift of law' can be related to both pre-Christian as well as to non-Christian traditions.[1] Indeed, S. N. Eisenstadt (1986) has made the claim that the key impulse of modernity – the notion that the world can be fashioned by human agency – was born with the great religions in Axial Age with the discovery of transcendence and the desire to bring the kingdom of God onto earth. There is much evidence to suggest that the modern quest for liberty was related to religious struggles. The political demands of dissenters and many of the Protestant Reformers for freedom of worship provided the conditions for the recognition of other kinds of liberty, although largely only for Christian churches. Luther's revolt for instance was made in the name of the German nation. This took many forms – in England leading to an established Church – the position that emerged from the end of the seventeenth century, while being very far from late modern pluralism, was part of the movement towards the democratization of state power and led to some of the early proclamations of nationhood.

There is also an important connection between Christianity and modernity. Christianity was a relatively modernizing religion in that it promoted a worldview that proclaimed the de-magicification of the world; it sought to eradicate paganism and replace it with doctrinal authority controlled by an ordained priesthood. It has often been observed that the term 'modern' was first used by Pope Gelasius in the fifth century to distinguish the Christian era from the pagan age. However we should not conclude from this that modernity was the paradoxical product of the rationalization of Christianity, a thesis that would appear to have been the view of Max Weber and Carl Schmitt. Modernity developed on quite independent foundations, however much it may have had a resonance in certain tendencies in the Christian religions. For instance, one of the distinctive features of modernity – modern experimental science – was greatly influenced by Christianity in that many Christian reformers believed that religion could explain the divine plan. There was too an integral link between the belief in the freedom of science and scholarship and the freedom of religious worship. Of the major world religions, Christianity was relatively late and effectively derives from the seventh century when ancient Christianity came to an end with the Carolingian Renaissance and the codification of new doctrines and the consolidation of the Church and its monastic orders. As is well known, Christianity in particular in its Protestant forms was more compatible with the spirit of capitalism than were the other world religions. According to Weber, it was this affinity that led to the victory of capitalism in the modern world.

Letting aside the complex question of the relation of Christianity to modernity, the cultural logic of Christianity was one that gave to

Europe a certain character and which might be said to be the source of its cultural model and one of the defining features of its heritage. The significant aspect of this, which may have been connected to the contestability of doctrinal authority, was the constant revisions of doctrine. Christianity was a religion that underwent considerable change in the course of its history and ultimately brought about its own secularization. In this socio-cognitive developments were significant. Shifts in doctrine occurred through reasoned disputes over the interpretations of the scriptures and in the course of its long history the church developed a considerable body of formal systems of theological interpretation. The intellectualization of religious belief in theology and institutionalized in universities gave rise to a cultural heritage that could be said to be characteristically European. The essential revisability of Christian doctrine was an expression of a religious movement that had conceived itself from the beginning as the source of all authority. Christianity repudiated the classical roots of Europe in the Greco-Roman civilizations, proclaiming itself as the new and the modern. There were certainly limits to this and eventually the modern world no longer saw itself in the terms of what had become a divided Christian church. This did not mean that modernity was characterized by a break from the past or from tradition, for tradition was reconstructed by modernity; at the same time the past exerted what might be best characterized as a non-determining power over modernity.

The discovery of the individual

Christianity was important in the shaping of the idea of the individual and gave rise to a different tradition than that of the Greek one, which rested on, to follow Brunkhorst (2005), civic solidarity. The Christian tradition instead established the idea of brotherly solidarity and, unlike the Greek tradition, it was apolitical. It made possible a conception of the individual as a member of a human and a divine community. Individualism and solidarity were two sides of the same coin that shaped the self as both an individual and as a collective actor. While Dumont (1986) traces the spirit of individualism to the origins of Christianity, it underwent major transformation in the first millennium.

In his account of the twelfth century Carolingian Renaissance, Colin Morris (1972) attributes to that century the 'discovery of the individual'. Self-knowledge was one of the dominant themes of the age as exemplified in a new concern with self-expression: 'We hear the authentic voice of the individual, speaking of his own desires and experiences' (1972: 67). The institution of the confession was a product of an age concerned with self-awareness as much as with punishment. The institution evolved as it was challenged by a new emphasis upon self-examination. Morris comments on the emergence of private confession, a new interest in psychology, the study of the passions and emotions, and the emergence of autobiography. The latter was part of a general tendency to examine and to publish one's personal experiences.

The arts, too, reveal the emergence of the individual as the object of artistic representations. Until the twelfth century portraiture was largely concerned with the representation of the rank and status of the individual. In this era it changed to record personal features. Morris speaks of the personalization of the portrait along with a transformation in vision. 'The twelfth century saw a distinct shift in the visual arts towards sensitivity to nature, and a more characteristically modern way of seeing the human form' (1972: 90). This can be found in memorial or tomb sculpture where there was an increasing emphasis on the display of the details of appearance and personal features as opposed to status and rank. It can also be found in busts of the Roman Emperors where there was an attempt to represent a certain individuality. Other examples can be found in the literature of the age, such as satire and the romance, which were both affected by the individualism of the age and the idea of following one's heart as well as protest against injustice.

The emergence of the individual can be found in the idea of friendship and the different area of love and eroticism. The self finds its identity in a relation with another self. Close personal friendship was a creation of the century and contributed to the emerging culture of humanism. Following Morris's characterization, the custom of the letter was a key vehicle for the expression of friendship, which in turn made possible the construction of the individual whose external acts are the products of an internal world that knows another reality. Letter writing was given a new emphasis in the twelfth century, many of which were simply stylistic devices for self-exploration. This was an age that had not yet discovered the writings of Plato and Aristotle on the subject, but had become the focus of a great amount of poetry. The cult of friendship found a natural place in the Church and the symbolism of human relations to God gave to it an additional religious dimension that reinforced the idea that every individual can have a personal relation to God. Of the many examples than can be given, the change in the appearance of the crucifix with a new devotional emphasis on the pains of Christ, who is increasingly represented in a more inwards and less formal spirit and in a manner that allows for the expression of personal grief. As Morris, argues, the importance of the individual's suffering with Christ is now paramount (1972: 141). Undoubtedly the most powerful impetus for the new individualism was the idea of participating in a divine mission and having a personal relation and place in the Kingdom of God. The modern age may have lost much of this devotion, but what survived and became the basis of Europe was the strong sense of the individual. This found its expression in many forms: in religious piety and dissent, philosophy, literature and in the self-questioning attitude and exploratory zeal of modern science, as well as in alternative political movements.

The social and economic order of the age made possible the first step in the direction of an autonomous life for an individual. At least for the upper classes and the citizens of the chartered towns, there were new professions as well as the higher ones, which might include being knight, a scholar, an administrator, or a monk. As Morris points out, there was as yet no clearly ordered ethic prevailing in these domains, for instance there were major disputes about the proper nature of knighthood or that of the monastic life. The institution of feudalism, may have created a space for people to think in personal as opposed to exclusively institutional terms insofar as it was based on personal bonds of commitment and obligation. Although there were hierarchical, they were also based on recognition of the other. However, it was in the cultural and religious developments of the age that the emergence of the individual is most evident.

The twelfth century discovery of the individual occurred within a narrow field of opportunities, mostly confined to the religious worldview of Christianity. In the following centuries, the exploration of individualism acquired more avenues for its expression. Medieval literature offers many examples of the search for the individual, such as the epic tradition and the new genre of biography and autobiography (Gurevich 1995). The injunction 'know yourself' by gaining knowledge of one's inner life rather than external acts opened the way for humanism and the cultivation of the European individual, leading eventually to Foucault's account of the birth of the modern self in the movement from sovereign power to biopower. (This theme will be returned to in Chapter 6 with respect to the augmented humanism of the Renaissance).

The present discussion can be concluded with an observation of the wider implication of the revolution of the eleventh century. According to R. I. Moore, the Carolingian elite brought about a social revolution in creating a new system of power which in its implications was more expansive than feudalism, which would eventually be replaced by capitalism. The result was a restless dynamism that came from 'their inner restlessness, their need to explore themselves and their destiny as well as the world they inhabited. The resulting combination of greed, curiosity and ingenuity drove these first Europeans to exploit their land and their workers ever more intensively, constantly to extend the scope and penetration of their governmental institutions, and in doing so eventually to create the conditions for the development of their capitalism, their industries and their empire. For good and ill it has been a central fact not only of European but of modern world history' (Moore 2000: 197).

Unity and division

Any account of the Christian nature of European civilization must consider that this heritage divided as well as united Europe. Christianity, like Europe itself, did not lead to a single church. The most important split occurred between Latin and Greek Christianity. Since the eleventh century this split became irreversible with the Orthodox Greek tradition, and a later Russian off-spring, representing a different version of Christianity. Hostility to the Orthodox Church was often greater than hostility to Islam. The fourth crusade was launched against the Byzantines rather than against the Muslims. This reveals a tendency to eradicate difference and impose and single belief system. The history of Christianity in Europe can be characterized by such tendencies towards intolerance and doctrinal uniformity. Where this was not possible through conversion, it was frequently imposed by force or the dissenters were either eradicated or marginalized. However, the resistance that such programmes provoked was as much a determining factor in the making of Europe, for the exercise of power attracts opposition. In the case of Christianity, dissent was never eradicated and its presence was an important factor in the internal transformation of Europe. It is also a reminder that not everything can be explained by external influences.

The history of Europe in the early modern period until the Peace of Westphalia in 1648 was shaped by the conflicts and upheavals that resulted in changes in the religions of the elites and masses. Since 1054 there was no pan-European religion, but three major religions: Catholicism, Orthodoxy and later Lutherism. For several countries in Northern and Southern Europe and in Russia these religions provided a framework of stability, while for others, unresolved religious conflicts had the consequence that modernity developed in an uneven manner. So whatever unity was established it was often at the cost of disunity on a wider scale and through the persecution and silencing of heretics and political opponents.

The Protestant Reformation and the Catholic counter-Reformation divided Europe to an extent that Christianity could never again be a source of unity. Divided in doctrine, ritual and language between an eastern Orthodox tradition and a western tradition that was itself divided between a Catholic south and a Protestant north, the European Christian heritage could only be a divided legacy. It can also be noted that some of the greatest religious divisions occurred within Protestantism where the conflict over rival doctrines was often greatest. In addition, the institutional and doctrinal reforms of the Catholic counter-Reformation, produced by the Council of Trent (1545–63) undermined a continuous Catholic tradition.

Yet, despite such divisions the important point is that the basic value orientations and the societal shape of Europe was already established prior to these divisions. The most immediate consequence of the Reformation was the disappearance of an official Christian civilization. The conflicts of the Reformation, at least for Western Europe, had positive outcomes in that the states that consolidated from the sixteen and seventeenth century onwards developed on fairly clear-cut confessional lines. The adoption of a state religion allowed Western European states to pursue policies of integration and ultimately to establish the foundations for models of nationhood. This was less the case in much of Central and Eastern Europe where the outcome of the Reformation and counter-Reformation tended not to provide the same degree of national cohesion as in Western Europe. So the crystallization of Christianity in relatively secular states in the aftermath of the wars of religion in the early modern period eventually put Europe on the path to nation-state formation. The resulting divisions of European history, which were most notably evident in the twentieth century, should not disguise a more deeply rooted unity. This unity is less a homogeneous culture than a matrix of orientations that provided common reference points for different cultures.

The secularization of Christianity

Secularization did not lead to the disappearance of religion from Europe.[2] From the seventeenth century many European states pursued policies of creating established churches. Those countries shaped by the political modernity that arose from the French Revolution rejected established churches, but almost exclusively gave a privileged role to the religion of the majority of the population. The pursuit of established churches was generally preferred by Protestant states, while the tendency in countries where Catholicism was stronger was a more radical separation of church and state. This led to two models of secularism from the late seventeenth century. The first, the constitutional conservative tradition whereby secularism entailed an official church established by the state and thus controlled by the state. The second, associated with the republican tradition, whereby the state separated the church from the public domain, in effect privatizing religion. European secularism is a product of these two traditions.

The important point is that in neither case religion did not disappear from society, but was institutionalized in the first case as an official religion and in both cases in the privatistic domains of family, education, and other social institutions, such as in health. Indeed, by keeping religion out of the domain of the state, the more likely it survived the transition to modernity. Churches also played a key role as charitable institutions. The Enlightenment itself was for the greater part fostered by the reformed Protestant churches in Western Europe. It was only in France of the Catholic *ancien regime* that it took an anti-clerical form. But in France, Catholicism had a firm basis in the society and, for a time, in the state when Napoleon re-established Catholicism as a state religion. The Enlightenment was a good deal less hostile to religion than is often believed. Many of the major Enlightenment philosophers believed that religion had a place in modern society, different from science and rationality but equally valid when judged by its own criteria. This was the basis of the philosophy of Immanuel Kant, who argued that religious belief and ideas could not be justified on the basis of reason. According to this view, faith was protected from the critique of rationalists such as Voltaire, who argued only reason was a criterion of belief. Belief based on faith and belief based on evidenced supported knowledge – have not always been equally acknowledged by the critics and defenders of modernity. Jürgen Habermas and Joseph Ratzinger, later Pope Benedict XVI, in a dialogue in Frankfurt in 2002 commented on this feature of modernity, which they both agreed cannot be reduced to the culture of rational science (Habermas and Ratzinger 2005). It would thus be wrong to see religion and reason as separate and thus assume modernity has simply two faces that never interact or that religion was a product of the world of tradition that was superceded by modernity.

The secularization of church and state in Europe is rather a case of degrees of separation. France did not separate church and state until 1905 in the wake of the Dreyfus Affair, although there was a gradual movement towards secularization from the late nineteenth century. Aside from the anti-clericalism of short-lived Second Republic in Spain, only the communist countries were atheistic, in the sense of actively discouraging religion. The European trend is one of neutrality, but this has been ambiguous since there has mostly not been a total separation of church and state and there are different interpretations as to the meaning of neutrality, ranging from non-recognition, to a principle of equality of all churches, to a position of privatization. In Ireland, for example, state neutrality was a means of maintaining the power of the church, especially in social policy, while in the Netherlands it has been a means of giving equal support to the main churches. Many states support the main Christian churches and do so in different ways, even if it is only in the official recognition of religious funerals or collecting tax. Several countries such as the UK, Norway and Denmark have state churches, which mostly have a minor official significance. An exception in this regard is Greece where the Orthodox Church is the official established church, with the salaries and pensions of the clergy paid by the state, which appoints bishops and gives exception to the clergy from military service. There has been a general increase in religion in the former communist societies, in particular in a rise in Orthodoxy in Bulgaria, Rumania and in Russia. However, the increase in religious activity in post-communist countries is not greater than the extent of religious worship in Western Europe (see Norris and Inglehart 2004).

While Europe has become secular, the vestiges of Christianity remain. There is no Christian unity in Europe, but there is evidence of a residual Christianity that is largely symbolic. Many countries have Christian parties and several have state churches and throughout Europe there are Christian commemorations and festivities which are all a reminder of the Christian background to European modernity. Most Europeans are affiliated to a church while being otherwise unreligious. The decline in religion in Europe is partly demographic in that the more traditionally Catholic countries, where religion was stronger, Ireland, Spain and Italy, have lower birth rates than the Lutheran countries. Religious practice is predominantly a matter of formal affiliation around birth, marriage and death, but is relatively unimportant for identity for the vast majority of Europeans. Christianity is no longer an important part of European societies, but in civilizational terms it was one of the major formative influences in shaping modern Europe.

It is difficult to conclude from this that the European heritage is primarily transmitted by Christianity since so much of it over the past 300 years has been a product of quite different cultural influences. Yet while the process of secularization has led to the decreased importance of religion in European societies, the very nature of secularization had its roots in the social organization of the Christian churches in relation to the state. In many cases the path to nationhood was achieved through state churches and there never was a concerted attempt to articulate a European wide church aside since the end of the quest for a universal Catholic monarchy. It can be concluded that Christianity shaped Europe history, but did so in a way that undermined the possibility of cultural unity. This was precisely the condition that made possible the formation of a European cultural model, for a paradoxical consequence of Christianity was despite the intolerance and eradication of difference that it promoted, it was not unconnected to a spirit of freedom, criticism and individualism that arose in the questioning of doctrinal authority and in demands for freedom of worship.

4
Between East and West:
The Byzantine Legacy and Russia

Most accounts of European civilization neglect the place of Byzantium. The Byzantine world is often dismissed as a chapter in the history of the decline of the Roman Empire, whose legacy in the conventional account was taken up by the western monarchies and modern Europe emerged from a path that supposedly goes back to Rome and Athens. In this account, which will be challenged in this chapter, the main off-spring of Byzantine civilization – Orthodox Christianity – was given a marginal role in European civilization in general and hardly figures in discussions on the place and significance of Christianity in that history. The general representation of the Byzantine tradition has been one of decline and irrelevance (see Arnason 2000a).

In the Grand Narratives the history of Europe has been essentially portrayed as the history of the Latin West, which was given an undue continuity and unity. This is a view that is increasingly challenged today in light of a more general recognition of a wider conception of the European heritage and the need to take into account the historical experience of those parts of Europe whose route to modernity was shaped by the encounter with Russia and the earlier legacy of the eastern Roman Empire. Any assessment of the European legacy today will need to consider the place of Byzantium in the history of Europe.

The historical significance of Byzantium for a broader conception of Europe as a civilizational constellation should not be underestimated. The argument in this chapter is that the Byzantine Empire, as it was known, was an important transmitter of classical antiquity and that consequently continuity in European history cannot be entirely considered without reference to Byzantium. In addition is the significance of that tradition for those parts of South-Eastern and Eastern Europe that came under the influence of Orthodox Christianity, most notably

Serbia, Bulgaria, Romania, Greece and Cyprus. The Byzantine Empire was the most important basis of Christianity for centuries before the rise of the West and transmitted the cultural, legal and political legacy of the Roman Empire to Europe. In the present day with the revival of Orthodoxy and the enlargement of the EU to include parts of Europe that had been previously marginalized, the Byzantine legacy needs to be incorporated into a broader understanding of Europe, including Russia, Belarus and the Ukraine. In view of the emphasis placed in this book on a conception of Europe as formed out of interaction with the cultures and civilization of those parts of the world with which Europeans came into contact, it seems essential to include in an account of the European heritage a consideration of the encounter with Russia. Russia, itself more than a nation and empire, but a civilization in its own right that is part European and part Eurasian, was deeply influenced by the Byzantine tradition and given its impact on Central, Eastern and South-Eastern Europe for much of the twentieth century, it is hardly marginal to the European historical experience.

Europe is constituted as much in its margins as in the centre. As is argued throughout this book, the very notion of a centre and margins needs to be replaced with a new emphasis on Europe as a world historical region comprised of borderlands. Borderlands are not present only in the periphery; they are everywhere and not defined by reference to a single centre but in terms of a multiplicity of centres. In the account offered in this chapter those parts of Europe that were influenced by the Byzantine world and later by Russia constitute not only a borderland, but an integral part of the wider European civilizational constellation. Russia itself is more than a nation-state and empire but a civilization that has been significant in shaping European and world history. Russia embodies both European and Asian civilizational components, but it is best seen as a Eurasian civilizational form in its own right. No account of the origin of the idea of Europe can neglect the Russia counter-discourse (Neumann 1996). This has been one of the main competing discourses of the idea of Europe and one that also played its part in the formation of a European consciousness.

Re-evaluating the Byzantine Empire

While Byzantine civilization did not survive the westward expansion of Islam and more or less disappeared in 1453 following the fall of its capital Constantinople to the Ottomans, it was important because the civilizational pattern that Byzantium established in Late Antiquity, between the third and seventh century, was based on a revival of the Greco-Roman tradition, which was later transmitted to Western Europe and had considerable influence on Russian civilization. Much of the Greco-Roman world other than what was continued by Christianity had been lost in the West after the fall of the western empire. The result of this legacy is that the Byzantine tradition was an important transmitter of the cultures of antiquity and to the extent to which one can speak of continuity in European history, the Byzantine world cannot be neglected. It offered a civilizational model of unity in the East while in the West the Carolingian kingdom gave to Europe civilizational unity.

Constantinople, renamed Istanbul after the Ottoman conquest in 1453, was founded in 324 AD as the 'New Rome', but the culture that consolidated there inherited much of the earlier Hellenic civilization of Alexander the Great, which was revived in Late Antiquity calling into question the older Eurocentric notion of the decline of the Roman Empire and a Dark Age prior to the rise of the Christian Middle Ages. The name Byzantium was the name of the empire that grew around it, generally regarded as beginning in 330. Byzantium was more a state than an empire and came to represent a cultural or civilizational world that was part a continuation of Rome and a new embodiment of the Latin civilization, which had re-encountered Greek culture and language. It was known as an empire as its leader was titled emperor and was an expanding territorial state with its centre at Constantinople. Its language was Greek, but its inhabitants considered themselves to be Romans. Its population was mixed and over the centuries since its foundation it became more hybrid so it is not possible to speak of a specific ethnic composition. This of course is true of much of Europe. Unlike the Roman Empire in the West, at least since the third century AD, as Averil Cameron points out, the Byzantines did not make a formal distinction between citizens and the non-citizens of the conquered provinces who formed the population, for 'what mattered was not ethnicity or local background but shared culture, connections and status' (Cameron 2006: 8–9). An education in classical Greek was the defining feature of Byzantine culture, but did not represent an ethnic category. The Byzantines incorporated groups who accommodated themselves to their Greek culture.

Historians of late antiquity are now generally in agreement that after the end of the Roman Empire in the West, the Mediterranean world remained interconnected and much of the social and economic links forged by the Roman Empire continued. The Byzantine Empire was important in this advancement of Europe and the preservation of Greco-Roman culture as well as its transformation into new forms. It was a pan-Mediterranean civilization and one that established lasting links with Russia and the Muslim worlds. The Byzantine Empire stood between East and West, occupying as it did a nodal point in the Eastern Mediterranean and Black Sea. It was a culture based on the Hellenistic legacy and Orthodoxy. The sixth century saw the building of the great cathedral Santa Sophia in Constantinople. The Empire experienced a renaissance of classical culture and from the sixth to the eleventh centuries during which time there was considerable cultural and intellectual energy not only in architecture and art, but also in literature. By the seventh century there was a final break from the old western Roman Empire and the foundations of a new civilization were established. The Byzantine civilization became increasingly Greek, especially since the reign of Justinian in the sixth century, and the version of Christianity that emerged was the Orthodox faith, which finally broke from the Latin tradition in 1054. For over a thousand years this was the only direct line of continuity with Greek civilization. The civilizational significance of Byzantine goes beyond the Byzantine Empire. The Greek, Roman, Judaic and Christian civilizational heritages were consolidated in the pivotal period of Late Antiquity and in the subsequent 1,000 years a distinct civilization developed based on Orthodox Christianity. Even though this finally shifted to Russia, the long-span of its earlier history was a defining part of the European heritage and illustrates the inter-civilizational composition of Europe. It played an important role in transmitting the art of government and the legal and cultural legacy of Rome to Western Europe. So here, too, structuring forming effects took place that had a formative influence in the making of Europe.

From the eleventh century the Byzantine Empire went into gradual decline, with many of its territories falling to the rising Islamic civilization as it expanded westwards. What survived was the Orthodox tradition, its major legacy. The term Orthodox emerged as a result of the defeat of iconoclasm in the seventh century and the exclusion of various heresies, such as the Nestorian and Coptic churches. With its roots in the Byzantine civilization, Orthodoxy preserved a direct link with the Greco-Roman world. Despite sharing the same Judaeo-Christian roots, Orthodoxy established a very different religious tradition to the Latin one. This was a culture that gave a stronger basis to spirituality and nurtured a different kind of subjectivity and one that had political implications which were most strongly felt in imperial

Russia. The contrast with Latin Christianity was more pronounced following the western Reformation, for Protestantism and Orthodoxy had little in common. The Protestant emphasis on freedom, questioning and individualism was a contrast to Orthodox spirituality and communality and, though the two traditions of Christianity placed a strong emphasis in the scriptures, the Protestant churches rejected the major tenets of orthodoxy.

After the burning of the papal bull issued to excommunicate the Eastern church in 1054 the break between Latin and Greek Christianity was definitive. This culminated in the sacking of Constantinople in 1204 by the Fourth Crusade, which unlike the earlier crusades was directed against the Byzantium Empire, though its ultimate aim was to recapture Jerusalem. The defeat resulted in the loss of a considerable part of its territories. The bizarre circumstances of the Fourth Crusade, which is probably best explained by political opportunism rather than religious zeal, illustrates the ambivalent nature of Europe's relation to the East, which by the thirteenth century did not appear to distinguish significantly between Islam and Orthodoxy as opponents, showing that the Eastern church could be as much a target as Islam. In 1261 the Byzantines regained control of the city, but the power of Byzantium had ebbed and the empire never regained its previous glory and gradually lost its territories to the rising Ottoman power. The Patriarch of Constantinople remained in the re-named city of Istanbul after its capture by the Ottomans in 1453, but it had lost its political power until the establishment of the Russian Patriarchate in 1589. Despite this the political legacy of Orthodoxy remained. This legacy has been described as one of complementarity (Agadjanian and Roudemetof 2006: 10–12). In this arrangement church and state leadership not just co-existed but the church complemented the state. This led to a stronger and more institutionalized role for the church than in Western Europe, where as argued in the previous chapter, the state gained greater control of the church.

In the dominant Eurocentric narrative of European history there is an apparent contradiction. On the one side, Byzantium has been regarded as a marginal imperial, a relic of the Roman Empire and destined to doom while on the other side, one of the main off-shoots of Byzantium was the emergence of Greek Orthodoxy. While in the Eurocentric grand narrative, Europe begins in Greece, but the representation of Greece is one that does not give any consideration of Orthodoxy and the inheritance of Byzantium. It is as though Greece's role in the European heritage was confined to its pre-Byzantine phase in an earlier antiquity. While Greece fell under western influence, especially since its independence from the Ottoman Empire after 1829, the other regions that were shaped by the Byzantine tradition remained for long under Ottoman rule and later came under Russian power, for example Bulgaria, Romania and Serbia. By the mid-fifteenth century virtually all the Orthodox peoples were under Russian or Ottoman rule, except in some cases Hungarian or Polish-Lithuanian domination. The Byzantine tradition had an important influence on the countries, which reflect a multiple civilizational background. The example of Romania illustrates the combination of the Byzantine model of political rule, which was modelled on a religiously legitimated autocracy, and a later adoption and politicization of western ideas of political community that made possible the construction of a national identity based on romantic nationalism (Blokker 2010). Since the early twenty-first century these countries have reasserted their European identity, with Bulgaria and Romania joining the EU in 2007. The accession of Serbia has already begun since its application in 2009.

It is not possible to ignore the different historical experience of South-Western Europe in an account of the European heritage or to separate Greece from the Byzantine tradition. In view of the current transformation of the wider region and the complex relation between post-socialist identity and post-secular developments there, European identity must be seen as being shaped in an on-going process of definition (Stoeckl 2010, 2011). The Byzantine legacy is part of that and a reminder of the inter-civilizational nature of the wider European heritage.

Russia, Eurasia and Europe

In addition to the significance of the Byzantine tradition for Europe, the Byzantine period was also important for Europe due to the influence it had on imperial Russia. In view of the influence of Russia on much of Europe, especially in the twentieth century, a consideration of its impact on Russia is in place. The Russian state, culture and people have for long been inextricably linked with much of Europe. The Russians, it should be recalled, were part of the wider Slav peoples. But the Slavs did not themselves constitute a civilization, divided as they were between the western (Poles and Czechs), southern (Serbian, Croatian) and the eastern (Russian, Romanian, Bulgarian) Slavs. It was the Russian Slavs who emerged as the most powerful within that broad diasporic group and the civilization that they established was inter-civilizational, divided between European and Eurasian orientations. The model of modernity that eventually emerged incorporated elements of both.

Byzantine culture played a formative role in Russian culture and religion in the aftermath of the defeat of the Mongols, which had effectively cut Russia off from the wider European civilization. The Mongols however did not leave a lasting influence on Russia, which later created new imperial institutions and a political culture very strongly influenced by Orthodoxy. Since the final abolition of the Byzantine Empire in 1453 after the Ottoman conquest of Constantinople, the Russian Empire inherited the mantle of Byzantine civilization and with it the link with the Greco-Roman and Christian civilizational heritages. More of Byzantine survived in Russia than elsewhere, although remnants of the Byzantine tradition survived in Istanbul until the Turkish nationalist movement eradicated the final traces of the Greek past in its attempt at Turkification.

Moscow was proclaimed to be the 'Third Rome' and the protector of Orthodox Christianity. The Patriarchate of Moscow, established in 1589, became the most powerful Orthodox church and was intended to be the continuation of the Roman legacy that Constantinople had all but surrendered. The messianic notion of the 'Third Rome' opened up the imperial vision of Christian conquest in Asia. The mission to be the religious and political heir of Constantinople – supposedly guaranteed by the political myth of the *translatio imperii* – also provided Russia with a major legitimation for expansion in the Balkan region.

Byzantine political and religious ideas also had a direct influence on imperial Russian notions of statehood. It has often been said that the Orthodox religion cultivated a culture of spiritualism that stood in the way of democracy and the creation of liberal institutions. It is doubtful that the path of Russian and eastern European history can be explained in this way since the cultural difference between Latin and Greek Christianity is not sufficiently large to account for major societal divergences, as the example of Greece shows. However, as Kharkhordin (1999) has argued, eastern Christianity cultivated notions of the self and ecclesiastical practices that lent themselves to Bolshevik collectivist methods of social control, such as practices of mutual surveillance. Kristeva (2000: 138–9) claims that the different conception of God – whereby the Holy Spirit proceeds from the father *through* the Son rather than in Catholicism from the Father *and* from the Son – cultivated an ethic that suggested the annihilation of the Son and the Believer, whereas in Catholicism there was a greater emphasis on the autonomy and independence of the person.

It has been for long debated whether Russia constitutes a separate civilization or is part of a wider conception of Europe. Southern Russia has been part of Europe far longer than many regions which we today consider to be core European countries. The original Rus, founded in Kiev in the ninth century, was a creation of the Vikings and through them a shared common heritage with other states conquered by the Vikings, including the British Isles, France and Southern Italy (Poe 2003: 18). Through the Byzantine heritage and Orthodox religion Russia preserves a distinct European inheritance. It has been argued (Lemberg 1985) that the idea of Russia as Asiatic was a nineteenth century German invention which replaced the older view that the main division in Europe was a north versus south one. According to Poe (2003: 59) the early Muscovite state had all the features of a European early modern state. Certainly by the nineteenth century the east-west divide became more pronounced and Russia increasingly ceased to be seen as part of the North as far as Western Europe was concerned. It may be the case that the new conflict between the Ottoman Empire and the Central and Western European powers increasingly came to influence views about Asia and Russia as Asiatic. However, political and cultural hostility between Russia and the Ottoman Empire and the role of Russia in the balance of power system tended to cultivate favourable views of Russia in Europe. It has been argued that the idea that Russia was essentially Asiatic was itself a Russian creation of the eighteenth century and expressed the desire of the pro-western Tsar Peter the Great to have Russia identified with Europe, where its capital, St Petersburg, was located while its colonies territories would be identified with Asia (Bassin 1991). After the victory over Sweden in 1721 the idea of Russia as a tsardom was abolished and replaced by the western and Roman idea of a colonial empire with the rural mountains as the newly invented boundary (Bassin 1991). So according to this view, it was Russia itself that invented the idea of Europe ending at the Ural mountains. Such identity constructions are always relative and serve political purposes such as establishing relations between groups. It has been argued that imperial Russia saw itself as European to define Russia in relation to China and in relation to their Asian regions (Riasanovsky 1972; Sarkisyanz 1954).

Russia is eastern in two senses, firstly there was a long association of Russia with the Mongols who had ruled the country in the thirteenth century and there was the conquest of much of North-Eastern Asia and in particular Siberia, which was to have an important part in the Russian national identity. The late nineteenth-century debate between

Slavophils and Westerners on whether Russia was a Slavic nation with its own indigenous civilization origins in Asia or was a European nation polarized not only Russian positions on its identity, but gave credence to the view that Russia was not European. Dostoevsky, for instance, believed Russia should oppose the British Empire and itself take up the imperial quest to overcome Islam and further the cause of Christianity (Hauner 1990: 49). The conclusion of this debate must be that Russia was neither Asian nor European, but Eurasia. However, the notion of Eurasia did not always imply anti-westernism, though it was certainly intended to signal a distinction between Asia and Europe. While the word was originally coined by a Viennese geologist in the 1880s to describe the unity of the combined landmass of Europe and Asia, it had its cultural origins in the attempt of Enlightenment intellectuals such as Alexander von Humboldt, to demonstrate the linguistic unity of the Indo-Eurasian family of languages (Bassin 1991: 10). However, by the end of the nineteenth century with the rise of the Eurasia movement, the idea of Eurasia had become politicized both within Russia and in the West and suggested not only a different and non-western civilization, but a divergent modernity that was politically and cultural anti-western. The school of thought, which had its origins in the writings of Nikolai Danilevsky in the 1870s, had many supports throughout the Soviet period, including the dissident writer Alexander Solzhenitsyn.

Despite its Janus face, Russia was in this period increasingly seen as a threat to the West and as representing a different and alien civilization. The facts of history support different interpretations. When it was under Mongul rule, Russia had cut itself off from the West, but not fundamentally transformed. The Mongul tribes, with a population of some one million had become the most powerful force in the world in the thirteenth century when they conquered China. When they turned westwards, Russia was unable to stop their advance and in the early thirteenth century Russia was conquered by the so-called 'Tatar Yoke', until 1480 when the Muscovite state under Ivan the Great was established. The Mongul conquest had severed Russia from the West from the mid-thirteenth century when the older centre of Russia based in Kiev was captured. The result of this was that Russia was weakened and unable to resist the rise of the Ottoman Empire and the spread of Islam. It also lost control of White Russia and the Ukraine, which were not regained until after 1945. But throughout the period of Mongul rule there was a basic continuity in the older social and political structures, making it difficult to claim there was a fundamental break and that Russia became more Asiatic. The relationship between Europe and Russia was influenced more by politics than civilizational differences. Much of this had to do with the ambitions of Russia to expand its sphere of influence.

Russia's westward mission was limited. The foundation of St Petersburg as a 'window into Europe' by Peter the Great as the new capital in 1703 consolidated Russia's western face, but ultimately Russian expansion into Central Europe was restricted and it did not succeed in its aim to gain access to the Mediterranean by means of the Balkans and Adriatic. The relative powerful state of Poland and the Grand Duchy of Lithuania prevented its western expansion into Central Europe while the Ottoman and Habsburg control of the Balkans prevented access to the Mediterranean. The rise of Sweden after the Thirty Years War prevented Russia from control of the Baltic region. Russia, after acquiring Finland in 1809 was effectively land-locked in the West (Thaden 1984). It was this failure to expand in the west and south that sent Russia on an eastward mission of colonization beyond the Urals. It was thus decisive that, at a point when the western powers were looking westwards and overseas, Russia began to look eastwards in its colonization of Siberia in the seventeenth century (Diment and Slezkine 1993). Russia was feared as much for its large empire as for its Eurasian identity.

The relation between Europe and Russia, as with the more general encounter of West and East, cannot be so easily summed up as one of conflict. While elements of a conflict of civilizations have been present, this was more likely to derive from groups within Russia, such as the Slavophils, than from the West. Since Russia was after all Christian, and however hostile the two traditions had been, it was more favourably viewed than was the case with Islam. Moreover, the acrimonious split and the circumstances of the Fourth Crusade had all been between Byzantine and the Latin West, so that when Russian Orthodoxy arose the conflict with Orthodoxy had lost its force. However, vestiges of that conflict remained. The myth of 'Holy Russia' as protector of Christianity was not only directed against the Ottoman Empire, but against its neighbours, Catholic Poland and Protestant Sweden. For the Orthodox Church Europe was still the land of the Antichrist. The Tsars invoked the idea of a European Christian order at a time when church and state were becoming increasingly separated in the West. Alexander I failed to impress Metternich and Castlereagh at the Congress of Vienna in 1815 with the idea of a 'Holy Alliance of Christian Monarchs'.

The Napoleonic invasions certainly widened the great gulf that had already been formed between Europe and Russia. However, Russia was instrumental in the defeat of Napoleon. Despite its alienation from the West, Russia was accepted by the Concert of Europe largely because of its foreign policy, which was based on an attempt to crush Prussia, secure the neutrality of France, and drive the Ottomans out of Europe. This led to military and political coalitions with French and Habsburg powers in eighteenth and nineteenth centuries. Russia was accordingly awarded with a generous measure of Poland. However the abiding idea remained that Russia was different. European perceptions of Russia in the nineteenth century were also deeply influenced by the rise of the United States. Europe was seen as hemmed in by the rise of two great powers to the east and to the west. Napoleon claimed that the world will soon be 'the American Republic or the Russian universal monarchy' (de Rougement 1966: 294). Alexis de Tocqueville (1948: 434) also reiterated this vision of a bi-polar world.

Despite these perceptions, at least before the rise of communism, it is not possible to speak of a frontier that separated Europe from Russia. The relation is better described as one mediated by borderlands and by shifting borders. Ever since the Roman Empire created a *limes* system along the Rhine in the days of Tiberius, the formation of borderlands became a long-term feature of Europe. The limes were as much borderlands as frontiers and were the site of exchange and negotiation. Russia, for instance, allowed its border, or marcher, regions to enjoy special rights in order to guarantee the overall security of the empire (Wieczynski 1976). Since the nineteenth century, the Ural mountains symbolically mark the division of a European Russia from its Asian territories, but this mountain range is of little geographical or political significance and as noted earlier was more a political construction than a geographical frontier. According to Szamuely (1988: 13) 'Russia had no frontiers: for many centuries she herself was the frontier, the great open, defenseless dividing line between the settled communities of Europe and the nomadic barbarian invaders of the Asian steppes.' In this view, Russia has been a frontier country until the end of the eighteenth century when it became an empire. It is undoubtedly the case than henceforth there was a general increase in the hardening of borders with the rise of Russian national consciousness in the nineteenth century movement. But in the longer perspective of history, Russia had many strong links with Europe. Two of its most northerly cities, Pskov and Novgorod, were part of the German Hanseatic league and a bridge to Europe. Russia in the eighteenth century was influenced by Poland and much of the arts were inspired by developments in Catholic Europe. The anti-western ideas of the Slavophil movement were also inspired by German intellectual currents and the ideas of Herder who emphasized the distinctiveness of national cultures (Matlock 2003: 232–4).

Despite the clash of different visions of Russia as well as different perceptions of Russia in the West, in terms of its model of modernity Russia is certainly different. Russia experienced a different historical path to modernity from that in the West. According to Marx and Lenin, feudalism was never fully established in Russia; it was the state not the feudal magnates that extracted the surplus from the population. Political domination and economic exploitation occurred primarily through the state, not society. This is the essence of the so-called 'Asiatic despotism' associated with the 'Asiatic mode of production' (Wittfogel 1957). Unlike western revolutions, the 1917 Revolution was a total revolution in its transformation of state, economy and society on a scale unprecedented even by the French Revolution. Most European revolutions preserved some continuity with what had gone before and even elements of the *ancien regime* were preserved until the twentieth century (Anderson 1974). In contrast, Russia's transition to modernity was accomplished with a more decisive break from the past, even if not all traces of the Byzantine and imperial tradition were obliterated. It was inevitable that would entail the rejection of the European face of Russia. This rejection of Europe was paradoxically supported by the Orthodox Church, which was to suffer under communist rule. The de-Europeanization of Russia was reflected in the choice of Moscow as capital and the renaming of St Petersburg first as Petrograd and then, after Lenin's death in 1924, as Leningrad. Russia's most Europeanized groups, the aristocracy and the intelligentsia, disappeared from Russian society after the Bolshevik Revolution. The western element of Russian was henceforth carried forward largely by the émigré culture in the West since the 1920s (Personen 1991). However it was also from that émigré culture that anti-western Eurasianism and the notion of Russian exceptionalism received its support (Sakwa 2006).

The communist period cannot be fully accounted for without a consideration of the civilizational context and a distinctive model of modernity (Arnason 1993). Although Marxism-Leninism was a western European ideology that had its origin in the industrial societies of nineteenth century capitalism, Russian communism developed in the context of a society that had only lately emerged out of feudalism and which did not have a strong civil society tradition in place of which was a tradition of collectivism that had civilizational roots. In many ways, the Bolshevik Party was a product of the imperial state tradition and, as previously mentioned, connections between Bolshevik methods of organization and surveillance and the ecclesiastical practices in the Orthodox Church (Kharkhordin 1999). Due to the supremacy of the Soviet Union, much of Central and Eastern Europe has been influenced by a civilizational pattern that has been very different from western civilizational patterns. The Orthodox tradition remains an important reminder of the existence of a different civilizational route to modernity, but one that interacted with the West and with modernity (Stoeckl 2010).

The idea of Russia as European made a brief return with Gorbachev's idea of a 'Common European house', but has not entirely disappeared. With the return of Orthodoxy the presence of the Slavic dimension of European civilization has been felt and with it a different route to modernity and a reminder of a different origin to the idea of Europe (Buss 2003). This has been asserted too by Putin, who sought to scaledown the idea of Russia as Eurasian of its anti-western connotations. According to Sakwa (2006: 218) anti-westernism remains an important component in Russian national identity, with its roots in the nineteenth century debate between the anti-western Slavophils and the Westerners. It can be considered an aspect of Russian Occidentalism and a defining feature of its national identity, which, like all kinds of Occidentalism and Orientalism, seeks to eliminate internal difference through the construction of a homogenized Other (Buruma and Margalit 2004).

To conclude this chapter, an important dimension of the European civilizational constellation was the revived Greco-Roman civilization established in Late Antiquity in the Byzantine Empire and which migrated to imperial Russia, where from the fourteenth century onwards a distinct Slavic Eurasian civilization developed based on the earlier Greco-Roman heritage and Orthodox Christianity. Rather than see a sharp line dividing East and West separating Europe and Russia a more accurate view of the historical experience would be to see the relation in terms of a 'cultural gradient' formed out of interactions, exchange and the space of encounters (Evtuhov and Kotkin 2003). Russia thus represents a hybrid civilization – Slavic, Eurasian, and European – that it is distinct from western civilization while incorporating elements of it. This mix of European and Asian components was the defining feature of Russian civilization and the basis of its route to modernity through the synthesis of the western (the national state tradition), Eurasian (Slavic) and classical (Byzantine) traditions (Tolz 2001). Its participation in the wider European civilization cannot be denied, but it is more than European. Neither exclusively European nor exclusively Asian, Russia is perhaps regarded as simply Russian, and thus as a civilization in its own right (Poe 2003).

5

The Islamic World and Islam in Europe

Rethinking the nature of the relationship between Europe and Islam in our own time requires a re-evaluation of perceptions of history. In this chapter the argument is made that Islam is a part of the European civilizational heritage and that as a result of migration in recent decades, a European Islam now exists and can be viewed as the latest expression of a long history of European-Islamic links. The place of Islam in European history has generally been considered in terms of a clash of civilizations and has ignored the possibility of contradictory belief systems within a civilization and positive encounters (see Davies 2006: 203–22).

Europe has never been purely Christian, despite the overwhelming importance of that tradition in shaping the European heritage. The Judaic and Christian traditions were mediated by the earlier Greco-Roman tradition and also by the Islamic world, which despite its huge internal differences, constituted a civilizational constellation in its own right. The place and role of Islam in Europe needs to be evaluated in light of the notion of a European inter-civilizational constellation as opposed to a narrow notion of a Western Civilization based exclusively on the Christian tradition. As we have seen, this tradition, important as it was, fragmented into quite different churches.

In terms of a notion of civilizational unity, the Judaic, Christian and Islamic religions are all expressions of Abrahamic monotheism, for common to all three was the belief that God revealed himself to Abraham. Their common roots suggests the existence of a wider Islamic-Judaeo-Christian civilizational matrix that underwent progressive variation. All three underwent much the same stages of development, which Fowden (2011) has characterized as the prophetic, the scriptural and classical or patristic. However, Islam was the later arrival and probably for this reason was more concerned to define itself against Judaism and Christianity, which at the time of the birth of Islam was firmly established.

European civilization cannot be seen only as a product of the Carolingian Empire, which represented only one pole in a wider and more polycentric European civilization. Decisive was the interaction of its Jewish, Muslim and Christian components. Islam played a greater role in European civilization than has often been acknowledged. While this cannot be exaggerated, or compared to the influence of the Christian heritage, a case can be made for Islam to be seen as part of the European civilizational constellation. However, in the course of history the different paths of development in Europe and in the main centres of the Islamic world ensured significant differences in their models of modernity. Yet, despite these differences there was never a clash of civilizations or an ancient rivalry. The radical and anti-western elements in modern political Islam cannot be projected back into history to tell a story of a clash of civilizations when much of the historical experience was one of co-existence and cross-fertilization.

Within the broader European civilizational constellation, Turkey is the best example of an Islamic country that was also formed through the active engagement with a model of modernity derived from Western Europe. The relation between Turkey and Europe constitutes the most important intersection of East and West and an example of the co-existence of Islam as a variant of the western model of modernity.

Europe and its Others

It is often argued that Europe emerged out of a process of self-definition in which Islam served as the 'Other' of the European 'Self'. Due to the highly-differentiated and internal divisions within Europe there was no central unifying cultural or political identity that could provide an identity for Europe for long. As a result, according to this view, the West became defined by opposition to the East, whose referent was variously Persia, Islam, the wider 'Orient', and Communism. As the East changed, so too did the West, redefining itself along with changes in its alter ego. This argument, which was influenced by the notion that Europe is a discourse in which power and culture are entangled, needs to be modified in order to avoid the wrong conclusion that the relation between East and West was always antagonistic and binary. So what was the relationship? Or should such terms be abandoned altogether?

The relation between Europe and Islam cannot be easily summed up as a single one or as a continuous one.[1] It can be described as threefold and that the three modes of relating to Islam have been present in every era, with some being more pronounced than others in particular periods: the first is a relation based on fear and xenophobia, the second is one of fantasy, and the third one of borrowing, translation and adoption. The nature of the relation between Europe and Islam was variable, with the Self also being in part an Other. There is no simple boundary between an European Self and an Islamic Other; rather Self and Other have been mutually implicated to a point that we need a new kind of analysis which recognizes such mutually interlinked histories.

Islam has certainly been an object of fear since its expansion into Europe in the eight century, when the European frontier was effectively the Pyrenees. From this period the idea of Europe came increasingly to be expressed against Islam and, as with all such collective ideas, an external threat made possible a unity that was otherwise not apparent. After the death of Muhammad in 632 his followers spread out from Arabia and conquered the Persian Empire of the Sassanids and gained control of the Fertile Crescent (the lands of Iraq, Syria, and Palestine). In the course of the seventh and eight centuries the Arabs conquered most of North Africa with Alexandria falling in 642 and Cartage in 698. Muslim power spread over Anatolia, Persia and Mesopotamia, and eventually reached India. The Arab Empire of the Umayyad dynasty, established in Damascus in 661, began to look westwards and advanced into Europe with the fall of Visigothic kingdom of Hispania in 711. The Muslim conquest of Spain was almost extended to France until its defeat at Tours in 732 and, although further expansion was halted by Charlemagne's defeat of the Moors in 778, Christendom was on the defensive against Islam.

Collective identities are often born at time of crisis and this was the case with the idea of a European identity. One of the first references to 'Europeans', as opposed 'Europe', was the army led by the Frankish leader, Charles Martell, who defeated the Muslims (Hay 1957: 25). The battle was of considerable significance for definitions of Europe since it marked a moment of Christian unity and vulnerability. It was the moment in which the idea of Europe as a geographical area became linked with the cultural and political domains of Christendom. This was a time when Christendom was relatively small and did not include the Vikings in Northern Europe. With the conversion of the Vikings to Christianity in the mid-eleventh century, the territory of Christianity was extended. For almost 1,000 years Christendom was on the alert against the rise of a large Islamic world that appeared to be seeking expansion westwards. However, the danger Islam presented was less religious – for it was a relatively new religion while Christianity has been in existence for several centuries – than military since it was the religion of a new and expanding empire. In this period, Christians knew very little about Islam, the Qur'an was not yet translated; and the Muslims were regarded as pagans.

This situation changed by the fifteenth century. To sum up a well-known story, the Fall of Constantinople in 1453 led to the rise of an Islamic power and the fall of eastern Christianity. On the western front, at much the same time, a considerably strengthened Latin Christian civilization defeated the Moors under the Spanish leadership, but on its eastern limits it was confronted by a formidable Islamic power, which laid siege to Vienna in 1688. What emerged in the sixteenth century, then, was a much divided system of Christian states, which were temporarily united by Christianity and who saw Islam as a threat, which was not only ideological but military. European fears of Islam derived from this period, when Christendom was relatively weak in relation to the Ottoman Empire. Spanish and Portuguese conquest in the Americas had of course begun, but these and other European powers were unable to match the might of the Ottoman Empire. It is difficult to assess the extent to which the Christian West needed Islam to define itself and exactly to what degree it was a threat (see Brague 2009). By the time of the last onslaught on Vienna in 1683, the Ottoman Empire's military strength had waned and probably did not present a threat to Europe at this time. But it is possible to speculate that the image of Islam as an Other continued to exercise a certain focus of hostility for Europe (Sayyid 2003; Yapp 1992). This should not be exaggerated. There is in fact not a lot of evidence to show that this was the most important expression of xenophobia. It is arguably the case that was the Jews who were the Others, for it was often the enemy *within* rather than the enemy *outside* that was more significant in defining European self-identity. Indeed, when many Europeans referred to the despotism of the East, this was often in praise. As Clarke points out, Enlightenment intellectuals, who were mostly *ancien régime* supporters, looked to China for an ideal model of despotism, a despotism based on the exercise of legal authority rather than whim (Clarke 1997: 4). It should also be recalled that the elimination of the heretic religions was more fiercely pursued than was Islam, which mostly lay outside the territory of Christendom, at least since the expulsion of the Muslims from Spain at the beginning of the seventeenth century.

The second aspect of the relation was one of fantasy and proclamations of European superiority. Since the Outside lacked a certain reality or was unknown, it had to be invented and imagined. The *Song of Roland*, circa 1100, is an example of an early representation of Islam as Europe's Other against which Europe is portrayed as superior. In early Christian times the idea emerged that the peoples of Europe, Asia and Africa were descendants of Noah's three sons. Japheth was the father of the Europeans, who included the Greeks, Gentiles and Christians, while Shem was the father of the Jews and Arabs and Ham the father of Africans. This idea of a divided humanity later became a basis for the creation of races. Since the Koran was translated into Latin in 1143, Christendom was familiar with Islam, but it is was generally a distorted version and one that gave rise to fantasies (Southern 1962). Islam was seen as a preparation for the final appearance of the Antichrist as forecast in the Book of Daniel and Muhammad was seen as a parody of Christ. Pope Innocent II characterized Muhammad as the beast of the Apocalypse. The idea of the barbarous Muslim world inhabited by evil tribes was a dominant theme in medieval literature (Metlitzki 1977). The medieval taste for the fantastic was not confined to fantasies about Muslims and of its many expressions was an interest in the existence of unusual races (Friedmann 1981). Another theme was the idea of an oriental despotism. For Dante, Muhammad represented evil and the opposite to Christ. The Orient was not only represented as despotic but evil and cruel. Machiavelli contrasted the despotism of the Orient with the free spirit of the West. The Orient was characterized by despotic kings as a contrast to republican government in Europe. It has been argued that western republicanism relied heavily on the notion of despotic oriental prince (Springborn 1992). In this was the idea developed that Europe based on a political tradition that was the opposite to the forms of government that prevailed in the Muslim world. These notions gave legitimacy to counter-offensives from the time of the crusades to later attempts to curb the spread of the Ottoman Empire.

Edward Said has written the most important examination of this culture of fantasy, which in his analysis was driven by the imperial quest to conquer the Other (Said 1979). Cultural and intellectual power invented the Orient in a way that prepared for its political and economic domination by the West. In order to define itself, Europe needed an Other. This was often an invented Other. According to Said, some 60,000 books were written on the Orient in the nineteenth century (Said 1979: 204). The orientalist thesis has led to a now huge literature on the unknowable Other where Islam appears to be an expression of the other face of the Enlightenment's Reason. However, it should be noted that orientalism as described by Said refers to a later period when western powers, mostly France and Britain, embarked on colonial conquest in Asia and Africa. It would be a distortion of history to see all representations of Islam in such light. Prior to the eighteenth century when the Islamic world and other Asian cultures were larger and more technologically and militarily more advanced than Christendom, negative representations and views about Islam were very much the expression of vulnerability and ignorance. A differentiated assessment, then, of European perceptions of Islam is needed and not all representations of the Orient had the consequence of bolstering a European consciousness. The notion of oriental despotism could also imply a critique of European monarchy and reflect a preference for republican government. Indeed it has often been the case that the Islamic world was used as a foil to provide a critique of western despotism. A famous example of this was Montesqueiu's *Persian Letters* in 1721. The contrast between democracy and despotism referred as much to two competing conceptions of political rule in Europe at a time when republican government was the exception and where it did exist, it was also far from democratic.

Europe did not have a single image of Islam but several. It should also be considered that Europe itself did not have a clear identity other than Christianity. Once Islam ceased to be a threat to Europe, the discourse and representation of Islam and the wider Orient changed. The contrast between Christianity and Islam became slowly replaced by one of civilization and barbarism (Jones 1971). The idea of the Turkish infidel was replaced by the notion of the Turkish barbarian. The old myth of Europa as an eastern migrant now becomes a triumphalist Queen Europe, who is portrayed in the sixteenth century as sitting on a throne holding the scepter of world domination (Hale 1993: 49). This vision of European superiority as far as Islam was concerned remained an aspiration until the nineteenth century. Until the colonial period, Europe feared but also respected Islam. As Christianity became less important in defining Europe, the contrast with the considerably more religious Islamic world grew. The European path to modernity, partially reproduced in the Americas, differed from the route experienced in the Islamic world in that it presupposed secularization and the relative privatization of religion in republican states.

This brings us to the third mode of relating to Islam, which can be termed the mode of translation and includes adaptation and borrowing. The first point to make is that despite the religious hostilities between Europe and Islam, Christianity had not gained hegemonic status at the time of the spread of Islam. The relation between Muslims and other groups was a good deal more diffuse than it was to become in later centuries. The notion of a clash of civilizations cannot be so easily projected back onto the early history of Islam and Christianity since these religions along with Judaism derived from the Near East and both Islam and Christianity aspired to be world religions. This possibly explains why it was sometimes thought that Islam was a Christian heresy.

As is well known, much of the culture of Greek antiquity, itself allegedly eastern in origin (Burkert 1995), was preserved by Muslim scholars; Cordoba and Toledo were important cultural centres, and, until the early modern period, there was considerable borrowing from Arabic culture. There was a large Muslim presence in Spain until Muslims were finally expelled in the early seventeenth century (see Kennedy 1996; Meyerson and English 2000). Much of the Iberian peninsula was Muslim not Christian during the Middle Ages. Significant pockets of Islamic culture survived until well into the fifteenth century (see Burns 1984). Throughout the Middle Ages, Europeans were indebted to Arabic achievements in science and Arabic scholarship was represented at many European universities. Sicily was for long a meeting place of two cultures. The Muslim civilization that emerged in the late seventh century was more advanced than much of what was later to be defined as Europe. Muslim civilization absorbed more of Greek culture than did much of Western Europe. We must not then see Europe and Islam as two mutually exclusive civilizations confronting each other. Much of classical culture, which had been extinguished in the West after the break-up of the Roman Empire, was preserved, and indeed, expanded, by the Arabs. Muslim Spain, in particular Cordoba and Toledo, was important in transmitting Islamic culture to Europe through a culture of translations, Latin translations of Arabic translations of Greek texts. For much of the middle ages three cultures co-existed in the Iberian peninsula, Islamic, Jewish and Christian. The importance of the twelfth century Arab philosopher Ibn Rusd, known in Europe as Averroes, has been widely commented on for his rehabilitation and commentary on Aristotle – who was unknown in the West prior to the eleventh century – and for his defense of Greek thought (see Brague 2009). Moreover, while Muslim Spain prior to the 'Reconquest' completed in 1492 has been portrayed as somehow outside Europe the reality was extensive trading links with Christendom and which continued long afterwards. Sicily and Malta had been for long the crossroads of two civilizations and it was there that many ideas entered the two worlds. Arab culture greatly influenced Europe until the sixteenth century. Even in the centuries of the crusades, in the eleventh and twelfth centuries, the crusades and holy wars occurred alongside considerable cultural exchange and trade. The significance of the crusades in defining relations between Europe and Islam has been a matter of dispute (Goody 2004: 33). Communication with the Arab world resulted in adoption of new methods in agriculture, architecture, and in the sciences and especially in astronomy and mathematics. There is much to suggest that Iberian centred Islamic world in fact saw itself as a distinct civilization from Northern Europe as well as from sub-Saharan Africa, thus calling into question continental notions of Europe and Africa as historically meaningful categories (see Lewis and Wigen 1997: 116–17).

According to Jardine and Brottom, the Renaissance was formed out of encounters between the Orient and the Occident and, in the fifteenth and sixteenth centuries, East and West met on more equal terms than was later the case (Jardine and Brottom 2000). These authors have shown how some of the most potent symbols in European culture derived from the East and how the borders between East and West were more permeable than was later thought. It also needs to be recognized that Islam in the Middle Ages was a good deal more tolerant than what it later was to become and also more tolerant than Christianity as far as polytheism was concerned. This tendency within Islam, which also did not have a hierarchical ecclesiastical structure, in fact allowed for great cultural transfusion that often has been recognized.

The Enlightenment, while being less influenced by the non-Western world, was in many respects possible only by a relation to otherness. The extreme interpretation, and now discredited, is that the Enlightenment was based on an Orientalization of the East, which was the necessary Other for the European 'we' to be defined and a strategy of colonial domination. While there is little doubt that the Western heritage was used to legitimate imperialism and that in many cases it entailed a fantastification of the non-Western Other, a more differentiated analysis is needed. The category of Otherness in Enlightenment thought can equally well be seen as an expression of the distance that many Europeans were to their own culture, which they could view only through the eyes of the Other. This Other was indeed very often the Orient, as in Montesquieu's *Persian Letters*, but in this case and in many others it was a critical mirror by which the decadence of Old

Europe could be portrayed. In many other cases the attempt for genuine understanding of the ancient cultures of Asia cannot be underestimated, not least because much of the Enlightenment culture was formed in pre-colonial contexts, such as eighteenth and early nineteenth century Germany (Clarke 1997; Halbfass 1988). There were many genuine attempts to understand Islam, especially prior to the imperial period. It would not be possible to explain all of this in terms of a hegemonic notion of Orientalism. The history of that relationship often has been misrepresented. A closer reading of Herodotus's account of the Persian Wars reveals in fact his view that the Persians were often more civilized than the Greeks. Certainly a more differentiated reading of this text shows that there are no grounds to project the later East-West divide back onto the Greek-Persian conflict, not least since the Greeks did not operate with such a distinction of East and West. The point, then, is to stress the threefold nature of the relation between Islam and Europe, this is not something that can be reduced to xenophobia or the fantasy discourse of Orientalism.

European Islam

The case for Islam to be included in a wider and more inclusive definition of Europe can now be made on several grounds. The first evidence is the cultural role of Islam in shaping European civilization since the decline of the Roman Empire. Indeed one perspective is that the Islamic Empire of the Umayyad and the later Abbasid dynasties was the successor to the Roman Empire (Robinson 2011). The early Ottoman rulers often saw themselves as the inheritors of the Roman Empire. According to Bang (2011: 326) the Ottoman version of supreme rulership involved a mixture of Roman, Islamic and inner Eurasian practices. Sülleyman the Magnificent competed with Charles V as the true heir of Rome. Throughout the Middle Ages, both Spain and Russia were under Islamic rule, in the case of Spain by Umayyad Empire and in the case of Russia by the Mongol Empire. Although these empires did not give rise to a permanent civilization in Europe and eventually disappeared, in the case of the Mongols more or less without trace, they are an important reminder of trans-continental flows of peoples and cultures in earlier times. It is true, too, that the major centres of the Islamic civilization lay outside the European area, but this was not a clearly defined geopolitical area. The notion of Islam as 'the other' of Europe has often been noted; however it was not only an enemy, but was also a cultural mediator. Despite the religious differences between Europe and Islam, Christianity had not gained hegemonic status at the time of the spread of Islam and differences did not always become the basis of hostilities. The relation between Muslims and other groups was a good deal more diffuse than it was to become in later centuries. It needs also to be recognized that Islam in the Middle Ages was more tolerant than what it was later to become and also more tolerant than Christianity as far as polytheism and heresies were concerned. The Muslims regarded the Jews and Christians living in their territories as 'Peoples of the Book' and tolerated them in ways that were often a contrast to the persecution of minorities by Christians in Europe. This tendency for tolerance within Islam, which also did not have a hierarchical ecclesiastical structure, in fact allowed for great cultural transfusion that has often been recognized. This should not be exaggerated since it was also discriminatory and became increasingly so. During the Reformation there were links between the Protestants and the Ottomans and the Renaissance's revival of antiquity would not have been possible without translations from the Greek by Arabic scholars. Western Europe borrowed heavily from the Muslim world, especially in science and agriculture (Hobson 2004, 2006). During the period of Muslim rule in Southern Europe, most of Northern Europe including Scandinavia and the British Isles was relatively backward. The spread of Islam in Europe occurred prior to the complete Christianization of Europe and at a time when the Islamic world was more territorially and politically integrated than was the case with Christendom.

The second example of the role of Islam in Europe concerns the Ottoman Empire and its modern successor, Turkey. Islam created a civilization that had a major European component. The Ottoman Empire was a multi-ethnic and multi-national trans-continental empire that brought Islamic civilization into the heart of what had been the Byzantine Europe. The Ottoman conquest of South-Eastern Europe, Greece and the Balkans, represents one of the more significant examples of the spread of Islam in Europe. Much of the Balkans was incorporated into the Ottoman Empire in the sixteenth century. The Albanians and Kosovians in Bosnia and Herzegovina converted to Islam between the sixteenth and seventeenth century, but other parts of the Balkan remained Orthodox Christian. In Albania Muslims were a majority, but in other parts of the Balkans they were minorities and were governed in accordance with the Ottoman millet system which based on administering populations according to their religion rather than enforcing conversion. The conflict in the former Yugoslavia in

1993–1995 highlighted the fate of Europe's largest existing historical Muslim population. More than 8,000 Bosnian Muslims were killed at Srebrenica by the Bosnia Serbs as part of Serbia's ethnic cleansing. To claim, as often has been the case, that this was the outcome of an ancient fault-line deriving from a clash of Christian versus Islam is a false characterization of the atrocity which was a state endorsed policy of extermination in the name of the Serbian nation. It should also be recalled that Muslims and Christians lived peacefully for centuries in the region. There was nothing in the course of Balkan history that made such an outcome inevitable. The pluralist political framework of the Yugoslavian federation continued the Ottoman example of peaceful co-existence.

The Ottoman Empire played a not insignificant role in the European civilizational constellation; today this civilization is principally represented by Turkey, which in itself can be regarded as a nation-state that has inherited some of the civilizational features of the Ottoman Empire. The Ottoman conquest was sufficiently enduring in political as well as in cultural terms to constitute a civilizational pattern that had long-lasting consequences for the region. The Ottoman Empire is a different case from the other historical examples of Islam in Europe, such as the Mongol conquest of Russia and the Umayyad conquest of the Iberian peninsula, since it had a longer and more continuous presence. Turkey is a reminder – especially in the context of the relation to the European Union – of a third route to modernity and one in which Islam is very much present. Mention could be made too of Bulgaria, which has a 10 per cent Muslim population, as well as other Balkan countries with Muslim minorities. The Mediterranean geopolitical face of Europe is becoming more and more important in the wider Eurasian and Mediterranean definition of Europe. Malta, for instance, is another example of this, albeit of a Christian country that has played a role in mediating the civilizations and cultures of the Mediterranean. The features of Turkey that gave to it a pronounced western identity was the adoption of western European models of republican government and secularization. Although the transition to democracy was slow, this was also the case in much of Western Europe. The Turkish route to modernity did not differ much more than the various models of modernity in Europe more generally. The question of the place and role of Islam in Turkey has mostly been worked out through democratic reform and is an example of the co-existence of Islam and democracy within a model of modernity that shares many features with western countries (Keyman 2006).

Despite the significance of Ottoman influence in the Balkan region, the question of modern Turkey and its relation to Europe draws attention to the wider civilizational context of Europe as an inter-civilizational constellation. The issue of Turkey and Europe is not a question of religion but of political modernity. Since the question of Turkey's membership of the EU first arose, its relation to Europe has been discussed for a long time. Despite the beginnings of accession talks in 2005, it would appear that Turkish membership of the EU will be for some time not a likely prospect. Yet the debate about whether Europe can be defined in ways that include Turkey continues (see Baban and Keyman 2008).

The third evidence of Islam in Europe is the rise of what can be called European Islam, or Euro-Islam (see Nielsen 1999; Alsayyad and Castells 2002; Göle 2004). Today at least 3 per cent of the population of the EU is Muslim. Some estimates suggest a figure of more than 15 million. Many are products of migration into Europe over the past four decades, especially in France and Germany. In this sense it is possible to speak of a European Islam formed out of the diasporic movement of peoples. Viewed in the longer historical perspective, Muslim migration into Europe from Turkey and North Africa in the last decades can be seen in the context of diasporic flows that have occurred throughout history.

This longer perspective also highlights the contours of a civilizational constellation that may be the best way to characterize Europe. Its major geopolitical components would be the western Christian, Russian-Slavic, and Islamic-Turkish civilizations. Europe and its modernity have been shaped by not one, but by all three civilizations which opened up different routes to modernity. Any account of Europe will have to include the active relation with Asia and the wider East (Delanty 2006). This is partly because the origins of European civilization lie in the appropriation of eastern civilizations and because a large part of the European civilization itself has been formed in relation to two Eurasian civilizations, the Russian and Islamic civilizations. Europe has been formed by precisely the interaction, cross-fertilization, cultural borrowing and diffusions of its civilizations. What this suggests is that Europe must be seen as a constellation consisting of links rather than stable entities or enduring forms.

In this view, the Ottoman tradition represents a third European civilization and one based on Islam. This is also the position taken by Jack Goody, who has argued for a trans-continental European civilization that includes Islam, which has the same roots as Judaism and

Christianity. Alongside the notion of a Judaeo-Christian civilization, is the idea of an Islam-Christian civilization (Bulliet 2004). Europe never has been purely isolated and purely Christian (Goody 2004: 14). This is a view of European civilization that stresses mutual borrowings, translations, and hybrid cultural forms. Europe can be identified by a mode of cultural translation rather than by reference to a particular cultural content (such as Christianity) or to allegedly universal norms (such as human rights or democracy) or territory or forms of statehood. Because of the different civilizations that make up the mosaic of Europe and the fact these were embroiled in each other through centuries of translations, Europe must be seen as a constellation consisting of links rather than stable entities or enduring traditions.

In conclusion, the argument of this chapter has that the traditional image of Islam as the 'other' of Europe is in need of some qualification. Viewed in the longer perspective of history Europe has been shaped by a model of modernity that itself has been influenced by civilizational encounters between West and East. While the relation between Europe and Islam has often been fraught with conflicts, there is nothing in it that forecloses possibilities for dialogue and mutual respect. The task today is to recover some of the cosmopolitan possibilities that have been a feature of the relation. The emphasis here is indeed one of dialogue rather than integration. Some of the modes by which Europe and Islam interacted have been far from xenophobic and there is evidence of the acceptance of differences that is an essential feature of the cosmopolitan imagination that is needed today. It would not be out of place to have a greater recognition of the place of Islam in European history than has been the case until now.

Part II
The Emergence of Modernity

6

The Renaissance and the Rise of the West Revisited

The Renaissance marks the arrival of both modernity and the crystallization of the initial form of Europe's cultural model. It refers to the cultural movement generally taken to be spanning the fourteenth to the sixteenth centuries. As the term suggests, the Renaissance means 'rebirth'. It stood for the rebirth of classical antiquity, which was mostly the Greco-Roman culture, and humanism, but it was also a movement that played a decisive role in the making of modern Europe. But the term is not to be taken at its face value, indeed it is a value-laden term and is an episode in the Grand Narrative of the European heritage as a continuous story from antiquity to modernity whereby Europe rediscovered itself in the past that it had broken from in the Middle Ages and thus made possible a continuity that was otherwise considerably ruptured. For this reason many scholars prefer to use the term 'early modern' to characterize the period that culminated with, and included, the Reformation, for the Renaissance did not simply end when the Reformation began; indeed the latter can be seen as a continuation of Renaissance humanism. The term 'Renaissance' will be used in this chapter with due caution on the grounds of its widespread currency to refer both to an era and to specific developments within that time. However, it needs to be re-situated in a more global context since the period in question was one that saw important encounters with the non-European world, which had as much a formative influence on Europe as had the rediscovery of the texts of antiquity. According to Jack Goody (2010), the European Renaissance was one of many such movements and should be located with the context of a wider rebirth of culture and knowledge that included the Islamic world from the ninth century when Greek texts were translated into Arabic.

The term Renaissance, which is French, was a creation of the nine-teenth century. It is important to note that much of what is taken to be European civilization were inventions of later periods and reflected the sense of historical time of that era rather the actual time of its contemporaries. In a famous work published in 1860 and translated into English under the title *The Civilization of the Renaissance*, the German historian Jacob Burckhardt celebrated the Italian Renaissance as the apex of European culture (the German title was *Die Kultur der Renaissance*). The reality was less coherent. The Renaissance is now generally seen as a European-wide movement, not as it was for Burckhardt an exclusively Italian development with universal significance. Almost every country in Europe in some way participated in a new interest in antiquity. It had particularly strong roots in Northern Europe (Kirkpatrick 2002).

The Renaissance marked the end of the Medieval Age and the birth of modernity. In this sense it was a movement in historical conscious-ness, which defined the present in terms of its relation to the past. As an era, the Renaissance covers some of the cultural aspects of what is now more commonly referred to as the early modern period. However it is best understood less as an era than a mood or consciousness that was variously present in Europe of the fifteenth century. The significance of the Renaissance as a European civilizational develop-ment was the relation it established between past and present. Periodization was one aspect of this, for since the Renaissance it became customary to divide European history into three eras – an ancient, a medieval and a modern period. The modern period was thus defined by a distance from the ancient. The revival of antiquity occurred simply because the present had already broken from the past, which was recovered by an age that had already perceived itself to have broken from its origin, but re-interpreted that origin for the purposes of re-orienting its identity in the present. This selective recombination of elements of the past that had as a whole been abandoned is a dis-tinctive feature of European cultural as well as political revolutions and marked the path to the Enlightenment in which the consciousness of modernity was more pronounced. The Renaissance, then, marks the point of transition to an emerging modernity; its embracing of antiq-uity can be explained by its rejection of the Middle Ages. This turning away from the Middle Ages was visually represented in the abandon-ment of the Gothic style of art and architecture and thus gave to Europe a means of projecting itself in the world (Rabb 2006).

The Renaissance constituted a cultural identity for Europe and laid the basis for a nascent political identity. This was achieved in the following ways to be discussed in this chapter. Firstly, it established through humanism a conception of human subjectivity and a self-questioning attitude along with new notion of authority based on science and exploration. Secondly, it also marked the birth of a new political imagination characterized by republicanism and which was to lay the basis for European political modernity. Thirdly, it was the moment that saw the emergence of a new consciousness of Europe in the context of an awareness of other worlds beyond Christendom. These three moments – the humanistic and scientific worldview, the republican imagination, and the encounter with the non-European world – were formative in the making of modern European identity. Burke (1998: 7) emphasizes the dimension of what he calls bricolage – the making of something new out of fragments – as a feature of the Renaissance, which was not based on a single cultural pursuit but many.

Humanism and the sources of modern subjectivity

One of the principal cultural achievements of the Renaissance was humanism, which was a view of human nature as shaped by culture, by which should be understood a body of texts that allows the individual to renew themselves. The culture of antiquity, as opposed to Medieval Scholasticism, was supposed to make possible a more self-conscious human person. This cannot be equated with modern self-identity, but was not too distant from it in the emphasis it placed on what Stephen Greenblatt (2005) referred to as 'self-fashioning'. It was a more of a modern than a medieval development. When William Shakespeare wrote in 1599 in *As You Like It* 'all the world's a stage and its men and women merely players', he was expressing precisely this insight that social relations are dramaturgical and that society is not a natural entity but something that can be literally staged and fashioned. It was a time when the recognition dawned that people are not God's creatures and that all is transient. Humanity was seen as occupying the place of God whose powers of creation were given to politics and to positive law. Modernity was born when transcendence became immanent and the idea of human freedom emerged. The result was a new relation to authority both in science and in politics. However, the culture of the Renaissance remained firmly within the Christian tradition, which is sought to change but not to abandon. Indeed, it was as much about its creative renewal than its rejection. If medieval Christianity rejected antiquity in order to advance the new Christian worldview, the Renaissance appealed to antiquity in order to revive Christianity. In this sense it is an example of a trend in European history of continuity through rupture.

The Renaissance was not about the disinterested study of antiquity. It was a period when new ideas about the social and natural world emerged. This was the age of the New Learning in both science and in humanism. The Renaissance world produced the Scientific Revolution that occurred at this time. Modern science based on the empirical inquiry began to separate from theological doctrines. Galileo, Bruno, Copernicus had de-centred humanity's place in the universe. The revolution they brought about established as the criterion on truth human experience and the related notion of experimental inquiry to be the sole source of truth. Instead of ecclesiastical authority or the received wisdom of the past, truth is now to be based on that which is subject to observation through experimentation. This had a democratizing impact on human knowledge since it separated scientific knowledge from other kinds of knowledge and made possible the freedom of science from ecclesiastical censorship. Aside from the scientific discoveries of the period, the most important legacy could be said to be the epistemic shift it inaugurated in establishing new foundations for authority. In principle, it meant that anyone in possession of technical instruments could establish claims to knowledge. In this period, science begins to free itself from subservience to non-scientific forms of knowledge.

Before its instrumentalization by the state, the new science of the Renaissance made possible a vision of knowledge that opened up for the first time the radical vision of a democratization of knowledge. This spirit of the freedom of science can be held to be a defining feature of the European heritage and one that has been preserved in the European university tradition. Even though the most important innovations in the European university took place later, the foundations were established in the Renaissance period with the movement towards the secularization of science. It is possible to see the network of European universities of the period as a basis for a cultural heritage that has endured to the present day and which constitutes a conception of Europe that is in tension with the imperial tradition that developed in later centuries. By 1500 there were about 100 universities and continued to grow in size and number as Catholic and Protestant institutions competed with each other (Rabb 2006: 87).

The Renaissance ushered in a scepticism that had to be reckoned with, though scholasticism and Aristotelian natural philosophy was to survive until the seventeenth century in the universities. The most important movement within it was humanism, which cultivated a critical approach to the reading of texts and made possible by the diffusion of printed texts since 1450, following the invention of printing and new methods of making paper (Eisenstein 1993; Nauert 2006). This was a way of thinking that stressed tolerance and especially tolerance in matters of religious worship. One of the most famous proponents of humanism in this tradition of critical humanism was Desiderius Erasmus of Rotterdam who argued for the cultivation of persuasion over force as well as pacifism. His work and that of Petrarch has often been taken to be a major expression of Renaissance critical humanism since it was rooted in the rhetorical tradition, which saw the revival of humanistic studies, principally grammar, rhetoric, poetry, history and moral philosophy (Remer 1996). Of these arts, rhetoric was particularly important and was linked to scepticism as well as moral and political tolerance. Rhetoric was an argumentative art that established a way of reaching truth without force, requiring toleration, moderation and persuasion. While the rhetorical tradition was rooted in the past and far from modern liberalism in its concerns, which ultimately were to arrive at truth, it was an important moment in the formation of modernity in that it admitted of the possibility of relativism and the need for a critical reading of texts and a questioning of conventional wisdom. For instance, Erasmus drew on early Christian thought to challenge the ideal of the crusade, which was still very much alive in this time, despite the military impotency of Europe in face of Ottoman expansion (Bisaha 2004: 174–5). Although Renaissance humanism operated largely outside the universities, it exerted an enduring aspect on almost all aspects of modern thought and scholarship as well as in politics in its non-dogmatic approach to life (Heller 1984).

While it is commonplace in recent times to stress the 'dark side' of the Renaissance (Mignolo 1995), it is important to see the Renaissance as differentiated and containing within its currents that cannot be explained only in terms of colonization and racism. Stephen Toulmin (1990) saw in the Renaissance a different foundation to modernity than one founded on rational mastery and the aspiration. In the works of the sixteenth century humanists, such as More, Erasmus, Montaigne, the sources of a different and more sceptical and benign modernity can be found than the one that he sees as emanating from the rationalism of Descartes in the seventeenth century. In Chapter 8 this theme of the conflicting currents in modernity will be returned to, but in the present context it can be noted that the Renaissance was both a mood and age in which Europe, outside Spain and Portugal, were not colonial powers with overseas territories; they had relatively weak central states and were very much overshadowed by the Ottoman Empire. The capacity for critique, and self-problematization that developed in later centuries was cultivated in this period by the humanist movement which can be seen as constituting a major current within the European heritage. Erasmus, for instance, was opposed to war and argued against war on both ethical and pragmatic reasons as both wrong and inefficient. The concept of human dignity was set forth by Pico della Mirandola in 1498 in his *Oration on the Dignity of Man*. The notion of human dignity along with the growing emphasis on the individual became an important dimension of the entire culture of modernity. At this time, what Marcel Mauss referred to as the category of the person, was developed into a conception of the individual from which arose the modern ideal of self-realization (see Carrithers et al 1985; Taylor 1989). The Renaissance gave expression to the emerging cult of the individual in the rise of portrait painting that in developing new techniques in perspectival painting was an innovative artistic feature of the era. The very notion of the modern self was consolidated in this period as an inner directed morality. As argued in Chapter 3 the beginnings of this were in the twelfth century, but it was not until the Renaissance that an augmented emphasis on the individual developed (Garner 1990; Martin 1997; Morris 1972; Gurevich 1995).[1]

The emergence of the modern self was crucial to the making of modern Europe. One of the distinguishing features of modern Europe was the cultivation of a concept of the self that made possible, which Burckhardt saw as a product of the Renaissance, a new emphasis on the human being as an individual as an objective of study and reflection. For Burckhardt this was simply the other side of the modern project of the state and institutions as something to be constructed (Garner 1990).

The basis of early modern discovery of the individual is a conception of the self as autonomous of the world. Jan Patocka (2002) in *Plato and Europe* and Charles Taylor (1989) in *The Sources of the Self* have shown in their pioneering analysis of the self that a defining feature of modernity in Europe was the inner self. For Patocka it commenced as early with Plato and the 'care of the soul'; for Taylor it was Augustine – who of course was influenced by Plato as transmitted through Plotinus – and marked the shift to the inner space of reflexivity through a distinction between an inner and an outer person, the inner being the soul and the path to God. For the European tradition, from Augustine through Weber to Foucault, the self is compelled to know itself and to discover truth within rather than in the objects of the world. Taylor (1989: 131) has argued: 'It is hardly an exaggeration to say that Augustine who introduced the inwardness of radical reflexivity and bequeathed it to the Western tradition of thought.' For Taylor this was formative of the entire western culture. It laid the foundation of a new cognitive shift: 'Augustine shifts the focus from the field of objects known to the activity itself of knowing; God is to be found here. For in contrast to the domain of objects, which is public and common, the activity of knowing is particularized; each of us is engaged in ours. To look towards this activity is to look to the self, to take up a reflexive stance' (Taylor 1989: 130).

Of course Augustine was just one figure, who for Taylor stood between Plato and Descartes, in the articulation of the western notion of the self. His thought serves as an illustration of how in Europe a particular and culturally specific conception of self and world emerged whereby the self saw itself to be separate from the world. This may explain how it was that the Europeans more than anyone else regarded their relation with the world to be fundamentally open and consequentially were not bound to Europe; it opened to them the prospect of finding the City of God anywhere in the world. This capacity led to a certain displacement and eventually to the great movement of Europe beyond the continent to the New World (Mota 2012). Without this notion of the inner self as the path to the City of God, Europeans would not have had the cognitive capacity to conquer other parts of the world or, compelled by curiosity, to seek out other parts of the world and to rule over them, acquire knowledge of them, and to convert them. One of the consequences of this was that the Europeans did not entirely see their world to be confined to Europe.

The birth of republicanism as a European legacy

The developments in science were reflected in new political ideas. The social thought of the medieval period subordinated society to the state, which in turn was embedded in a largely theological worldview. The pact of state and church began to be questioned with the advent of the modern age, which inaugurated new ways of thinking about society. One of the most striking aspects of this new thinking was the idea that society was an artifact, something that can be fashioned by human design. This insight marks the beginning of social theory. The idea that society is not a natural entity, created by divine will and based on fixed principles, led to a view of society as something than can be created and thus changed by people. Suddenly, then, in the sixteenth century politics ceased to be seen as an exclusive instrument of royal and ecclesiastical authorities, but a medium by which society could shape itself in new ways.

One notable outcome was utopian thought. Sir Thomas More's *Utopia* in 1516 was the first of a genre of political allegories on the foundation of a new society. The political tradition of utopian thinking, which goes back to Plato's *Republic*, was in part a response to the discovery of Europeans of other civilizations and in part a consequence of humanism, which in cultivating a questioning attitude opened the political imagination to new possibilities, including the possibility of human beings creating a new kind of society. Such works were both a critique of the existing society – and often, as in the case of More, written under conditions of political censorship – and explorations of what an ideal society might be (see Kumar 1991). While utopianism was to become an important part of modern political thought in the following centuries, arguably the most important legacy of the Renaissance for the European political heritage was republicanism.

The Renaissance re-introduced the ancient idea of the citizen and the idea that society can be rationally planned by a benign state, ideas that were to be influential in shaping the Enlightenment and modern utopian and republican thought. A work of huge significance was Machiavelli's *The Prince* which offered one of the first modern visions of the state and the work of politics as a secular undertaking. In this work, published in 1513 and dedicated to the Florentine ruler, Lorenzo de' Medici, the ruler is not the servant of God but the representative of citizens. Until Machiavelli politics was generally seen as the extension of morality and the state was primarily moral and legitimated by theological principles. Machiavelli changed all that in advocating a theory of politics that broke the connection between morality and politics. *The Prince* was written as a guide to modern politics as a purely instrumental art: the state is not founded in the image of God or on ethical principles, but on the need for protection in the context of a corrupt society.

The theory of politics advocated by Machiavelli was a very modern one and challenged all organic conceptions of the state. He believed people could govern themselves and he believed in the idea of a republic, but saw absolute monarchy as an expediency. He was writing at a time when political and financial corruption was rife in the Italian city states. A viable social order required a strong state, but the state is only a means to an end. His famous principle that the end justifies the means must be seen in light of humanism, namely the idea that a political order requires an act of political foundation rather than of legitimation by preordained moral or religious principles. In this he differed from More, who was more concerned with the ends of politics and the ideal society. Machiavelli shifted the focus to the means and was more acutely aware than was More that the ideal society cannot be achieved. Despite his authoritarian tendency, Machiavelli was first and foremost a humanist, seeing society as something that can be fashioned by secular rulers and shaped in the image of humanist values. He is one of the founders of modern republicanism and believed in the idea of citizenship, that is, sovereignty is invested ultimately in citizens rather than in the state.

The republican idea – the vision of a self-governing political community based on citizenship and the consent of the governed – could be said to be one of the major achievements of the European heritage as it consolidated in the Reformation. It has often been commented that this tradition constitutes a uniquely European political legacy (Van Gelderen and Skinner 2002). While it origins go back to Greek and Roman thought, modern republicanism is different from classical republicanism in its view on liberty and rights. The sixteenth century Spanish philosopher of the Salamanca school, Francisco Suarez, was one of the first proponents of popular sovereignty. It was not until the early modern period that republicanism became a pervasive political movement as well as a social and economic reality in several parts of Western Europe. The notion of citizenship on which it is based refers to a status based on rights that is held by a community of individuals who constitute the public realm. The republic is thus an autonomous political community that governs itself. In republicanism, sovereignty is located within the people rather than in the ruler, who acts in the name of the people. Early European republicanism developed alongside nationalism since it asserted the principle of self-determination that was to become the defining principle of modern nationalism. Rousseau, in the eighteenth century, was a central figure in combining republicanism with nascent nationalism. However the republican imagination is prior and largely a product of Renaissance thought and political practice. Republicanism while not reducible to democracy was important in shaping the progress of democracy insofar as it emphasized the right of a people to rule themselves and that political rulers ought to be answerable to the people in whose name they rule. However, much of modern republicanism was undemocratic.

Springborn (1992) has argued that Renaissance republicanism was constructed out of a self-made myth that it was a stark contrast to 'oriental despotism'. While many republicans promoted democracy others did not see an immediate link, as was the case with Immanuel Kant, who strongly believed in republican government but distrusted democracy, which he believed could weaken the foundations of republicanism. The American and French revolutions, too, appealed to republicanism in general but did not embrace any single system of democratic government other than a general appeal to the principle of the consent of the governed. Republicanism was also in tension with liberalism and variously included a commitment to liberal values, such as the rights of the individual. While the contrast between liberalism and republicanism was not sharply drawn before the nineteenth century the difference was present. Republicanism is properly speaking a political philosophy about the nature of political rule and takes the political community as the primary reference point, not the individual. Unlike liberalism, it does not proclaim freedom but autonomy as the overriding principle for the legitimation of a political order.

Whether in the Renaissance city states of Northern Italy or in the later revolutionary movements of the eighteenth century, republicanism was to become a core feature of European political modernity, although it was often over-shadowed by liberalism. The republican tradition makes sense only in the context of an arrangement between state and society whereby the former never entirely dominates the latter. The basic structure of political modernity in Europe was determined in the early modern period when political authority developed in a way that required the consent of the governed; in other words, state and society evolved in ways that the state rarely for long was able to assert itself over society. Rulers have always had to take account of demands emanating from civil society. In earlier times, the sovereign had, too, of course to seek the consent of the governed, but until the early modern era this was generally confined to the elites, initially the nobles and clergy but increasingly the burghers. Republicanism brought a new dimension to political rule in Europe in placing the source of sovereignty in the people rather than in the elites.

The republican idea can be contrasted to another aspect of the European heritage, namely the cosmopolitan idea: the vision of the global context and human life as shaped by participation in a universal order. This was also present in the Renaissance period and existed in a relation of tension with the republican current. One of the hallmarks of the social and political thought of the Renaissance mind was the idea of a common humanity. This had its origins in the medieval notion of a universal monarchy and in the Christian idea of a universal church, but marked the transition to modernity with an emphasis on equality, human dignity and rights. This was embedded in humanism and in the movement towards the recognition of dissent and toleration (Headley 2008). The notion of a common humanity can be found in most civilizations and has taken many different forms within the European tradition. In some forms it was simply a Eurocentric vision of the world while in other forms it was the belief all peoples are equal and can learn from each other. The notion of a common humanity, too, could be used as much against the colonial drive as in its name. To appreciate the cosmopolitan currents within the Renaissance a consideration of the encounter with the non-European world is necessary since it was in these encounters that European self-consciousness becomes more clearly defined.

Cultural encounters between East and West

The humanism and republicanism of the Renaissance had a global dimension that has only recently been given much attention. The Renaissance should not be seen as an entirely inward movement, but was part of the European age of discovery and exploration, when European explorers ventured to many parts of the world far beyond the limits of the Mediterranean. The sixteenth century witnessed the beginning of European colonialism, especially in the Americas. It is impossible to think of that century without considering the significance of 1492, when Europe began to look westwards in the aftermath of Columbus's voyage to America. However, it was largely an age that as far as much of Europe was concerned was pre-imperial. The period between 1492 and c.1800 was one in which Europe was relatively weak in relation to the Asian empires to the East. The conventional Eurocentric account of the relation between East and West has neglected not only the global context, but also ignored the positive moments in the encounter of Europe with the Asian world, emphasizing only hostility and the penchant for exoticism.

The encounters with other worlds that began in this period had the consequence that European civilization increasingly began to be defined in terms not just of a distance from its own origin, as Brague (2002) has argued, but also in terms of a relation to an Other, a relation that varied from being one of superiority to one of co-existence to one of mutual interest and respect to one of a goal to be reached. In this a tension was set up between the republican idea, with its relatively closed vision of political community, and the open horizon of cosmopolitan idea. In short, the Renaissance was an era of major reorientation in terms of culture, politics and territory for Europe. The Renaissance period was one in which new contacts with the East were established and when the allure of the tropics was also present. A major dimension of the Renaissance was not only the recovery of classical antiquity, but also a fundamental shift in spatial perspective, which was reflected in the exploration of new worlds. Headley (2008) draws attention to the recognition by Renaissance thinkers of the habitality of the new lands the Europeans encountered. This was a challenge to the Christian myth of a common human descent and the denial of an inaccessible yet habitable antipodes. The problem of the accessibility of a habitable world beyond the seas required a redefinition of the Christian *ecumene* in order to affirm the universal redemption of the human race. The complex entwinement of cartography, theology, racism and the history of exploration in the sixteenth century was the ground on which the medieval notions of universal empire and a universal church gradually underwent transformation and increasingly so in the direction of a non-religious way of imagining the world.

A neglected aspect of this new way of imagining the world was the vision of globality that was made possible by cartography (Inglis and Robertson 2006). As argued by Inglis and Robertson, following Brottom (1997, 2002), while cartography was, on the one side, a tool by which Europeans gained control over new territories and an instrument of colonization, it was also a medium that made possible a nascent global consciousness for maps and globes which depicted the 'whole world'. Europeans could thus place themselves in a larger context, the context of the whole world, and this shaped their own self-understanding as part of a larger whole which they might try to gain control over, but could never succeed given the overwhelming presence of global powers and civilizations. The vision and imagination of globality gave not only a sense of nationhood, but also helped to define Europe. Europe thus took shape in the imagination of people as part of an interconnected world. Developments in navigation, cartography and shipbuilding made possible greater exploration than was previously possible. The result was not necessarily the affirmation of a unified European continent but one that was globally connected. In the conventional grand narratives of Europe, this global sensibility has been insufficiently emphasized and instead a picture painted of Europe growing in self-confidence as it re-discovers its allegedly true self in the cultures of antiquity. An alternative view, more in keeping with recent scholarship, rather stresses interactions with those parts of the world with which Europeans came into contact. This should also include the capacity for a critique and a self-questioning attitude towards the relation between the Old and New Worlds, as the one that can be found in the writings of the Salamanca School of political and legal philosophers in sixteenth century Spain. As the lectures of Francisco de Vitoria attest, colonization was not always regarded as self-evidently justifiable and opposed the view that the native Americans had no rights and that the Spanish were justified in appropriating their land.

It should be noted that the rise of global consciousness in the Renaissance period was largely in a pre-imperial context when East and West met on different terms than what was later to be the case. Europe was relatively weak in comparison to the wealth of Asian civilizations. The Renaissance is often mistakenly taken to be a celebration of the European heritage based on a narrow conception of an inward looking humanism without due consideration of the fact that much of that heritage was based on an active engagement with the East. It would not be inaccurate to suggest that the openness to the cultures of antiquity was also reflected in openness to the cultures of the non-European world. It is important to note that in this period the consciousness of being European or the consciousness of nationhood was not particularly pronounced and there was nothing obstructing the emergence of a global consciousness. The turn to a fixed conception of the self and the concern with the obliteration of otherness was a development that came with modernity, whereas by the sixteenth century there was less certainty about such matters. This was what the Renaissance expressed. It articulated a cultural identity that was not the unified culture it was often claimed to be, but a worldview that was open to cultural influences from antiquity and from the wider world. Such forms of consciousness certainly included colonial and racial views. In this sense, then, the Renaissance was very much the cultural expression of the European civilizational constellation, which, as demonstrated earlier, is an interconnecting web of civilizations and cultural flows that was constitutive of modern Europe.

The basis for much of this was trade. The overseas missions of Europeans was initially for trade. This was the rationale for the Portuguese explorations in the Far East. The accidental discovery of present-day Brazil in 1500 by the Portuguese was regarded as unimportant, since it was believed that the newly discovered lands did not contain riches. The Spanish-led conquest of the Americas did not have an impact on all of continental Europe and only later did the rising powers of England and the Dutch seek to participate in the westward conquest. The encounter with Asia occurred at a time when the global economy was largely Asian. Europeans where in effect inserting themselves in this Afro-Asian economy which was the dominant world economy c.500 to 1800, when a new world economy more weighted to the West emerged (Hobson 2004, 2006). But until then the world economy centred on the Indian Ocean, which was the real focus for the Iberian explorations. The vast bulk of silver imported from the Spanish dominions went to China via Spain between 1500 and 1640 where, as Pomeranz argues, it became the monetary and fiscal basis of the greatest economy in the world (Pomeranz 2000: 271–2). Europe gained a new identity through the Renaissance that marked it off from the Asian world, but at the same time Europeans borrowed from the Asian civilization, from the Ottoman to the Chinese Empires. They borrowed extensively from them in science, mathematics, agriculture, and navigation. Islamic, Indian and Chinese innovations were appropriated by early modern Europe much of whose rise to supremacy was made possible only due to inventions outside Europe (Bala 2006). The Scientific Revolution was greatly assisted by Islamic science and it is conceivably the case that the European conquests of the rest of the world would not have been possible without the adoption of navigational techniques learnt from the Muslims. This does not mean that Europe only borrowed from Asia or that its rise to global supremacy is due to such borrowings, but that without the prior Asian innovations there would have been far less advancement both in science and technology as well as in European power. Such borrowings were possible in the first instance only as a result of centuries long interaction between Europeans and Asians. The later divide of West versus East that came with the age of empire in the nineteenth century should not be taken to have defined all relations between Europe and the civilizations of Asia.

It is now increasingly clear from recent scholarship that before 1800 East and West met on more equal terms, and frequently it was the Europeans who were in the weaker position. Recent studies on the relation between Europe and the Ottomans show a differentiated picture than exclusively one of hostilities between ancient rivals (Birchwood and Dimmock 2005; Bisaha 2004; Jardine and Brottom 2000; Goffman 2002). These studies question the existence of a binary divide between an infidel East and a Christian West, showing instead a more entangled geopolitical configuration. Some authors more than others stress an interconnected world (Bitterli 1986; Jardine and Brottom 2000; Goffman 2002; McLean 2005; Springborn 1992) while others emphasize constantly shifting attitudes, which included a willingness to learn from the Turks in the arts, civility and government (Bisaha 2004). Bisaha (2004) emphasizes the fact that Europeans were conscious of being weaker than the Ottomans, who they both respected and feared. This was not an era of aggressive European expansion in the East and no single Europe power, let alone Europe as a whole, had anything like the military power that the Ottoman Empire commanded, which by the fifteenth century ruled over Greece and much of the Balkan area. The discovery of the Americas was largely accidental and an effect of a search for a new trade route to the East. Yet there can be no doubt that Ottoman expansion made possible cultural alterity in which a European consciousness was defined. After the conquest of Constantinople in 1453 and the subsequent conquest of the Balkan area, the writings of the Renaissance humanists clearly gave expression to a European consciousness confronted by an advancing Islamic power that was a threat to Christendom. This was reflected in the increased preference for the word 'Europe' over Christendom. However, this was far from being a racial category or even a political category, since in this time there was no pan-European power and the various powers continued to make alliances with the Turks. It is also evident that despite increased use of the term, the idea of 'Europeans' was a later development, illustrating that alterity was limited to a vaguely defined geographical and cultural area. It is clear that a re-evaluation is needed of relations between Europe and Asia in the period prior to 1800 as far as the Ottoman Empire is concerned and more generally concerning relations with the wider Islamic world as more complicated than previously assumed.

The capacity of the Renaissance to provide Europe with a unified identity was limited. While establishing a cultural orientation and a nascent cultural model, the Renaissance also divided Europe. Politically, the ideas that emerged in the period that is more generally defined as the early modern period provided a foundation for sovereign states which gradually consolidated from the seventeenth century. The Renaissance was also the age of the Reformation, which led into the early modern revolutions and wars of religion that were to define the modern history of Europe, which henceforth was a story of national conflicts. As regards what can be said on the end of the Renaissance, Paul Hazard (1953) in a classic work published in 1935,

The Crisis of the European Mind, argued that by 1700 the Renaissance was finally over due to a new and deeper level of scepticism and critique that did not look primarily to the past.

What can be concluded from the present discussion is that the shape of modern Europe was set in the Renaissance period, but that was far from being predetermined as the outcome of long-run historical forces; nor it is something that can be explained teleologically by what happened in later centuries when Europe achieved near global supremacy either directly through empire-building or through the global diffusion of capitalism. It can also be concluded that the formation of modern Europe in this period cannot be explained internally as a self-induced process. What is needed is a global perspective that takes account of how the dynamics of the process were shaped by the interaction with the non-European world, which itself must be seen as a globally connected one (Abu-Lughod 1963, 1989; Bayly 2004; Darwin 2009; Gunn 2003; Hopkins 2002). Despite its marginality in the early modern period, which should now be considered in light of a wider global economy that was centred in the Indian Ocean, it is nonetheless the case that in this formative period the seeds were set for its later advancement, which is now generally located much later than was previously assumed (Darwin 2009; Goldstone 2008; Pomeranz 2000). The nearest the Europeans had come to a world empire before the nineteenth century was the Spanish one, but Spain lacked the resources for significant conquest in Asia and there was no imperial strategy to make Spain the ruler of the world; Philipp II was more concerned to defend Christianity against the Reformation than seek further overseas conquests (Darwin 2009: 97). As Arnason has argued, the formative effects of inter-civilizational encounters played a decisive role in developing capacities and institutions that could later serve to sustain new initiatives in a changed global environment (Arnason 2006: 78–9).

This all suggests that the formation of modern Europe can only be understood in a multi-dimensional and global context in which both internal as well as external factors played a role. The older accounts tended to stress only the internal forces that shaped Europe and in the traditional and somewhat Eurocentric historiographical accounts of the rise of West Europe did not suffer from the 'oriental despotism' that supposedly impeded Asian development. Recent accounts, such as Frank (1998), have over-stressed the external context, such as the claim that Europe's rise was due to the decline in Asia rather than due to anything it did on its own or the view that Europe's rise was due to having borrowed everything from the East, a thesis implicit in Dobson (2004).

The truth lies somewhere in between and it is difficult to disagree with Arnason's argument for an intermediate position that emphasizes the interaction between East and West without downplaying Europe's capacity to develop in unique ways that which it learnt from other civilizations. Darwin has argued for caution about assuming the relative dynamism and wealth that Europe acquired in the early modern period was sufficient for empire-building ventures and that much of early colonization was in fact limited, at least in Asia and Africa. John Darwin is struck by the limited influence of Europe until well into the nineteenth century (Darwin 2009). The *ancien regime* states were, he argues, ill-equipped for the conquest of the non-European world and there was often little material incentive to do so. Dynastic struggles within Europe weakened Europe's capacity for anything like an imperial order comparable to the Ottoman Empire. However, the warring nature of Europe was inevitably a breeding-ground for colonial wars as well as a basis for advances in military technology and organization (Darwin 2009: 114). It is clear that Europe can be understood only in a global context and this must include an appreciation of earlier waves of globalization that had a formative impact on the wider Eurasia world.

7
Unity and Divisions in Early Modern European History: The Emergence of a Westernized Europe

The very notion of European history suggests that there is a pattern that constitutes the basic unity of its history. Indeed, the very notion of a historical process seems to presuppose a structural pattern. Yet, a closer look at the historical experience reveals a more complicated situation. Instead of unity one finds divisions that undermine claims to significant unity. Much of the narrative in this book has stressed internal civilizational differences and has invited scepticism about proclamations of unity, at least without showing how they came into existence. This is not to deny the existence or possibility of a unity, but urges caution in assuming its existence as a self-defining reality or a teleological ideal that should be reached when divisions are overcome. In the traditional Grand Narratives the assumption was that out of the divisions in history a greater unity would be possible due to an underlying common civilization that provided it with its basic orientations. Yet some notion of unity is needed, if only to make sense of diversity. The argument in this book is that European civilization is to be understood as a constellation of civilizations whose interaction produced the basic matrix of modern Europe, which as a consequence is composed of multiple forms that were later solidified with the emergence of modernity and its different routes. The key feature that makes possible a structural pattern is the mechanisms and processes that establish connectivity and development, rather than a system of values that is somehow foundational or an underlying subjectivity or a path-dependent course. It is in this sense that a basic pattern of unity can be established from which diversity develops through internal logics of development and the creativity of social actors.

Rejecting the notion of unity in favour of divisions does not entirely answer the question of how should European history be understood especially if, as has often been the case, a notion of division stresses the binary divide between an internal European self versus a non-European external other. The notion of unity, understood in the above terms, is a basis on which to conceive of diversity, rather than assuming diversity is prior to and generative of unity. This does not mean that it cannot be argued that because the history of Europe has been characterized by divisions arising from strife and competition between different regions, nations, geopolitical units, elites etc, the only unity possible is that made possible by the existence of an external enemy. This has been one corrective to the traditional account of a common European civilization (see Delanty 1995a). However, as argued in the preceding chapters, the view that the only unity possible is one formed against a common enemy must be relativized, not simply because of the scale of internal divisions, but because there has rarely been a constant external enemy and alterity has been as much internal as it has been external. Yet, it cannot be denied that at crucial moments – 1453 (fall of Constantinople) 1688 (Ottoman Siege of Vienna), 1917 (October Revolution), 1939 (Second World War) – in the history of Europe the vision of the enemy outside has been significant in shaping European consciousness. However, alterity is not always negative; as argued, in earlier chapters, the external other has also been a focus of positive identification. Other significant moments – 1789, 1989 – for instance were not built on constructions of an external enemy.

The thesis of the unity forged against an external enemy assumes a degree of continuity that in fact has not continuously existed and sits uncomfortably alongside the recognition of major ruptures, which question any assumptions of continuity. If there is less continuity in history – from antiquity to modernity – than has traditionally been assumed in the Grand Narratives it is difficult to postulate the existence of an external Other that gave to Europe its identity. This would not entirely explain the singularity of Europe – which requires some notion of a cultural and social structure – nor account for relative similarity in social and economic structures or other sources of the idea of Europe that can be more easily accounted for in terms of endogenous developments. The previous chapters have questioned the claim that the exteriority of Islam or the East was the defining tenet in European identity, for it oscillated between positive and negative positions too often to be of sufficient force for a long-run identity to emerge. The argument has in fact been stronger, namely that Islam is a part of the constellation of civilizations that make up Europe.

The problem of unity and divisions cannot be disengaged from the problem of continuity and rupture. Recent approaches would appear to stress divisions over unity and rupture over continuity and in so doing relativize both the existence of a common European self as much as cast doubt on the possibility of an external Other that provided the enduring terms of alterity. As argued in the previous chapters, an inter-actionist account of Europe is needed to relativize the older emphasis on internal explanations of the rise of Europe, for European history cannot be entirely accounted for without taking into account the rela-tion with the non-European world. The context for exploring this is Europe's insertion into the global world of Asian trade and commerce, which had preceded the rise of Europe and its later colonial path and provided it with opportunities for innovation and expansion. This broader context offers a more comprehensive interpretation of the external relation than one focused only on responses to an external threat, whether real or an imaginary construction.

These tensions between internal versus external, unity versus divi-sions, continuity versus rupture are related to another set of contradic-tions, which altogether define the formation of the European heritage as it unfolded over the centuries: the relation between homogenization versus pluralization. On the one side, it is possible to see history in terms of processes of increased uniformity arising from the consolida-tion of new centres of power which exert homogenizing influences through cultural, political and economic forces. This may lead to unity in terms of durable geopolitical units or societal frameworks, for instance states and markets, but such homogenization may also take a more varied form, as a particularization of the universal in the sense of different countries creating similar institutions. Thus, law has been one way Europe achieved a certain homogenization, while at the same time pursuing different national routes. The wider framework of modernity, to be discussed in the next chapter, is also a way in which to situate national patterns of differentiation within a wider context that pro-vides a degree of commonality. This will require due attention to the ways in which disparate units – elites, regions, nations, etc – connect up with others. Rather than look for uniqueness and singularity on the level of the internal composition of the entity or subject in question, or Europe as a whole for that matter, more significant is the means by which the various components interconnect. The formative process that constituted Europe can be best understood as one in which versa-tile structures of connectivity were created that made possible rapid innovation and learning in technology, science, government, and the

formation of cultural models that facilitated individualism and progressive social movements that challenged authority. All of this made
possible a degree of contingency that has undermined any notion of a
path-dependent view of history.

Some of these issues will be taken up in the third section of this
chapter and in the next chapter. The main focus of this chapter will be
on those attempts to establish new patterns of unity through homogenization and new relations between interiority and exteriority. The
first section deals with the rise of the West in the wake of the conquest
of the Americas when a major shift occurred in the borders of Europe
from an eastern to a western oriented one. The second section looks at
the internal homogenization of Europe. The third section shifts the
focus to network-based forms of integration and the tradition of
popular rebellion and social movements that can be said to constitute
the European heritage in ways that challenge the dominant homogenizing trends and suggest a model of integration through differentiation.

Empires and borders: Expanding, limiting and over-lapping

By the end of the early modern period a basic divide became evident in
the cultural and the geographical definition of Europe. The geographical notion of a Europe, broadly the territory of Christianity, ceased to
be a meaningful frame of reference following the westward expansion
of the Ottoman Empire and the beginnings of the Iberian conquest of
the Americas. This was a time when the gravity of Europe shifted westwards. From then onwards, the idea of Europe became increasingly a
cultural or political construct that did not refer to a specific geographical territory. This was the beginning of the loosening of any underlying reference point for the idea of Europe, which first lost Christianity
and then a specific geographical territory, as the reference points for its
specificity. The older ambivalence between Christendom and Europe
was replaced by a new one with Europe now becoming associated with
the notion of the West. In this shift in the signifiers with which Europe
has been identified, the ground moves in the direction, first, of western
and, then, the north west of Europe in a process that can be termed the
'westernization' of Europe. The encounter with what was to become
the New World gave to Europe a new identity as the Old World, and
along with this came a new notion of civilization, which in turn was
contrasted variously to 'primitive man' and to the barbarian who had
to be remedied by civilization.

By the seventeenth century Europe as a world region became more discernable, though its rise to global supremacy did not take place until well into the nineteenth century. The late fifteenth century witnessed several defining moments in the emergence of Europe as a distinct entity. As argued earlier, the year 1453 was a turning point in that it gave a certain geopolitical identity to the Latin West, if not culturally, certainly politically in that the Ottoman Empire had more or less encircled Europe to the East and South-East closing off any expansion in that direction. To the North, Russia since 1480 became a rising power under Ivan the Great when it became free of the Mongols. The year 1492 symbolically marked the westernization of Europe with the completion of the Catholic 'Reconquest' of Spain following the seizure of Granada, which had been the last stronghold of the Muslims – and it was too the year that Columbus sailed for the Americas claiming those lands for the Spanish crown. So after 1492 the ground had been prepared for the emergence of Europe as the West: Columbus replaced Charlemagne as the harbinger of the new age and with this the notion of the West became transformed into an outward movement.

Spain, united under the union of the Catholic monarchs, was at the forefront of European homogenization. From being a frontier land, it had become a bastion of a revived and imperialist Catholicism. 'Europe conquered the Peninsula', Braudel has written (1990: 824), 'by way of the Pyrenees by the Atlantic and Mediterranean shipping routes: along this frontier zone it defeated Islam with the victories of the Reconquest which were victories for Europe.' The marriage of Isabella and Ferdinand and the subsequent unification of Castile and Aragon in 1479 laid the foundation for Spain to become a leading power. In 1516 with accession of Charles V to the Spanish throne, the Habsburgs ruled Spain and its emerging empire, which was also linked from 1520 with the Holy Roman Empire following Charles V's election as Holy Roman Emperor. In 1521 Hernando Cortes conquered the Aztecs and 11 years later Francisco Cortes defeated the Inca Empire, thus opening the path for Spanish dominion of much of the New World. Spanish expansionist policy led it into conflict with the other rising powers, in particular England, France, the Dutch who all competed for control over the new territories.

Until the completion of the 'Reconquest', Spain, under Muslim rule, was not in the 'West' as far as Christendom was concerned. Alfonso VI captured Toledo from the Muslims in 1084 but further advance was halted until the thirteenth century as a result of Muslim revival. By the end of the fifteenth century this had all changed and the pluri-civilizational world that had developed in the Iberian peninsula linked to Northern Africa had dissolved. This Ibero-African frontier became what Hess (1978) has called the 'forgotten frontier', which after the 'Reconquest' had become a closed frontier and Europe ceased to have any inclination in expansion beyond the Mediterranean. With the closure of the extended Eastern frontier, the vast border stretching south and east of Europe, a new and different kind of border was opened up to the west. This crystallized in what Webb (1952) has referred to as the 'Great Frontier', which has been one of the primary factors in modern history. While the eastern frontier became increasingly one of defence, the western frontier was one of expansion. The Atlantic Ocean replaced the Mediterranean Sea in setting the terms for a new conception of Europe as the West.

The western frontier of course was not initially regarded as a frontier, but a passage to the east and it was not for several decades that it had an impact; indeed, when the Portuguese landed in present-day Brazil in 1500 they did not know it was the same landmass as the one the Spanish landed a few years earlier. But when it became known that the newly discovered lands were part of one single continent it was decisive in the re-orientation of Europe westwards. The Portuguese were the first to set up a vast trading empire and were followed by Spain, which established from the beginning a colonial empire. England and the Dutch followed with the foundation of the English and Dutch East India Companies in the early seventeenth century and the bid to gain control of North East Brazil. In England the Cromwellian 'Western Design' to colonize the Caribbean began the march to empire. Internal conquest within Europe has come less attractive to the rising western sea powers than overseas conquest, first in the Americas and later in Asia and Africa. European mastery thus passed to the control of the sea with the decline of the agrarian-based economies of the Middle Ages. It was the belated mastery of the sea that that helped to shape modern Europe as a westernizing civilization.

It may, too, have been the case that the western re-orientation in Europe made it less confrontational with the Muslim east. Though the struggle to gain control over the seas continued, Europe had abandoned its desire to conquer the Ottoman Empire, which remained a formidable power. It is significant that as the western sea-based powers were looking increasingly westwards, the main Central Europe power was still landlocked and fostered a different civilizational identity that marked off east and west within Europe as an internal division that had a lasting consequence for the later history of the Europe. The developments of the sixteenth and seventeenth century favoured nation-states with overseas territories and mercantilist trading economies. The result was the formation of two Europes, an 'Oceanic' Europe and a 'Continental' Europe (Cahnman 1952). These two notions of Europe found their embodiment in the two imperial traditions: the colonial sea-based empires and the Central European land-based empires. Thus the relation to the exterior and the opening up of a new expanding frontier created the conditions for the future internal division of Europe. Imperial Russia was a slightly different case in that while being a land-based empire, it was an expanding one and extended to the pacific with the conquest of Siberia, but like most land empires it did not have a strong separation of core from colony, as was the case with the nascent sea-based empires in the West.

The existence of a relatively open and expanding western frontier and an increasingly closed eastern one, should not detract attention from the fact that many of Europe's frontiers in this period took the form of overlapping borders, or borderlands where a clear division between internal and external cannot be easily discernable. This was particularly the case with Europe's internal borders, which have continuously changed, and its borders to the north, which were less clear-cut, since, as argued in Chapter 4, Europe's relation with imperial Russia did not have the rigid character it was to take in the twentieth century. Despite the separation of imperial core and colonial periphery that was a feature of the sea empires of the West, the reality was that much of Europe was also outside of the geographical territory of Europe. The largest European empire in modern times, the British Empire, was not considered to be European. The rise of empire created a hybrid Europe, which became increasingly shaped by its overseas colonies. In the case of Portugal, the colony overtook in importance the colonial country and shortly before its independence and the creation of the Empire of Brazil, the Portuguese crown was forced to relocate there following the French invasion of Portugal in 1808. The 13 colonies that formed the basis of the United States eventually grew to become the world's largest power and overshadowed their European origins. Later emigration from Europe to the Americas, especially in the nineteenth and early twentieth centuries, led to settler societies that were in part European, but developed distinctive national and transnational identities (Hartz 1964). The result was a new definition of the notion of the West that reduced its reliance on the Old World.

All of these New World societies were shaped by the history of slavery, a reminder of the interconnected worlds of the Americas,

Europe and Africa. While politically the turn to empire brought about a division between colony and imperial centres, which was later consolidated by the formation of independent states in the New World, the economic system that developed in the New World tied it to the colonial powers. Until its abolition in the nineteenth century, for almost three centuries slavery made possible the accumulation of wealth in both colony and in the imperial centres. This again belies the importance of a consideration of the global context for an understanding of the formation of Europe and an assessment of its political heritage. The factors that shaped the rise of Europe are simply not integral to Europe, but were constituted in a relation with many other parts of the world as is vividly illustrated in the case of the history of empire and slavery. As Stuart Hall has written: 'colonization was never simply external to the societies of the imperial metropolis. ... It was always inscribed deeply within them' (cited in Magubane 2005).

The prevalence of overlapping borders was particularly a feature of the geopolitical shape of Central and Eastern Europe where the major land-based empires – Prussian, Habsburg, as well as the Russian and Ottoman Empires – were spread across multi-ethnic territories. In these empires the divide between interior and exterior is less clear-cut, especially given the tendency towards a constant expansion of the core to include the semi-periphery. The shape of Europe was very much the product of their complex ethnic and cultural composition. The outcome of this was a civilizational background that made the creation of territorial nation-states difficult, since most territories did not have a single ethnic group that could be the basis of a national community, due to greater discontinuity in nation and state formation. This brings us to the question of plurality and the notion of Europe as less defined by external borders than being itself a borderland.

Homogenization and plurality

One of the most important accounts of the question of the unity and divisions in Europe is that of the Polish historian Oskar Halecki's *The Limits and Divisions of European History* (1950). In this work, which reflects the historical experience of Central Europe, he identified four historical regions of Europe: a 'Western Europe', West Central Europe', 'East Central Europe' and an 'Eastern Europe'. These four regions effectively amount to two, since the first two are essentially part of what became known as Western Europe and the latter two became part of Eastern Europe. The fourfold division however draws attention to a more pluralized historical experience and the division within the Central European area between the Germany and the less clear-cut line between the western (Poland, Bohemia) and the eastern (Slovakia, Romania, Bulgaria) areas. This fourfold approach was later revised in another well-known essay in 1981 by a Hungarian historian, Jeno Szücs, 'The Three Historical Regions of Europe' in which he argued for three historical regions: Western, East Central and Eastern Europe (Szücs 1988; see also Arnason and Doyle 2010). The debate around Europe's historical regions is of particular relevance to Central Europe – and will be returned to in Chapter 10 – but in the present context it can be noted that it draws attention to the question of a conception of Europe that arose from within the land-based empires that shaped the history of Europe from the early modern period until the middle of the twentieth century.

In this approach to Europe – which seeks to identify the regional specificity of Central and Eastern Europe – the external dimension is less significant, though with due consideration of the relation with Russia as far as East and Central Europe are concerned and the fact that all these regions had to define themselves in terms of a relation to Russia. The civilizational basis in the history of Christianity is taken as a basis for regional variations that later gave rise to distinctive national traditions. So Europe should be understood less in terms of a singular 'Western Civilization' than in terms of inter-related regions that while having common roots, in particular in Christianity, developed different trajectories. In view of the meaning that the notion of the West took on with the project of overseas expansion in the Americas, it is not surprising that the historians of Central and Eastern Europe would find in the designation Western Civilization a less than meaningful application to histories that were influenced by very different imperial traditions.

The notions of a regional diversity of Europe is an important correction to over-generalized concepts of Europe as a unified region or as something than can be accounted for in terms of the notion of the West. From a continental perspective, geographers and historians have often implicitly attributed a unity to Europe in contrast to the great diversity of Asia or Africa. But understood as a world region, Europe is varied in much a different way and of course is considerably smaller and, if we take civilizations based on writing, it has a much shorter history. Plurality might be the best starting point for an adequate appreciation of the shaping of Europe since the Middle Ages in that Europe is constituted out of different units, which include nations and wider regions, while having common characteristics and backgrounds that give to its commonality. To explore such commonality, a formative civilizational background can be postulated, but a stronger notion of a constitutive process is also required in order to explain change and variability. One such way to theorize the unity of Europe is to identify structure forming processes of homogenization and the regional geopolitical variants that emerge from them.

Empires can thus be seen as agents of homogenization and, with respect to the role of the Central European empires in making of Europe, as we will see, they were also agents of pluralization, due the nature of their internal organization and too because of their eventual fragmentation. Indeed, much of modern Europe is the product of the fragmentation of empire. Empire was the dominant form of state organization in Europe until the end of the nineteenth century when the nation-state emerged as an alternative model. The German Empire has been one of the most important, for in many ways it was the *de facto* basis of a large part of Europe in much the same way that the present-day European Union is. From the tenth century onwards in the wake of the break-up of the Carolingian kingdom, the Germans under Otto I, shifted the centre of gravity to the east from the Franks and claimed the mantle of the Roman Empire, in 962 when Otto was crowned Holy Roman Emperor. The imperial title thus passed to the Germanic lands. In this a tension was established between the Germanic kingdom and the Frankish legacy of Charlemagne and the eventual emergence of two contenders for the leadership of Europe: the French and the German.

The German Empire – an alliance of counts and princes under an oath of allegiance to an elected emperor – was itself sufficiently large to be able to claim to be Europe, though this was more an aspiration than a reality and one that was also intertwined with Christendom. It was the Holy Roman Empire of the German Nation, under Hapsburg leadership since 1520, that gave a certain geopolitical reality to what was to become Europe in aspiring to link the Germanic lands with Europe – it was to include the Iberian peninsula, which Charles V inherited – and Christendom. When that somewhat artificial confederation collapsed following the Napoleonic occupation, the result was a certain reality to an undefined European space that no power ever fully controlled. The German world itself became divided between two imperial traditions, the Prussian and the Austrian-based Habsburg empires. The Polish-Lithuanian state, a large and powerful dual state in the sixteenth and seventeenth century, disappeared in 1795 following the partition of Poland.

Homogenization through empire formation in Central Europe is one way that the formation of modern Europe can be seen and in ways that duly give a place to a plurality of regional traditions, before the arrival of the modern national state. To develop this perspective further an additional dimension is needed in order to capture the geopolitical dynamics of the process by which imperial cores consolidated themselves and established a system of political role over larger territories and in doing so constituted what has become known as Europe. In this regard the notion of 'internal colonization' is useful. As already mentioned in Chapter 3, the shape of medieval Europe arose from a continuous process of the expansion of cores into the different regional centres of Europe. While some of this can be understood in terms of a process of pluralization – since it was spear-headed by different centres – it was effectively achieved through the homogenization of those territories it came into contact. Since many earlier such movements at empire-building – Norman and earlier Roman – were later incorporated into larger units, a secondary process of homogenization took place, leading to a greater degree of geopolitical integration. Since such process were rarely in any sense complete and often co-existed with others, the result of a certain degree of polarization and conflict.

The background to this was the collapse of the Carolingian kingdom in the tenth century and the consequent emergence of different political units, significant of which was the rise of Norman power and its extension after 1066 into England and Wales and Southern Ireland. Bartlett (1993) has referred to this as a process of internal colonization, which led in time to the creation of entirely new states (see also Chapter 3). In this case the process of internal colonization produced a state that later broke from its original base and became a world power. The incompleteness of such processes of internal colonization can explain the nationalism of the periphery, as in the case of the incomplete conquest of Ireland by the later generation of Normans who had gained control of England and Wales but only partially conquered Ireland and did not extend their dominion into Scotland.[1] The loss of control of Sicily and Southern Italy was a basis for Catalan colonization of Sardinia, the Kingdom of Naples and Sicily, and for a time Athens. The example of Catalonia is itself an interesting instance of the incomplete colonization of Castile and Aragon, though it formed treaties with the latter, it was never fully absorbed into the Spanish state; yet, as a significant economic power, it acquired its own colonial dominion with Europe, of which only a trace remains today in Western Sardinia where a dialect of Catalan is still spoken, but the process of internal colonization had the cumulative effect of creating larger, more uniform and more linked geopolitical units, many of which remained part of the original colonizing project. Other such movements would include the migrations of the Vikings and the Magyars in the ninth century. The history of Europe is very much the story of how some of these projects succeeded and others failed and the fact that none succeeded overall in dominating Europe. The shape of Europe is as much due to the failure of internal colonization as to its success, since by 1919 all the European land-based empires – Prussian, Habsburg, Ottoman and Russian – collapsed, having been defeated by the more successful western sea-based empires with the help of the New World offspring.

Since these imperial projects were frequently in conflict, if not at war with each other, it is not surprising that the internal colonization of Europe took an uneven form. The notion of uneven development is highly pertinent to the wider regional variation of Europe and to an extent can explain the above mentioned difference between a western and an eastern Europe. This in part resides in different experiences of state formation and capitalism, in particular in the transition from feudalism to modernity and the transition from the absolute state to the constitutional state. In Western Europe the transition took place relatively earlier, while in many parts of Eastern Europe the transition was slower and more incomplete. The regional divisions within Europe, especially between north and south and between east and west can be in part explained by the different patterns of state formation.

To account further for the homogenization of Europe in the Middle Ages and Early Modern period would require an extensive discussion on the different trajectories of empire formation. The above remarks suggest possible avenues for further exploration of how nations, regions such as Europe as well as smaller ones, become constituted in power relations between core, periphery and semi-periphery. The fact that some of these configurations have endured should not lead to the conclusion that these entities are somewhat the natural building blocks of Europe. The nature and logic of all homogenizing processes is the elimination of difference, except where it lies outside the process. In this sense, internal colonization can be consideration in much the same terms as Norbert Elias's notion of a 'civilizational process', namely a process of increasing homogenization in the organization of social relations (Elias 1982). In this case, any notion of unity is not a starting point for the identification of basic similarities in societies but a condition that is produced and the more we approach the emergence of modern societies the greater the extent of similarity will be.

Despite the various processes of homogenization that led to the formation of modern Europe none succeeded in creating a lasting geopolitical framework. All imperial projects – the early Germanic and Frankish Empires, the later French, Habsburg, Prussian one – eventually collapsed, as did the Roman Empire. There were about 200 states in Europe in 1500, but by 1900 only 20 (Mann 1993: 70; Tilly 1990). Europe is as much the product of the failure of empire as it is of its success (see also Kennedy 1987). Despite the relative victory of the western sea-based empires, the eventual retreat from empire in the post-1945 period, is a further phase in the long history of the breakdown of empire in Europe and can be viewed as constitutive of the European historical experience. In this sense, then, plurality is a creation of the failed attempts at homogenization that began with the collapse of the Roman Empire.

A consideration of the processes of homogenization should not neglect those that were less a direct product of empire-building project than those explicitly concerned with the elimination of difference. Throughout the early modern period the persecution of minorities and in particular anti-Semitism was rife. The regional diversity of Europe disguised a drive towards cultural homogenization. Since the 'Reconquest', the Jews were expelled from Spain and the Muslims were forcibly converted to Christianity, but were finally expelled by the early seventeenth century. The destruction of the mosques, the burning of the Moorish libraries and the establishment of the Inquisition in the late fifteenth century further enhanced the homogeneity of western civilization as Christian. After the twelfth century the segregation of the Jews established a fear of pollution in Europe which underwent forcible homogenization. Europe became what Moore has termed a 'persecuting society' from the eleventh century when minorities, such as Jews, witches and heretics, became the object of policies of homogenization (Moore 1987; Cohen 1993). It is a reminder that the homogenization of Europe was often a forced one.

Networks and social movements

Finally, to complete the present discussion of homogenization and plurality in the early modern period when a 'westernized' Europe emerged, attention should be given to processes of integration that fall short of homogenization, but which were constitutive of modern Europe insofar as they reduced deep divisions without at the same eliminating pluralization. Significant in this respect are the processes that made increased interconnectivity possible between diverse regions and which brought about forms of integration than rested on societal differentiation rather than highly homogenized units. It has already been stressed that Europe was not endogenously created, but emerged from centuries long interaction with the non-European world. This obviously also applies to the genesis of Europe from internal encounters, which extend beyond the dynamics of core and periphery relations discussed above in the formation of empires to relations that take place within the context of both formal and informal networks. It is important not to lose sight of the myriad of networks that linked up different parts of Europe that from a different perspective might be seen as separate. In the early modern period Europe become increasingly interconnected through trade, the circulation of cultural products, scientific knowledge, travel, the lives of elites and dynastic lineages. The outcome of the networks that make such interconnectivity possible was not a more homogenized Europe, but a more transversally connected one.

If the tendency of the modern state towards territorial expansion produced a more homogenized Europe, capitalism and the nascent market economy tended to produce more and more heterogeneity insofar as it needed to seek out new markets, for by its very nature trade required access to markets beyond the context of production. While the state was a homogenizing force, capitalism was more likely to produce heterogeneity. The variety of transitions from feudalism is in itself an example of the logic of differentiation within capitalism, which of course is also not tied to state structures. (The tension between capitalism and the state will be returned to in the next chapter). The gradual abandonment of mercantilism and the turn to the free market was one such way capitalism escaped the bounds of the state, which increasingly had to confront a capitalist class whose interests increasingly were widening beyond the national to the international context.

Going back further into the early history of Europe we can see several examples of how Europe became slowly constituted from processes that depended on establishing links between different centres than on a core subjugating and domesticating a periphery. Although it is not known for certain, the Celts for example were probably not a unified people but either inter-linked peoples with common cultural practices and it may have been the case that it was their cultural artifacts and practices that was mobile and adapted by diverse peoples. A later and less speculative example is that of the Vikings, who were not only warriors, but also traders and established links between many different parts of Europe as far as Byzantium and left an indelible mark on the shape of Europe in examples as diverse as the English language and the foundation of Dublin, which was originally a Viking settlement. Within the examples discussed early of empire-building, one can also find many instances of interconnectivity working alongside more pronounced processes of homogenization. This was certainly the case with regard to the Roman Empire, which did not sustain itself only through military subjugation but also required the operation of more networked-based processes. The Portuguese Empire is also a pertinent example of a trading-based empire than one based only on colonization, as were the Spanish, British and French Empires. However, a more differentiated analysis will require separating the institutional forms of empire-building from the unintended effects they produced.

The period from the second half of the fifteenth century was one of relative growth for Western Europe, which began to recover from decline in the previous century. Earlier in the mid-fourteenth century, the Black Death, which reduced Europe's population, may have created some of the conditions for economic growth (see Herlihy 1997). The rise of autonomous cities not subject to the homogenizing power of other political structures such as empires was crucial for the making of Europe even if they became absorbed into centralizing nation-state in later times (Benevolo 1993). New trading centres emerged, for instance Antwerp, which was the centre of an extensive trading empire that stretched across Europe and beyond. The Baltic region acquired an enhanced importance with the foundation of the Hanseatic League, which played a decisive role in linking different parts of Northern Europe for some three centuries from the thirteenth to the seventeenth century (Tracy 1993). The Hanseatic League linked the major trading cities, or Hansa cities of Northern Europe, thus giving a basis to a Nordic Europe. At its zenith there were 170 cities in the network, which represented an alternative form of social, economic and political organization to the nation-state, the rise of which eventually saw the demise of the Hanseatic League. The existence of networks of integration such as the Hanseatic League draw attention to forms of commonality that do not obliterate unity or provoke the nationalism of the periphery. Trading networks played an important role in laying the creation of modern Europe and offer further evidence of the interconnected nature of Europe and the rest of the world. They can in fact be seen as having a constitutive role in the making of the modern world and reflect a different modality of unity to ones that set it against divisions (see Bayly 2004; Curtin 1984; Parker 2010; Tracy 1993). Trading networks are of course not specifically European, but what was distinctive about the European experience was the location of these highly organized networks in urban and relatively autonomous centres. It was this that gave to Europe a distinct advantage in the accumulation of wealth since it combined trade with the pursuit of self-determination. Although the rise of the centralized nation-state and the overall dominance of major centres of imperial power ultimately brought about a decline in the tradition of the autonomous city, its legacy remained and shaped modern Europe in multiple ways.

The question of unity and division in European history is in danger of being overly concerned with the analysis of geopolitical unity. The above discussion has attempted to draw attention to different modalities of unity than ones that are essentially regionally-based. However network-based conceptions of societal integration are insufficient. Any account of the question of unity and divisions must address the ways in which power itself undergoes transformation. In this sense what is needed is an account of the impact of social agency in the making of Europe. When viewed in global terms, the distinctiveness of Europe resides in the popular radical tradition of dissent and protest which since the early modern period had a constitutive role in the shaping of the modern state and in the relationship between economy and society.

What was unique in Europe was the opposition that the exercise of power received. Europe was never fully integrated from 'above' by the state or by an ecclesiastical authority due to long-standing traditions of popular rights that had evolved since the early Middle Ages leading to the constant challenging of power by civil society. According to Szücs (1988: 300), 'the stability of the West was ensured in the long run precisely by the impossibility of integrating it "from above". The integrative lines of force began "from below", and in the first phase (9th–11th centuries) these displayed a specifically vertical orientation.' The thirteenth century medieval state was a solidaristic self-organizing polity based on the different interests of the clergy, the nobles and the burghers or merchants who resisted the attempts of royal authority towards centralization (Ertman 1997). In the twelfth and thirteenth centuries various groups succeeded in winning liberties from central authority, leading to what Szücs (1988: 306) has referred to as a 'plurality of small freedoms' and the birth of the idea of society. While most of these were the liberties of the elites, other groups also benefited from attempts to limit royal power. This was achieved both by increased representation and by limiting centralization through increased autonomy for factional interests, such as those of the clergy, the nobles, and burghers. By the early modern period there was a well-established popular tradition of revolt and dissent. The basis of much of it was in urban populations and in guild-based organizations that had formed in the cities. In these organizations craftsmen, artisans, the professional classes, merchants, established statutory rights for their activities. Such economic-based rights were the basis for many challenges to power. This had the long-lasting consequence of making possible a model of political modernity in which civil society would play a central role in the relationship between economy and state. In the course of the eighteenth century there was a relative decline in the growth of the state, in terms of its size and spending, in relation to the growth of civil society (Mann 1993: 394). This was reflected variously in the republican tradition, religious dissent deriving from the Reformation and Renaissance humanism, agrarian rebellion, the socialist movement, the mixing of liberalism and republicanism and resulting constellation of forces that led to the French Revolution and its legacy for a tradition of political community based on collective self-determination. This will be discussed further in the next chapter.

In conclusion it can be said that by 1800 the basic structural shape of modern Europe had been created and that this was a considerably more westernized kind of Europe than had been previously the case. It was westernized in the sense that the geopolitical gravity had shifted to the western half and that this was due to a shift in the wider global context from the Asian world economy to one based in the Atlantic. The emergence of a westernized Europe, too, was accompanied by homogenizing trends that were spear-headed by the new centres of geopolitical power. Since the French invasion of the Iberian peninsula in 1808 Spanish and Portuguese colonial power came to a final end with the independence of Spanish Latin America in its immediate aftermath. The new centres of colonial power were Britain and France, and to a lesser extent the newly created Belgium. Plurality was never eliminated and nor was opposition. The regional divisions within Europe survived the geopolitical frameworks that sought to eliminate them.

8

The Enlightenment and European Modernity: The Rise of the Idea of Europe

From the end of the seventeenth century the idea of Europe took on a more concrete form as a result of the crystallization of new political structures and geopolitical frameworks in the wake of the Thirty Years War, 1618–1648. The post-1648 Westphalian political order that ushered in the age of sovereign states saw the end of the era of the wars over religion and schisms that followed. The early modern period was an era of wars over religion and related dynastic struggles, at least since 1713 with the Peace of Utrecht that saw the end of the War of the Spanish Succession. The emergence of the idea of Europe can be seen in the context of what Rabb (1975) has called the 'struggle for stability' in the seventeenth century. The eighteenth century, in contrast, was one of relative stability and consolidation for the post-1648 order. In this period new political ideas emerged in response to the crisis of the wars of religion and the recognition that the unity of Europe cannot be a political unity. One concrete outcome was the rise of the nation-state and the European inter-state system which shaped world politics for the next three centuries (Tilly 1990). The Reformation had led to a major division between the Catholic south and the Protestant north, and as discussed in the previous chapters, a division had also taken root between the sea-based empires of the West and the land-based ones of Central Europe. The period that has been variously character-ized as the Enlightenment and modernity is one in which new concep-tions of European political community emerge in response to the historical experience of the age.

From the late seventeenth century to the early nineteenth century the idea of Europe emerged with a certain ambivalence: it reflected consciousness of a broad cultural or civilizational basis and a politically divided reality. On the one side, the emerging idea of Europe is a reflection of the cultural unity of Europe that comes from its civilizational background and, on the other side, it is a response to the divisions that have resulted from its history. This partly explains the distinction that arose since the eighteenth century between civilizational unity and cultural diversity, where culture in this instance refers to national cultures. A distinction that is not without problems, given its assumptions about the nature of civilization, it does express the deep political discord that had become apparent within Europe. Whatever the civilizational basis of the idea of Europe, it had acquired a certain meaning and reality in face of divisions that increasingly took a national form. This was a period of creativity in the arts and in science, but especially in social and political thought when religion ceased to offer a basis for political community. In the seventeenth and eighteenth century some of the major intellectual developments took place that defined the self-understanding of modern Europe and gave to it the means to interpret its own heritage in a more secular age.

This chapter will examine three ways of looking at what can be termed a cognitive shift in European consciousness leading to the emergence of a new cultural model. The first is the Enlightenment, including the Romanticism of the nineteenth century. The second is the idea of Europe itself. The third is the idea of modernity. The argument of the chapter is that it is the latter, the idea of modernity, that should be seen as the context in which to view the emergence of the idea of Europe and that the Enlightenment is also best understood as a movement that forms part of modernity. From c.1800 it makes more sense to speak of Europe in terms of a model of modernity than in terms of a civilization, since the civilizational basis of Europe did not lead to a lasting political or cultural framework; it should rather be seen as providing orientations that were differently appropriated. As will be argued later in this chapter, the notion of modernity is better equipped to capture the contested nature of political community and divergent interpretations of the European heritage. This is because the idea of modernity signals a greater recognition of conflicting interpretations of the world than does the idea of a European civilization, however pluralized it may be understood. The cultural model of modernity was shaped by both the ideas of the eighteenth century Enlightenment as well as the romanticism of the nineteenth century.

As we approach the present day, it becomes increasingly clear that Europe cannot be understood in terms of a model of long-run continuity. This does not mean that the degree of rupture has been so great that no continuity can be possible. European history has witnessed major ruptures – the wars of religion of the seventeenth century, 1789 and the Napoleonic wars, 1914–18 and the Russian Revolution 1917 – that opened up new visions of social and political order and new interpretations of the past. These moments of rupture are themselves constitutive of the European heritage and have been moments of creative renewal. But it is only with modernity that they enter the self-consciousness of Europeans, who also become more the bearers of a nascent European identity. The perception of crisis is one way in which the idea of Europe has been perceived. This is also why the idea of Europe since the early modern period acquired also a certain normative character as a critique of the prevailing order. As such, it is best seen as a cultural model that formed part of a wider emergence of modernity in Europe and in which has contained conflicting interpretations of how Europe should be governed in an era of political crisis.

The Enlightenment

The Enlightenment is often considered to be the epitome of European civilization and the birth place of its modernity. In many ways it was a continuation of the Renaissance's concern with globality, republican freedom, the emancipation of the self, and the quest for knowledge unfettered by intolerance and dogmatism. As with the Renaissance, the standard interpretation is in need of some correction. Often associated with France, just as the Renaissance was characteristically associated with Italy, the Enlightenment was in fact a European wide movement and took a wide variety of forms. However, there is little doubt that French ideas played a major part of its legacy. The Enlightenment can be taken to be both a particular period in European cultural history – roughly from the end of the seventeenth century to the early nineteenth century – and a specific mode and style of thought characterized by the celebration of the intellect, freedom and progress. The 36-volume *Encyclopedia*, which was edited by Denis Diderot and published from 1751, epitomized the Enlightenment in its aim to be a repository of all human knowledge. The freedom of knowledge was to be the basis of progress.

The Enlightenment cannot be equated with an actual age, since the ideas it espoused were often in tension with social reality. However, the ideas and ideals of the Enlightenment arose at the time they did and not in other times and places, so in a sense the Enlightenment was a historically specific event in the history of Europe. It was a time when ideas – cultural and political ideas – took on a new significance in shaping a world in which the consciousness of modernity was emerging.

The world of the Enlightenment was a product of social change. New cultural and political elites began to challenge the received wisdom of the past. These elites were products of a social order in which intellectuals were becoming increasingly autonomous. This was a period when bourgeois society emerged along with the rise of an educated reading public and a commercial market for intellectual and cultural products. The Enlightenment, although an elite movement, was not confined to the closed world of the court society and constrained by patronage. Commercial independence nurtured intellectual autonomy and a radicalness of spirit that often led to conflicts with political authority. There was also an important popular Enlightenment as reflected in the diffusion of science and scholarship in the wider public.

Yet, it would be wrong to see the Enlightenment as only a radical movement or as a product of social revolution. While it is often associated with the American Revolution and French Revolution, it should be noted that many of the Enlightenment thinkers were functionaries of the *ancien regime* and did not encourage rebellion. Condorcet, who embodied the spirit of Enlightenment thought, was a high ranking aristocratic official, and was executed by the French Revolutionaries during the Terror. In Germany the leading representative of the Enlightenment, Immanuel Kant, made a clear distinction between the cultural and the political aspects of Enlightenment thinking with the argument that intellectuals should be allowed to argue as long as they want so long as they obey their rulers. Kant epitomized the spirit of the Enlightenment as one of intellectual autonomy and cosmopolitanism, but he did not challenge the prevailing political order. Indeed, the version of republicanism he espoused was hostile to democracy, as Kant did not think that popular rule would be desirable. His critical philosophy confined critique to an analysis of the conditions of knowledge and to separating empirical knowledge from pure reason or faith, neither of which are grounded in the other. One of his most important ideas was that morality derives from the moral law, not from natural law and that human beings are therefore characterized by moral freedom. This had far reaching implications for the philosophical and political understanding of modernity as a condition of autonomy and ultimately of freedom.

The emphasis on freedom, which in many ways was the leitmotif of the Enlightenment, gave a tremendous legitimation to republican nationalism, which although having independent origins, were very much products of the Enlightenment. Both nationalism and republicanism are based on the central belief in the principle of self-determination, the notion that civil society ought to be self-legislating. This was championed by Jean-Jacques Rousseau who gave a defence of the idea of the republic as a self-governing political community based on a notion of civil society rather than the state. In his thought, which greatly influenced nineteenth-century nationalism, the nation was for the first time associated with the republican idea of a self-legislating civil society. What this did was to set up a tension between nation and state, since what Rousseau was arguing for was a Europe of free nations (see also next chapter). The reality of course was one of *ancien regime* style states. In this example republicanism expressed the radical side of the Enlightenment. The republican ideal was not always associated with the idea of a self-governing society and could be undemocratic and autocratic. In France the republic became an empire. The beginning of the end of the Enlightenment is often taken to be 1804 when Beethoven withdrew the dedication of the Third Symphony to Napoleon who betrayed the republican and cosmopolitan spirit that Beethoven admired by declaring himself emperor. As a political movement, the Enlightenment came to a final end in 1848, when a new age of social and political unrest emerged in the aftermath of the revolutions that occurred in Europe in the spring of that year. By then, as will be argued below, romanticism had offered an alternative to the rationalist vision of the French influenced Enlightenment.

One of the enduring features of the Enlightenment was the secularization of religion. But this needs to be placed in its context, as argued in Chapter 3. Although it was to be one of the signatures of the Enlightenment, the anti-Catholicism of the French enlightenment intellectuals was an exception, even if it left an indelible mark on Europe. Secularization did not mean anti-clericalism, but the separation of church and state. But even this was not unambivalent. Indeed, it was not long after the French Revolution that Napoleon re-established Catholicism as a state religion. The Enlightenment's separation of science and law from religion, occurred precisely in order to preserve faith from the critique of science (Chadwick 1993). Virtually all the major Enlightenment philosophers sought to place religious faith on a separate level from scientific reason or knowledge. This was encapsulated in the philosophy of Immanuel Kant, who argued that religious belief and ideas could not be justified on the basis of reason. In this respect faith was protected from the critique of rationalists such as Voltaire, who argued reason was the sole criterion of belief.

The Enlightenment, like the Renaissance, was cosmopolitan. On the one side, it was a European-wide movement, which took different forms in Scandinavia, Germany, Scotland and France, and of course it was particularly evident in the United States (see Porter and Teich 1981). On the other side, it was a globally-oriented movement in that it was characterized by a great interest in non-European cultures. As a European movement as opposed to a specifically national movement, the Enlightenment had different faces ranging from the rationalism of the French intellectuals and the celebration of knowledge to the romantic cult of the heroic individual and the republican quest for a self-legislating community. In addition there were the moral philosophers of the Scottish Enlightenment, which was an important movement in the development of new ideas about the social and economic order (Strydom 2000).

The other aspect of the cosmopolitanism of the Enlightenment was its fascination with otherness, and in particular non-western civilizations. While this has often been dismissed as an orientalization of the East, which was the necessary Other for the European 'We' to be defined in terms of a dualism of civilization versus barbarism, this accusation is too simple. While there is little doubt that the European heritage was used to legitimate imperialism and that in many cases it entailed a fantastification of the non-western Other, a more differentiated analysis is needed. The category of Otherness in Enlightenment thought can equally well be seen as an expression of the distance that many Europeans felt from their own culture, which they could view only through the eyes of the Other. This Other was indeed very often the Orient, as in Montesquieu's *Persian Letters*, but in this case and in many others it was a critical mirror by which the decadence of Old Europe could be portrayed. In many other cases the attempt for genuine understanding of the ancient cultures of Asia cannot be underestimated, not least because much of the Enlightenment culture was formed in pre-colonial contexts, such as eighteenth and early nineteenth-century Germany (Clarke 1997). It was the capacity for distance that gave a crucial cultural foundation for the critical and reflexive dimensions of modernity to develop. European cultural modernity thus came to be very strongly associated with the critique of tradition and scientific reason. This self-questioning attitude was as likely to be used against Europe and as much as against the non-European. Eurocentrism and the critique of Eurocentrism were intertwined. As Sankar Muthu (2003) has argued, many of the major Enlightenment thinkers, including Diderot, Herder, and Kant, were critics of imperialism and accepted the pluralism of different cultural forms of life. Others such as Alexander von Humboldt criticized slavery in his *Political Essay on the Island of Cuba* in 1856 and sought to find a way in which all human societies could co-exist through mutual understanding and exchange (Walls 2009). There was not then one Enlightenment, but a variety of Enlightenments. Moreover, many Enlightenment thinkers, such as Kant, were not consistent in their views about other cultures. In this vein, Bronner (2004) defends the legacy of the Enlightenment for democratic and critical thought against both the conservative and anti-modern critique of thinkers such as Leo Strauss and against the leftist critiques of the Frankfurt School and post-modernism.

The romantic critique

The Enlightenment encapsulated the idea of modernity. The idea of the 'modern' comes from the Latin word *modus*, meaning now, but the term 'modernity' has a stronger meaning, suggesting a new beginning based on human autonomy. It is in this emphasis on the present as newness that finally marks the Enlightenment from the Renaissance. Where the latter looked to the past, the Enlightenment was firmly rooted in the present and in a mode of thought that emphasized argument and the critical exercise of Reason. The seventeenth-century French 'Quarrel of the Ancients and the Moderns' on whether modern culture is superior to classical culture is often taken to be the point at which the Enlightenment embraces modernity. One of the most famous uses of the term was in 1864 when the French poet Baudelaire wrote: 'By modernity I mean the transitory, the fugitive, the contingent'. This definition of modernity was reflected in part in modernism to indicate a particular cultural current in modern society that captured the sense of renewal, revitalism and the cosmopolitanism of modern life.

The idea of modernity ultimately goes beyond the Enlightenment, which is a term that is generally not applied to developments beyond the middle of the nineteenth century. Some consideration must be given to the Romantic reaction to the Enlightenment, for the notion of modernity by the mid-nineteenth acquired a second face, namely that of the romanticist pursuit of the creativity of the imagination and artistic freedom as opposed to reason and the advancement of science. This had two orientations, both radical and, unlike the mainstream Enlightenment, anti-bourgeois; one, a left leaning revolt in favour of

artistic and political liberty; a second and later one that was anti-
modern and favouring an aesthetization of politics. In place of the
intellect and science, the themes of life and nature became more attractive to a new generation of intellectuals whose world was more that of
the nineteenth century than of the previous century. The object of
their critique was not only the *ancien regime*, but bourgeois society. The
romantic reaction has often been termed a 'counter-Enlightenment',
but this over-states the divide and suggests greater coherence to the
two movements than was in fact the case. Most of the Romantics, for
instance, supported the ideals of the French Revolution, while depart-
ing from the cultural and philosophical assumptions of the French
intellectuals. Yet, there was a stronger emphasis in it on the pursuit of
meaning as opposed to reason and science.

   The post-Enlightenment period was thus marked by the rise of
romanticism, which challenged many of the assumptions and proposals of the Enlightenment for the creation of a rational and largely
secular society. Its emergence was decisive for European modernity.
The romantic movement was especially prevalent in Germany –
though very influential in England – and reflected a disenchantment
with the French Revolution and with the ideas that were associated
with France: rationalism, classicism, abstract thought, progress.
German intellectuals in philosophy, literature and the arts generally
developed new ideas that offered a new and very different vision of
history and the future of Europe from the ideas of 1789. Schlegel distinguished between classical and romantic cultures and argued that the
romantic culture was the truly modern one (Gouldner 1973; see also
Ossewarde 2007). Unlike the so-called classical culture – which he associated with the French Enlightenment – Schlegel, and the romantic
movement in general in Germany, saw the present as situated in the
context of a history, which was less broken from than revitalized.
Schlegel was less concerned to deny the Christian heritage than to
diminish the significance of science as the innovative feature of the age
and at the same time engage in a critique of the present situation of
German society. The romantic movement sought to give expression to
a notion of modernity that accommodated the past as much as the
present. The romantics rejected both the German present and the
dominant French ideas about the world. The romantic movement
cannot therefore be understood as backward looking or exclusively
concerned with German culture; it was European in its view of cultural
revitalization and progressive in seeking an alternative possibilities
within the present through a re-evaluation of the past and the

affirmation of sensibility and the emotions. One of its legacies was the belief in the unity of the world and the essential unity of a people. This had important consequences for collectivist movements, including Marxism and for nationalism but also provided a basis for a conception of Europe that transcended the particular.

In philosophy, Hegel, Schelling, Fichte, Schlegel, and in literature Schiller and Goethe and the *Sturm und Drang* movement, developed a new conception of freedom very different from the dominant French Enlightenment tradition; this placed at the centre of modernity the idea of aesthetic individualism and the pursuit of cultural creativity. It was a movement that had many affinities with romantic nationalism, with its stress on heroic individualism and emancipation from tyranny. This tie between romantic modernism and nationalism was exemplified in the figure of Byron and the cause of Greek nationalism in the 1820s. Other representatives of the Romantic tradition were the poets Coleridge, Blake and Wordsworth. This movement has often been portrayed as reactionary and a conservative nostalgic defence of the lost world of Medieval Christendom. This would be to misunderstand the place and significance of romanticism in European culture in the nineteenth century, a movement that provided both the idea of the nation and the idea of Europe with new possibilities. A famous example of what has often been taken to be the reactionary current in romanticism was Novalis's *Christendom or Europe* in 1799. However this was more an exploration in mysticism than in serious political analysis and also had a cosmopolitan dimension (see Kleingeld 2008). William Blake, for instance, invoked the idea of Europe in 'Europe a prophecy' in 1794 by means of visionary images of how Europeans had become victim to an enslaving religion and morality, while beyond Europe America was in contrast inspired by the revolutionary impulse.

In rejecting the classicism the Enlightenment and its emphasis on a universal order of reason, the romantics sought instead to uphold the imagination. In this tradition what is modern is the capacity to be creative. Modernity thus requires the liberty of the imagination and in the German romantic tradition it had a strong relation to the pursuit of individualism. Hence, the romantic movement stood for artistic freedom, which was often promoted above the cause of political freedom. German intellectuals unable to bring about social change sought refuge in the world of culture that was often divorced from politics. The result was a contradiction, for while they were more radical in their critique of bourgeois society and in the cult of the creative imagination than the proponents of the French Enlightenment, they were politically impotent and ultimately became more concerned about artistic freedom than political freedom. The legacy for Europe was the movement towards modernism and a conception of modernity as a cultural critique of the present. In the case of Germany, they tended towards a divorce of culture and politics, ultimately leading to the retreat of culture from political responsibility, as Fritz Ringer demonstrated with respect to the German universities and the rise of Nazism (Ringer 1990). In the second half of the nineteenth century a second orientation developed from the romantic movement, namely cultural pessimism and a general drift towards anti-modernism. This will be considered in Chapter 11. It will suffice to mention in the present context that one outcome was an orientation within European modernity towards the aesthetization of politics.

In the course of the nineteenth century the European cultural model consolidated; it was not composed of one coherent set of ideas, but was comprised of diverse orientations, which had emerged from the Enlightenment and the romanticism of the nineteenth century, as well as from earlier developments. On the one side, was the Kantian ideal of a republican order of states, the rule of reason, freedom, autonomy and progress and, on the other side, was the pursuit of the creativity of the imagination, individualism, the revolt of nature and of art against bourgeois society. Both of these orientations, and their numerous off-shoots, shaped the European imaginary and gave form to its cultural model.

The idea of Europe as a cultural model

The idea of Europe is a product of the modern age. It had antecedents in earlier centuries, but as argued in the preceding chapters, an idea of Europe did not exist as a cultural or political entity and was generally a term to refer to the territory of Christendom. The increased conscious-ness of Europe since the eighteenth century can be understood in terms of the emergence of a cultural model in which Europe signalled both a normative and an interpretative response to the crisis of the age and the perception that out of the present new possibilities could be realized. This fate in a new kind of society in which the conflicts of the past might be overcome was central to the idea of Europe. Rousseau envisioned an age when 'there is no longer a France, a Germany, a Spain, not even England, there are only Europeans. All have the same tastes, the same passions, the same way of life' (cited in Hampson 1984). Voltaire believed that Europe was replacing the nation-state. In a much quoted statement that echoed Rousseau's, he wrote: 'Today, there are no longer Frenchmen, Germans, Spaniards, even Englishmen: whatever people say, there are only Europeans – all have the same feelings, the same customs, because none has experienced any particular national formation' (cited in Dann and Dinwiddy 1988). In 1796 Edmund Burke wrote that 'No European can be an exile in any part of Europe' (cited in Hay 1957: 123).

These somewhat lofty claims need to be considered in the context of an age when the nation-state was not yet established as the primary territorial form of political organization. The idea of a European order that Enlightenment thinkers had in mind was more a product of a new kind of political imagination than one that followed from anything concrete. Such ideas, despite their background in *ancien regime* aristocratic society, are best seen as having a critical function in exploring new possibilities for political community in Europe at a time when it appeared that no durable solution had been found. It was evident that the age of the autonomous city state, which Rousseau admired, had no future and that the future also did not lie with empire. The idea of a nation-state was still in its infancy and had no real meaning until well into the nineteenth century when the nation began a focus of mass identification. The idea of Europe arose at a time of political uncertainty on how Europe should be governed. Inevitably it was implicated in various national interests as well as in reactionary politics.

The major European powers were expanding and many, such as France, saw their mission to contest the Habsburgs for the political leadership of Europe. These proclamations to be sure were the notions of a small group of intellectuals and had a little reality in terms of concrete political movements. Many of the ideas of Europe had the function of providing France with a wider association with Europe. Thus Bismarck dismissed the idea of Europe as incompatible with the interests of Prussia: 'I have always found the word "Europe" on the lips of those statesmen who want something from a foreign power which they would never venture to ask for in their own name' (Crankshaw 1982: 352). But he could also find it useful in countering Jacobin rebellion, as when in 1863 he promised help to Russia to suppress rebellion (Wittram 1973: 105). For Metternich, the architect to of the *ancien regime*, Europe was an Austrian necessity (Taylor 1942: 34). This was also reflected in Peter the Great's statement: 'We shall need Europe for a few decades, and then we can turn our backs to her' (Szamuely 1988: 136). Other conceptions of Europe had a colonial dimension, as in Leibnitz's 'Egyptian Plan' in 1672 which he proposed to Louis XIV arguing that the most effective means of securing peace in Europe would be a concerted European invasion of Ottoman ruled Egypt and led by France. Such an invasion would be in the interests of France which would then be 'the avenger of outraged justice, leader of Christendom, the delight of Europe and of mankind' (cited in Yapp 1992: 146). There was little consistency in such views, for Leibnitz promoted the idea of 'unity in diversity' as a motto for Europe and believed Chinese civilization was superior.

The French Revolution – though not supported by many who invoked the idea of Europe – was the single event that gave force and meaning to Europe as a political construct. The French Revolution was both a European event, a global event and a French revolution.[1] Initially it had a wider European relevance, but its nationalist zeal was to have a contrary impact. The universalistic ideas it fostered were ultimately subordinated to the nationalist interests of the revolutionary government, which launched a war against the other major European powers until it was finally constrained. Underlying Napoleon's plans for the reconstruction of Europe was the idea of recreating Europe in the image of France. At first there was widespread support for the French Revolution which brought about the abolition of the last vestiges of feudalism and was seen as signalling the end of the *ancien regime* and absolutism. Republics were set up in many parts of Europe and Europe itself seemed like it might become a republic. In 1812 the first liberal constitution was proclaimed in Cadiz and it was there that the term liberalism was first used. But since 1814 the idea of Europe could just as easily have signalled an anti-French position, as in the so-called Holy Alliance of Russia, Prussia and the Habsburg empires (Cahnman 1952: 609). Republicanism, so often associated with Europe, was in fact more advanced in Latin America in the nineteenth century.

The appropriation of the idea of Europe in romantic ideas is another illustration of its ideological. One of the most famous was Novalis's *Christendom or Europe* in 1799 which was an early Eurosceptical and romanticist nostalgic critique of Europe in the name of the vanished past. In this work Europe is associated with the Reformation, modern philosophy and the Enlightenment, all of which he regarded as inferior to Christianity, which held out the promise of unity in contrast to the idea of Europe which appeared to symbolize division. Novalis epitomized the organic conception of political order in contrast to the modern acceptance of pluralism. However, as noted earlier, it was a work that was essentially an exploration of mysticism than of political philosophy. Nonetheless, romanticist ideas in Germany easily lent themselves to obscurantist political philosophies. Fichte regarded Germany as the cradle of civilization and the Germans were 'to serve Europe' by bringing it under their control (Taylor 1988: 38). Hegel saw Europe as the synthesis of German culture and Christianity. Leopold von Ranke believed that there was a natural bond between the Latin and the Germanic nations and that this cultural unity constituted the basis of the cultural unity of Europe (Schulen 1985). Europe could be invoked in the name of liberal and republican ideas as much as in the name of organic notions of culture. There had earlier been a strong association of Europe with the Orange cause. In the late seventeenth century the English Whigs promoted it and it was in the name of Europe that William of Orange landed in England in 1688 to claim the English crown at the invitation of the Whig dominated parliament (Schmidt 1966). The subsequent Battle of the Boyne in Ireland, in which William defeated the Catholic and the French supported James II, was seen as a battle for the future of Europe. The idea of Europe was later invoked on behalf of Protestant interests in the context of the War of the Spanish War of Succession in 1700 in opposition to the French cause and the Hanoverian succession after 1701 in opposition to the Catholic cause of the Stuarts.

As a normative idea, the idea of Europe was institutionalized in the congress system of the Concert of Europe, following the Congress of Vienna in 1815. This was a response to the rise of 'international society' in the early nineteenth century when in the wake of the defeat of Napoleon it became increasingly important for the European powers to regulate the world stage. The beginning of the scramble for colonies was one reason, as was the desire to keep Russia out of the Ottoman territories. The idea of a European order, too, was a pragmatic necessity to prevent either the Habsburgs of the Bourbons from dominating the continent. It was of course a devise to preserve the *ancien regime* and was composed of a negative unity: more of one power meant less of another. It was a balance of powers and did not signal any other kind of unity than the collective pursuit of self-interest. Thus the Ottoman Empire joined the Concert of Europe in 1856 after the Crimean War in order to contain the Russian Empire. The Concert was redefined as around 'a law of civilized nations' as opposed to 'a law of Christian nations' (Alting 1975: 53).

The idea of Europe also became a compelling reality in view of the rise of the United States of America. Europe became increasingly seen as occupying the space between Russia and Europe. Indeed, this was to be the major defining element in its identity in the twentieth century, but was already foreseen by Alexis de Tocqueville (1948: 434). Since the early nineteenth century it was the background for many federal notions of the unity of Europe. In this respect the idea of Europe moved beyond *ancien regime* designs to preserve the *status quo*. If one looks beyond these notions, which ranged from the lofty to the bizarre and reactionary, to the broader aspiration to link the idea of Europe with programmatic ideals for the re-organization of European society and new political philosophies, such invocations of the idea of Europe have a more normative and critical function. The idea of Europe was attractive to Enlightenment thinkers as a utopian ideal. The leading Enlightenment utopian thinker Saint-Simon argued that Europeans should organize themselves in a new framework in order to preserve their independence. Kant in *Perpetual Peace* in 1795 put forward an argument for a republican order of free states as a solution to the problem of war in Europe and to secure a lasting peace. The association of the idea of Europe with visions of a peaceful Europe united into some kind of a republican transnational order survived the context in which they were originally put forward. (In the next chapter the cosmopolitan implications of these developments will be discussed in relation to the rise of nationalism and the arrival of the nation-state). The ensemble of ideas that Europe was associated with since the early eighteenth century point to the emergence of a European cultural model rather than a specific political meaning to what the notion might embody. The idea of Europe never had any clear basis in geography and it never coincided with a single civilizational tradition. By the 1800 it became apparent that it was not going to fit into a single political design or ideology. Yet the development of modernity found within the idea of Europe a way of reflecting upon the nature of how Europe should be governed in light of the absence of agreement on how this might be possible. For this reason the idea of Europe is best seen in terms of a cultural model rather than a substantial political entity or a fixed idea underpinned by politics, culture or geography. As argued, this cultural model was influenced by diverse Enlightenment and romanticist ideas which gave to Europe different and often incompatible cultural orientations.

European modernity: Cultural and societal models

The idea of Europe is a product of modernity and as such it needs to be contextualized as a reflective discourse on the state of European modernity. In other words, it is an idea of modernity, along with the many other 'ideas' that modernity in Europe produced about itself. The idea of Europe can be seen as a way European modernity has reflected upon itself with respect to the relation with the past and an orientation for the future. The notion of modernity itself was a product of the modern age and a way in which the present age defined itself in relation to past and future. A consideration of modernity is in place in order to better situate both the Enlightenment and the idea of Europe, which are different expressions of European modernity. The notion of modernity has greater relevance than the idea of civilization since the constellation of civilizational influences on modern Europe produced both ruptures and divisions that undermined the very possibility of a European civilization. The theoretical framework for the analysis of the idea of Europe is the general context of modernity.

S. N. Eisenstadt has argued that modernity is a new civilization that has replaced the axial age civilization and that it takes multiple forms depending on how it has been appropriated in different parts of the world. The rupture brought about with modernity can indeed be seen as constituting a significant re-orientation for all societies, but its features cannot easily be regarded as akin to a civilization. The emergence of modernity while being influenced by a civilizational background is better seen as a new matrix for all parts of the world rather than a civilization in itself. The interpretative order of modernity along with its constitutive components involves significant differences from anything than can be called civilizational. However, one of Eisenstadt's key insights, that modernity takes multiple forms, is an important corrective to conceptions of modernity that see in it only one form. We return to this later and in Chapter 10 in a discussion of the multiple forms of modernity in Europe.

The present discussion will focus on clarifying the theoretical framework of modernity. This can be summed up as entailing two dimensions, a cultural model and a societal model. Firstly, it involves an interpretative level in the sense of a particular kind of consciousness or way of thinking as opposed to being an age or a specific time period. The cultural model of modernity can occur in any time or place. Fragments of modernity can be discerned in societies that can be termed pre-modern and it is a condition that is not confined to Europe or the West. Secondly, modernity refers to what has been variously called modern society or the process of modernization and thus concerns the institutional order of society, which here will be defined in terms of a societal model based on relations between the state, economy and civil society (organized interests, social movements, the public).

As an interpretative order, modernity has often been seen in terms of a social imaginary. This is the basic argument of Castoriadis (1987) for whom modernity involves a radical imagination that is always a projection of itself and an expression of the creative potentiality of the present. Arnason (2003) has developed this idea, as has Charles Taylor (2004), who has formulated the notion of a social imaginary.

Peter Wagner (1994) has developed the most clearly defined conception of modernity that makes further advances on the basic vision of modernity as entailing a central conflict emanating from its radical imaginary, which in the most general terms resolves around the tension between the pursuit of autonomy or freedom or liberty, on the one side, and on the other mastery in that all societies must be able to reconcile the pursuit of autonomy with the need to master the material and institutional reality of power. For Wagner a singular and generalizable definition of modernity is required before seeking its multiple forms. In later works (Wagner 2009, 2012) identifies central 'problemátiques' or questions that all modern societies seek to answer and which defines their self-understanding in terms of this tension between autonomy and mastery. The self-understanding of modern societies has not been constant but has undergone change with the result that modernity is an on-going process of interpretations in light of experiences made earlier. He highlights three such interpretative questions that modern societies seek to answer: the nature of knowledge, the rules for a common social life, and how to establish the rules to solve the basic material needs of society. So what is finally common to all modernities is also what defines the specificity of their 'societal self-understandings': all societies need to find answers to these problemátiques in its own ways. The fact that these problemátiques are open to interpretations means that different answers will be found and thus there will be a plurality of modernities. To show what kind of answers can be found to these questions is ultimately a more fruitful approach to the analysis of modernity that a civilizational approach tries to discover historical paths.

As an approach to modernity understood as a consciousness or a condition this has many advantages, in particular it divests modernity from western path-dependent assumptions, since in principle any society can pose such questions. This conception of modernity can be related to other notions of modernity, such as what Arnason has termed 'a field of tensions' or Habermas's theory of modernity as a conflict between communicative and instrumental rationality. Modernity is thus a condition that is irreducible to one element and is essentially open. A further implication is that modernity is not reduced to an age that has a clear end point that culminates in an 'end of history scenario' or one that is superceded by post-modern or a new global age. Instead of seeing modernity as temporally limited or sequential, it should rather be conceived of as a condition that is continuously reconstituted as opposed to being a condition that is defined by the transition from tradition to modernity. So rather than being marked by transition – as in the transition from pre-modern to a modern age – it is more characteristically marked by the condition of transformation. To capture the sense by which modernity is continuously reconstituted the notion of an interpretative order of conceptions or key questions is important. This interpretative dimension to modernity constitutes the cultural model of modern society and – drawing on Habermas, Eder and Strydom – moreover involves potential advances in learning.[2] Thus the cultural model of modernity opened up new ways of solving the problem of violence and of accommodating difference with notions of the constitutional state, the idea of collective self-determination, the idea of the citizen as the bearer of rights. Many of these remained for long only on the level of ideas, that is to say they were articulated within the context of the cultural model of society. In this respect, too, the idea of Europe was a product of the formation of a modern cultural model in which new conceptions of Europe were advanced. Without these 'ideas' the modern world would not have been possible. It follows from this that the cultural model of modernity precedes the realization of its ideas and that many of these remain unrealized. An additional implication is that the core ideas of modernity have not always commanded widespread agreement. As the history of democracy and modern political philosophy attests, there have been many major differences of interpretation on how normative ideas should be realized. This is quite evidently, too, the case as far as the idea of Europe is concerned, which, as will be argued in later chapters, has been subject to major conflicts of interpretation.

Since the cultural model of modernity involved major disputes over its key ideas, the real significance of it resides not in simply offering normative ideas, but in opening up a cognitive order by which modern society could make sense of itself. The contents of the cultural model of European modernity were ways in which the various crises of the age could be interpreted. As Strydom has put it: 'over a period of approximately two centuries the cognitive order of modernity arose which would henceforth, in interaction with the prevailing social practices, constitute, generate, guide and regulate the formation of modernity and the actualization, realization and expansion of its multilevel potentialities' (Strydom 2012: 26). The cultural model of modernity as a cognitive order is made of ideas that present themselves in part as rules or reference points that are reflexively related to social contexts, but realized in situations of conflict between opposed social actors who may form different interpretations of them. The cultural model of modernity is thus a generative resource for social actors and may have a transformative impact when it comes into conflict with social reality in contexts of dispute.

For the notion of modernity to be useful it should also address societal structures and institutions, such as the relation between state formation and economy. In this sense it refers to a societal model which in part bears the influence of the cultural model of society, but, and especially in times of major crisis, there is a tension or contradiction between both. The history of modern Europe can be written in terms of a conflict between the ideas of modernity and the concrete form it has taken. As a societal model, modernity refers to the ways in which the modern state, capitalism or more generally the modern market economy, and civil society interacted. This has been the subject of classical sociological theory, which concerned itself with the macrolevel development of the major structures on modern western society. For present purposes, the relevant points are that the specificity of European modernity resides in a model of modernity in which a particular relation between state, economy and civil society developed such that the neither the state nor capitalism succeeded in becoming the other and that the relationship was one mediated by civil society.

The relation between these forces, which defines the matrix of political modernity, gives rise to a societal model that in turn offers a way for modernity to interpret itself and articulate an identity, or what is better characterized as a social imaginary. Solidarity, democracy, autonomy and social justice, for instance, are not concrete institutional realities, but transcendental ideas or social imaginaries that make possible institutional arrangements and guide political practice. The concrete outcome has been a certain balance between capitalism and democracy. This has been variously reflected in the nation-states of modern Europe. T. H. Marshall's famous 1949 essay on the formation of modern social citizenship reflected in part this view of democratic citizenship as a counter-balance to the inequalities of capitalism (Marshall 1987). Of course this conservative and perspective was limited by the absence of any sense of social struggles, seeing as he did the social contract as an achievement of the state and not as negotiated outcomes of political mobilization spear-headed by trade union-ism, socialist movements, labour and various social democratic parties. European modernity is a *European* modernity and not the only form modernity has taken. Modernity can take many different forms, as has been noted in what is now a significant body of literature on compar-ative modernity.[3] The difference between modernity in Europe and elsewhere resides in the ways in which the cultural and the societal imaginary have been constituted and in the temporal development. The basic structures of both can be said to be relatively constant in that most societies have within their cultural model some conception of the individual and collective self-determination and in more general terms a particular way in which their social imaginary articulates a vision of freedom or formulates the key questions Wagner claims are constitu-tive of modernity. The specific form these take will vary as will the level of cognitive development and the relation to political practice.

Regarding the societal model, this too can be broadly generalized as relevant to all societies in that the inter-relations between state, economy and civil society tend to be the most important forces shaping modern society. In the case of Europe the state was constantly challenged by forces within civil society with the result that the power of the state was relatively constrained. This is a contrast to many other parts of the world, for instance Russia, and the various models of modernity that developed in Asia, with notable examples being Turkey, Iran, and China. In these instances, civil society was less devel-oped and as a consequence the state was subject to less constraints. The period of totalitarianism – to be discussed in Chapter 11 – is an illustration of the fact that modernity also entails regressions and is not unilinear. The same can be said of capitalism, which was variously constrained by, on the one side, and on the other by civil society. In the United States, in contrast, a different model of modernity emerged that laid a greater emphasis on liberty and the market; it was one that was less based on rights and set less limits on the market. The route that Europe took towards modernity was considerably shaped by church and state relations. As argued in Chapter 3, a feature of Europe, in contrast to much of Asia, was that the church – which can be seen as a civil society actor – was relatively constrained by the state, which by 1648 had gained the upper hand. The result was that the subse-quent history of European secularism was one of compromises between church and state. This was ambivalent in that the state proved it could exert final power over rival forces, such as the Church, but it also had to make compromises. The history of civil society in Europe is one in which the power of the state is constantly challenged by organized social interests, which often become incorporated into the sphere of the state. The outcome of modernity for Europe was in the creation of a specific kind of societal model that while taking variable forms can be characterized as one in which the demands of social solidarity and social justice had to be accommodated. According to Claus Offe (2003: 442) if there is anything distinctive about a specifically European model of capitalism it is the prominence of state-defined and state-protected status categories, which set limits to the rule of markets and of voluntary transactions. Stressing the diversity of types of capitalism in Europe, Offe notes that viewed in a global perspective it is possible therefore to speak of a European model of social capitalism that under-lies the diversity of these different national models. This social fabric and the guiding principles of solidarity and social justice are more important in the formation of Europe than the specific form the consciousness of Europe took.

A comparative analysis of modernity would reveal a more compli-cated story, but the basic societal model of European modernity can be described as a world regional variant of forms that have a more general applicability while having variable relations. The result is not progress as once understood as a cumulative and unilinear Grand Narrative of improvement, but a more varied, multi-dimensional and multi-directional field of orientations that operate on the cultural model and on the societal model in ways that are highly contingent rather than the product of necessity of path-dependency.

Globality and modernity

With regard to the earlier discussion of unity and division in European history the implication of the above analysis is that the context of modernity provides the basis for a conception of unity in the sense of a way in which commonality can be understood. As various theorists have argued, modernity is primarily a singular condition whose basic elements make possible plurality. In this way, as with the notion of civilization, the assumption of unity can be made as a basis from which diversity follows. The implications for diversity are as follows: on the level of the cultural model there is a diversity of interpretations as to the meaning of modernity's core ideas; on the level of the societal model there is a diversity, within some broad parameters, of institu-tional arrangements concerning the state, capitalism and civil society. It is possible to speak of a European model of modernity where there is relative cohesiveness in these structures. It follows from this that some parts of Europe may be more modern than others and that this is in part a temporal matter, in that modernity unfolds at different speeds. With regard to the question of modernity as an age it can now be suggested that the association of modernity commencing with the Enlightenment – broadly defined as the period from the mid-eighteenth century – makes sense so long as modernity is not reduced to the Enlightenment itself, which instead should be seen as part of the articulation of the cultural model of modernity. But modernity ultimately goes far beyond the Enlightenment and the early formative period in the emergence of European modernity. Other modernities will not necessarily have been framed through the European Enlightenment. However, as argued through this book the underlying reality of globality means that societies are mutually influenced by each other. The Enlightenment itself was like the Renaissance influenced by contacts with other parts of the world and cannot be considered entirely on its own. When viewed as an aspect of modernity, the wider global context is essential for an understanding of the genesis of modern Europe.

The closer we approach the age of empire the more essential a global view of Europe becomes. In this respect we can add to the emphasis on civilizations as a formative early influence on Europe and modernity as the wider framework, globality as a condition that makes possible the encounters of different civilizations and modernities. Without such a concept, and in the absence of a universal model, there is no way to explain how modernities and civilizations came into contact and how even within specific models of modernity similar orientations developed. So globality can be taken as a context which is variously present and the degree to which it is present will be decisive for the spread of modernity. In the present day it is unlikely that there is any part of the world that has escaped at least some of the consequences of modernity. However, in earlier centuries in the formative period of modern Europe, and even earlier in the early civilizations of the axial age, such contacts were limited, but where they occurred they were decisive for the emergence of modernity and within the European context for the formation of modernity. Indeed, it was the case that due to global connections between different parts of the world the emergence of modernity was often more advanced than in parts of Europe (for instance Buenos Aires was more modern than parts of most Spain outside a few metropolitan centres). Globality should not be seen as derivative of modernity or a latter development, but integral to modernity and also integral to the axial age of civilizations.

What has changed in the course of history is the scale and speed of globalization, rather than the fact of global connectivity. Globalization arises when different parts of the world come into contact with each; it may be driven by economic or cultural forces, but it is ultimately made possible by the movement of people, goods, or ideas from one place to another. The more extensive this is the greater the impact of globality, which becomes a condition in itself when the extent of global connections makes possible a global imaginary, a social imaginary that extends beyond the immediate context to includes an orientation to the world (see Robertson 1992). The emergence of the idea of Europe as with the emergence of national idea is part of this process of the broadening of the horizons of the present in both spatial and temporal directions. A European space opens up with the increased connectivity of different parts of the region due to the diffusion of cultural, economic or political forces with the result that previously separated areas become linked and the element of a shared history emerge. So by the mid-nineteenth century the diffusion of Enlightenment and romanticist ideas, the ideas of the French Revolution as well as the idea of Europe had spread to most parts of Europe through networks of cultural and political communication. The diffusion of a new cultural model opened up new ways of imagining Europe. This will be explored in the next chapter with respect to the rise of the national idea and cosmopolitanism in the age of the nation-state and empire.

9
The Rise of the Nation-State and the Allure of Empire: Between Nationalism and Cosmopolitanism

Two events that loom large in the making of European modernity occurred in the eighteenth century: the Lisbon earthquake in 1755 and in 1789 the French Revolution. Both events had a European-wide significance in that they had a considerable impact across Europe in both the shape of the natural and political landscape of the continent. While the Enlightenment emphasized a narrative of progress and freedom, consciousness of crisis also lay at the source of the imagination of the age. The Lisbon earthquake had a huge impact on Europe due both to the physical effects that were widely felt across Europe of the earthquake that struck on 1755 and due to the destruction it brought to Lisbon, which was mostly burnt and destroyed following a tidal wave that followed in the aftermath of the earthquake. It was the first example of European-wide consciousness of a catastrophe that brought a certain sense of a wider unity to European intellectuals who debated its causes and significance. The event was not perceived as divine retribution – in fact it marked the end of theodicy – nor as a Portuguese catastrophe, but as a European event and a challenge for European science.

Voltaire's *Candide* is the most well-known work inspired by the Lisbon earthquake, but Kant wrote three short essays on it, Rousseau regarded it as evidence of his republican philosophy that small self-governing cities rather than imperial metropolis are the ideal places for people to live in for the future (Larsen 2006). Catastrophes are occasions for political reflection and political renewal, as was the case too with the Great Fire of London in 1666 when London was rebuilt. While the latter was largely a national crisis, the Lisbon earthquake in contrast had global ramifications. The Portuguese empire, long in decline, was considerably weakened due to the destruction of the

169

imperial core. However, the main consequences were largely in a consciousness of the physical vulnerability that it brought to Europe in a pre-risk age that its cities are subject to destruction by natural forces. This sense of vulnerability seemed to be in tension with the new belief in science, freedom and progress that the Enlightenment had proclaimed. It is a reminder that the experience of crisis and the imagination of catastrophe was not only political, but could also take a physical form. The Lisbon earthquake was reflected in a new discourse about the physical foundations of European societies and of the need for a new kind of knowledge about nature. It is possible to see the later development of natural science as a response to the need for greater mastery of nature.

The example of the Lisbon earthquake illustrates how from the beginning of the modern age a cosmopolitan current accompanied modernity. It expressed the consciousness of an objective crisis and a challenge for European science and thought. The second major event, the French Revolution in 1789, was the marker of the modern age insofar as it demonstrated the vulnerability of the *ancien regime* state to destruction and the beginning of a new age of social revolution that had ramifications for the rest of Europe and the wider world. In this instance it was of course presaged by the American Revolution in 1766, where republican thought was more advanced. However 1789 was not just a French Revolution; it was also a European one in that its consequences changed the political landscape in Europe due both to the spread of new political ideas and to the expansion of the post-revolutionary state in its aspiration to create a French-led Europe.

In this paradox we find the basis of European political modernity: the entwinement of nationalism and cosmopolitanism, the particular and the universal. On the one side, 1789 signalled a new age of freedom based on republican government while, on the other side, the consequences was the assertion of national supremacy and leadership. Modernity witnessed both particularism and universalism as exemplified in the rise of nationalism and the nation-state and, at the other end of the spectrum of modernity, the consciousness of common problems and the need for common solutions. This is not to say that the cosmopolitanism and the nation-state were antagonistic or somehow incompatible. The aim of this chapter is to show how the rise of the modern nation-state contained cosmopolitan possibilities and that both nationalism and cosmopolitanism are not contrary, despite the gradual uncoupling of both. This chapter is broadly concerned with the long nineteenth century, from 1789 to c.1919. This is the period that falls between the two major movements of social and political crisis in the modern age: the French Revolution and the First World War. The first section looks at the rise of nationalism and considers the significance of the nation-state; the second section is concerned with the relation between nationalism and cosmopolitanism as two sides of modernity; the third section discusses the nature and limits of the idea of Europe in the context of political modernity and the prevalence of crisis and critique as ways in which the very notion of the political has been experienced. The next section is a discussion of the emergence of a European society. While a European polity as such did not emerge, given the irreversible trend towards a Europe of nations, it is possible to speak of the rise of a European society by the end of the nineteenth century. Finally, the chapter concludes with a discussion of the place and significance of empire in the making of Europe, for Europe was not simply internally constituted, but was formed in encounters with the rest of the world, much of which were through colonization and the accompanying category of race.

The rise of the nationalism and the nation-state

The idea of the nation, which precedes the nation-state and nationalism, signifies the idea of a people who share a common birth right. The word itself, *natio*, means birth and suggests the notion of the creation or establishment of a political community. In early modern Europe it coincided with the rise of republicanism in that both the notion of the nation and the idea of the people referred to the public as the source of sovereignty. This understanding of the nation as a *res publica* was primarily civic insofar as it saw the nation as a public rather than a private category. Hence was born the modern idea of the nation and with it the notion of collective self-determination, for the nation must seek its autonomy if it has been denied. Thus opposition to tyranny was a driving force in the rise of nationalism.

Although not in itself a democratic philosophy, it had a democratizing effect insofar as the nation referred not to the court society of the elites but to the masses: the *demos* was the nation as a public body. It roughly corresponded to the rise of civil society and colonial independence seeking movements in the Americas where the break with the European *ancien regime* was most decisive. Indeed it was in the Americas that some of the most important experiments were made with liberalism and republicanism. As such, early republican nationalism was civic in its essential self-understanding in the sense that it was based on a notion of peoplehood that was defined in terms of rights and thus linked collective self-determination with a notion of the individual as a rights bearing citizen.

The idea of the nation can be considered to be primarily a feature of modernity. The question whether the notion of the nation is a product of long-run ethnic identities or is a product of modern society has been much debated. Much of this concerns the question whether nationalism precedes the emergence of the nation-state or is largely, as Gellner and others have argued, produced by modern states for the purpose of social integration (Gellner 1983; Breuilly 1982; Delanty and O'Mahony 2002). Nationalism for Gellner is a development of industrial capitalism and the arrival of a new 'high' culture that can provide cultural cohesion for diverse people and replace local 'low' cultures. While having in many cases pre-modern roots in the memories and histories of ethnic groups around whom many modern nationalisms were created, the idea of the nation is not in itself an ethnic category. The association of the idea of the nation with a dominant ethnic group, an *ethnos*, was a gradual development of the nineteenth century. To the extent to which the notion of the nation was invoked in pre-modern times, it was more likely to have been an identity of elites than a mass identification, though exceptions will be found. As we have seen, the America and French Revolutions gave a tremendous boost to popular sovereignty and the idea of self-determination, which can be contrasted to the idea of sovereignty embodied in the ruler and can also be contrasted to the British political tradition that emerged from 1688, which posited the source of sovereignty neither in the monarch nor in the public, but in parliament, as in the doctrine of the sovereignty of Westminster. In contrast, 1766 and 1789 gave rise to the notion of popular sovereignty, which challenged what in effect was the continuation of the British *ancien regime*. However, it should be noted that the rupture brought about by the French Revolution was not total and elements of the *ancien regime* survived and post-revolutionary Europe continued much of the older absolutism in new forms (Anderson 1974; Mayer 1981).

The ideology of modern nationalism emerged out of this background. Nationalism effectively came to mean the right of a people who define themselves as a people and who occupy a certain territory and the right to exercise collective self-determination. This was the principle of nationalism that was advanced by Giuseppe Mazzini, who was a proponent of Italian unification and independence and influential in establishing an ideology of modern republican nationalism. This was in every sense an ideology, in the sense of a programmatic project for the re-organization of state and society in accordance with new political ideas. Influenced by the French Revolution and modern liberalism, he advocated the necessity of national unity as an aspiration for modern Europe and promoted the vision of a united Europe of nations. He believed the nation-state was the most democratic unity of political organization. Mazzini's liberal nationalism was highly influential across Europe in the nineteenth century and helped to reshape the map of Europe in favour of nation-states as opposed to empires. Although primarily an Italian nationalist, he promoted the cause of European nationalism. He put forward the idea of a 'United States of Europe', essentially an early version of a united Europe based on democratic nation-states, and founded 'Young Europe' in Berne in 1834 to provide support for independence movements, such as Young Italy, founded three years earlier. The association led to the creation of Young Ireland, Young Poland, Young Germany and many others. This was a kind of nationalism that was underpinned by republicanism and liberalism and was an expression of a new wave of democratization that had begun with the French Revolution and culminated in the 1848 revolutions that occurred in many countries.

Between 1789 and 1848 nationalism was generally associated with republicanism and liberal reform movements seeking to overthrow the *ancien regime*. Irish, Italian, Polish, Greek nationalism was inspired by Mazzini's ideals, which were also influential in Germany where liberal nationalists promoted the cause for German unity. The independence of Greece in 1829 was one of the first examples of national independence that reflected Mazzini's ideal of national unity and the ideals of freedom, constitutionalism and self-determination. Despite the failure of the 1848 revolutions to bring about a lasting constitutional order based on liberal democracy and national independence, the vision of a Europe of nation-states was an enduring legacy and continued to inspire nationalist movements everywhere: Belgium was created in 1831 and, after the Treaty of Berlin, Romania, Bulgaria, Serbia and Montenegro were carved out of the Ottoman Empire, as was later in 1913 Albania; in 1905 Norway became independent of Denmark. The British Liberal Party under W. E. Gladstone embraced the cause of liberal nationalism in the case of Bulgaria and the Irish Home Rule movement.

However, despite the prevalence of liberal nationalism from 1848 nationalism gradually lost its earlier revolutionary direction and association with a civic conception of the people and became increasingly an ideology of the existing state. After the unification of Italy in 1861 and the unification of Germany in 1871, nationalism became the ideology of the nation-state as opposed to revolutionary movements seeking national autonomy. Secessionist movements continued to seek national independence, such as Irish nationalism, but, as in this case, nationalism became increasingly open to diverse interpretations as to the meaning of nationhood. In the case of Irish nationalism, for instance, one movement sought independence within the UK and another, which became increasingly more powerful, sought the creation of an independent republic. In addition, nationalism also took on a more cultural direction with the emergence of cultural nationalism from the late nineteenth century with the romantic rediscovery of national histories and a pre-modern past; it moved in the direction of an ethnic as opposed to a civic conception of the people. The idea of the people became defined as a community of descent; it was a powerful ideological instrument that located the nation ultimately in everyday life. According to Hobsbawm (1994: 121), the very term 'nationalism' was coined as late as the 1890s to describe reactionary lower-middle class militancy in countries where the ideologies of liberalism and democracy were weak.

Not all nationalists movements asserted political aspirations, for they emerged at a time when there was little consciousness of the nation-state as a natural geopolitical organization. Empires were the norm, not nation-states. National communities were discovered or invented by national intelligentsias who created in many cases a national language and defined national heritage around a national literature, music and folklore. Such cultural programmes were made possible by new national institutions, such as museums, universities, art academies and mandatory schooling; they have been variously described as fabrications or the inventions of traditions that had in fact a relatively recent origin while projecting their history into early times and thus portraying a picture of continuity regardless of the record of history (Hobsbawm and Ranger 1983). Nationalism was a product of the age of ideology and along with other ideologies of the age it was promulgated by intellectuals who formulated the key ideas which were transmitted to the masses. In many cases a national language had to be created where it did not previously exist or where it did, it had to be standardized. With few exceptions, almost every nation-state was based on a common language, which made possible greater communication and identification, even if such forms of identifications were based on an imagined national community, as Benedict Anderson (1983) has argued.

One of the most important instruments for the diffusion of the idea of the nation was education and in particular the creation of a national curriculum. National schooling and literacy made it possible for the national community to be given a symbolic reality in the lives of people through the creation of a dominant national memory, the homogenization of cultural practices, sport, and patriotic political culture based on xenophobia and the exhalation of the state as the embodiment of the nation. In this way national identity became not just an identity of the nascent elites and an ideology of the modern state, but a collective identity for industrial society. Such forms of identification were underpinned by the growth of centralized state bureaucracies, which created new integrative mechanisms and systems of surveillance – such as passports and visas – to define the link between state and individual (Giddens 1985; Torpey 1999).

In sum, the French Revolution popularized the notion of peoplehood, which was equated with the nation, but in doing so opened up new conceptions of peoplehood that quickly lost the earlier meaning. The idea of nationhood in many cases was not a clearly defined consciousness and when it was defined it generally took a largely ethnic kind. The confluence of an ethnically-based definition of peoplehood with the notion of nationhood brought about a transformation of nationalism from a civic notion to a cultural one. This shift in the meaning of nationhood opened up nationalism to entirely new projects of nation-state building. Central to all of these was a strong emphasis on an external Other against whom the national Self had to defend itself. It was frequently the case that the Other was associated with an oppressor and the history of the nation had to be told in terms of a narrative of emancipation from such tyranny. Indeed, almost every nationalism has such a narrative of a founding moment that was related to liberation from tyranny or occupation by another power. The French Revolution gave a basis to this notion of emancipation from tyranny, but modern nationalism converted it into a territorially defined 'us' versus 'them'. An inevitable aspect of this was xenophobia, since it became easier to know who the enemy was than to know who the nation was and all too often the external enemy was related to a national minority. Given the multi-ethnic nature of much of Europe, the formation of nation-states frequently resulted in the marginalization and persecution of national minorities, who were associated with a neighbouring nation-state or who did not fit into the emerging ethnic definition of the nation-state.

A related development to the equation of ethnicity with nationhood was the emergence of the nation-state around a dominant region, as Eugene Weber has demonstrated in a classic study of the formation of the modern French state (Weber 1976). Many nation-states were constructed out of a single region whose cultural identity became the basis of the national culture and resulted in a process of homogenization or in the case of the UK, where one region, England, was constituted the core. Where homogenization was incomplete, as in Corsica, Ireland, or Catalonia, the result was a peripheral nationalist liberation movement. Federalism was for some the solution, but in many federal arrangements a dominant core – Prussia in the case of Germany – dominated. The tendency was for a dominant region to be a basis for nation-state formation which occurred alongside the simultaneous elimination of regional autonomy and the concentration of centralized systems of power in national capitals (see Watkins 1991). Hence the project of state-building entailed the construction of national capitals with the characteristic monumental style of neoclassical architecture that was designed to show-case the symbolic power of the nation-state (see Jones 2011).

Different traditions of nationalism arose in the second half of the nineteenth century and can be roughly characterized as: (1) republican independence movements, which were generally secessionist or seeking to assert national unity; (2) cultural nationalism that was inspired by organic notions of a historic peoplehood who constitute the soul of the nation; such types of nationalism were predominately ethnic in their self-understanding; (3) nation-state nationalism that asserted the territorial identity of the existing state; and (4) civic nationalism that was primarily inspired by republican ideas as opposed to an ethnic conception of the nation. The latter tended to be marginal or was variously present within the other dominant traditions. However, it was the third variety that became the dominant political force in the making of the modern Europe. By the end of the nineteenth century nationalism had become the patriotism of the state, which in turn came to constitute a territorial nation-state. Newly created states, such as those that gained independence at the end of the nineteenth century and after the Treaty of Versailles in 1919, were all organized as highly militarized nation-states and set about the codification of a national identity. The re-drawing of the map of Central and Eastern Europe after the end of the First World War and the creation of independent nation-states out of the territories of the Habsburg and Ottoman Empires demonstrates the power of the idea of the nation-state which had become the accepted solution to the problem of statehood. Nationalism increasingly lost its civic and emancipatory orientation and became an instrument by which the state secured loyalty from the masses. In many cases, it was easily reconciled with monarchy and with the pursuit of empire and congealed into new forms, such as fascism and authoritarian state socialism (see below and Chapter 11).

This is not to say that nationalism severed any connection with the civic definition of the nation or that nationalism entirely lost its emancipatory significance. The notion of the nation, like the idea of Europe, continued to be open to diverse interpretations, with different groups making different claims in the name of the nation. However, it is clear that the notion of the nation became increasingly associated with ethnic definitions of the nation, on the one side, and, on the other, with a territorially defined state. This confluence of statehood, territory and ethnicity gave to the modern state what it previously did not have, namely a territorial identity. This became the basis on which other claims could be made, such as citizenship rights and the related duties that the state could expect from its citizens. The legacy of republican nationalism in the end was a territorial conception of the nation. However an ambiguity continued to exist between nationality and citizenship: the rights of the individual as a citizen and the rights of the individual as a member of a nation-state. The modern nation-state achieved a degree of inclusivity for its populations, but this was at the cost of the exclusion of those who did not belong to the nation; where this concerned national minorities it often led to resentment that in turned fuelled secessionist nationalism.

Nationalism provided the essential ideological bond that linked the individual with the state in ways that proved to be highly effective. By the end of the nineteenth century a system of centralized states was in place in Europe. The record of history shows that it was the liberal democratic nation-state that was the most durable state form and that in time all of Europe became organized on the basis of the nation-state, with constitutional monarchies as variants on what was broadly a common trajectory. National identity made possible the identification of a rapidly growing industrial population with the state, which required the compliance and loyalty of the individual. Nation-states were also warring states and instituted military conscription as part of the duties of citizenship. This also produced strong bonds of identification between citizens and the state. The modern nation-state proved to be an effective organization for the control of populations and the pursuit of power on a global level. With few exceptions, since 1648 European states ceased to conduct wars within their own territory and concentrated wars with neighbouring countries, as well as colonial wars. This permanent preparation and engagement for war was a crucial aspect of the state tradition in Europe and which was critical in the formation of relative strong states in contrast to other parts of the world where there was a higher degree of internal warfare (Centeno 2002). The pursuit of imperial projects from the middle of the nineteenth century possibly provided some of the conditions for relative stability within Europe and the consolidation of homogenized central states (Tilly 1990: 167). The nation-state was not only a territorially organized national community, but a state organization and like all states it acquired a monopoly over the means of violence, since in Europe since the eighteenth century the capacity to exercise violence was concentrated in the state (Tilly 1990). The European nation-state was a centralized and bureaucratized apparatus designed to extract resources and engage in war and territorial expansion; it devised effective powers of taxation and, since the mid-nineteenth century, military conscription; it regulated markets; provided a back-up for law, which is essentially a command secured by the states capacity to enforce it; and secured relative loyalty from their populations through the institution of citizenship.

As argued in the previous chapter, the modern European national state developed alongside the formation of a European societal model in which the state had to negotiate settlements with demands from civil society. This was achieved through the creation of legal frameworks that defined rights and duties for citizens and at the same time set limits to both state power and to the rule of the market. The modern nation-state as a law-governed state was the principal vehicle by which the state was constituted and the basis of a model of modernity for Europe that resulted in both unity and diversity. The success of the modern nation-state was due in no small measure to the degree of social justice that it made possible, through in part to the creation of welfare systems and due to the constant need to negotiate between capital and labour. The expansion in claim-making was increasingly incorporated into the domain of the state, which can be seen as both a system of guarantees and a negotiated political order based on the rule of law. The popularity of the nation-state was due to the capacity of the state to meet demands from social interests as much it was to the appeal of nationalism as an ideology.

Cosmopolitanism and political community

The homogenization that the nation-state achieved within its territory was at the cost of a more divided Europe. It was inevitable that the idea of Europe would be subordinated to the idea of the nation and that Europe could firstly be a Europe of nations and then only European. Since no pan-European state existed and due to the balance of power system no state succeeded in overall supremacy. This does not mean that European modernity is to be understood exclusively in terms of the nation-state. International institutions were created, such as The Red Cross in 1857 and the Universal Postal Union in 1874. In 1861 the Suez Canal was opened linking European seafare directly to Asia, the Panama Canal in 1914 and the adoption of Greenwich Mean Time as a global time standard in 1884 reflect the rise of internationalism. Internationalism did not decline in the age of the nation-state, but increased due to the need for cooperation between states and the needs of the capitalist economy. It also took numerous other forms that were not dependent on states, such as scientific and cultural institutions, including the expansion of universities.

In terms of the distinction made in the previous chapter between a cultural and a societal model of modernity, it can be seen that that the nation-state formed the institutional basis of the European societal model in that the various forms that modernity developed were largely mediated by the nation-state. However, the cultural model of modernity is not reducible to social arrangements with respect to the relation between state and economy that formed the basis of the modern nation-state. The cultural model of modernity offered a horizon beyond the institutional order and has been frequently in tension with the societal model of modernity. Part of the cultural model of European modernity was a cosmopolitan orientation that in part was expressed in certain nationalist movements, but was more generally in opposition and only in part realized in concrete political institutions.

The thesis advanced here is that cosmopolitanism was an integral part of modernity in Europe and that it is no less important than nationalism. Modernity does not consist of one form, but is composed of different orientations, which have different degrees of significance. The cosmopolitan currents with modernity are not derivative of nationalism or secondary, but form part of the social imaginary of modernity. It has already been argued that the logic of globalization produces a more connected world in which consciousness of globality becomes part of the condition of modernity. The emergence of cosmopolitan thought was a product of such a consciousness of an interconnected world and influenced the idea of Europe as a normative idea. Indeed, the genealogy of cosmopolitanism is prior to the very idea of the nation (Delanty 2009a). Despite its ancient origins, however cosmopolitanism, like nationalism, is largely a product of modernity and existed alongside the early notions of the nation. The French Revolution itself embodied cosmopolitanism in the universalism it claimed for its notion of the rights of the individual. The eighteenth century notion of a commonwealth of nations was essentially a cosmopolitan proposal for an alternative to nations and a way to secure lasting peace in Europe. Many of these proposals were based on the federal idea as a political framework for Europe to accommodate its diversity within a wider political order. While many of these programmatic ideas for a federal state of Europe did not progress beyond the level of ideas, one concrete outcome was the rise of international law theory, as espoused by Grotius and Pufendorf (Hochstramer 2000).

Political modernity could not be confined to a world of nation-states; some kind of commonality had to be found in order to prevent constant warfare. The balance of power was one way in which states were contained, but this could never be enough without a normative international order as opposed to a purely contractual system based on treaties, which in effect was what the Post-Westphalian state system was. Kant believed that republican states are less likely to go to war with each other and need to be embedded in a cosmopolitan order governed by the rule of law. Kant's notion of a cosmopolitan legal order went beyond international law, which is a law of states. In *Perpetual Peace* in 1795 he championed the idea of a principle of hospitality as basis of cosmopolitan law. The right to hospitality, by which he meant the right of a foreigner to be recognized by the state whose territory they enter, must be upheld by all states. Although it was unclear how this was to come, it was eventually realized much later in the incorporation into the national legislation of European countries of international human rights. This illustrates how the elements within the cultural model of society become progressively embodied in the societal model, generally following an extended period of crisis in which increased claim-making forced a new wave of democratization.

The cosmopolitanism of the eighteenth century Enlightenment may indeed have been more a state of mind than a depiction of reality and it took more than 100 years for the first major normative international order to be created in the form of the League of Nations following the First World War. It would be wrong to claim than in face of the objective reality of the nation-state that cosmopolitanism was a fanciful world of ideas that were not politically effective. Cosmopolitanism was present within republican and liberal thought, though undoubtedly more in the latter than in the former, since republicanism has been predominately concerned with a bounded conception of political community. However, cosmopolitanism is not exclusively an aspiration to create a normative international order and nor is it opposed to the nation-state or the idea of the nation. Cosmopolitanism, as a condition of the broadening of the moral and political horizon of society, is compatible with the idea of the nation insofar as this is the basis of political community. Thus some national traditions more than others are open to external influences, while others are more closed. Both nationalism and cosmopolitanism were inspired by the modern idea of freedom and by the notion of self-determination. On the whole, nationalism tended to give expression to the notion of collective self-determination, while cosmopolitanism gave expression to individual self-determination. In this way, both complemented each other in articulating the social imaginary of modernity. The emphasis on individual self-realization within cosmopolitanism was further embedded in liberalism, which more than republicanism emphasized the centrality of the individual. Both republicanism and liberalism were further complemented by the socialist tradition and its various offshoots, including democratic socialism, social liberalism and social democracy, with a concern with collective self-determination around social justice. This tradition contained within it cosmopolitan aspirations that were famously voiced by Marx and Engels in *The Communist Manifesto* in 1848, that 'the proletariat has no country'. However this tradition later developed along national lines, thus defusing its cosmopolitanism. The liberal conception of political community preserved the strongest link with cosmopolitanism, undoubtedly because it was easier to think of the individual having wider loyalties than collectively organized groups such as entire nations and, too, the negative conception of justice within liberalism was easier to achieve than positive justice, as associated with republicanism.

Yet, it would not be correct to confine the cosmopolitan imaginary to the level of individual self-realization, which is one strand within it. It had a wider resonance in the search for a normative international order as well as in the very notion of a democratic political community that is inclusive. In this sense, cosmopolitanism might be seen as constituting the open horizon of modern political community while nationalism constitutes the tendency towards closure. In other words, political community is neither defined by nationalism nor by cosmopolitanism; both are present and the history of political modernity – mediated variously by liberalism, republicanism and socialism – can be seen in terms of the ever-changing relation between both sides of its Janus face. Both nationalism and cosmopolitanism reflected the homogenizing logic of modernity and the tendency in modern culture towards pluralization and dialogue (Delanty 2009a). The eighteenth century was a period when the cosmopolitan current was in many ways more prominent, while in the following century the balance had shifted towards the national ideal, an argument put forward by the German historian Friedrich Meinecke in 1907 (Meinecke 1970; Schlereth 1977). However Meinecke mistakenly believed that the nation-state required the abandonment of cosmopolitanism which could not find a political embodiment; he did not see that that both were linked and that the development of political modernity required these two sides. As Harrington (2004) has argued, until at least 1914 German intellectuals could find within the nation-state a means of reconciling German particularity with European universalism. More generally, the spirit of cosmopolitanism was kept alive by a global consciousness that was never entirely dominated by a narrow nationalism, with some pertinent examples being the re-founding of the Olympic Games, the Nobel Prizes, Great Exhibitions and other 'Mega Events' which while show-casing the nation-state did so in ways that fostered cosmopolitanism (Roche 2000; Inglis and Robertson 2008). European elites continued to circulate as much of the world of art and music was cosmopolitan. Yet, it is clear that by the end of the nineteenth century, nationalism was in the ascendancy and it was not until after the destruction of two world wars that the cosmopolitan current became once again influential and a necessary compensation for the tendency within nationalism towards closure.

The emergence of European society

The nineteenth century saw the consolidation of modernity and the emergence of a Europe of nation-states. The global significance of Europe only becomes evident by the middle of the century when its economic, technological and political structures proved to be highly resilient and innovative. This had a lot to do with the nature of state-formation within Europe and, as argued earlier, to the particular kind of societal model that predominated whereby a balance had to be constantly secured between the interests of capitalism and the homogenizing tendency of the state. A feature of this was the opposition from civil society and the need to accommodate demands from diverse groups as well as to regulate capitalism. The result was a model of modernity that was marked by what Koselleck (1988) has referred to as 'crisis and by critique'.

The constant application of critique to the exercise of power – whether in the economic or political order – was a decisive feature of European political modernity which generated new expectations. Thus, at the heart of modernity was not the state as such, but various processes which generated variety and opened up alternatives that were variously selected and often institutionalized as a result of a period of extended social struggles. These processes within European modernity provided the primary ideas of modern Europe influencing both left and right conceptions of social order and political community ranging from social democracy, Christian democracy to democratic socialism and other radical democratic movements. As with all such models it crystallized into different forms due to the ways in which it was taken up and transformed by different social actors. So in civil society claim-making and the broadening of the scope of democracy led to tensions between state and society, on the one side, and, on the other, between capitalism and democracy.

It was not surprising then that the idea of Europe did not lead to the functional equivalent of the idea of the nation. The idea of the nation contained one ingredient that the idea of Europe did not have, namely a notion of peoplehood. There is not a meaningful sense to speak of a European people in the way nationalism can invoke a notion of peoplehood. There is no European-wide equivalent of the ethnic component that has been the basis of almost every national tradition. Most nations have a common language – Belgium and Switzerland being exceptions – while on a European level there has never been a common medium of communication at least since the vernacularization of Latin. French functioned for long as a common language of elites, but never became the basis of a European ethnos; nor did religion, which, as argued in Chapter 3, was more likely to be a source of division than commonality on a European level. The symbolic and emotional ties that made possible national identity around a notion of a people with a common history is clearly possible on regional or national levels, but not so easily on a multi-national level. Moreover, as argued earlier, the idea of a national people was closely tied to a historical memory of emancipation from tyranny while on a European level there had never been an enemy that was sufficiently threatening to constitute an Other against whom an enduring sense of a European people might be defined.

The idea of a Europe does not entail a specific people as such, but refers more to a model of society and cultural orientations that has come to shape a historical world region. It is true that by the late twentieth century the notion of a European identity has become more tangible and it is possible to speak of Europeans, though it is arguably the case that this has not resulted in a European people as such. The important point in the present context is that the idea of Europe should not be approached from a subject-centred perspective as the expression of a collective subject, such as a notion of peoplehood. Instead of a notion of a European people or a European identity it is more meaningful to speak of a European society. By the end of the nineteenth century, while a transnational European political order was not created and would not emerge until after the Second World War, it is possible to see the direction of social and economic change leading to common structures. As Michael Mann has written 'What we call societies are only loose aggregates of diverse, overlapping, intersecting power networks' (Mann 1993: 506). European societies were not only entangled in each other, but were embroiled through colonization in the wider global context.

Already in 1893 Emile Durkheim in *The Division of Labour in Society* saw signs of an emerging European society emerging from increasingly common ways of life. What happens, he wondered, when two collective consciences confront each other. 'For one people to be penetrated by another', he argued, 'it must cease to hold to an exclusive patriotism, and learn another which is more comprehensive.' Durkheim goes on to argue: '… this relation of facts can be directly observed in most striking fashion in the international division of labour history offers us. It can truly be said that it has never been produced except in Europe and in our time. But it was at the end of the eighteenth century and at the beginning of the nineteenth century that a common conscience of European societies began to be formed' (Durkheim 1960: 281). Durkheim like many of the *fin-de-siècle* thinkers was deeply pessimistic that a genuinely European collective conscience would emerge and overcome the aggressive nationalism that was bringing Europe closer to war. Though he opposed the negatively defined conservative view of the move from the cohesive world of community to the individualistic world of society he was ambivalent about the merits of society; he did not think modern society, because of its differentiated structures, could recover the traditional idea of community as a fusion of culture and society; yet, 'the social' was something deeply ambiguous. It could provide the individual with more autonomy, but it could also undermine it in the formation of anomie. Durkheim was one of the first thinkers to reflect on the idea of a European society as an emergent reality. The specificity of a European society for Durkheim lay in two dimensions. In terms of its social structures it was characterized by the growing differentiation in institutions and by increasing size in space and demography. However, what is more central, is the question of solidarity in a differentiated society. His sociology pointed to the view that social integration required a cooperative framework for social groups and one in which education would play an ever greater role in generating cultural cohesion around the formation of generalized values. The idea of how a society represents itself and creates a space which constitutes, what he called, the 'meeting ground' between two collective consciences is an issue of central importance in understanding the cosmopolitan dimension of social change.

Durkheim's reflections on social change and the making of European society remained undeveloped. Later sociologists offered more comprehensive accounts that are important correctives to the one-sided emphasis on nation-state formation in the making of European modernity. Talcott Parsons (1971) noted three social revolutions that laid the societal foundations of modern society: the industrial revolution, the democratic revolution, and the educational revolution. Despite the limitations of his evolutionary approach and its conception of transition to new stages, his characterization of the emergence of modern society through these three social revolutions provides a useful perspective on major societal change. By the end of the nineteenth century the basic shape of European society was made as a result of social and economic change deriving from these social revolutions. Since c.1800 industrialization transformed Europe from an agricultural to an industrial society in which class structures emerged. It was accompanied by urbanization and population growth. The second industrial revolution, which was based on new technologies such as electricity and chemicals made possible mass production, enhanced this momentum and brought about a transformation in all aspects of social life. In this period, the second half of the nineteenth century, there was a huge drop in fertility rates as well as in infant mortality along with a rise in life expectancy. This development, the so-called demographic transition, brought about population growth. In 1800 the population for Europe as a whole including Russia was 188 million. By 1900 the population for England, France, Spain, Italy and the Netherlands was more than 400 million, while in 1550 when these five countries represented more than 50 per cent of the population of Europe excluding Russia it was c.80 million (Livi-Bacci 2000: 7). This was mostly a development of the second half of the nineteenth century. The nineteenth century was not only the century of the rise of the nation, but it also saw the rise of classes. Classes and nations were of equal importance in the making of modern society; both arose alongside each other. The result was less uniformity than a more complicated picture of class conflict and the growth of industrial capitalism, which exerted the most pervasive impact on Europe. Within a relatively short span of time European societies had become highly urbanized with manufacturing and commerce replacing agriculture; social relations everywhere were transformed by new kinds of conflicts that arose from the inequalities and exploitation produced by industrial capitalism. The growth of industrial capitalism, in particular from 1850, had as much significance for the shaping of European society that nationalism had, and as suggested earlier the idea of the nation was very much a product of the formation of class society, for the nation gave a political and cultural expression to class. In the view of Marx, it gave to class a false consciousness that defused it of its potential capacity to bring about political change.

The democratic revolution was in part a response to the need to extend political representation to a wider spectrum of society and to accommodate the demands of class, including the new middle class and professional groups. The process of democratization, while having its roots in earlier developments, increasingly brought about the widening of political inclusion through the extension of the franchise and political reform to the working class and later to women. As argued in the previous chapter, the basis of the process of democratization was a societal model in which political and economic power had to be compromised to meet the demands of civil society and in particular the demands of organized labour. However, nationalism too tended to make demands for greater representation.

Class and nation may have been the two most consequential developments for the shaping of modern European society. Often neglected in accounts of European modernity is the educational revolution. The expansion and development of education since the second half of the nineteenth century was one of the notable features of European modernity. Europe was relatively advanced in the development of education and science more generally. Despite educational segregation along class and gender lines before the twentieth century, the development of educational institutions was decisive for the formation of nation-states and national identity. Its gradual democratization was an essential condition for individual self-realization as well as for collective identities. The extension of education made possible citizenship and extended the sphere of rights to include the right to education. More fundamental was the extension of literacy and the growth of new media that all depended on literacy. The creation of universities and institutions of higher education and training since the early nineteenth century was a further crucial feature of European modernity that established a knowledge basis for social development.

By the beginning of the twentieth century major social and economic transformation that took place over the previous century brought about an increased homogeneity in social trends. It is not possible to speak of societal convergence and the disappearance of divisions or plurality, since national and regional differences remained, for the uneven development of industrialization ensured that societal convergence would not be possible. Conflict far from declining, increased as a result to greater democratization as well as due to militarization and the creation of war-oriented economies. However, it is possible to speak of an increased homogeneity brought about by nation-state formation, industrialization and the formation of classes, a new range of social and cultural institutions, whereby common structures and institutions became adopted; the specific form that these took varied and all produced different outcomes in terms of patterns of consensus and conflict and the relationship between elites and masses. Underlying these differences, some of which were very large and generated outcomes as different as fascism, state socialism, and constitutional democracy, were relatively similar societal processes. Moreover, European societies were also increasingly intertwined to an extent that it does not make sense to speak of separate societies. Nationalism and the nation-state was a principle of separation, but the social and economic reality was different. The economies of Europe were becoming increasingly interlinked and underpinned by the gold standard; indeed, though they went to war with each other, France and Germany were closely linked by the beginning of the twentieth century. Railways connected more and more parts of Europe. It is possible to speak of similar logics of social and system integration at work in different parts of Europe whereby similar dynamics and processes produce both common and different outcomes.

The technological forces that connected Europe were not unrelated to the wider global connectivity that linked Europe to the rest of the world. The railway was not only a European development but was an effective tool of colonial expansion by which industrial capitalism could gain access to new markets; the steamship and the telegraph were also other technological means by which Europe in the age of empire and industry became linked to distant parts of the world.

The allure of empire

Any account of formation of a European self-understanding in the nineteenth century will have to consider the place and significance of colonialism. Europe cannot be understood endogenously as somehow creating itself but, as argued in earlier chapters, was formed through relations with the rest of the world. As Said (1994: 4) has claimed, what is required is a perspective on history as shaped by 'overlapping territories and intertwined histories'. Such a perspective must be a global one, for Europe was shaped by encounters with the rest of the world, which from the mid-nineteenth century were largely colonial and involved the construction of race as a category through which Europe was constituted. Both race and empire were constitutive of Europe.

The nineteenth century was not only the century of the rise of the European nation-state, but was also the age of empire; indeed, both were connected. In this period most European countries were colonial empires, either land- or sea-based. Much of Central and Eastern Europe was ruled by either the Habsburg, Russian or Ottoman Empires, while in the west were largely sea-based empires with overseas colonies. Several of these sea-based empires also acquired European territories and many sought territorial expansion within the European area: Britain ruled over Ireland, the French sought universal dominance over Europe until defeat in 1815, Denmark ruled over Norway until 1814 when it acquired Greenland as a Danish colony. However, the imperial drive lay in overseas colonization. Following the decline of Portugal and Spain and the independence of their colonies in Central and South America by the early nineteenth century, the independence of the United States in 1776, the age of European empire-building began with the conquest of Africa and large parts of Asia. Most of the Western European nation-states acquired overseas territories in the course of the nineteenth century. Between 1870 and 1900 virtually all of Africa, except Ethiopia and Liberia, was under European control, largely British, French, Dutch, Belgian and German. However, most Western European countries were involved in the so-called 'scramble for Africa', including Sweden and Denmark; Italy finally acquired control of

Ethiopia in 1936. Many of these were minor acquisitions, such as the Danish overseas empire which included a number of islands in the West Indies or the German acquisition of Western Samoa and did not lead directly to colonization, as in the case of Ethiopia. Empire-building and colonization did not always go together. Britain acquired direct rule over India by 1858, occupied Egypt since 1882 and gained considerable power over the Chinese by 1900 but with the exception of Hong Kong, neither colonized it nor incorporated it into its expanding empire. By 1914 Britain had created the largest world empire since the Roman Empire. France built up a considerable overseas empire but did not rival Britain, which concentrated on overseas colonization. France gained control over Algeria by 1847 when it became a French colony.

There was no overall pattern to European imperialism and economic advantages did not always follow, as illustrated by German colonialism in Africa or the French bid for the control of Egypt; and in the early decades of the century not all of it was under state control as in King Leopold's colony in the Congo before it was taken over by the Belgian state. By the late nineteenth century Spain, once the leading colonial power, had become an improvised minor European nation. Many colonial missions were originally neither attempts to build empires nor efforts at conquest, but the outcomes of colonial companies that operated with state sanction and in many cases had to struggle to gain state support, as the early history of the Spain conquistadors illustrates. The earlier exploration of the South Pacific prior to the nineteenth century did not always lead to colonization (Bitterli 1986). By the 1870s colonization became a national project for almost every country and was related to nation-state formation and industrialization (Halperin 2007). The rush to acquire overseas territories was often driven by no better reason than to prevent another country getting there first. Imperialism as a state policy became too a means of buying off class discontent. The term 'imperialism' lost its earlier pejorative meaning when it was associated with the Napoleonic wars and acquired a positive goal for states (Kumar 2009: 292–4). The Berlin Congress in 1884 was a pan-Europe attempt towards organized European colonialism. The major imperial powers with stakes in Africa (Britain, Belgium, France, Germany and Portugal) met to agree on how the continent should be divided. In effect, since the mid-nineteenth century a state of exception had existed whereby the norms by which European states were governed were suspended in the territories they acquired. Genocides were common, as in the German led Herero War in Namibia, 1904–07.

However it is difficult to speak of European imperialism in general, since these were very different processes and belonged to different eras. Spanish imperialism was based on conquest and the pursuit of gold and silver, while French and British empire-building was primarily driven by trade and commerce rather than the search for natural resources (Pagden 1995: 66–8; Halperin 2007). The striking aspect of European imperialism in general is that it occurred on a significant scale outside the Americas relatively late, and when the rush started, it occurred with great speed, fuelled by the industrial revolution and technological innovations. European overseas imperialism in Asia and Africa was driven by two kinds of expansion: commercial and territorial, neither of which entirely coincided, but both were connected, with the latter a kind of 'battering ram' for the former: territorial imperialism could break open markets that resisted free trade (Darwin 2009: 16). The French favoured assimilation while the British preferred indirect rule though local elites (Cannadine 2001). By the end of the nineteenth century indirect rule at least within the British Empire had become the norm and was backed up by the coercive power of the state. Despite the conquest of large parts of the world by European powers, much of Asia lay outside direct European territorial colonization: the major examples being Iran, Turkey, Thailand, Nepal, Korea, Japan, much of China, and Afghanistan (until the Russian and later US and British invasions). Only Africa was entirely colonized, though the Islamic west resisted and Ethiopia was never colonized as such. This was an era when colonization was normal, for it was not only western countries that practised colonization. Before the arrival of the modern nation-state, empires have generally been the norm in world history, as the examples of the Alexandrian, Roman, Russian, Ottoman, Ming Empires, Persia under the Safavids as well as the Inca and Aztec Empires in Central and South America. Indeed, whether the notion of empire is the right word to characterize these different political orders is another matter. The notion of empire, like the notion of nation, is a contested term that has often an imprecise meaning when it comes especially to the pre-modern age when empires were the normal forms of state formation rather than the exception.

It is evident that by the mid-nineteenth century both nation and state-building process were embedded in colonialism. The acquisition of overseas empires brought great wealth to Europe and had a formative impact on nationalism. The nation was seen as having an imperial mission to rule as much of the world as it could. Bismarck decided it was in the interests of Prussia to abandon attempts to rule the German-speaking world and instead acquire territory in Africa. Imperial nationalism, or social imperialism, was one way in which the masses found identification with the state. The title of Empress of India, given to Queen Victoria, was for such domestic purposes. The allure of empire too was irresistible for liberal nationalist movements seeking autonomy, as the example of the Irish Home Rule movement in the nineteenth century illustrates. The Irish Parliamentary Party supported Home Rule for Ireland, but wanted Ireland to remain loyal to the crown and empire. The Catholic Church too supported the British Empire, which was seen as an indispensable for the worldwide spread of Christianity. European liberalism was also enthusiastic about empire. While the leadership of the British Liberal Party under Gladstone was opposed to imperial expansion, many liberals were strongly in favour and promoted imperial liberalism. Some of the main figures in political philosophy, such as de Tocqueville, Locke and Mill were deeply implicated in imperialism. Mill opposed liberal government in India, for instance, and de Tocqueville supported France's colonization of Algeria. Generally, liberalism did not see a contradiction between democracy and human rights at home while depriving the colonized of rights and self-government. Nineteenth century liberalism had accepted social Darwinism and the idea of a struggle of nations and races.

Underlying imperialism was a myth of western civilization and of the racial superiority of Europeans. This was part of a system of knowledge that made imperialism possible, which Said has characterized as 'orientalism' (Said 1979). This system of knowledge was embedded in sciences such as anthropology, criminology, geography and cartography as well as in literature and travel writing. Europeans acquired great skill in collecting, translation, categorizing artefacts, languages and information which provided a cultural basis for economic and political mastery of much of the world. In all of these modes of knowledge the category of race loomed large. Although European countries were in competition in the race to acquire overseas colonies in Africa, Asia and the Pacific, they were conscious of belonging to the same race and constructed a notion of a European race. The older principles of legitimation used by the Spanish to justify their conquests were less suitable for the age. The notion of a hierarchy of races and the superiority of Europe provided a justification for colonial rule, which was based on the separation of colony from metropole. This geographical and political difference was mirrored in a distinction of different races, which was variously interpreted as having a biological or a cultural basis.

The idea of Europe as a racial entity gave to Europe what it was otherwise lacking, namely a foundation in something other than politics. In this way, the idea of Europe acquired a reality it had previously lacked. Europeans who worked in the colonies as soldiers, administrators, educators, traders etc gained a European consciousness as much as a national consciousness; many too were able to acquire status and power that they would not have had at home. The notion of belonging to the white European race served to link colonial civil servants, soldiers, officers, merchants etc into a community that was not only national but racial. The British poet of imperial nationalism, Kipling, celebrated this in his famous poem, 'The White Man's Burden', whose message is that Europe has a mission to bring civilization to the world. The inconvenient facts of history that the civilizations of Asia were older and more superior to those of Europe was solved with the notion that these were in decline and that Europe was their inheritor and saviour. The missionary zeal of Christianity lent itself to colonization. The introduction of race and the idea of racial superiority by Europeans may have helped to define Europe, but it also could be used against European colonialism when it was taken over and used to re-define non-European cultural identities, as in the notion of the racial superiority of the Han Chinese race or the idea of a Bengali race and Hindu race (Darwin 2009: 348–9).

Much of European thought and culture was embroiled in empire and in racism, but this took many different forms, ranging from cultural to biological notions of race. Eurocentrism was pervasive, but this did not necessarily always amount to racism or a pan-European ideology of imperialism. The Boer War in 1899–1902 was a war fought between two groups of settlers, British and Dutch born farmers. Opposition to empire and to slavery is also an important current of the age of empire. In Britain there was considerable rethinking of empire after the Indian Mutiny in 1857. Some of this was opposed to empire, but it was mostly an attempt to rethink the imperial project in face of major resistance. Cannadine (2001) has described this in terms of the construction of a monumental 'ornamentalism', namely a vast imperial structure based on the instrumentalization of status designed to incorporate local elites into the metropolitan project. However, this edifice based on alliances with local elites was not simply a matter of negotiation and accommodation, but underpinned by notions of civilizational differences. As Mantana (2000) has demonstrated, 1857 marked a turning point in British imperial ideology when the earlier liberal and reformist approach based on the idea of a civilizing mission was abandoned as it was seen to have been a failure. In place of this universalistic ideology a new and pernicious one emerged that recognized unbridgeable cultural differences. Rather than embark on a project of reform and modernization, a new culturalist project was put in place that aimed to rule through native categories, indirect rule, and managed by the crown rather than being left to the East India Company. Thus was born the notion of a traditional society locked into a different cultural world that was a contrast to the imperial modern world which henceforth would cease to try to transform its belief structure. While liberal discourse had constructed natives as amenable to reform and civilization, the new ideology proclaimed them un-redeemably different. In effect, as Mantana argues, this left empire without a moral justification. This was the source of a new colonial racism.

Awareness of the evils of colonization and slavery had a major impact on European publics in the nineteenth century. However opposition to slavery, abolished in Britain in 1807 was compatible with colonial rule, which did not require slavery, and was generally regarded as inefficient before it was considered to be immoral. From the abolition of slavery to colonial independence, the debate over empire had a formative impact on European democracy and exerted a long shadow over the twentieth century. Most European countries were shaped by their colonial past. The consequences of empire for domestic politics was right-wing and often fascist trends. The Spanish Civil War and the subsequent defeat of the Republic was in effect an outcome of the loss of Spanish dominance in Africa and the creation of a large and dissatisfied cadre of officers who found themselves in a clash of culture with the newly created republic. The coup of 17 July 1936 that led to Franco's eventual seizure of power was made possible by the Spanish African Army which spear-headed the invasion that led to one of the most repressive regimes in modern European history. The French-Algerian war and the eventual independence of Algeria had a formative impact on France which in effect led to a civil war. Since its incorporation into the France, Algeria had not been a colony but a *department* of the French state (Hansen 2002). Until 1975 Portugal retained a rigid control over Angola and Mozambique, which gained independence only after a long struggle against the Portuguese dictatorship.

The thesis, then, is not that Europe and empire are the same or that everything is to be explained by imperialism. Colonization was not external to European societies; the territories may have been overseas, but it was also inside them in their economies, the modes of government, systems of knowledge and in their cultural self-understanding.

Europe gained knowledge of itself through gaining knowledge of the peoples it had colonized. This was not always despotic or in the service of imperial power. The advancement of democracy in Europe was in some respects due to the developments in the colonies. The Haiti slave revolt in 1791 was important not only in leading to the end of slavery there and to colonial independence of the colony Saint-Dominique, but sparked off much debate in France on the meaning of freedom and democracy (James 1980; Buck-Morss 2009). The Haiti revolution is also a reminder that democratic change in the colony is not only the result of the diffusion of European ideas, but that the opposite might be the case. The impact of the ideas of the American Revolution, too, had such a formative influence on European democracy, as did the later twentieth exit from colonization when the former colonial power became multi-ethnic societies. Europe was shaped by its colonies in both positive and negative ways; but in the end it lost its colonies and much of its identity in the twentieth century has been shaped by the exit from empire.

Europe is thus best seen in terms less of separate nation-states than of transnational states, connected to each other as well as to overseas territories. This means that these states should be seen as shaped by the context of the transnational rather than the exclusively national.[1] However, the formative processes that led to the European state system were primarily the outcome of the internal transformation of what Tilly (1990) has referred to as capital and coercion. The condition of empire was constitutive of Europe from the nineteenth century, but not before; it gave to Europe a subjectivity based on race and made possible a new global economy in which European powers gained global hegemony. Above all empire gave to Europe a new global imaginary that was both complemented and competed with its national imaginary. Even if Europeans could not in the end rule the world they succeeded to a considerable extent in shaping it. As with all empires, imperial over-stretch was reached and European decline began not long after Europe ruled the world. But what survived was the world-wide diffusion of European ideas, products and institutions and within Europe the legacy of empire created post-colonial societies that remained tied in multiple ways with newly independent nations. The history of the world in the twentieth century was in many ways the outcome of the adoption of European aspects of Europe's own model of modernity, in particular its model of statehood, to vastly different conditions. The outcome was in many cases as detrimental to Europe as it was to those countries that sought to adopt European modernity.

10
The Historical Regions of Europe: Civilizational Backgrounds and Multiple Routes to Modernity

The topic of this chapter returns to a theme discussed in Chapter 7 concerning the plural nature of Europe and offers an interlude before a more detailed survey of the twentieth century, which follows in the next chapters.[1] The emphasis so far has been on identifying underlying processes of unity and departures from broadly common civilizational structures. The civilizational background has itself been diverse with routes within it that were shaped by the western and eastern currents of Roman civilization, the Russian offshoots of the Byzantine tradition that developed in the east, and the multifarious impact of Islam on the Iberian and the south eastern regions. Four inter-linked civilizational currents formed, what was termed, the European inter-civilizational constellation: the Greco-Roman, western Christianity, the Byzantine-Russian and Ottoman-Islamic traditions.[2] The unity and diversity of Europe derives from its civilizational diversity, which as we have seen also established the basis of different traditions of empire.

However, this does not offer a sufficient basis for an assessment of the unity and diversity of Europe, for with the unfolding of the project of modernity new dynamics come into play bringing about a more complicated tapestry that cannot be so easily accounted for in terms of civilizational forms alone. Modernity brought about a major transformation in the moral and political horizons of European societies. It placed the individual on a new level and put forward new ideas about political community that gave to the modern world a cultural model that both united and divided it, for the new ideas were not only differently interpreted in terms of their application, but were also differently formulated. Yet, certain trends unfolded that can be said to constitute the basic matrix of a European societal model; moreover, the ideas of modernity, including the idea of Europe, gave to Europe an imaginary that defined its identity. As with the civilizational background, modernity, too, crystallized into different forms and were taken up in different regional routes. The objective of this chapter is to examine the historical regional diversity of Europe as a product both of civilizational backgrounds and the trajectories of modernity. This will entail in part a forward perspective to the twentieth century, since the shape of these routes was altered in the course of that century with the rise and fall of the Soviet Union and the creation and expansion of the European Union.

The notion of modernity offers a useful way to view the diversity of Europe since it includes a perspective on both unity and diversity. As argued in Chapter 8, modernity is based on a cultural model that provides a general framework of ideas and a cultural orientation; it is also based on a societal model, which can be seen in terms of relations between state, economy and civil society. A feature of European modernity in general was the fact that civil society remained relatively strong. The state was constantly challenged by organized social interests, which often became incorporated into the sphere of the state domesticating both the state and civil society and both exerted a strong influence over the market so that capitalism was constantly held in check by the state. In this view, the varieties of modernity that developed in Europe can be in part understood in terms of the different ways this societal model crystallized in the different historical regions of Europe. The notion of a historical region, despite the problems of definition, offers a fruitful approach to the analysis of the idea of Europe and an alternative to purely national histories. The regions in question are historical regions and do not necessarily coincide with present-day transnational regions that are of a later origin.

A broad definition of Europe's historical regions would identify three, namely Western, Central and Eastern Europe, to follow Jeno Szücs (1988) classification in his famous essay 'The Three Historical Regions of Europe' in which he argued for three historical regions: Western, East Central and Eastern Europe. In an earlier classic work Oskar Halecki (1950) identified four historical regions: western, west-central, east-central and eastern. However, a more differentiated and systematic approach is needed given the especially complicated nature of Central Europe and the post-1989 context that led to a major reconfiguration of Central and Eastern Europe and the system of states established in 1919. A systematic typology or comparative analysis does not exist and there is relatively little literature on the topic (see Arnason and Doyle 2010). The proposal in this chapter is that a sixfold classification is needed to capture the diversity of routes to modernity without reducing all such routes and models of modernity to national trajectories or collapsing them into more general civilizational categories. The forms of modernity that constitute Europe as a world historical region correspond to North Western Europe, Mediterranean Europe, Central Europe, East Central Europe, South Eastern Europe, North Eastern Europe.

As with all such classifications there is the problem of defining specificity and taking into account overlap as well as broader contexts of commonality. Furthermore there is the complication that historical regions do not remain constant with the result that different configurations may be relevant in different periods. The map of Europe's regions will have been very different from the standpoint of the tenth century or the seventeenth century. However for the purpose of the present analysis assumptions will be made about the *longue durée* from the perspective of the present. An additional problem is the degree to which self-identification should be taken into account. In the case of historical regions self-identification can be regarded as less important than in defining national identity, not least since regional identity is not the most important feature of a historical region whose specificity may be the basis of different but related identities. To add a further level of complication, many regions are the product of ideological constructions – for example the notion of *Mitteleuropa*, or Eastern Europe or the notion of the Balkans – and can be hegemonic in the ways in which they establish taken-for-granted relations between peripheries and centres. The more general categories of western, central and eastern, or a dichotomy of West and East also do not offer a sufficiently rich basis on which to explore the variety of models of modernity in Europe.

The case for the specificity of these regions will be made below in more detail. The notion of a historical region implies that there is a common historical experience that can be discerned in the *longue durée* and that common features of the region's history are more significant than the differences (Müller 2010: 114). The general rationale in this chapter for a differentiated approach to Europe's historical regions is, firstly, each must correspond to a distinctive route to modernity and which is a variant of the more general form that European modernity took; secondly, there should be a broad background in civilizational contexts. Together civilizational background and routes to modernity define the identity of a historical region and give to it a certain unity which in turn is the basis of a 'mental map'. In short, it is necessary to define the regions as transnational historical spaces in terms of their relation to Europe – as variants of a more general historical space – and in terms of their specificity in relation to each other as areas of close interaction and historical commonality.

A final preliminary observation is that all these historical regions are not self-enclosed enclaves, but over-lapping and in many cases their historical experience entailed at different points a shared history, as in the case of those areas that fell under Soviet rule in the post-1945 period. For these reasons, Europe's historical regions might be seen as borderlands. The borders that have shaped the historical regions of Europe changed so many times that they are best seen less as lines of division than as lines that constitute intersecting spaces. For Balibar (2003) Europe is itself a borderland in that it is made up of multiple spatialities in terms of state formation, markets, social and cultural institutions and identities. In this view, any reference to a geopolitical or historical region must recognize its interconnections with other regions. Europe's regions should thus be seen in terms of hyphenated spatialities than as separated territories. The following discussion of Europe's six major historical regions will consider the interconnected nature of these regions as much as their singularity.

North Western Europe

The very notion of a North Western Europe is itself an acknowledgement of a borderland. Rather than speak of Western Europe in general, it is more meaningful to take the more circumscribed category of North Western Europe. This includes the British Isles, Scandinavia,[3] France, the Low Countries and Germany. As a borderland, the inclusion of Germany ties the area to Central Europe, given the overlapping nature of Germany, which includes more than one historical region. The region may be extended to include Northern Italy and parts of the Iberian peninsula could arguably claim to be part of a wider notion of Western Europe. However, the notion of North Western Europe puts the emphasis on the northerness of the region and for this reason it is best seen in more limited terms as an area that can be located within the broader category of Western Europe, but which exhibits distinctively northern features.

North Western Europe has been influenced both by Central Europe in general and more specifically by Mediterranean Europe. In earlier periods, Southern Europe provided the basic civilizational orientations for all of Europe and North Western Europe bears this influence. However, in the course of history the western area of Europe became progressively distinct from Southern Europe and its shared character-istic with the regions of Central and Eastern Europe too became less formative. The Frankish leadership under Charlemagne gave to the region its essential identity, which according to Henri Pirenne (2001) in his famous thesis in 1935 – 'without Mohammed there would have been no Charlemagne' – was made possible by the rise and advance-ment of Islam across the southern shores of the Mediterranean.

As we have seen, state formation since the nineteenth century tended to move in the direction of sea-based empires and with a rela-tively high degree of democratization in the metropole. With its histor-ical basis in the Carolingian kingdom and the area west of the Rhine, the North West region became what has often been called modern or core Europe and formed the basis of what was eventually to become the European Union. However misleading the idea of a core Europe is and despite the many wars fought within the region between the dynastic powers and the later national states, North Western Europe exhibits remarkable similarity in its political, economic and wider soci-etal structures and institutions. It has undeniably played a major role in the shaping of modern Europe both for good and for bad. The diver-sity of its regions in terms of cultural factors, such as language and national identity, disguises a certain unity that is discernable more in the myriad of interconnections than in a common framework. No such structure developed, at least until the formation of the European Economic Community (EEC) in 1958; yet, the region has had a relatively common history in terms of both its civilizational background and its model of modernity. A crucial fact in its uniformity and overall dom-inance has been the fact that the region enjoyed relative uninterrupted growth and consolidation over several centuries, while the eastern regions underwent major changes in their civilizational directions. The Mongol invasions of Russia, the latter's expansion over Eastern and Central Europe, and the Ottoman conquests of the South East, the German onslaught in the 1940s led to more turbulent histories.

The civilizational roots of North Western Europe were formed by Latin Christianity and in part by the Roman Empire. However much of the area lay outside the territory of the Roman Empire, which can be considered to have been less important than the state tradition and the institutions that developed in the medieval age. A key aspect of this was the struggle between Church and State and the fact that in the balance that was finally achieved the state retained juridical autonomy and was not subordinated to ecclesiastical authority. The result was a clear separation of state and society. The states that formed in

200 Formations of European Modernity

Northern Western Europe have been relatively settled in their basic structures and territories and the nation-states that consolidated there witnessed greater stability and continuity than in most other parts of Europe where the state tradition and nationhood led to less peaceful outcomes. Earlier, feudalism established the conditions for economic and political stability as did its relatively early abolition. The 'Great Transformation' that led to the emergence of the modern market society that Karl Polanyi (1944) characterized as the basis of modern society was most vividly present in North Western Europe where the industrial revolution and the formation of the modern class structure was also most advanced. In addition to these factors relating to state formation and market society, North Western Europe had a long tradition of the autonomy of the city *vis-à-vis* the countryside. The rise of civil society, decisive for the emergence of modernity, was possible only because of the autonomy of the city and the kinds of authority that it cultivated. Later patterns of democratization were built on these foundations.

The societal model of modernity that developed in North Western Europe can thus be characterized as a relatively distinct one whose early crystallization has been important in the overall shaping of Europe. The Cold War and the rise of military and fascist regimes in Southern Europe in the post-1945 period gave to it an additional identity based on democracy and capitalism. For instance, Spain, under Franco until 1975, was relatively isolated and experienced a different transition to the European social model in the twentieth century that clearly demarcates it from the experience of North Western Europe. In this region democratic capitalism enjoyed a period of uninterrupted growth since 1945 in contrast to Eastern and Southern Europe, where the democratic tradition was variously interrupted. Italy, at least until the 1980s, was the exception, but there the huge divide between north and south and the power of the Mafia in Italian politics, put it on a different trajectory from Northern Europe. North Western Europe contains the most powerful economies in Europe and in the world, Germany, UK, France, the latter two having had the largest overseas empires. It can finally be noted that North Western Europe was western in another sense: it was part of the wider West world with its centre in the Atlantic rather than in the Mediterranean or Black Sea. Today, in the twentieth-first century, this may have lost much of its force, but in the previous century it gave to the area an identity that consolidated an historical trajectory that might otherwise have had less specificity.

Mediterranean Europe

The notion of a Mediterranean Europe presents some obvious difficulties since it covers a wider and diverse area stretching from the Iberian peninsula, Southern France, Italy, part of the Southern Balkans and Greece. As with all of the historical regions of Europe it does not have clear-cut boundaries and more or less all of its constitutive countries are not entirely Mediterranean in their entirety. Unlike the other historical regions it is more difficult to specify a historical core area, though arguably that core is Roman. The case of Greece is a complication, since its civilizational background and path to modernity is markedly different from the countries of the Western Mediterranean. For this reason it is probably best located as part of South Western Europe. Another complicating case is Portugal, while not having a Mediterranean coast and more Atlanticist in orientation is nonetheless from its civilizational influences clearly not too far removed from the wider Iberian context. Despite these qualifications it is possible to speak of the specificity of a Mediterranean Europe as a historical region.

This region is above all a civilizational one that was shaped by the Roman Empire and Catholicism. The Roman Empire provided the most enduring cultural and geopolitical framework for the emergence of Europe, but this was primarily a Mediterranean civilization rather than a northern or western one. The cities founded by the Romans as well as the roadways they built gave to the region a matrix that laid the basis of a civilizational orientation. However, the post-Roman empires were all greatly shaped by its legacy as were the national cultures and the modern nation-states that emerged in the area. The Holy Roman Empire is one such legacy that for almost a thousand years from the tenth to the eighteenth century gave a certain unity to much of Europe. While this had a pronounced Habsburg dimension since the early sixteenth century, when it became known as the Holy Roman Empire of the German Nation, it was modelled on the memory of Rome. The cultural heritage of the Roman Empire is easily discernable along the shores of the Mediterranean in ways of life, language, religion, climate and the built environment. Greece, different in its language and religion from the largely Latin influenced western areas, is equally part of the Southern Eastern historical region; its state tradition is different from the Western European one, as its model of church-state relations, and the slow development of capitalism marks it off from the wider Mediterranean area.

The Roman origins of Mediterranean Europe draw attention to the wider unity of the Mediterranean and the fact that the Roman Empire was not simply European but included North Africa and parts of the Middle East. The Roman Empire, as argued in Chapter 2, was itself shaped by Greek antiquity and by the numerous cultures it encountered. Entailed in this is the idea of a Euro-Arab region, for both the European and the Arab shores of the Mediterranean form part of the wider unity of the region. This was not only in the distant past. Much of the Maghreb was part of Europe in the twentieth century and several wars were played out in the area as a result of the imperialist ambitions of the European powers. Algeria was an integral part of France until after the war of independence in 1962; the circumstances that led to the Spanish civil war emerged from the loss of Spanish dominion in North Africa; fascist Italy sought to control Ethiopia. The notion of a Mediterranean Europe as a historical region is best understood as a borderland region formed out of cross-cultural encounters and the civilizational legacy of Rome. This borderland can be considered the basis of what Ian Chambers (2008) has termed a 'heterogeneous modernity' which is a particularly striking feature of the area.

The examples of Malta and Cyprus capture the spirit of Mediterranean Europe as a borderland and one deeply influenced by the Roman origins, as well as the later Byzantine Empire. The two islands had been for long part of the Muslim world. Malta's chequered history was marked by various periods of conquest by the Normans, the Arabs, the Germans, Spanish, British and was the scene of numerous wars. Cyprus is an example of Greek, Greco-Roman, and Ottoman encounters and divisions. Today these islands are part of the EU and constitute the heart of the wider Euro-Mediterranean area, an identity that was revived in the 1990s with the enlargement of the EU.

The idea of a European Mediterranean took on a new form in 1995 with the Euro-Mediterranean partnership between the European Union and the countries of the Southern Mediterranean, and revived in 2008 with the idea of the Union of the Mediterranean, which was created to promote economic integration and democratic reform across 16 countries in Southern Europe, North Africa and the Middle East (these being Albania, Algeria, Bosnia and Herzegovina, Croatia, Egypt, Israel, Jordan, Lebanon, Mauritania, Monaco, Montenegro, Morocco, the Palestinian Authority, Syria, Tunisia and Turkey). The EU has been effective in giving shape to the European Mediterranean as a regional identity (Pace 2004; Featherstone and Kazamias 2001).

In terms of patterns of modernity that developed in the region, Mediterranean Europe, the historical models of modernity associated with France, Italy and Spain can all be considered to be firmly within the wider Western Europe tradition, albeit with large variations and uneven development, such as the contrast between Southern and Northern Italy. The twentieth century fascist and military regimes in Italy, Portugal, Spain, and Greece – and the civil wars within the latter two countries – are a reminder of a weaker state tradition and an interrupted transition to democracy. The case for the distinctiveness of a Mediterranean Europe is largely made on the basis of its civilizational influences. However, considered as a whole the pattern of modernity in terms of state formation, capitalism, and civil society bears the mark of the European societal model insofar as the democratizing influences of civil society are concerned. In all its areas the national state was established by the nineteenth century, a feature it shares with North Western Europe and a contrast to Central and Eastern Europe. For all these reasons the idea of a Mediterranean Europe can be regarded as a distinctive transnational historical region.

Central Europe

Of all of Europe's historical regions, Central Europe is the one that comes closest to having a regional identity rooted both in civilizational currents and in a model of modernity.[4] The idea of *Mitteleuropa* has a long resonance in the German-speaking world. Although not an identity as such, it invokes a heritage that is distinct from both Eastern and Western Europe. Like the term Europe itself, it has always been a contested term and has had different uses depending on when and by whom it has been used. It had pan-German origins, but with the political instrumentalization of the pan-Germanism with the Nazis, it became most widely used as an Austrian nostalgic term for the Europe of the Austro-Hungarian Empire. In the 1980s it acquired a more pronounced political meaning in Hungary and Czechoslovakia as a way of defining the European heritage of those countries against the Soviet Union and communism. In this use of the term, as advanced by Milan Kundera and George Konrad, it signified civil society. As a historical region, Central Europe – as opposed to the idea of *Mitteleuropa* – includes Southern Germany, Austria, Switzerland, and much of what will be discussed separately as East Central Europe, namely Poland, the Czech Republic, Slovenia and Slovakia. The historical heart of the region is the area once covered by the Austro-Hungarian Empire. Its centres were Vienna, Prague, Ljubljana, Trieste, Bratislava and Budapest and could be extended to parts of South Eastern Europe, such as a Zagreb. In this sense it is a poly-centric historical region.

The idea of *Mitteleuropa* has been the subject of several influential works that have contributed to the regional identity of the region. The most well known are Friedrich Naumann's *Mitteleuropa* in 1915, Thomas Masaryk's *The New Europe* in 1918 and Claudio Magris's *Danube* (2001). The geographical and political notion of *Mitteleuropa* by definition can only be a relative term since its definition rests on assumptions on the borders of Europe. In the case of the eastern border, which has been the most important in the self-definition of *Mitteleuropa*, this has shifted numerous times. As Milan Kundera (1984: 35) has written, 'Its borders are imaginary and must be drawn and redrawn with each new historical situation'. Obviously, the notion is essentially cultural rather than geopolitical.

The idea of *Mitteleuropa* had been part of German economic policy since Frederick List promoted it as an area of free trade, but it should not be equated with Prussian expansionism. For Naumann *Mitteleuropa* referred to the larger German-speaking lands as well as the non-German regions of the Habsburg Empire, and was as much a political and cultural category as it was economic; Thomas Masaryk, the first president of Czechoslovakia, in contrast, used the term to exclude German and Austria, essentially meaning the smaller countries of East Central Europe (see below). In this view, *Mitteleuropa* is not located between north and south and could include Greece and Finland. A related idea, influential in Germany in the inter-war years, was the notion of *Zwischeneuropa*, first coined by the geographer Albrecht Penck in the early twentieth century, and which can be translated as a borderland Europe, though literally meaning 'in between' Europe, that is the in between areas between East and West. The term was revived in Austrian nationalism to connect the country to the Habsburg past. Any discussion of the notion of *Mitteleuropa* runs the risk of either polemics or simplification. Like Europe as a whole it lacks clear borders, suggesting it is more like a state of mind or a culture or fate, as Kundera has argued, than a state or territory.

The notion of *Mitteleuropa* should not be dismissed as nostalgia for the Habsburg Empire, Catholicism or as a German expansionist ideology, simply because it had too many meanings, which include a certain cultural cosmopolitanism. In a region where the nation-state developed later than in North Western Europe, there is some value in re-assessing it in light of the region's multi-ethno nationalism. In addition, there is the relevance of the wider appeal in the region for a supranational ideal. Without this the very possibility of Czechoslovakia or Yugoslavia, as a union of states, or the Dual Monarchy of Austria and Hungary would not have been possible. These now vanished confederal states were a feature of the political landscape of Europe in the mid-twentieth century and their disappearance has not been without a certain loss of opportunity to a create multi-national state. It was this sense of the term that the Austro-Marxists sought an alternative to the nation-state in the aftermath of the first world, for they believed that the political structure of the Dual Monarchy could be used to construct a new post-imperial political framework.

The idea of Central Europe/*Mitteleuropa* had considerable appeal to civil society intellectuals (such as Michnik, Konrad, Havel) in Poland, Hungary and Czechoslovakia in the 1980s. Kundera's famous 1984 essay 'The Tragedy of Central Europe', although written in exile, captured the mood of the period with his notion of a 'return to Europe' and thus signalled an anti-communist appeal to the European traditions of the region. In the 1989 discourse on *Mitteleuropa* Russia is the Other. It was a contrast, too, to the western triumphalist narrative of the 'end of history' and instead called for the 're-birth of Europe'. In this use of the term, modernity as a societal condition is most evident, for by Europe is signalled the political assertion of the autonomy of civil society against the absolute state and the suppression of individual and collective liberty. Viewed in such terms, *Mitteleuropa* is not just a civilizational milieu, but reflects a model of modernity in which the conflict between civil society and the state has been central to its identity. It is possibly this post-socialist conception of *Mitteleuropa* that has the most relevance for the present day; it offers a way to re-address the question of the inter-cultural and multi-national legacy of a polycentric region whose borders have continued to change.

East Central Europe

In recent years the notion of East Central Europe has emerged less as an alternative to the idea of Central Europe than a demarcation within it of a more narrowly defined region (see Arnason 2005a; Arnason and Doyle 2010; Troebst 2003). Unlike the broader category of Central Europe it does not have the same resonance in terms of an identity and has been mostly used by historians of the region, such as Szücs (1988) and Halecki (1950, 1953), who noted an inner dualism within Central

Europe between its western and eastern orientations. Yet a case can be made for its relevance as a distinctive historical heritage. While Central Europe refers to a wider area that includes the German-speaking world and much of the Habsburg territories, the notion of East Central Europe pertains specifically to Poland, Hungary, the former Czechoslovakia. The notion should be extended to include Slovenia, which can also be regarded as part of Central Europe's eastern face. However, the core has generally been taken to be Hungary, the Czech lands, and Poland. The notion of East Central Europe in many ways approximates to the non-Austro-German *Mitteleuropa*, and a contrast to what might be more accurately termed West Central Europe. As a region, it is located between the Baltic and the Adriatic, on the one side, and on the other between Russia to the east, the Ottoman Empire to the south east and the various incarnations of the German empires in the west. For this reason, it accords most precisely with the idea of 'the lands in between'. The region is thus to be distinguished from the Ottoman influenced South Eastern Europe and from North Eastern Europe, in the sense of the western Russian-speaking world and the Baltic region (see below). Szücs, in his classic essay written in 1981, argued it lay between two areas of expansion: the western zone of expansion and the Russian one to the east (Szücs 1988: 313).

In civilizational terms, East Central Europe is a product of western Christianity, but represents the interface of the Carolingian tradition with Slavic, Hungarian, and eastern influences. Its identity was shaped against the Ottomans to the south east and the Russians to the east. As Arnason (2005a: 392) has argued, its heritage is more intra-civilizational than inter-civilizational, since the dominant influences were variants of western Christianity. However, the inter-civilizational dimension is also present in view of the older conflict in the region between western and eastern Christianity before the final alignment with the western tradition in the ninth century. Before the formation of the Polish, Bohemian and Hungarian kingdoms, the area was the scene of struggles between the Magyars and the Christian kingdom of Moravia, until power shifted to the other Czech kingdom to the west, namely Bohemia. The three kingdoms that consolidated in the region and gave to its identity as a historical region were themselves expansionist. Of the three kingdoms, though all integrated into western Christianity, the Bohemian kingdom was more closely integrated into the western tradition, being part of, and for a time, the capital of the Holy Roman Empire. Due to the Hussite movement, it has a good claim to be seen as the beginning of the Reformation and Counter-Reformation.

There is another sense in which the region can be considered to be an important area of inter-civilizational influences. In the three core areas, Bohemia, Poland and Hungary there has been for long a large Jewish population that was fully integrated into the social, cultural and economic life of the societies. The Jewish dimension of the region, by far the most important in all of Europe, added to its multi-ethnic diversity. The loss of this after the Shoah represents a major cultural loss for the region and for Europe.

While Hungary and the Czech nation remained relatively intact in their borders over the centuries, the case of Poland is rather more complicated. Its borders have shifted many times in history and, as with much of Central Europe, it has had a divided heritage between its eastern and western orientations. Of these it is undoubtedly the western pull that has been decisive and led to the creation by the Jagellonian dynasty of the Polish-Lithuanian kingdom in the sixteenth century. Stretching from the Baltic to the Black Sea, this was a powerful and large multi-national state that was created in 1385 when the Jagellonian dynasty came to the Polish crown, consolidated into a closer union in 1569 and lasted until its demise in 1795 following the partition of Poland. This episode is also an illustration of the involvement of the region in a wider borderland area. The Lithuanian link did not endure, though arguably a case could be made for the inclusion of Lithuania and the Baltic states in the category of East Central Europe. However, their different historical paths and later patterns of state formation and societal modernization put them on a trajectory different from that of Poland, Hungary and the Czech Republic, a region that can be extended to include both Slovakia and Slovenia.

An example of the civilizational current in the region, pan-Slavism was for a time a reflection of a transnational identity that tied the region to a broader trans-region. Although it did not endure, due not least to the diverse Slavic traditions, significant cultural differences between the Russian and Polish Slavophiles, and the different routes that the Slavic peoples had embarked on, it illustrates a departure from the wider Central European region. The eastern versus the western faces of the region were less strong in the Czech lands and in Hungary, while in Poland the search for a Slavic nativism based on a peasant culture ceased to be significant by the twentieth century and in all parts of the region a pronounced European consciousness was present and, especially in the Czech case an integral part of its national identity.

From the perspective of modernity, the core countries of East Central Europe can all be seen as within the broader category of what has been referred to earlier as the European societal model. Their historical experience has been marked by resistance to absolutism. In the early modern period, especially in Poland and in Bohemia, but also in Hungary, there was considerable resistance to absolutism; in the case of Bohemia resistance to the Habsburgs and in the case of Poland to the Russian Empire. Within their territories absolute rule was curbed by traditions of rights and privileges of the nobles that set limits to imperial power without representation and eventually provided the ground on which nationalism would rise. This has been described as a political culture of government by estates and differs from western monarchical and absolutist rule as well as from Muscovite autocracy and Ottoman centralized statehood (Müller 2010: 115). This tradition gave to the region a political heritage that can be seen as basis of a democratic tradition, albeit a weak one. Unlike, other parts of what was once called Eastern Europe, such as Romania and Bulgaria, the area shared with the West a similar history based on feudalism and private ownership, though the transition to industrialization took place much later (Berend 2005: 402). Western influences were stronger than in the areas further east, to the south in the Balkans and to the north where Russia exerted more influence. Despite these similarities, nation-state building since 1919 put the region on a different course from the mainstream North Western and Mediterranean regions, for in this region the problem of linguistic, ethnic and cultural plurality were very great and not easily accommodated into the mono-cultural design of the national state.

In the twentieth century, East Central Europe was massively transformed by the double impact of German fascism from the West and from the East by communism and Soviet occupation. This experience ensured that modernity would take a different form in the region, which also experienced an experiment with state formation. The creation in 1918 of Czechoslovakia can be seen as a variant of modernity that eventually proved too fragile to last and the two nations finally separated in 1992 (Arnason 2005b). Though it should be noted that in all of the Soviet bloc in Central and Eastern Europe, it was in the previously more European and western-oriented Czechoslovakia that communism received considerable domestic support. Some of the most significant debates on the meaning of democracy and civil society took place in the countries of East Central Europe in the second half of the twentieth century (see Garton Ash 1993). The assertion of civil society by dissident intellectuals against the totalitarian state has been a significant aspect of European political modernity that had a transformative impact in the region leading to the eventual collapse of Soviet domination.

South Eastern Europe

As a historical region South Eastern Europe presents a number of difficulties of definition, being in part an extension of both Eastern and Central Europe. However, the specificity of the region marks it off from both in very distinctive ways. The region in question concerns the Balkans including Bulgaria, Macedonia, Albania, Greece and Romania. The latter two, especially Greece, are by no means self-evident. The case for the inclusion of Greece within the category of South Eastern Europe is made on the basis of its participation in the Byzantine-Orthodox civilizational background, which has been arguably more significant for its history than its entry to the western world since its independence from the Ottoman Empire in the early nineteenth century. Moreover, in the course of that century Greek culture had a formative impact on the rest of the Balkans. As argued earlier, Greece can also be considered as part of Mediterranean Europe. However, in consideration of the overall historical, civilizational and geopolitical context, Greece can be seen as part of South Eastern Europe, as can Romania. Since Romania was formed in 1859 out of the historical region of Moldova, along with Wallachia, the present state of Moldova can be located with the wider region of South Eastern Europe. As a historical region, South Eastern Europe while not being entirely reducible to the Balkans is unavoidably more or less synonymous with it, thus giving to the area a certain identity.

From a civilizational perspective the region is defined by two orientations. Firstly, the Byzantine and Orthodox heritage has been an important civilizational influence. The entire Balkan region differs from the other regions of Europe by the Orthodox faith. Orthodoxy, deriving from the Byzantine tradition, has also remained an enduring feature of Bulgaria and Romania (Blokker 2010). The second civilizational influence is the Ottoman-Islamic heritage. Since the Ottoman conquests of the Bulgarian and Serbian kingdoms, the region underwent a very different history to that of the rest of Europe. Due to the nature of Ottoman rule, Islam was not imposed on the populations of the conquered countries, but Islamic influences were present and in many cases there were conversions to Islam, examples being Albania and Kosovo. More important than Islam was the wider Ottoman influence in the region. In European historiography the area was once referred to as Turkey-in-Europe and was the object of much western, especially British, Prussian and Habsburg foreign policy-making in the nineteenth century (Müller 2001). In addition to these factors, the Slavic component has been significant, uniting at least linguistically the Croats, Bosnians, Bulgarians, Macedonians, Montenegrins, Serbs, and Slovenes. Yugoslavia – meaning 'the land of the Southern Slavs' – derived its name from this civilizational unity. The link between the Slavophile movement and orthodoxy adds an additional layer of weight to the civilizational specificity of the region and has often been regarded as a basis for anti-westernism. Many Bulgarians and Serbs, influenced more by Russian than Greek culture, saw Europe as a distinct cultural form different from the Byzantine legacy of Slavdom and Orthodoxy (Mishkova 2008: 245).

As a geopolitical and civilizational space South Eastern Europe can be seen for much of its history located between the Habsburg and Ottoman Empires. In the case of Bulgaria, the Russian influences were significant, although in this instance to be explained less by the direct impact of Russia than by appropriation by the Bulgarian intelligentsia of Russian culture in order to combat the dominance of Greek cultural superiority in the Balkan region (Mishkova 2008: 242). In the second half of the twentieth century, the area along with much of Central and Southern Europe other than Greece fell under Russian domination. The Russian and Ottoman moments, in particular the latter, shaped the region in ways that mark it off from the rest of Europe. These amount to a civilizational influence and attest to the presence within Europe of neighbouring civilizations, which give to the European heritage its character as a constellation of interacting civilizations.

Europe has been greatly shaped by the seas that surround it. This is especially true of South Eastern Europe. The Black Sea is as important, if not more, than the Mediterranean and the Adriatic seas in the region. Its place and significance in European history has been neglected. The Balkan region is generally seen as a mountainous region – the name Balkan means mountains – and one that is cut off from the rest of Europe. Placing the Black Sea rather than landmasses at the centre of stage gives a rather different view of the region. As Neal Ascherson (1995) has argued in his travel history of the Black Sea, over many centuries the Black Sea united cities and regions in Greece, the Ukraine, Turkey, Bulgaria and Romania. In this perspective the Black Sea is, like the Mediterranean Sea, a zone of interconnections between Europe and its neighbouring regions. The Black Sea, which receives five rivers including the Danube and the Don, has been important in

European history since antiquity. The Crimea was one of the most important centres of the trading networks in the Greek world and it was especially important for Classical Athens; it was the site of a major war in the nineteenth century and the location of the Yalta conference, which symbolically represented the post-war division of Europe between East and West (Ascherson 1995: 10; Feher 1987). Such a view of South Eastern Europe would place it in relation to the Caucasus area, in particular linked to Georgia and Armenia. Instead of seeing the area as cut off, as in mainstream Eurocentric accounts, it should be seen as constituting links between the different cities and regions drawn together by the Black Sea. In this view, William McNeill (1964) locates the region as part of a wider Danubian and Pontic European region and constituting what he termed Europe's 'Steppe Frontier'.

Any discussion of the modernity of South Eastern Europe is unavoidably complicated by the perceived view of backwardness with respect to Western Europe and a representation of the region in terms of 'Balkanism', which Todorova (1997) regards as another kind of Orientalism. Representations of especially the Balkan area as the opposite to the West and as an extension of the Ottoman East have also been reflected in the ways the Balkans have also perceived themselves. Such positions operate on the basis of a distinction of core and periphery whereby the periphery is always defined in relation to the modernity and high civilization of the core. This fails to capture the diversity of Europe and its multiple civilizational logics. By reducing the Balkan region to an extension of the Ottoman East, it also fails to understand how a different route to modernity is possible. This Eurocentric tendency should not be exaggerated, for it would appear that it was more recent than previously thought (Mishkova 2008). Larry Wolff (1994), for instance, claimed this hegemonic discourse was part of the eighteenth century Enlightenment, but it may have been a later nineteenth development. As Mishkova (2008: 251) has argued, while the 'gaze of the Other' was always a feature of the Balkans, in reality there existed many gazes often in conflict with each other.

North Eastern Europe

Any account of the historical regions of Europe is complicated by the question of what constitutes Eastern Europe or the East of Europe today in light of the absence of any clear lines of demarcation. All such designations are relative – the northern tip of Norway is as geographically east as Istanbul – and generally based on the assumption that the core is the west. The Cold War division of Europe has left a lasting mark on the face of Europe, but in the longer perspective of history the division it created between an East and West needs to be differentiated. However getting entirely rid of the notion of an Eastern Europe is also fraught with difficulties. There is a sense in which as a consequence of the developments that have occurred since 1990 that Eastern Europe should now be projected further to the east and refers to the western regions of the Russian-speaking lands. In this view, Eastern Europe refers to Belarus, Kalingrad, and, with some difficulty, the Ukraine and Modova.

The approach taken in this paper is to define the eastern component of Europe by a logic that configures the mental map in terms of East Central, South East and a North East. According to this reasoning, Eastern Europe is best seen in terms of three inter-related zones. Of these the latter is the more complicated one; instead of being termed Eastern Europe – or even 'far Eastern Europe' or some such formulation – the term North Eastern Europe is the more accurate one. The area comprising it includes the Baltic Republics in addition to Kalingrad, Belarus, Ukraine, and possibly Moldova. While North Western Europe would then extend inland into the vastness of Ukraine, as a region the area is centrally defined by its relation to the Baltic Sea which gives it its European character as a borderland area of interconnected cities.

These areas are clearly primarily influenced by Russia and were for a long time part of the Soviet Union (Szporluk 1991). The three Baltic Republics, forcibly incorporated in 1940, have always been part of the wider European area and cities such as Tallinn and Riga were important Hanseatic cities and where German was widely spoken. Unlike other parts of the region, they are also part of western Christianity, Lithuania being predominantly Catholic and also the most northern Catholic nation. Kaliningrad was the former German city and province of Königsberg in East Prussia. Moldavia, which was partially colonized by the Romans, was considerably influenced by Romania, the modern state of which was formed in part of Western Moldova. In the case of Moldova, North Eastern Europe merges into South Eastern Europe.

Belarus and Ukraine are clearly only partially European and the latter does not entirely fit into the designation North Eastern, which as used in this chapter is partly as an alternative to the notion of Eastern Europe (which is perhaps a more pertinent term in the case of the Ukraine). However, both have strong European civilizational influences. Polish influences in Ukraine and Belarus have been historically strong, and of course Lithuania was part of the Polish-Lithuanian kingdom. Parts of

Poland were incorporated into Belarus after 1945. Western Ukraine has traditionally been regarded as European and was the least Soviet area in the USSR (Szporluk 1991: 475). Russian and Ukraine historiography has traditionally distinguished both Belarus and the Ukraine from the general course of Russian history and have emphasized its Europeanness (Halecki 1950: 137). However, there can be little doubt that the Ukraine in general is more closely allied with Russia than with Europe, for Kiev was the common birth place of both Russia and the Ukraine. The trajectory of Russian history begins with the Kiev Rus before the foundation of Muscovite state which became the successor of the Kievan kingdom. Due to the overlapping and entangled histories of the area, there is then a good case to include these countries in the mapping of the historical regions of Europe.

In sum, in civilizational terms North Eastern Europe has been shaped by the Russian influence and to varying degrees by other civilizational currents. As a historical region it possibly has the weakest identity as a region, given the divisions of its history and the forcible incorporation of its territories into the Soviet Union. The Baltic republics themselves do not have a clearly articulated collective identity as a region; each having quite different histories prior to their incorporation into the Soviet Republic. The model of modernity in the region has been equally fragmented, depending on the degree of Russification. Of the historical regions of Europe it is the one that, with the exception of the Baltic republics, had the weakest civil society tradition and where democratization developed only relatively lately and incompletely. Again, with the exception of the Baltic Republics, where the modern market society was relatively advanced prior to their incorporation into the Soviet Union, virtually all these countries experienced a very late transition to capitalism. As a result the model of modernity that evolved there was shaped more by a feudal legacy – a term to be sure that can be used only with some difficulty in the Russian context – left by German, Nordic and Russian conquerors, and the subsequent rise of Soviet totalitarianism.

The six historical regions discussed in this chapter are historically variable and overlapping. They do not simply overlap with each other, but are also closely linked spatially and culturally with areas that lie outside the European region as a whole. The chapter has stressed in this regard the formative influence of the east in the west, and the importance of the Russian and Ottoman-Islamic worlds in the making of Europe. This serves in part to correct the older Eurocentric view of the making of Europe that tended to see Europe as shaped by itself and to define all its regions in terms of their relation to the North West. In approaching the question of the historical regions of Europe from such an inter-civilizational perspective, it may be possible to avoid an account that sees unity only as possible in face of a common enemy, for as we have seen there was neither one enemy that predominated nor was there a single core that gave to Europe its identity. To the extent to which it is possible to speak of the 'idea of Europe', this must be found in the plurality of its regions, which offer an alternative to accounts of European history in terms of national narratives. The emphasis on a plurality of regions with their own civilizational backgrounds and routes to modernity does not, it must be noted, mean that there is no unity since all these regions interacted with each other and ultimately such interaction made possible the genesis of modernity and the formation of Europe as a world historical region.

11
Europe in the Short Twentieth Century: Conflicting Projects of Modernity

From the perspective of the twenty-first century the previous century as far as Europe is concerned can be seen as defined by the two world wars and the political systems to which they gave rise. It is now commonplace to observe that 1918 did not mark the end of an era, but the beginning of a new one, which ended not in 1945 with the defeat of Nazi Germany but in 1989, with the break-up of Russian domination in Central and Eastern Europe and within a year the collapse of the East versus West divide. This is what Eric Hobsbawm (1994) has termed the 'short twentieth century', which can be regarded as the most apt characterization of the century (see also Badiou 2007). Instead of a periodization that sees 1945 as the threshold to a new era in which democracy returned to Europe, a longer view of the century would see the era 1918 to 1989 as constituting a certain unity. From both a global and a wider Europe perspective a conceptualization of the twentieth century is needed. Conceived of in terms of models of modernity, which places any consideration of the twentieth century in the context of a longer-term view, the emphasis is less on the beginning and ending of wars than on the formative moments in the making of modernity. Such moments of great crisis as major revolutions are more significant than the cessation of wars. European wars such as the Franco-Prussian war of 1870–1, the First and Second Worlds, the Cold War, important as they were in shaping the course of European history, need to be understood in a larger framework of analysis. The year 1945 did not mark the end of an era for much of Europe. It may have been once possible to tell the story of Europe from the perspective of European integration as commencing in the aftermath of World War Two or from an Anglo-American perspective. Judt (2012: 214–15) has commented that the Second World War cannot be contained within six years and the period 1936 to 1956 constituted a single period, from the beginning of the Spanish Civil War and to the Soviet intervention in Hungary. In any case assumptions of such a narrative collapsed in 1989. Undoubtedly many still adhere to this conventional periodization and see the post-1989 context as one of the 'enlargement' of what was a Cold War inter-state system. This approach relies too much on the European Union's own narrative of its short history and forces a view of European history from the vantage point of the West, with the East reduced to a deviation from a grand narrative that sees in the European post-war project the latest chapter in the rise of the West.

Against such grand narratives of the idea of Europe an alternative approach would give more weight to revolutions in defining the shape and identity of Europe, for revolutions were sites of contestation over modernity and the implementation of its basic programmes. The Russian Revolution of 1917 and the revolutions in Central and Eastern Europe in 1989–90, which we may term the 1989 Revolution, can now be seen as the formative events that shaped Europe in the twentieth century in much the same way as 1789 did two centuries earlier. In addition to bringing into the picture the Russian dimension of a wider Europe, as opposed to a narrow conception of Europe based largely on the North West, it has the additional advantage of placing modernity at the centre of the analysis, since what was at stake for much of the previous century can now be seen to be rival projects of modernity with entirely different visions of how state and society should be organized. There were essentially four such programmatic models of modernity experimented between 1917 and 1989: state socialism or communism, fascism, liberal democracy, and European transnational governance. Of these the first two failed and the second two succeeded with varying degrees of success. All four were products of Europe and to varying degrees appealed to the idea of Europe for legitimation; they were also quintessentially products of political modernity insofar as they articulated a social imaginary for the creation of political community on new foundations and the reconfiguration of the relationship between the individual, the state and society.

It would be tempting to reduce the course of European history in the twentieth century to national patterns, such as aggressive German nationalism or the catastrophic path of nation-state formation in many countries or to tell the story as one that sees the Shoah as the final destructive outcome of European civilization. Certainly no account of the idea of Europe can omit the 'dark side of Europe', the eclipse of democracy, and what Walter Benjamin referred to as the tie of civilization and barbarism. For all its brutality, the legacy of the twentieth century is ambivalent; it was not only the century of totalitarianism, but of peace-making and new experiments with democracy, emancipation and cosmopolitan justice. It would be equally wrong to see the destructive events of the twentieth century from 1914 to the Yugoslavian War of 1993 as the outcome of long-run historical forces driven by deeply-rooted cultural identities rather than the contingent outcome of the times. The aim of this chapter is to offer an assessment of the idea of Europe in the short twentieth century around the conflict of rival models of modernity rather than national conflicts or civilizational conflicts. As argued earlier, there was not a single European civilization, but a plurality and which have been too inter-linked to be considered as mutually antagonistic. As far as the twentieth century is concerned, the advent of modernity and the competing interpretations of how to realize and organize society and state according to its principles, has had greater consequences than the civilizational backgrounds that lay behind the different projects of modernity. The diversity of Europe, which may have been greater than its unity, was as much an outcome of rival modernities, than a civilizational condition. The pursuit of these projects was decisive in shaping the course of European history in the twentieth century. These projects of modernity will be discussed as follows: beginning with an account of the background *fin-de-siècle* – c.1890s to 1918 – period of crisis, the four main projects of modernity will be discussed, namely western liberal democracy, communism, fascism, and European transnational governance.

The *fin-de-siècle* crisis of modernity

The two decades or so preceding and following World War One marked a shift in European modernity away from the legacy of the French Revolution. The ideas of 1789 did not fade, for if anything they became stronger, for the period saw the rise of more extreme interpretations and new and rival notions of modernity stemming from all parts of Europe, and especially from the German-speaking world. The *fin-de-siècle* was a watershed in modern Europe; it was a period of cultural and scientific creativity and one in which new social and political ideas emerged. Throughout the nineteenth century the ideas of the French Revolution greatly influenced European political modernity in all its expressions, from liberalism to nationalism and socialism. This was an age when the political ideologies of the nineteenth century crystallized into potent political programmes with different and incompatible emancipatory agendas.

By the end of the century a major crisis of modernity developed with the recognition that the social fabric and cultural form of modern societies might be degenerating. The general diagnosis of the age was that European civilization was in crisis and that a new order had to be created, if necessary by violence. It is possible to characterize this as a crisis in modernity comparable to the crisis brought about by the French Revolution. The Russian Revolution of 1917 was the most consequential expression of this crisis in modernity, for it led to an entirely different project of modernity to the one begun in 1789. It was not the only such departure from modernity. The intellectual currents of the age presaged the crisis that was to come in 1914 and which led to a new European order in 1919 when the European state system was re-organized by the principles set down in Versailles.

Towards the end of the nineteenth century European thought underwent an anti-modern turn marked by a rejection of the Enlightenment. The promises of the Enlightenment were seen as failures. Against the universality of civilization came a new pessimism about its prospects. Oswald Spengler's influential work, *The Decline of the West*, published in 1918, captured the mood of crisis and pessimism. The theme of the crisis of civilization influenced how Europe might be understood for an age that was also becoming aware that Europe might be falling apart and overshadowed by the United States of America and Russia. In this period we see a clear shift from Grand Narratives of Europe to one of critique and crisis and a search for an alternative idea of Europe. Arnold Toynbee, who produced the most elaborate analysis of world civilizations in his monumental 12-volume *A Study of History*, took up the Spenglerian theme with an explanation of why civilizations decline (Toynbee 1934–63). In his view it was due to a failure in creativity among elites and this was the fate of Western Civilization, which he saw entering a period of decline akin to that of the Roman Empire.

The crisis of civilization theme often assumed a distinction between culture and civilization whereby culture could redeem civilization. Thus civilization was deemed decadent, but European culture could overcome civilization. Nietzsche's critique of the 'malaise of modern European civilization' was written in this mould of thought. He believed modern Europe had lost its way due to collectivist ideologies and what was needed was the creation of a new individualism, whereby 'the Good Europeans' would not rely on elites or values other than what they can create themselves. In *Beyond Good and Evil* in 1886 he wrote of the 'slow emergence of an essentially supranational and nomadic type of man', but saw 'the democratization of Europe' a potential breeding ground for the emergence of tyrants (Nietzsche 1973: 145–4). Yet, Nietzsche saw himself as a European: 'I am a *Doppelgänger*, I have a "second" face in addition to the first one. And perhaps also a third…Even by virtue of my descent I am permitted to look beyond all merely locally, merely nationally conditioned perspectives, it costs me nothing to be a "good European"' (1979: 41). The greatest danger is 'that of losing the voice for the soul of Europe and sinking into a merely nationalistic affair (1973: 159). The spirit to which he appealed is that of a 'transvaluation of all values' which will rescue Europe from corruption by national cultures. The retrieval of the Dionysian elements of the European 'will to power', which is also 'the return of the Greek spirit', is the basis of Nietzsche's idea of Europe, which is more like a state of mind than a political reality. His philosophy was one of radical autonomy that saw within the present the possibility for a new beginning. It was unfortunate that his argument for a regeneration of Europe would become the intellectual basis of the fascist ideology for a new modernity.[1] A generation later Nietzsche, along with other German thinkers, most notably Heidegger, whose relation to Nazism was more direct, became the principal inspiration for French post-structuralist thought, which was to find in the German tradition the sources for the overcoming of the Enlightenment legacy.

Other examples[2] are Carl Schmitt's attempt in a work in 1943 to find a new and authentic European jurisprudence based on the idea of seeking an alternative the *Jus Publicum Europaeum*, which he saw coming to an end; Husserl's examination of what he called the 'crisis of European science' in 1935 and the search for a new kind of philosophy beyond positivism that would be capable of articulating meaning; Heidegger's critique of western philosophy from Plato to the Enlightenment in the name of a new philosophy of 'being' based on the pre-Socratic thinkers who he believed had an alternative to the dominant European tradition; Freud's critique of civilization in works such as *Civilization and its Discontents* in 1930 where civilization is cast in the throes of a death wish and ruled by the destructive forces of the unconsciousness. Max Weber's motif of the 'Iron age', although not specifically a characterization of Europe, was another such image of European modernity having rationalized itself to a point that all meaning had vanished from the social world leaving room only for an inner directed spirituality and individualism to find meaning.

Many of these interpretations of the crisis of European civilization were also critiques of mass society. Bourgeois society was regarded as in decline and the nascent 'mass society', a theme of the era, was seen as lacking authenticity. Hence the appeal to an historical authentic Europe as an alternative to the *status quo*. The idea of Europe could then be a way of expressing hostility to mass society. As Ortega y Gasset (1932: 195) wrote in *The Revolt of the Masses* in 1930–2: 'The world today is suffering a grave demoralization which, amongst other symptoms, manifests itself by an extraordinary rebellion of the masses, and has its origin in the demoralization of Europe.' The idea of Europe came increasingly to reflect the transformation in consciousness and much as in the structure of society and the nature of the state. The appeal to the 'spirit of Europe' or the European mind or consciousness in the early decades of the twentieth century reflect as much a sense of crisis and decline than anything forward looking. In a period in which Catholic thinkers were active, there were several pleas for a conservative organic conception of culture resisting politics, as in Henri Massis's *Defence of the West* in 1928, the writings of T. S. Eliot, Jacques Maritain and Hilaire Belloc who thought that culture could overcome the crisis of civilization, which included for them democracy. Paul Valéry, for instance, in a later work in 1974, 'The Grandeur and Decadence of Europe', saw the crisis to be the descent of high culture into the low culture of mass society. Karl Jaspers (1948) in his book, *The European Spirit*, in 1947 proclaimed in more positive terms the need for the idea of Europe to be associated with freedom (see also Harrington 2012).

The crisis of modernity that culminated in the 1914–18 war was fuelled by the transformation of the social and economic order. Changes in capitalism, in work and in the class structure led to a more volatile situation that could not be managed by the existing structures. Economic policies shifted towards protectionism, a massive increase in industrialization, urbanization, and a trend towards monopoly capitalism and Fordist style production, all transformed the nature of work producing the conditions for a shift in political consciousness around social issues. Modernity appeared now to be in perpetual change and no longer could be made sense of through the categories of the previous century. The emergence of the social sciences and new theoretical insights as in the work of Marx, Durkheim, Weber, Simmel, was the beginning of a fundamental rethinking of the nature of social life, the individual and modernity. Within psychology and philosophy, too, new breakthroughs occurred in the analysis of consciousness, language and the nature of subjectivity, as reflected in Husserl, Heidegger, and

Freud. In literature and the arts the modernist movement and its various offshoots led to a new emphasis on consciousness, time and the possibility of new realities beyond the empirically given. Above all it was the thought of Marx and Freud that encapsulated the search for a new modernity. Both the individual and society henceforth could no longer be conceived in terms of a conception of modernity derived from the old social struggles of bourgeois emancipation. The individual now occupied the centre of stage and in a way that tied subjectivity to the pursuit of new collective goals, many of which involved the creation of a new kind of individual and the reorganization of the relation between state and society. While Marx declared a new goal for collective determination; Freud declared individual emancipation from domination as the goal. In short, the project of the realization of human autonomy was open to new definitions; it was inevitable that some of these would be self-destructive.

In the terms of the conception of modernity outlined in Chapter 8, it is possible to characterize these developments as part of the genesis of a new modernity insofar as they involved the articulation of diverse social imaginaries about how the social world should be organized and how human emancipation could be achieved. They had both a generative and transformative effect on the age in that they opened up new perspectives, which were in turn variously taken up by social, cultural and political movements in the early decades of the twentieth century. These new ways of seeing world in time became the basis of new societal systems, as well as the inspiration of many abortive attempts at social reconstruction. The following sections consider four such projects that can be seen both as attempts to create new models of modernity and entailing conceptions of Europe that had cast a long shadow over the twentieth century.

Western liberal democracy

Democracy has often been associated with the European political heritage and the defining feature of its modernity. The experience of the twentieth century is a sober reminder of both the limits of democracy and of what Michael Mann (2006) has referred to as the 'dark side of democracy', namely their capacity for 'ethnic cleansing' and xenophobic nationalism leading to the persecution and elimination of minorities. The tendency of the democratic nation-state was to equate the demos with a singular notion of the people. Democracies were nation-states and, on the whole, it was the nation-state that was the principle vehicle for the diffusion of nationalism in the twentieth century. The driving force behind liberal democracies was nationalism, especially from 1914 to 1945. Democracy was fragile in many European countries during the first half of the century and it was not until 1990 that all countries made the transition to liberal democracy. The only countries that did not have a break in their democratic tradition during the inter-war period were Britain, Ireland, Finland, Sweden, and Switzerland (Hobsbawm 1994: 111). Even where the constitutional state survived internal or external challenges, as in Britain, nationalism was a powerful force. The modern state, it is often argued, aimed at the homogenization of the population, through policies of assimilation, forcible repatriation, population exchanges or even elimination (Wimmer 2002). There are of course important differences between ethnic cleansing and policies of assimilation. Liberal democracies based on the constitutional state have generally resorted to less extreme measures for the control of their populations. Yet those liberal democracies that have had the longest history of constitutional and democratic government were the ones that presided over colonial empires for much of the short twentieth century and embarked on colonial wars while promoting peace in Europe.

Imperial nationalism was one of the major features of the liberal democracies of Europe until 1945 and continued for several decades later. While 1945 has generally been taken to be the point at which democracy returned to at least Western Europe, it is often forgotten in such conventional accounts that the western liberal democracies continued to rule over colonial territories. India finally became independent in 1947, but Britain continued to rule over what remained of its empire and fought a war against Egypt in 1956 over Nasser's nationalization and closure of the Suez Canal. Britain fought a brutal war in Kenya in the 1950s following the Mau-Mau Rebellion in which thousands were killed and many tortured. France was liberated from German occupation in 1945, but engaged in a war against an uprising against French rule in Madagascar in 1947 and continued to rule over Algeria until 1962 where it fought a war from 1952–62 in which one million were killed. France also fought a war in Vietnam in 1950 at exactly the same time as France opened the way towards European integration with the Schuman Declaration. European integration itself was implicated in the legacy of colonialism since several overseas territories were incorporated into the then EEC in 1958 following the Treaty of Rome, including Algeria, which was an integral part of the French state, French Guyana, Réunion, Martinique, Guadeloupe and the Spanish territories of Melilla and Ceuta (Hansen 2002). British reluctance to join the EEC was not unconnected with the view that membership would be against its colonial interests. However, it has been argued that the project of European integration, when it finally gained momentum, was in part driven by the failure of the British and French to defeat the Egypt and the desire for greater military control over the canal, which was regarded as critical for access to its colonial dominions. The fact that the United States put pressure on Britain to withdraw drove the French more firmly towards a plan for European cooperation (see Hansen 2002; Anderson 1997: 57). Eventually Britain came to see that the EEC might be a substitute for its diminishing empire insofar as economic policy was concerned and too a possible source of international influence. The shadow of war never entirely left Europe, despite the overcoming of internal wars between the European states since 1945. Iraq became the scene of a global war led by the US and the UK in 2003 and despite massive public protests, with the exception of the French and German governments, most EU member states directly, such as Poland, Spain and Italy, or indirectly gave their support to the war. Democracies may no longer go to war with each other, but so far they there is nothing hindering them from going to war with non-democracies on the dubious grounds of enforcing democracy upon them.

Despite the experience of war, both internal warfare and external colonial and neocolonial, liberal democracy from the end of the nineteenth century onwards provided Europe with a means of solving the major challenges produced by modern society. The disastrous experience of war in the twentieth century should not detract from the fact that liberal democracy was the principal model for the realization and organization of modernity in Europe. Peter Wagner (1994: 73–4) has termed this the period of 'organized modernity', roughly from the 1890s to the 1960s when the exit began to a different model of modernity from the nineteenth century's 'restrictive modernity'. In this period European societies achieved a degree of stability and certainty following a long period of uncertainty. This was not finally achieved until the post-Second World War period, since the two world wars undermined the initial move in the direction of organized modernity, understood in Wagner's terms, as state-led projects organized on national lines for the classification of social phenomena. The broad categories of organized modernity were the nation-state and social classes. Liberal democracies thus spearheaded programmes for material allocation and reward through institutions such as education, citizenship, health and welfare reform. These programmes went far beyond the nineteenth century methods of state control for they required more extensive apparatuses of government and had to become more embedded in democracy. Democracy was no longer seen as a product of the free-market, but required state-led pr ogrammes of integration including economic protectionism, technical shifts and changes in the nature of organization management, such as scientific management along the principles of Taylorism. The capital and labour increasingly became incorporated into this organized model of class conflict.

Liberal democracy in the twentieth century brought about a transformation in citizenship in the direction of social citizenship. The notion of social rights, in addition to political and civic rights, as in the famous theory of citizenship of T. H. Marshall (1987) in 1949, was an achievement of the twentieth century, though not specific to liberal democracy, as it was also a feature of the Soviet Union. However in Europe it was more firmly tied to a belief in individual and collective determination and made possible a more expansive degree of democratization, even social citizenship was, in the terms of Marshall, a compensation for the inequalities of capitalism. This was a project shared by the right as much as by the left. Indeed, some of the major drives towards the welfare state were undertaken by the centre right before it discovered neoliberalism. Liberal democracy within the model of organized modernity increasingly became wedded to the normative goal of equality and in theory the vision of an egalitarian society articulated the basic imaginary of the era which was animated by the idea of meritocratic achievement. The various national variants tended towards the egalitarian or the meritocratic ends of the normative spectrum of organized modernity. The societal model that underpinned social citizenship can be characterized as democratic capitalism, namely the integration of capitalism within a basic democratic framework; however this is relevant only to the three decades after 1945, when economic growth sustained a more social kind of capitalism, an expanding welfare state and public sector, full employment, the general acceptance of Keynesian economics and the assumption that capitalism had to be compatible with democracy (Streeck 2011).

Thus, it can be said the one of the major features of the short twentieth century was the transition to organized capitalism. This was orchestrated by the democratic nation-state and essentially in the direction of Fordist style industrialism. It was inevitable that this would not be a smooth transition, just as the transition from feudalism to capitalism or the transition from absolutism to the constitutional state did not produce uniform results. Democracy was weak in much of Southern Europe: in Spain Franco ruled until 1975, Portugal was ruled by a military dictatorship until 1974 and in Greece the colonels ruled from 1967 to 1974. However, in a relatively short space of time, it had become the dominant framework for the organization of state and society in Western Europe. With the transition to democracy in Spain and Portugal by 1980 and the return to democracy in Greece in 1975, liberal democracy within the framework of organized modernity had become stabilized, at least until the late 1970s when its edifice unravelled, though not before the demise of its main alternatives. Until then the nation-state, industrialism, and liberal capitalism formed the basis of the era of organized capitalism.

There was of course nothing specifically European about it. This was a model already in operation in North America. It was a period in which Americanization had become a pervasive force in Europe, due not least to the Marshall Plan for post-war recovery, and when the wider context of the West served as an ideological orientation. The notion of the West competed with the idea of Europe, a development that was not surprising given that for most of this period Europe was confronted by a hostile and anti-western Russia. For this reason the notion of organized modernity could be contrasted to a wider idea of a 'western modernity' as part of the social imaginary of the twentieth century. There was certainly widespread belief in the idea of Europe as part of a wider civilization of the West from 1919 onwards. This was a period when the Anglo-Saxon world was influential right across the world outside the USSR and the Warsaw Pact countries (see Katzenstein 2012).

The communist experiment and its aftermath

The Russian Revolution in October 1917 marked the emergence of one of the major experiments in modernity and can be conceived of as an alternative to western modernity. In some six decades of its existence it reshaped the map of Europe. State socialism was not only a political system, but a project of modernity, which may have been an experiment that failed, but was nonetheless an experiment with the making of a new kind of social and political order that sought its legitimation not in the French Revolution, but in the idea of the Russian Revolution of 1917 (see Arnason 1993, 2000b). Modernity, as argued earlier, does not take a singular western form, but has taken many different forms. Non-western variants of modernity should not be regarded as un- or anti-modern, traditional or aberrations from a universal model. As argued in the previous chapter, the historical regions of Europe all had different models of modernity, albeit variants of a broader European modernity. The Soviet Union is a particularly pertinent example of the plurality of forms of modernity in that it was one of the most radical experiments with modernity and one that cannot be considered a product of pre-modern tradition. The civilizational influences have often been noted in that the Soviet state inherited certain aspects of the Russian imperial state. However, there can be no doubt that 1917 brought about a major rupture with the past and the new state was a radical departure of greater proportions to the rupture of 1789, when part of the *ancien regime* survived or adjusted to the new order.

As an experiment with modernity, the Soviet Union instituted a new societal system in which state and society were to be organized in an entirely new way. The planned economy, rapid industrialization and the authoritarian state took to an extreme what the model referred to as organized modernity set out, namely an ideologically grounded programme for the total reconstruction of state and society. According to Feher, Heller and Markus (1983), the Soviet system, with its command economy, was the carrier of a modernizing trend. This was a self-proclaimed universalism based on growth driven by the two forces of maximization and control (see also Feher 1987: 13). State socialism was thus based on a societal model and a social imaginary. Without the social imaginary of communism such a project probably would not have been possible since it was necessary to create an ideological blueprint and a project of emancipation in order to conceive of the possibility of an alternative society. As Furet (1999: 63) has commented, '[W]hat was so spellbinding about the October Revolution was the affirmation of the role of volition in history and of man's invention of himself – the quintessential image of the autonomy of the democratic individual.' This vision crystallized in the Soviet Union's pursuit of education and science as a means of transmitting its vision of modernity to its citizens. Despite its authoritarianism, it was another and extreme facet of the Enlightenment project of enlisting knowledge for social advancement. However, the course of Soviet history since Stalin set it off on a different trajectory to that of the rest of Europe.

The Marxist Leninist project originated in Western Europe in terms of the genesis of its ideas, but it was implemented in Russia under very different circumstances in a society that had not yet fully emerged out of serfdom; it was also potentially, as propounded by Leon Trotsky, a universal movement of 'permanent revolution', probably with greater appeal in the colonies of Europe and in Asia than in the West. It did not see itself as a specifically European movement, since its aims were universalistic, though for a time the notion of a republican United States of Europe was voiced by the Bolsheviks and had the support of Trotsky (Anderson 2007: 483). However in the end it settled for the model of 'socialism in one country'.

In 1919 there were two competing social imaginaries for the reconstruction of Europe in the aftermath of the collapse of the European empires. One was the Marxist Leninist project; the other was Western Liberal Democracy. The defeat of the Prussian, Austrian Habsburg, Ottoman and Russian Empires, along with the weakening of the British and French overseas empires, was a turning point in European and world history. The Bolshevists, especially Trotsky saw it as the opportunity to create a new modernity according to the principles outlined by Marx and Engels in the 1848 *Communist Manifesto*. The outcome was the creation of the USSR and the eventual extension of its area of influence to the countries of the Warsaw Pact in the aftermath of the Second World War. The western powers that signed the Versailles Treaty in 1919, including the United States of America, had a different vision for Europe, namely the introduction of western liberal democracy for a European of nation-states, a project that had the support of Churchill who believed enigmatically that Britain should be the leader of it without becoming part of it. The League of Nations, founded also at the Paris Peace Conference in 1919, was created to oversee the new international order, which included Russia until 1939 when it was expelled following the offensive against Finland. While the western powers invoked the idea of Europe for the post-1919 world order, the Soviet Union did not and generally saw its project as anti-western and rooted in Russia's own Eurasian tradition. In that sense it had a distinct civilizational dimension to its modernizing impulse. At stake, then, were not just two ideologies, but two competing models of modernity, each having their own variants and imaginaries of emancipation. In the case of communism, the Chinese route since 1949 was the other major one and a reminder of the potential for communism to adapt and endure to become what is still the main alternative to the western liberal democracy.

The Second World War brought a new dimension to the emerging division between Russia and Europe. No European power ever succeeded in defeating Russia, as both Napoleon and Hitler discovered. Both Russian and the West were united in their resolve to defeat Germany. Indeed, without the Red Army the outcome of the Second World War would have been very different, for it was Russia, which also incurred the greatest losses that ultimately secured the first major defeat of Germany following the Battle of Stalingrad in 1943. For the second time in the century Germany was at the centre of the division of Europe. In the race to Berlin, the allied powers did not beat the Russians leading to the compromised division of Germany, which was a prelude to the division of Europe. The Cold War began with the occupation of Central and Eastern Europe by the Soviet Union and the subsequent construction of the Berlin Wall in 1961.

The introduction of state socialism into Central and Eastern Europe in many ways was simply the forced extension of Soviet totalitarian rule on countries whose political heritage and civilizational background was closer to the European model of modernity. The reality was more complicated since there was also considerable domestic support both from elites and the masses for socialism in these countries; in several cases there were innovative attempts to create different models of socialism, the Czechoslovakian experiment to liberalize socialism being the most far reaching one, if also the most short-lived. The Yugoslavian route was also a different path, as was the Hungarian. The fact that state socialism in the end failed does not mean that it was fated to do so or somehow incidental to history or an eastern import and thus not really part of the European legacy. The four decades of state socialism in Central and Eastern Europe should not be seen as a departure from an authentic historical path but as constitutive of modern Europe. Few ideologies, with the exception of religion and occasionally nationalism, were more powerful in commanding obedience and commitment than communism. Though in the final analysis it required barbed wire, terror and armed police to maintain it, and the destruction of political modernity, in both the East and for the myopic left in the West it offered a vision of an alternative society. State socialism achieved a significant degree of social rights for workers as well as gender equality. The experience of making history, as Badiou (2007) has argued, the sense of living in historic times, was a powerful motivating force for many people for whom communism was a utopia that could be realized regardless of the amount of suffering involved. The example of China shows that there was no inherent reason for the Soviet system to fail. Lack of flexibility and adaptability to a non-western context was a factor, but above all it was its incapacity to see through reforms that proved fatal. In the terms of a conception of modernity, it failed because it did not succeed in securing a workable balance between autonomy and power; in the end it eroded the conditions of the possibility of modernity.

The notion of a Cold War between East and West is in many ways a misleading picture of the short twentieth century. Despite a number of potential threats of war, both Russia and the western NATO alliance were reconciled to the existence of each other and the war was, as often claimed, a phony war, especially since Khrushchev's de-escalation of hostility. The real race was to gain as much control over the so-called Third World. The Trotskyist notion of worldwide permanent revolution had long been abandoned and the West saw no real advantage or possibility in bringing about the defeat of the USSR. The industrial war economies of East and West found more uses in the Cold War as the only source of justification that existed for their own hegemonic systems that required high levels of military spending and political control of populations and the suppression of dissent (see Kaldor 1990, 1991). The existence of one provided the conditions of the other with the threat of a politics of what E. P. Thompson (1982) called 'exterminism'.

The end of state socialism following the revolutions in Central and Eastern Europe in 1989 and the subsequent break-up of the USSR in 1991 was an event that was as momentous as 1917. Firstly, the events of 1989 can be regarded as revolutions even if they were not based on fundamentally new ideas or new conceptions on the foundation of political community. They can be considered revolutions due to the transformational consequences for state and society in those countries and due to the global significance the outcomes had for the rest of the world. Secondly, the ideas that led to the collapse of state socialism were of considerable significance despite their short-lived consequences, such as the *Perestroika* (reform) and *Glasnost* (openness) initiated by Gorbachev in 1986 and the civil society movements in Hungary and Poland where the idea of civil society was revived not only for Central and Eastern Europe; in addition there was the earlier movement to create democratic socialism. These movements, in particular the civil society ideas, were also ideas of Europe and of how political modernity should be organized. The outcome was not only transformational for Central and Eastern Europe, but too for the rest of Europe and for the future direction of the European Union. It was not, then, that western modernity was simply embraced and that henceforth liberal democracy triumphed over all competing political ideas – the so-called 'end of history' thesis – but instead a transformation occurred within European political modernity leading to a plurality of outcomes (see also Blokker 2005, 2008).

Fascism, civil war and path to destruction

The first half of the short twentieth century was a period of extremes, on the left communism and on the right fascism; the varieties of liberal democracy and nationalist movements occupied positions in between these extremes of right and left. But it was the extreme position that shaped the century. Fascism can be viewed in a number ways. In Germany it was initially a peculiar mixture of nationalism and socialism, though this became less important with the rapid development of Nazism and anti-Semitism; in Italy fascism, the original birthplace, emerged in the 1920s with Benito Mussolini as the leader of a right wing nationalist movement primarily opposed to the left; in Spain under Francisco Franco an authoritarian ultra-nationalist movement was established that opposed the liberally-oriented Second Republic and various socialist and communist movements operative in it. While Franco parted from the fascist Falange movement and won power by military conquest, the regime he established embodied fascist characteristics despite relying on an anti-modern ideology of legitimation. The German, Italian and Spanish variants were the most important, but many other countries experienced the creation of fascist states, such as Romania and Hungary during the 1930s, and Portugal under the *Estado Novo* movement led by the military dictator Antonio de Oliveira Salazar. Other countries had fascist parties, such as Oswald Mosley's party in Britain in the 1930, which did not gain control of the state. Mussolini was the inspiration for European fascism, which like state socialism, can be viewed as an attempt to create a new political order of modernity. Indeed, it was a rival to the socialist alternative to liberal capitalism. Fascism sought a position that was not mid-way, but an entirely different course. In the 1920s and 1930s, before liberal democracy in the West and state socialism in Russia consolidated, it appeared to many that the options were open and included the fascist alternative, which can be seen as a third variant of modernity in Europe in the twentieth century. Both fascism and communism offered to many intellectuals and political figures a credible alternative to liberal democracy. Those attracted to fascism were generally inspired by the movement's opposition to communism. Despite the obvious similarities in that both were authoritarian one-party political systems, fascism was heralded as the most promising alternative to communism.

Fascist ideology was very much a creation of the twentieth century. It lacked the intellectual and ideological sources that communism and liberal democracy could draw on, since it did not have in any significant sense than its nineteenth century origins, being largely a counter-revolutionary movement that arose in opposition to the political modernity that came with the French Revolution. Fascism was based essentially on an ethnic notion of nationalism and a belief in the organic unity of the nation, but was more than nationalism. Fascism promoted violence as a political philosophy to create a new social and political order; although primarily a statist ideology of national regeneration, it also sought the radical reconstruction of society, often in the image of an idealized past of imperial glory and resentment against the present. For Hitler, German resentment against the Versailles Treaty, which imposed heavy penalties and humiliation on Germany for the First World War, was the driving force; for Mussolini it was the mythology of the Roman Empire and the prospect of a new imperial state; for Franco it was the loss of Spanish dominion in Africa and hatred of communism that drove him and the Falangist movement to repel against the liberal and secular Republic. The centrality of the leader and charismatic authority was a feature of fascist politics as was the symbolism of masculinity and redemptive violence. A characteristic of all fascist movements was the worship of the state as the total expression of the nation. The fusion of society, nation and state defined fascism which sought the revolutionary transformation of society. The notion of totalitarianism strictly speaking derives from the Italian fascists, who used it in the positive sense of the state as the total representation of the nation. The fascist political order is better defined as authoritarian populist, and often embodies aspects of democracy and republicanism. All fascists were opposed to what they regarded as the internal enemies of the nation, who generally were the left, but also the liberal establishment; for Hitler this included the Jews. The place of anti-Semitism in German fascism gave to it a different character since this characteristic became the dominant one in Nazism, while being more or less absent from Spanish and Italian fascism. In all cases, the capacity to gain control of the military and bring about effective mass mobilization ensured the relative success of fascism as a formidable political movement in the twentieth century.

It may be considered to be as much a project launched against modernity than a movement of modernity. However to regard it as anti-modern would be to neglect some of the modernizing dimensions within fascism and some of its core tenets which proclaimed the creation of a new kind of human being, innovative social and economic engineering and the assertion of the autonomy of the nation overall else. It was driven by a peculiar modernist aesthetic that proclaimed new transcendent values that would be realized through violent rebirth and revolution (Griffin 2009). It was closely linked with Futurism, which glorified modernity as a regenerative force. Gentile (2003: 61) has shown that fascist modernism sought to realize a new synthesis between tradition and modernity without renouncing the goals of the nation. Riley (2010) has argued that fascism was a form of 'authoritarian democracy' and was a product of civil society associationism, which did not contrary to de Tocqueville always block despotism, but facilitated it by providing it with a means of anchoring itself in local sources of power. Fascism drew from revolutionary movements and, according to Hobsbawm (1994: 127), owed its support to people who were attracted to its anti-capitalist and anti-oligarchic edge. Its modernity was a different one from that of Enlightenment liberalism. The sources on which it drew, which varied from political romanticism to nationalism and republicanism, were all products of modernity, however much convulsed they became in the fascist imagination, which did not have the same project of emancipation that communism had. As a project of modernity, it was a force of economic and political modernization but without the assertion of freedom and human autonomy. Through the creation of a monolithic state apparatus, it destroyed most of the foundations of modernity and failed in the end to create a viable alternative.

While the principal ideology in fascism was nationalism, it had also a European dimension in terms of its appeal to the idea of Europe, such as Hitler's vision of a 'New Europe'. Fascists proclaimed the essential unity of Europe as both an ideal and a reality. In the case of Hitler this was taken much further than by Franco, who confined his movement to Spain, and Mussolini (see Roseman 2011). It was a supranational ideology that in its extreme version sought the creation of a new European civilization. Hitler and Mussolini believed in the Roman Empire as the model for a new fascist Europe. The One Thousand Year Reich was to be a European order. The inspiration for Hitler was Mussolini who articulated many of these ideas for the revival of the Roman legacy in a new fascist Europe. Despite its lack of philosophical foundations, fascism was embraced to varying degrees by many intellectuals, such as the philosophers Carl Schmitt, Martin Heidegger, Ernst Jünger in Germany, in Italy Gabriele D'Annunzio, in France Charles Maurras and Andre Gide, in Britain the poets T. S. Eliot and Ezra Pound, and in Ireland W. B. Yeats (see Herf 1986).

The fact that fascism ultimately failed does not detract from its importance as one of the major political movements of the twentieth century. It was not confined to Europe, but it was in Europe that it had the greatest impact in the twentieth century. Fascism received its first and most important defeat by Russia and by the western liberal democracies in 1945, but in the case of Portugal and Spain it survived in the form of authoritarian and repressive regimes until the 1970s; until 1974 in Portugal following Salazar's removal from power and in Spain in 1975 following the death of Franco. Indeed, in the case especially of Spain fascism proved to have been a durable system of rule for almost four decades. Franco's restriction of the fascist project to Spain made possible its survival for several decades after the defeat of Hitler and Mussolini. Francoist Spain was arguably more repressive than any of regimes in the Warsaw Pact countries, with over 500,000 people being charged and persecuted by the Political Responsibilities tribunals between 1939 and 1945 and more than 35,000 official executions of republican supporters during the Francoist Terror (Beevor 2006: 450).

The rise of fascism in the 1920s and the challenge it offered to both liberal democracy and the variety of socialist alternatives was not entirely surprising and is a reminder of the vulnerability of democracy and the fragility of modernity, which was not entirely wedded to the democratic state. Parliamentary or liberal democracy was not firmly rooted in the political traditions of many European countries, and in those with relatively strong democratic traditions there was nothing preventing mass mobilization to subvert democracy, which without strong institutional structures can easily take populist forms. For these reasons caution must be exercised in associating Europe with the spirit of democracy. It was a feature of fascism that it gained considerable popular support, though not in all cases democratic legitimation. Since the First World War, in which 8 million died and as many as 13 million due to diseases that followed (Mazower 2000: 80), the reality of violence as part of the nature of the political had become apparent. Violence thus seemed for many as a way to rebuild a new world through creative destruction. Fascism was a product of this climate that also produced support for communism. As mentioned earlier, Badiou's (2007) claim that underlying these radical projects was the sense of living in historic times rather than in the past. In many countries in North Western Europe Hitler offered a vision for the future that was more appealing than what liberal democracy could offer. The notion of submission to Hitler was not entirely objectionable to elements of an elite for whom mass democracy was not particularly attractive and the prospect of Bolshivist victory spreading to Western Europe was equally unappealing. The idea of a total state that controlled economy and society offered elites and masses alike certainty and stability. One of the major attractions for fascism was its social and economic programme of full employment. It was this more than anything that made it more appealing than liberalism (Luebbert 1991: 275).[3]

The reality of such illusions and the collapse of the fascist modernist project was the social and political destruction for Europe in a war that left over 40 million dead, half of whom were civilians. One outcome was that the European legacy would be redefined around the centrality of the persecution and extermination of the European Jews. The Shoah would henceforth be the central event in the twentieth century for Europe and an illustration of Walter Benjamin's claim in his 1940 *Theses on the Philosophy of History* that 'There is no document of civilization that is not also a document of barbarism.' The idea of Europe could no longer be invoked without recognition of the destructive forces that modernity could unleash. The writings of Hannah Arendt, Max Horkheimer and Theodor Adorno, and Zygmunt Bauman, explored the relationship between modernity and the holocaust. Their work offers a perspective on how fascism and in particular the Shoah was not simply a product of a national mentality or a path dependent course of national history determined by the cultural characteristics of the Germans or can be explained by the weakness of German culture to resist the Nazis. In *Eichmann in Jerusalem* in 1963 Arendt (1963) argued that a significant factor was the way in which the Holocaust had been bureaucratized by the state leading to the removal of individual responsibility. In *The Dialectic of Enlightenment* in 1944 Adorno and Horkheimer (1979) placed the holocaust in the context of the instrumental rationalism within western civilization. Bauman (1989) in *Modernity and the Holocaust* argued in a similar vein that the holocaust was an expression of modern instrumental rationality and made possible by a self-perpetuating technological and administrative apparatus which led to the growing distance between action and responsibility. Of the many genocides of the twentieth century within Europe – those of Stalin, Franco, the Turkish massacre of the Armenians – the singularity of the Nazi's genocide of the Jews stands out from all others. In this case genocide was the primary aim of the state; rather than being a means to an end, it was an end itself. Virtually every aspect of the state was involved in a programme of extermination that had no rational aim while paradoxically requiring complex rational organization to achieve its objective.

The conflict of rival projects of modernity – between liberal democracy, communism and fascism – led to major divisions within Europe in the short twentieth century. These divisions are also illustrated by the prevalence of civil wars from 1919 to 1949, the major ones being the Russian Civil War 1917–22, the Finnish Civil War in 1918, the Spanish Civil War 1936–9, the Greek Civil War 1943–4. Others, such as the Irish Civil War in 1922–3 emerged out of a split within the nationalist movement and did not involve major ideological disputes. These wars, which could be seen as part of a wider European civil war, were more than national conflicts, but entailed conflicts over the nature of political modernity; all arose following revolutionary changes leading to different conceptions of nationhood and statehood and in all cases the international context was important (see Casanova 2000; Minehan 2006). The Russian Civil War – the most fateful of all civil wars – resulted in the victory of the Bolshevists over the White Army, but in the other examples, it was the counter-revolutionary right that won. In the case of Finnish Civil War the Red Guards won, but within weeks the Grand Duchy of Finland was invaded by Germany leading to their flight to Russia. The Spanish Civil War is undoubtedly the most vivid example of the conflict of modernities.

The attack on the Second Republic, created following the collapse of the dictatorship of Primo de Rivera in 1931, by Francisco Franco's African Army in 1936 was a struggle between a democratic state, in which socialist and anarchist groups sought to reform, and a fascist counter-revolutionary movement that sought a return to an autocratic Catholic national state that could command total obedience from society. For the fascists, the Republic represented the worst excesses of secularism and socialism, which from 1936 took a more radical egalitarian direction, as recalled by George Orwell in *Homage to Cataluña* in 1938. The struggle took on a wider European dimension with the involvement of the International Brigade in support of the communists. Franco's victory, aided by Nazi Germany, over the republicans and communists led to the creation of an authoritarian state that survived until Franco's death in 1975. The Spanish Civil War was the scene of some of the clash of most radical political projects in modernity and involved an unprecedented level of violence, which continued long after the end of the civil war.

The project of European integration

The post-Second World project of European integration was a product of the experience of war and the expression of a desire by a new generation of visionary political leaders for a new beginning. It had pre-1945 antecedents in various pan-European movements and proposals for federalism on a European level, but these rarely progressed much beyond the level of ideas and ultimately could not compete with nationalism and the appeal of the nation-state as the crucible for modernity. The circumstances of both the 1939–45 war and the subsequent division of Europe between East and West was the context for European integration, a project that ran parallel to the building of socialist republics in the Warsaw Pact countries. It can be viewed from the perspective of modernity as an alternative course, albeit with uncertain outcomes, to the three main models of modernity that clashed over the preceding four decades. European integration was in the first instance born of the desire to overcome the destruction that fascism had brought to Europe, which in its original goal was a bid to unite the economies of Germany and France, countries that had gone to war three times since 1870. Indeed, even after 1945 there were still fears, especially in France of a potential Nazi revival in Germany. But it also a product of the emerging Cold War and designed to integrate Western Europe against the spectre of communism and Soviet expansion. Finally it was a project aimed at the transnationalization of the European nation-state.

As a project of modernity, European integration was less radical than the two major modernities it sought to overcome, its inception was not entirely opposed to the democratic constitutional nation-state, but in time it sought the transformation of political community and the creation of a new kind of polity. For these reasons it can be considered a project of modernity, even if it did not seek the overcoming of liberal democracy in the way the earlier competitors did. The post-1945 period was marked by a movement away from nationalism in the recognition of the need for a new international normative order. The foundation of the United Nations in 1945, the creation of UNESCO also in that year, the Declaration of Human Rights in 1948 and the establishment of a new legal principle of 'crimes against humanity' were the most prominent signs of the emergence of a new cosmopolitan imaginary that sought to embed the pursuit of national interests in a normative order beyond the nation-state. Initially this did not seek anything more than to avoid war and in the case of Europe to bring about lasting peace between countries whose entire economies and national psyches had been organized for war for several decades. Such an ambition required the diminution of nationalism and a commitment to international cooperation. The experience with fascism had corrupted nationalism, not least due to the fact of very widespread collaboration and a political legacy of violence that few countries could overcome through a myth of fascist resistance. Resistance to fascism, where it occurred, was often weak and due to the extent of collaboration and rival interpretations of who resisted and in what cause, it was not always a viable basis for a new beginning, except in the case of Britain where it played a major role in national identity. The result was widespread amnesia, as Judt (2005) has documented and which was probably necessary for post-war recovery. European integration in contrast held out the promise of a new beginning and it had the advantage that it was without memory. As a memoryless project, it was not burdened by the legacy of the past. This may have proved to be in the long run a weakness, but in the decade or so after 1945 it had advantages for those wanting to escape from history. Peace and prosperity were attractive goals to be achieved by moderate social engineering in an age when state intervention and planning was regarded as normal (Schrag 2013).

The escape from history was incomplete, for as discussed earlier while within Europe the conditions for a lasting peace were secured, with only the serious prospect of war being between Greece (which joined in 1981) and Turkey over the question of Cyprus.[4] However, while France and Germany appeared to bury the past, war was not far from the horizon. In the early decades of European integration the exit from imperialism had begun, but it was a slow one: France embarked on a war in Indochina in 1950, the year the French foreign minister, Robert Schumann opened the path to European integration, and between 1954 and 1962 France was involved in a bloody war in Algeria in which one million were killed. Both France and Britain went to war against Egypt in 1956 (see Hansen 2002). As discussed earlier, Britain fought a brutal war in Kenya in 1956 following the Mau-Mau Rebellion and in 1971 Britain fought a war in Northern Ireland in which there was a suspension of civil liberties and a state of exception created. Such developments are an important reminder of the importance of situating the history of European integration in a global context, and as illustrated by these examples of European self-deception, one that can be situated in the longer perspective of Europe's colonial history (see also Böröcz 2010).

The political circumstances in any case had changed. Europe was effectively reduced to Western Europe and economically, politically and militarily weakened, it aligned itself with the USA at the same time as pursuing its own uncertain course, which was also one for many of its members of the exit from colonization. From the Schumann

Declaration in 1950, which made the first step, to the Treaty of Rome in 1957, which created the European Economic Community – renamed the European Community in 1993 – European integration began with the objective of economic integration, though the higher political aim of securing peace was for some the ultimate aim. The economic rationale earned it the opposition of the left, especially in Britain, while it enjoyed almost total support from the centre right as it was seen in the interests of capitalism. European integration was mostly advocated by the right and the European idea since the early twentieth century was often invoked in the context of opposition to both Americanization and to communism. However, by the 1960s the project of European integration had won general support by the centre left and centre right. The EEC was founded to make possible four kinds of mobility, those of capital, labour, services and goods. While it acquired complex legal competences in the course of its history and evolved a range of other policy objectives, these remained the primary objectives of European integration on which there was widespread consensus. Created to make possible market integration and to remove obstacles against internal trade within Europe, European integration was initially based on a model of negative integration in terms of the removal of barriers to integration rather than the creation of new structures.

This is not to say positive proposals for integration did not exist. The post-war project was also inspired by the New Deal in the United States and generally by Keynesianism, giving to it an additional social dimension. In the first phase of European integration from 1950 to the Single European Act in 1986 political integration was kept low key with the emphasis on economic cooperation; from 1986 positive modes of integration became more prominent, with greater coordination in order to achieve the objective of what was now to be a single market. With this move towards enhanced integration, the question of political integration became an issue. However, European integration was never designed to supplant the nation-state, being largely a market-based conception of Europe. Yet the logic of European integration was such that the creation of a common market necessitated ever greater political coordination, which led not entirely inexorably but steadily in the direction of political unity. However, the normative nature of European unity was never clear and remained contested. This was in part due to the nature of its design which did not set constitutional restrictions on its future course. On the one side, the proponents of Euro-Federalism sought the progressive transnationalization of the nation-state through the strengthening of the European level of supranational governance; while others saw in the project of European integration nothing more than inter-governmental cooperation with sovereignty remaining on the level of the nation-state.

Academic debates in political science and the new field of European Studies highlighted two perspectives, the largely realist school that argued the nation-state was the primary driver of integration, which could remain only inter-governmental; and the neo-functionalist school that saw a deeper level of inter-dependence at work and which was more than international cooperation. The nature of the process was such that it was able to foster two competing interpretations of its direction: the vision of a Europe of nations – with the emphasis on European diversity – and a federal Europe – where the aspiration would be unity. Underlying these positions is a difference of view as to whether the EU is driven by normative goals – which are more evident in the second position – or by functional requirements, including political bargaining between the nation-states. These interpretations fed into the political process influencing its direction, which in effect was multi-directional. European integration was not one, but several kinds of integration. It also won the support of the social democratic left who saw in it the prospect of greater egalitarianism and, for a generation who still believed in it, progress.

Prior to the so-called deepening of European integration from 1993 with the Maastricht Treaty, the aspiration to unity was tolerable within certain limits. With the consolidation of the EEC in the 1970s there was a widely felt need for a stronger political identity in order to give it greater weight in the world. So long as it remained a European inter-state regulative order this was not important, but with its growing importance the leaders of the EEC saw the need for greater political unity and with this an identity that went beyond the general desire of the post-war period for peace and prosperity, which as Schrag (2013) has argued was frequently invoked in appeals to the common European good in this period. Thus, in 1973 the Copenhagen Declaration of European Identity pronounced a strong notion of a European political identity founded on 'common values and principles' that provide a basis for the pursuit of a 'united Europe'. It referred to a 'common European civilization' based on a 'common heritage' and 'converging ways of life': 'The diversity of cultures within the framework of common European civilization, the attachment to common values and principles, the increasing convergence of attitudes of life, the awareness of having specific interests in common and the determination to take part in the construction of a united Europe, all give the European identity its originality and its own dynamism.' Notions of unity, such as this one, were of course sufficiently vague and lacking in political substance.

With the enlargement of the original EEC to include Denmark, Britain and Ireland in 1973, Greece in 1981, and in 1986 Spain and Portugal the EEC included most of the core western countries except Norway and Switzerland, which never joined. There was only one secession: Greenland in 1985, after having secured Home Rule from its former colonial master Denmark, voted to leave. The EEC could claim to represent Western Europe. The prospect of further enlargement – beyond the inclusion of Austria, Sweden and Finland, who joined in 1995 – was not a serious prospect given the objective and apparently permanent existence of the Iron Curtain. The EEC constructed a political identity for Europe based on the values of liberty and grand narratives that celebrated the received values of European civilization. The appeal to Christianity as the basis of the European heritage along with the capitalist free market gave additional weight to the emerging idea that European unity will blossom from national diversity.

Interpretations of European history that stressed unity, and often a grand narrative of unity, played an important part of the construction of a European identity. Historians such as Jean-Baptiste Duroselle (1990), Henrik Brugmans (1966, 1987), Christopher Dawson (1932) and, and author of voluminous writings, Hugh Seton-Watson are among the most notable Europeanists who wrote explicitly pro-Europeanist histories of Europe. In both academic and in popular writings as well as in European policy a discursive shift occurred towards the idea of a common European identity that has progressively unfolded in history revealing a unity of purpose that finally takes a political form with the foundation of the EU. Such grand narratives were often attempts to offer counter-rival accounts. Thus Karl Jaspers (1948) argued for a vision of the European heritage in terms of a notion of freedom and diversity and which was conceived in opposition to the pessimistic Spenglerian theory of the decline of the West and notions of European decadence. Other forward looking grand narratives include the writings of the Swiss philosopher of history, Daniel de Rougement (1965, 1966), who sought to articulate a notion of a common European identity that was intended to be an alternative to purely market notions of European integration. The short twentieth century was a period in which such grand narratives were the most common ways in which the European heritage was conceived as an alternative to national histories. However, these grand narratives of the

European heritage were largely modest, if not naïve, attempts to provide alternative approaches to history and politics and to articulate a different conception of modernity beyond that of liberal democracy and the free market.

It is easy to be dismissive of such grandiose concepts of heritage, especially today in light of more critical theories of culture and post-Foucauldian approaches to history that stress rupture over continuity, but to conclude that if there is no grand narrative there can be no meaningful sense of a European heritage is unwarranted and something like a post-universalistic and post-western conception of the European heritage is possible. In recent years there has been considerable questioning of some of the assumptions that lay behind the grand narratives. The idea of Western Civilization as a singular and universalistic condition with a capital 'C' has been mostly refuted. Such developments have been linked to reconsiderations of the ontological assumptions of the values on which civilizations are supposed to be based. It is becoming increasingly difficult to see these values as primordial or as given. The political Left since the 1980s has attacked the very idea of civilization, which has generally been seen as a legitimation of colonialism. Post-modernism, which emerged out of this Left discourse, and post-colonial thought declared not only the obsolescence of modernity but also the civilization that modernity was based on. The idea of a 'western canon', based on the core texts of 'Western Civilization' came increasingly under fire since the late 1970s. As a result of the discrediting of a universalistic idea of European civilization, the idea of culture moved into the fore bringing about a concern with identity as an attribute of individuals. With this was born the notion of Europeans as bearers of European identity, leading to a new concern in the 1990s within European policy-making around cultural issues, such as the European Capitals of Culture programme, Erasmus exchange programmes, European research, and a communication policy, the idea of a European citizenship (Sassatelli 2009; Schrag 2013). In this, the concern increasingly shifted from a focus on unity to one of diversity. Since its creation in 1974, the Eurobarometer was to be an instrument to determine, and at the same time influence, the degrees to which Europeans were becoming European.

As a project of modernity, European integration was part of what was earlier referred to, following Wagner, as organized modernity; it was conceived in programmatic terms as a major attempt at inter-state coordination and became more and more a transformative project in the economic, social and political realms of all countries. Whether or not it can be seen as a Europe of nations or as a transnational polity, on balance it is evident that European integration has become a rival to a conception of modernity based on national models of liberal democracy. Notwithstanding the realist interpretation of the EU as a project of states or the modified position that the EU is nothing more than a coordinating mechanism, it is evident that five decades of Europeanization have produced one of the most significant experiments in statehood and in the articulation of normative ideas of post-national political community. One of the key aspects of this is the question of sovereignty and the prospect of the EU – re-named as such in 2009 replacing the term EC – being a post-sovereign political order in which sovereignty is shared between national and European levels of governance. The shift from a conception of the state in terms of government to governance in the 1980s was too an expression of a wider change in the nature of the state which increasingly is seen as an order of governance in which different political actors are involved, the political parties, civil society organizations, various governmental and non-governmental organizations, as well as the increasingly important transnational level. However, in the period under discussion there never was anything like a European social imaginary with a clear articulation of political community. As an institutional project based on treaties, the creation of an identity was limited to slogans such as 'ever greater union' or a unity to come.

The short twentieth century ends with the revolutions of 1989 and the break-up of the Cold War system in the following two years. This was also the end of the period of organized modernity when the impact of globalization was felt everywhere with the return of uncertainty and the search for a new framework to re-establish stability. Thus the end of the short twentieth century did not lead to the 'end of ideology', for instead of liberal democracy becoming the unquestioned normative alternative to the death of state socialism, a plethora of alternatives were opened up leading to new visions of modernity. The post-1989 world order and its implications for the idea of Europe will be explored in the next chapter.

Part III
The Present and its Discontents

12
Europe since 1989: Nationalism, Cosmopolitanism and Globalization

The revolutions in Central and Eastern Europe and the subsequent transformation of those countries occurred at much the same time as the project of European integration entered into a new phase with the Maastricht Treaty in 1992. On the one side, the countries of the Warsaw Pact underwent a transition to capitalism and to democracy, as well as in many cases a transition to national autonomy, while on the other side in Western Europe the EU was embarking on a major project of enhanced integration (see Offe 1997). Alongside these processes, other changes took place all of which had implications for the making of political community: German unification in 1991, which led to a shift in the balance of power in Europe towards Germany; the emergence of a global multi-polar world; changes resulting in major technological developments in information technology; the steady rise of the new centres of economic and political power, most notably China and India and later Brazil; the growing significance of global civil society; the end of apartheid in South Africa by 1994.

For all these reasons, the post-1989 period marked the beginning of a new era in the history of Europe producing new ideas of Europe and a major shift in modernity towards the inclusion of the post-national dimension. In this shift cosmopolitan tendencies can be found alongside contrary ones, which include nationalism, racism and xenophobia, and neoliberalism. The dynamic of European integration moved in the direction of greater constitutionalization and transnationalism, while on the other side, partly in reaction but also an outcome of 1989, the nation-state was re-asserted and the period saw a revival of nationalism. The result of this was not only multiple directions of travel for Europe, but greater uncertainty since the different understandings of political community mutually challenged each

245

other. Unlike in 1957 with the Treaty of Rome and the beginnings of European integration there is an absence of consensus on the future of Europe. The political challenge in the formative years of European integration was largely an intra-European one and required commitment to cooperation. The present situation is characterized by the more complex environment of a globalized economy and the apparent systemic failure of the model of integration that had been created hitherto.

Towards a post-Western Europe

The revolutions in Central and Eastern Europe in 1989–90 were unpredictable, but had huge implications for all of Europe, which in the subsequent two decades underwent major social and political transformation. The events of 1989 mark the end of the era shaped by the First and Second World Wars. Old states disappeared – Yugoslavia and Czechoslovakia – and new ones were created, suggesting a possible return to a 'Europe of Nations'. The unification of Germany in 1991 was one of the most significant events to arise out of the collapse of the Warsaw Pact countries. Despite the rise of nationalism in the period and the Yugoslavian civil war, it would be a simplification of the tremendous changes that occurred to see only the return to the nation-state or the assertion of national sovereignty. One of the possible alternative narratives of European identity that has emerged in the wake of 1989 in opposition to the more familiar western narrative of Europe is what one could call a 'post-Western Europe', in which the emphasis is on a recognition of the cultural plurality and pluri-civilizational background of Europe.[1] This notion includes recognition of Europe's participation in a wider West, but it is now increasingly recognized that western civilization is one among other foundational sources of Europe. Moreover, a post-western understanding of Europe requires critical reflection of the notion of the West, entailing its relativization, and the acknowledgement of Europe being the result of encounters with other European, peripheral cultures and civilizations. This is not to say that such a pluralist understanding of Europe is now a dominant vision, or that it is the only alternative to the now less prominent idea of Europe as part of a more or less homogeneous wider western world.

Significant other definitions of European identity often include a more essentialistic and homogeneous understanding. Such an identity is in most cases understood as more distinctly European rather than western, and Europe is supposed to represent the authentic core of western civilization as such. In political terms, this is then often translated into a need for protection of such a core identity (as in the idea of a 'Fortress Europe'). Other narratives take a more open, but nevertheless distinct, understanding of Europe as their core idea, in which they sometimes find Europe's significant Other in the United States.

The end of the Cold War has often been hailed as a triumph of the West, in particular in the sense of its liberal understanding of democracy and a market model of capitalism, suggesting that we are all western now, or soon will be, while others have claimed more durable, civilizational divides that prevent western culture from spreading easily. However such accounts of the post-1989 context as leading to either an ultimate triumph of the West, or to its contrary, i.e., the clash of a western with other civilizations, is difficult to uphold when considering the complex evolutions of, and contestation over, European identity. In contrast to such claims, it has become increasingly clear since the diminishing significance of the East-West divide that European identity is not entirely based in the acceptance of a western ideology of liberal politics and free markets. In this, a search for a specifically European identity has increasingly come to the fore.

The necessity of such a quest for a specific European identity is stimulated even more by an increasingly complex situation in Europe, in which there is no clear significant Other anymore. It can be argued that the old East-West divide is difficult to uphold, now that a good part of former 'Eastern Europe' is part of the European Union, while the eastern borders of that same union are difficult to define, in the light of pending membership of some other Eastern European countries, and evolving forms of cooperation between East and West through the eastern dimension of the European Neighbourhood Policy. It can also be argued to a degree that Islam has become the substitute for the Communist East and that the post-September 11th context has confirmed this trend. However, such a view simplifies a more complicated situation in which positive relations with the Islamic world are also present along with negative ones. Negative images do not in any case translate easily into a new European identity, which has become considerably pluralized (see Chapter 5).

The disappearance of the Cold War bifurcation of East and West, and the subsequent rapprochement between Eastern and Western Europe, has made an exclusive identification of Europe with the modernist integration project of the early EU (as it had emerged in the 1950s), and by implication with the West and western modernity as such, increasingly difficult. The idea of a reunification of Europe, or as Gorbachev put it in a speech in Strasbourg in 1989, a 'common European home', entails a shift away from a larger western identity to an identity with a more specifically European substance. The enlargement of the EU brought to the fore various historical traditions and legacies that do not fit in a strictly western reading of Europe, even if they are not necessarily incompatible with it. As a result in the post-1989 period European identity has been open to various interpretations and has been essentially contested. The events of 1989 have clearly had important consequences for the European integration project and the idea of a European identity. At least three issues are significant in this.

Firstly, as noted, 1989 meant the collapse of an East-West distinction as providing an almost unchallenged identity marker for both East and West, thereby putting any proposal for Europe as part of the West to the test. The collapse of the Cold War constellation meant not so much the triumph of western liberal democracy and the unquestioned continuation of the subordination of Europe to the idea of the West. Rather, the end of the binary division of the world into East and West in important ways unravelled the older grounding of Western Europe in a wider notion of the West and opened up new directions that only in limited ways pointed to a continuation, or in some cases a reinvigoration, of a US-dominated idea of the West. The disappearance of the rigid division between East and West in Europe meant that ways were now open to search for new identity markers, which has also meant a return to older ideas (such as in the case of the re-emergence of Islam as Europe's main significant Other). Europe as the West has thus not disappeared, but is now more critically challenged by alternative narratives of Europe. The new context for Europe is a more global one than a more narrowly circumscribed one defined by the United States and Russia.

Second, 1989 made possible the political, economic, and cultural reunification of Europe, i.e., the inclusion of the former East into the Western European integration project, thereby strengthening any proposal for a more distinct European identity, neither necessarily fully coinciding with (the older notion of) the West, nor with a notion of Western Europe. The unification of Eastern and Western Europe in the form of the inclusion of the former into the integration project of the latter has often been taken to entail a mere fortification of the Western European integration project, as expressed in the notion 'return to Europe'. From the point of view of the old, Western European member states, the eastern enlargement of the European project often did not seem to imply much more than the further diffusion of this normality, and the confirmation of the unviable nature of what had arguably been the most successful alternative interpretation of modernity, i.e., communism, and any alternative, for that matter. At the same time, it seems undeniable that the reunification of Europe has induced the calls for more distinctly European notions of European identity, i.e., as different from a wider notion of the West and a narrow understanding of a West-European identity.

Third, with the enlargement of the EU there was a prominent (re-)emergence of forms of cultural and civilizational diversity, rendering more difficult any proposal for homogeneous forms of a European identity, particularly in an explicitly western understanding. Those promoting a more or less homogeneous understanding of European identity – either grounded in a wider notion of the West or not – have now to reckon with the cultural diversity that the reunification of East and West brought with it. The predominant grounding of the European project in the Western European states that mostly identified themselves with Christianity, the Roman and Greek heritages, and the hallmarks of western modernity was now to be reconciled with re-emerging awareness of different traditions. The Western European project did not reflect Slavic culture, nor eastern Orthodoxy or Islam, and was not designed to deal with the complex legacies of state socialism.

In sum, Europe emerged out of the short twentieth century with the task of fundamentally redefining political modernity. The post-Second World War consensus no longer existed and the global context had entirely changed by 2001 when a new security order emerged and in the same period a tremendous transformation in capitalism took place. The three key dynamics that would shape the future of Europe are: pluralization, integration, and globalization. The pluralization of European societies in culture and politics; the emergence of new processes of integration led by the EU; and the diverse and often catastrophic impact of global forces including global capitalism and global wars (the latter will be discussed in the next chapter).

Europeanization and the transformation of political community

How should we understand political community in Europe today? Has nationalism attained the upper-hand over cosmopolitanism? Has the social project of European modernity been strengthened or abandoned? It has been widely recognized that there have been major shifts in collective identity and political culture more generally in Europe since 1989 due not only to the impact of Europeanization, but because of the wider context of globalization and global politics as well as within Europe of developments that are not specifically linked to the EU, which is not the only initiator of change. Political community can no longer be discussed as a nationally specific matter, but it is also not entirely in the hands of EU's transnationalizing institutions. The shape of European post-national political community is far from clear. Proponents of cosmopolitan politics argue for the existence of political community beyond the nation-state, while their critics dismiss such visions as either undesirable or unrealistic. Nationalism has clearly become a potent force in most European countries and increasingly the national interest is asserting itself over the European level of policy-making. Despite this assertion of the national interest, the European Union has advanced its transformative project and the logic of Europeanization has increasingly worked towards a kind of post-sovereign political order that has brought about a significant trans-formation of both the institutional framework as well as the political imaginary that lies at the core of every society's political self-understanding. But this is at best incomplete and uncertain. Since 1989 nationalism has emerged as a significant challenge for most countries whose models of national identity have paradoxically incorporated significant reflexivity and post-national consciousness, even though it is undeniably the case that these cultural models fall short of what might be termed cosmopolitan.

The European transnationalization of the nation-state is one of the most significant developments in the wider transformation of political community. Since the Single European Act in 1987, there has been a steady growth in the power of the EU with more and more power in the hands of non-elected politicians. It is also one of the most con-tested political experiments since its implications for democracy are unclear. Democracy developed within the bounds of the nation-state and in the view of any attempt to erode the foundations of the nation-state will have adverse implications for democracy. However, the EU is primarily a development of the state system and was never intended to be an instrument of democratization. Democracy was never mentioned in the founding treaties. But in transforming in fundamental ways the nature of the nation-state it would inevitably have implications for democratization.

The main institutions of the EU – the EC, the Council of Ministers, the European Central Bank – have acquired significant powers over their member states; other institutions such as the European Parliament and the European Court of Justice have also considerable influence, if on a smaller scale. The result of the huge expansion in the scale of European institution-building, as discussed in the previous chapter, is post-sovereignty, with sovereignty shared between national and European levels of governance. The national level still retains sovereignty over the traditional areas of the state, namely a monopoly over the means of violence: powers of taxation and of defence. It also retains control over social policy and migration, though with the Schengen Agreement since 1995 control over borders has been much diminished. However, this does not lead simply to a two-tier political system with the European level of governance impacting on the national level bringing about its transformation. The EU is no longer an instrument for the member states to pursue their interests, as Milward (1982) claimed in a classic work, *The European Rescue of the Nation-State*. The member states have surrendered their veto powers in several arenas of policy-making. However, the political form of the EU is not simply a super-national state or merely a regulatory order. Eriksen (2009: 418) has referred to the constitutionalization of the treaty system which has led to the transformation of the EU from an inter-state governmental organization into a quasi-federal legal system based on precepts of higher legal constitutionalization. As far as democracy is concerned, the EU is closer to what Colin Crouch (2004) calls, 'post-democracy', since it relies only on indirect democratic legitimation via the nation-states.

The relation between the EU and nations is a reflexive one as opposed to being a hierarchical one and consequently nations, generally, are 'Europeanized' such that Europe is not an external entity, but integral to its member state. This is the case even where Euroscepticism is predominant. Indeed, one could argue Norway has been Europeanized more than some of the recent member states and in many ways Switzerland is the most 'European' of countries. Depending on what indicators one chooses – identities or institutional arrangements or lifestyles and mobility – the UK may be more European than countries that often see themselves as European. So European identity can be conceived of as an Europeanization of identities, that is an internal transformation of national identities. The result is a pluralization of Europe into different national projects.

For some time now there is growing recognition that the European project cannot be conceived entirely within the conceptual lens of political science of European integration, which has traditionally operated with an empirically reductive concept of integration drawn directly from the EU's own discourse. This has failed to discern different logics of integration that may be at work. For this reason many theorists have preferred the term Europeanization in order to avoid the difficulties associated with the term European integration, for instance, the notion of European integration as an EU-led project that integrates diverse units into a new framework, the notion that integration leads to societal convergence or the notion that underlying the cultural diversity is a logic of unity (see Delanty and Rumford 2005). Instead, Europeanization should be seen as multi-directional and extending to include a broader reach of the political beyond the level of government. From the perspective of a notion of governance rather than government, a different interpretation of the state and the transformation of political community can be arrived at.

The EU is a framework of governance in which different groups, be they nations or regional governments, civil society actors, pursue different goals. It offers opportunities for social actors to pursue their interests, often through lobbying and in opposition to the EU itself. Like all states, it is not an homogenous entity, but a complex ensemble of different interests and includes within it political contestation. The EU is itself only one political actor in a more complex political field involving elites, masses, the media, and technocrats of all kinds. From being an elite driven project, European integration is now a more pluralized framework and operates within a context of the structural weakness of the state and a more globalized capitalist system over which its regulatory order does not control.

As theorists of the state have argued in recent years, the state can no longer be understood as separable from civil society, which has expanded the sphere of the political (Johnson 2011; Sassen 2008, 2009). The result is the incompleteness of democracy with a perpetual challenge to democratic legitimation (Trenz and Eder 2004). This, then, is one of the paradoxes of Europeanization: while the growth of non-democratic organs of governance on the EU level appears to undermine representative democracy and has not put in place alternative forms of democratic organization, it has widened the scope of the political in numerous ways, in particular through the domain of the law and the incorporation of huge areas of civil society into the sphere of the state. States operate in an increasingly complex field of rights and which they do not entirely control, as Benhabib (2011) has argued.

The EU has produced a political system that has the capacity to bring about change in areas of social and political life that it does not itself control. This is due not least to the fact that Europeanization is a medium of legal communication and one that very often is open-ended in terms of consequences, but in many areas, such as monetary policies, the capacity of social actors at national levels is very limited. The various measures the EU created to redress the democratic deficit – the European Parliament and the notion of a European citizenship – have not solved the basic problem of European integration, namely democratic legitimation. Instead its legitimacy is mostly derived from its capacity to be an effective problem-solving apparatus; moreover, as has often been noted, EU the sphere of activities it generally deals with are of secondary importance for national politics and thus do not normally require direct democratic support. So long as the EU delivers on its promise, legitimacy is not in question, but when problems of coordination happen, the result is a withdrawal in legitimacy and an increase in demands for democratic legitimation. This is now the case since the financial crisis of the Euro-zone area and the apparent failure of the EU to provide a framework for long-term stability.

The size of the EU – with currently 27 members and a population of 500 million – has certainly not helped. The enlargement of the EU to include much of Central and Eastern Europe, as is generally recognized, has worked to undermine the prospects of extending democracy to the transnational level. The new member countries found in EU membership a means of asserting national autonomy, many for the first time. The rapid inclusion of a large number of very small countries also imposed a further burden on democratic representation leading to a return to a Europe of nations as far as the democratic state is concerned. However, the conflict between 'widening' and 'deepening' did not lead to a change in the course of European integration, for the same period saw the increased expansion in the institutional edifice of the EU at the expense of democratization.

The two decades or so since 1989 thus saw the expansion of the EU to include more or less the entire Warsaw Pact countries and the Baltic Republics, with plans for the inclusion of the former Yugoslavian countries, and concomitantly the construction of a novel type of state system. The result of such processes of integration was not the founding of a new polity, such as a constitutional republican state, as envisaged by Habermas. Yet something had changed on the level of the state, which had been considerably transnationalized. Political community entered a post-national phase in which there were gains and losses for democracy. The gains the EU was responsible for are often ignored: increased social rights for workers and for women and children, anti-discriminatory legislation, increased rights of mobility, environmental policies, progressive initiatives in research and in education, the incorporation of human rights into national legislation. Although falling considerably short of a social project, these were not insignificant gains for social citizenship and a social conception of democracy.

Given the open nature of European integration and the wider context of uncertainty and contingency, caution should be exercised in any prognosis of the where the EU is heading. In view of the current situation – to be discussed in more detail in the next chapter with respect to social and economic questions – it may be suggested that the transnationalization of the European nation-state has reached its limits as far as major societal change is concerned. The foreseeable future will probably see a greater emphasis on multiple levels of memberships, with more opt-out conditions, and too a multi-speed EU, or at least a two-speed Europe. The logic of constitutionalization will undoubtedly continue its present course, though it is unlikely that Joschka Fischer's call in 2000 for a European Constitution will become a reality. The nation-states of Europe have been for ever changed as a result of the EU and now exist in what is best termed a post-national polity rather than a supranational state, for the national state has not disappeared, however much it has been changed. The problem of democratic legitimation is a problem not only for the EU, but is also a challenge for nation-states, which also have to operate in an increasingly globalized context that presents perpetual challenges for democracy. Looking at the EU from the broader perspective of modernity, the major development undoubtedly has been the transition to a post-national political community. The European experiment can be seen as one step in the direction of a more general shift towards cosmopolitan forms of governance worldwide. The inevitable short-comings of European integration should be viewed in a broader context of the need everywhere for transnational cooperation and global solutions. Much of the debate has been confused by a concern with the loss of national sovereignty. This however fails to distinguish popular sovereignty from state sovereignty, for the loss or erosion of the latter does not necessarily mean the loss of the former.[2] The existence of state sovereignty in itself does not in any case guarantee popular sovereignty and it may be the case that post-national forms of governance may be more effective in affirming popular sovereignty. One of the major challenges for the EU is to enhance popular sovereignty and, what such kinds of sovereignty have traditionally fostered, social citizenship.

The pluralization of political community

Rather than look for a new post-national or cosmopolitan European identity beyond the nation, a more fruitful line of inquiry is to examine the national imaginary or the cultural model of the nation, which is fragmented and the site of diverse orientations around the figure of the migrant. So the answer to the question whether post-national political community can become cosmopolitan and democratic will largely depend on how national models of society develop. Post-1989 nationalism has not foreclosed the possibility of a cosmopolitan Europe, for both nationalism and cosmopolitanism are intertwined elements in the cultural models of all societies today since these concern problems of the definition of self and other. If this is correct, then, the conclusion is that the resurgence of nationalism since 1989 has not fundamentally altered the situation, despite the comfortable illusion of security that national sovereignty cultivates. A second conclusion must be that the chances for a more cosmopolitan Europe do not lie in transcending the nation as many cosmopolitan theorists claim, but in introducing greater reflexivity into it and extending the national horizon in the direction of a socially inclusive model of political community.

Europeanization – in the sense of the transnationalization of the European nation-state and the project of European integration – has brought about a major transformation of political community, producing for instance a European public sphere (Eder 2006a; Trenz and Eder 2004). However, it has not brought about the end of national identity and its replacement by a post-national or cosmopolitan European identity. This is the wrong way to look at the situation. While it can be argued that the EU has created a European political identity, this has not replaced national identities, but sits alongside national identities to varying degrees of tension. A different perspective, informed by the above reasoning, is that what has come about is a pluralization of European identity as opposed to a supranational EU-based political identity. The extent of the latter is limited and stands in contrast to a more pervasive Europeanization of identity. The impetus here is not the impact of an EU political identity, in the sense of more and more people identifying with the EU, but rather the influence of a European cultural model. The cultural model of Europe is less an identity construct than a medium of self-interpretation that is mostly worked out in a huge variety of public spheres (Fossum and Schlesinger 2007). The consolidation of a European symbolic culture based on the EU is not the only dimension of cultural Europeanization. The symbols of the EU – the blue and yellow flag, anthem, currency icons, burgundy passport covers, pink driving licences etc – have in most cases been absorbed into national cultures and are not in a significance sense the basis of collective identities.

European identity, understood in this sense of a European cultural model, is more diluted than the concept of identity normally suggests, but it is also open to more and thus involves more interpretations. The result is that there is more, not less, contestation as to the meaning of Europe as well as greater uncertainty as to what it consists. For this reason, again, what is at work here is not an identity that is progressively assimilated or adopted by different people, but the internal transformation of identities. National culture and national identities are themselves highly diverse and there is often greater internal differences within a given country than between countries. It is not the case of a coherent national identity resisting a dominant European identity any more than it is a matter of national identity being replaced by a new European identity. The main form that European identity takes is, as argued earlier, a Europeanization of national identity, that is an internal transformation of national identity.

The logic of cultural Europeanization is not unlike the logic of political Europeanization. The EU does not erode the nation-state, as argued earlier, but brings about its transformation through a reflexive relation between the national and the European levels. The nation-state is not disappearing, but is being reconfigured. Nations are adjusting to the EU rather than being rendered obsolete. Sovereignty, like identity, has been relativized and pluralized today in the European polity. The notion of a network state, as proposed by Castells (1996), is one way of understanding the European political order which is connected by nodes rather than to a centre in which sovereignty resides. The simple fact in all of this is that Europe is in nations as much as it is outside then (see also Stråth 2002). Europeanization is not a project of unity or of integration as such and, it follows from this, that the absence of unity is not itself a reason to conclude that Europeanization has failed. The logic of Europeanization is rather one of internal transformation arising out of the reflexive relation between the national and the

European whereby each acts on the other. The relation is reflexive as opposed to being one of co-existence, since each level acts on the other (Eriksen 2005, 2009). This is particularly evident in the case of the European citizenship, which is a phenomenon that makes sense only when seen as a Europeanization of national citizenship. The European space has now become a part of the national space as a result of trade, tourism, consumption. In addition to these factors, it is also the case that European societies are more and more connected for reasons that have nothing to do with the EU, for instance due to wider processes of globalization. The result of these transversal processes is inter-societal interpenetration and a greater hybridized modern Europe, as suggested by Balibar's (2003) notion of Europe as a borderland.

If Europeanization is not only a project of integration, what then is it? Integration does not simply produce a unified framework in which differences disappear. Integration in complex societies proceeds through processes of differentiation, including pluralization, and reflexive adaptation where by one unit undergoes change in response to interaction with another unit. In other words, Europeanization cannot be understood in terms of a state or a EU-led project integrating diverse societies into a unified framework. Indeed, in recent years it has been increasingly recognized that Europeanization has become a kind of unity in diversity (Sassatelli 2009). The nation has been the instrument by which it has achieved its goals. It follows from this that the nation is not going to disappear, but rather will change its form and it is inevitable that as it does so it will become more and more implicated in a certain discourse of Europeanization.

A European cultural model is taking shape around debates within the public culture about Europe. Europe is thus not prior to the political but is expressed in debates that are often about national identity. All of identity and culture has witnessed a loss in markers of certainty; it has become fragmented and fluid. This situation has led to a greater emphasis on a communicative conception of culture and it is in this that we can see the signs of a European cultural model in which Europe becomes a frame of reference that exists alongside and in tension with national frames. The notion of a cultural model is then different from a shared collective identity; it operates at a more general level as a cultural process that cuts across collective identities and is best exhibited in zones of interaction, as in the debates in the public culture. As a cultural model, Europe is not a clearly defined political project as in a collective identity that distinguishes between self and other, but is marked by contradictions, ambivalences and paradoxes.

The European post-sovereign polity has contributed to the formation of a highly pluralized post-national culture. This post-national culture is one in which a diversity of cultural models and collective identities compete with each other. It is post-national culture in the sense that national identity is no longer the dominant or only collective identity that shapes the cultural model of nations and Europe more generally. National societies have been pluralized and their political identity has been challenged by different cultural models. The paradox in this is that cultural Europeanization can lead to more nationalism, not less; but it can also lead to a greater role for European identity, the significance of which is not always apparent from opinion research of personal identifications with Europe.

Making sense of post-1989 nationalism

Against this background, the nature and significance of nationalism can be discussed. Despite the rise of nationalism since 1989, there has been a considerable Europeanization of national community and cosmopolitan trends are in evidence. Post-1989 nationalism is largely anti-systemic and an expression of the crisis in social justice and solidarity than the product of long-run national identities. It is a defensive kind of nationalism that seeks to assert closure to political community, where cosmopolitanism seeks to establish openness. Nevertheless, despite this difference, nationalism and cosmopolitanism are not mutually exclusive. Both, too, can be seen as different responses to the current situation of political community.

However, nationalism is not a single phenomenon, but takes a huge variety of forms and many expressions are not compatible with cosmopolitanism or post-national trends. The term is best reserved for organized movements, as opposed to being over-generalized to include all aspects of national culture and identity. We can distinguish three main types in Europe today. First, there is nationalism in the sense of the assertion of national identity by mainstream parties and which feeds into notions of nationality by the general population. This is connected to perceptions of national interest and is generally an expression of nationalism that is represented by various national elites. For the greater part, this kind of nationalism has been compatible with Europeanization and both are frequently mutually reinforcing. In this case nationalism is just one register of meaning within a wider political culture. It can take political, cultural and civic forms depending on whether its objectives and rational are the pursuit of the national interest on the international level, cultural discourses of national belonging, or issues of rights and citizenship.

Second, there is the growth in populist nationalist parties, who generally pursue a single issue – such as anti-EU or anti-migration – which is supposed to reflect the national interest usually against an external threat. In this case, nationalism can be related to an organized political movement, which is generally a marginal party, and a strong as opposed to a weak notion of collective identity that is hostile to plurality. The majority of such parties have shifted from being racist to anti-migration parties and operate to varying degrees on the margins of the political system. Such parties are characterized by cultural authoritarianism, anti-establishment populism, and combine in different ways anti-capitalism and anti-European Union.

Third, related to the second, but distinct, from it is the rise of extreme nationalist movements, who mostly operate outside the official political system. Such movements represent a more extreme version of nationalism than populist parties and take a huge variety of forms, ranging from right-wing youth culture to neo-fascist movements. With some exceptions, their capacity to dominate mainstream politics is limited and they generally operate on the margins of the political system.

Since 1989 there has been an overall increase in all these expressions of nationalism. With respect to the first there has been a certain normalization of nationalism within the mainstream political culture. In the case of Germany, for instance, there has been a tendency towards a 'normalization' of national identity and which can be seen as a development that has come in the wake of the unification of the two German states. It is also an outcome of generational change as the memory of the Second World War becomes increasingly a historical memory as opposed to a collective memory for the generation who lived through it or whose parents were born in the period. Historical memories are nonetheless powerful sources of national identity, as is exemplified in the case of the UK, where what Paul Gilroy (2005) terms an imperial nostalgia still defines the dominant national culture. In Central and Eastern Europe the tendency has been towards an increase in nationalism, since for many countries the post-1989 context has been one of national autonomy. Democratization and European integration opened up for many countries the prospects of national sovereignty with the inevitable result that national identity was considerably strengthened.

One of the significant developments was the decline in some of the traditional forms of nationalist mobilization and the increase in new forms. Since 1989 there has been a steady decline in the older violent secessionist nationalist movements that were a feature of the earlier decades of the twentieth century. In Northern Ireland the Irish Republican Army (IRA) formally abandoned the armed struggle in 1994, leading to the Good Friday Peace Agreement in 1998, and in 2011 the Basque nationalist organization ETA announced a definitive ceasefire. However, peaceful and constitutionally-based secessionist movements still exist and have acquired a new impetus fired by the financial crisis, with the most pertinent examples being Catalan, Flemish and Scottish nationalist movements for independence. There has also been a general rise in populist parties and neo-fascist political movements. However it would be a mistake to see these forms of nationalism as a product of post-communist transition. While it is certainly the case that such movements are now widely present in Central and Eastern Europe, they are also a feature of several Western European countries, in particular the smaller social democratic countries. The major cleavages in Europe are not between East and West, but between different nationalist and post-nationalist groups. It is arguably the case that the differences between East and West are not significantly different than the differences within western countries (Laitin 2002).

Post-1989 populist nationalism can be characterized as having the following characteristics. It is primarily anti-systemic and derives its support less from ideology than from widespread disenchantment with the political mainstream. It is anti-systemic in the sense of being anti-statist and anti-mainstream. The rise of the British National Party (BNP) is a relevant example of this. The party derives its main support from the white working class in areas with high unemployment in the north of England and stands for anti-immigration and the view that migrants are not British and should be deported. Following a controversial BBC Question-Time TV debate in October 2009, when the leader, Nick Griffin, was openly challenged for his statements, he made the claim that he was a victim of 'a lynch mob' audience drawn from a city that had been 'ethnically cleansed' and was 'no longer British'. The BNP leader's reasoning illustrates the anti-mainstream tendency of right-wing populist nationalism that the establishment and political class have lost touch with people. As primarily anti-systemic, and anti-elites, such parties do not have a project of their own. They are rather defensive and reactive. A recent and potent example is the rise of the New Dawn movement in Greece.

A second characteristic of post-1989 nationalism as reflected in right-wing populism and in extreme neo-fascist style movements is that their capacity to articulate a national identity is limited. Nationalism is not based on a stable set of values, but is highly volatile and fragmented. There are major differences between the three kinds of nationalism as noted above and their projects are intermeshed with diverse strategies. The nationalism of the mainstream and the nationalism of right-wing populist movements and parties is clearly in tension and many of these movements are highly marginalized and regarded with suspicion by the mainstream. Opposed to the EU, many of their leaders, as for example Le Pen, have been themselves Members of European Parliament (MEPs). Europe and nationalism are thus mixed in a constantly changing process of repositioning in which local, national and transnational circumstances intersect (see Holmes 2006). Much of post-1989 nationalism is played out in the European space of political communication. As noted above, the European space has become part of all national imaginaries. An illustration of this was the position of the Irish electorate on the Lisbon Treaty in June 2008 while in the second referendum in October 2009 they voted yes. The no vote can be explained as the expression of a certain national confidence that had come from economic prosperity and the embracing of market liberalism and a certain Americanization that was in tension with Europeanization. It was also – as was the case in May 2005 in France and the Netherlands – the outcome of diverse groups, ranging, in the Irish case, from the authoritarian right and the extreme left as well as nationalist parties, who all found in a no vote the means of pursuing their different projects. In all cases anti-systemic tendencies were in evidence. The yes vote in 2009 was the outcome of different circumstances and which can be easily explained as the result of the economic crisis and the perception that the EU was after all important. In this instance a re-Europeanization of national identity can be evidenced.

A third characteristic of post-1989 nationalism is that much of it is fuelled by social fragmentation, which has driven a politics of insecurity. A particular characteristic of populist nationalism is a discourse of insecurity around issues of social justice. With many of these parties moving from out-right racist movements to anti-immigration parties, a discursive shift has taken place in their political rhetoric whereby cultural and social issues are given central place. Moreover, such parties also seek to offer political justifications for their slogans. Thus hostility to migrants is justified not in racial terms *per se*, but in terms of protecting jobs; opposition to the EU is not primarily in the name of national purity, but is driven by an association of Europe with

262 Formations of European Modernity

neoliberal market liberalization. This tendency to capture the middle ground is also in line with the trend towards constitutionalization in secessionist nationalism. The relative success of populist nationalism can be attributed to its capacity to operate within the democratic process. This belies the earlier point above that nationalism is not always easily separated from other identities and values and nationalist rhetoric is often a trope for diverse issues. It may be suggested that the success of nationalism is due in large part to its ability to permeate the symbolic and moral fabric of political community.

This is also true of the relation between nationalism and cosmopolitanism. Nationalism and cosmopolitanism may ultimately be incompatible, but from the perspective of a critical cosmopolitanism the category of the nation should be seen in terms of a conflicting constellation of cultural and political forces. These include nationalist movements as well as post-national orientations including cosmopolitanism. European identity is thus a field of interacting cultural and political orientations and identities. Nationalism and cosmopolitanism are not mutually exclusive, except in highly normative terms or where two extreme positions are contrasted. Cosmopolitanism is present in degrees as opposed to a condition that is either present or absent. One is more or less cosmopolitanism and similarly one is more or less local (see Roudemetof 2005). This position differs, then, from, for example, the Habermasian post-national position or, in a different key, from Beck and Grande's argument for a cosmopolitan Europe (2007), in that it does not require the overcoming of the nation-state. A critical cosmopolitan approach, in contrast, would see European post-nationalism in more interactive terms as formed out of the interaction of multiple publics and chiefly realized through nations. It follows from this that one of the challenges for a cosmopolitical European project is to capture and transform the ground of the national imaginary, rather than seeking to overcome it.

Nationalism and cosmopolitanism are embroiled in each other in many ways. In normative terms there is no essential contradiction between value commitments to a nation or to a wider sphere of community, in particular since both rarely present a challenge to each other and mostly tend to pertain to different contexts. As argued above, European transnationalization has mostly been realized through nations and most nations today have been transformed as a result of European integration. Nations adjust to the EU, rather than simply being eroded, and as they do so they are themselves transnationalized. While nationalist movements and nationalism more generally understood as a collective identity has expressed hostility to Europe and to cosmopolitan values, it is important to see that collective identities do not fully capture the entire space of cultural signification.

Europe as a social space and a space of identities

To begin some clarity needs to be established on the vexed question of European identity as a meaningful term. The notion of European identity has been increasingly used as an alternative to what was once referred to as the 'idea of Europe' or the even more elusive 'spirit of European'. The literature on it is now vast. It gained currency due to the recent interest in identity and cultural politics in social and political science, on the one side, and on the other, as a result of a clear shift in the project of European integration from a concern exclusively with the integration of states and markets to the integration of peoples and cultures. But systemic forms of integration did not lead directly to social integration and we do not have neatly formed European identities, however understood. Identity cannot so easily replace integration and it has been criticized for being an elite-led view of Europeanization, a construction imposed by elites on people (Shore 2000).

The notion of a European identity can mean at least three different things and clarity needs to be established on which sense is being used. Much of the debate on Europe identity commits basic category errors, looking for evidence of one type by using evidence of another, or simply conflating the different levels into a single undifferentiated category of 'European identity'.

First, European identity can refer to processes of identification by which individuals identify with a referent that can be designated 'Europe'. To speak of European identities is to refer to the personal identities of individuals. Such identities are often vague in their European self-understanding. Europe may be the EU or it may be an undefined imaginary that lacks political content (Bruter 2005). As with many identities, a European identity may co-exist alongside other identities, since individuals generally have more than one identity. Moreover, as has been often noted in identity research, identities are not static, but in continuous formation and, too, are often ambivalent and contested (Calhoun 1994; Jenkins 1996; Melucci 1996; Woodward 1997). This all applies to European identities as a form of identification (and for clarity it is probably best to speak of European identifications). There is considerable empirical research demonstrating the existence of European identification at least as a secondary identity that complements national and regional identities (Herrmann et al 2004; Risse 2010). In this instance what is interesting is the combination of identities in the sense of the relation of the components than the replacement of one by another.

Second, European identity can exist in a somewhat more coherent form as a collective identity of a collective actor, such as an organization or movement. For instance, to an extent it can be argued the EU and EU-oriented organizations have a collective identity that is specifically European. However, this does not mean that it underpins the identities of individuals. Such identities may be strong or weak. Unlike personal identities, collective identities are by their nature more likely to be singular (movements generally have one aim which defines their identity). The EU may have an evolving political identity, but this is quite a separate matter from the question of whether Europeans have a European identity or identity with the EU. The institutional complexity of the European and that fact that it operates through the language of law has made it difficult for the EU to articulate an identity. There is clear evidence of a progressive expansion in European institutions and organizations many of which have identities that can be described as European. But of course there is also considerable contestation as to the identity of the EU (is it a post-national polity, a supranational federation, a Europe of Nations etc?). Nonetheless after some five decades of consolidation, its symbols, legal competence and the Euro currency, the EU has become a reality in the lives of many people. In this sense it is possible to speak of the symbolic and juridical reality of the EU and its collective identity.

Third, quite separate from personal and collective identities are wider and much more fuzzier societal identities, such as the identities of whole national societies or of Europe broadly defined. Societies have identities – often called national identities – but unlike collective identities such identities are less clear-cut and more likely to be ambivalent, contested, and multiple. Whether or not the EU has a political collective identity does not mean that this is the equivalent of a European identity. It is on this level that one can speak of the European heritage or the cultural legacy of Europe. It may be more useful to refer to this as the level of European cultural identity, as opposed to the question of collective identity, since any notion of a collective presupposes a specific actor and there is no such actor as a 'European people'. European identity in this broader civilizational sense can be discussed in much the same terms as national identity can be, that is as a societal identity it is not a coherent identity or one that is neatly encapsulated in personal or collective identities. In this sense European identity can perhaps be better understood as a consciousness – the broad awareness of a cultural heritage – rather than something that can be understood in social psychological terms.

Three further points can be made. As with many identity constructions, European identity in all these senses is not static but changing. This raises the question of how and where we find it as an ever-changing and contested category. As a cultural and social activity, identity can be understood variously as performative, as a discourse or as a narrative depending on the theoretical position adopted; it is expressed in concrete form in communication and in cultural acts of meaning. If anything of a general nature can be said about identity, it is that it is about self-interpretation: an identity is the expression of how an individual or group sees itself; it is a specific kind of self-understanding (Kantner 2006). It follows from this that it involves re-interpretations and a relation to both the past and future. Generally identities tell something of the history or memory of the subject, its project, and its present situation in the world.

Rather than look for identity as an underlying structure of meaning or a holistic system or a cultural system, it is best evidenced in specific sites of communication. In the case of European identity one such place to look for it is in debates about Europe. In this view, then, Europe is not an objective entity – a geographical or political structure that confers meaning that it becomes the basis of identities – but a cultural construction that is variable and contingent on specific circumstances. So, a concrete methodological implication is that European identity is expressed in debates about Europe.

The second point is that European identity can be conceived of as an Europeanization of identities. A national identity, for instance, emerged out of a process of nationalization of regional identities or in some cases of other collective or societal identities. But as an identity it evolved through the transformation of other identities. It is in much the same way that European identity can be understood, less of an alternative kind of identity that one that variously co-exists or operates through local, regional and national identities (see Risse 2010). As argued earlier, Europeanization is best understood as a transformation of nations rather than entirely as a supranational process. Thus many national identities have found within the project of European integration the means of advancing their interests, but too of re-orienting their self-understanding (Spain, Germany and Ireland being three clear examples). This is not to deny that there are also projects that seek to advance a conception of Europe that is hostile to nations, though many of these do use the language of Europeanization to advance their cause and are, as in the case of the UK, embroiled within Europe.

It follows from this, finally, that European identity exists on different levels and is expressed less in zero sum terms than in degrees, that is to say it is always more or less present (though this is an empirical matter).

A methodological point is that identity is best seen in contexts of interaction as opposed to being reduced to the mind-sets of individuals or the objective structures of cultural systems of meaning or societies. Looking at identity, on any of the three levels referred to above, requires an interactive perspective: identity takes shape in contexts of interaction, be they the interactions of individuals, collectivities, or of large-scale entities such as societies. Viewed in such terms, the objective reality of identity lies then in contexts of interaction where one group seeks to advance its interests or assert its self-interpretation. Moreover, as indicated, given the discursive and contested nature of, in this case, European identity, the most interesting sites are debates and controversies. Indeed, it has often been noted that identity arises most strikingly in moments of crisis.

The prospects of cosmopolitanism for Europe

What does it mean to say that Europe has become more cosmopolitan or that there is a European cosmopolitanism emerging? Various authors have argued that Europeanization can be understood in cosmopolitan terms (Beck and Grande 2007; Rumford 2007; Robertson and Krossa 2012). By this is usually meant that the internal national borders have been eroded and that Europe has acquired the features of a political community or polity. In this view, Europe is a post-national polity. This position has been advanced by Habermas (2001a, 2001b, 2003, 2006) and Eriksen (2005) who have argued that the European Union needs to take up the republican political legacy of Europe and that European identity is best defined in terms of citizenship rights, constitutionalism and democracy which henceforth must be conceived of in European terms than in national terms. In this view, it remains unclear whether the resulting polity will have no national structures of organization. Benhabib (2008) has drawn attention to cosmopolitan norms of justice embedded in the juridical structure of the EU. Another view, put forward by Beck and Grande (2007) is that Europe has become cosmopolitan due both to the alleged obsolescence of the nation-state and to the transnationalization of European societies. Others have argued that many characteristics of the EU can be seen as being either cosmopolitan or bearing meanings and implications that point in a cosmopolitan direction (Roche 2010). It is certainly the case that the collective identity of the EU embodies cosmopolitan ideas, such as the general concern with human rights or the pursuit of a unity in diversity (Sassatelli 2009). It has also been argued in numerous studies of European identities that there is increasing evidence of a European dimension to identities and an increase in the number of people with primary and especially in secondary European identity (Hermann et al 2004; Pichler 2008; Risse 2010). These latter arguments are not generally related to cosmopolitanism and in others cosmopolitanism is roughly equated with post-national trends or with transnationalism.

A general assumption also in the literature is that cosmopolitanism is a European political legacy that has become somehow more real today to the alleged transnationalization of the nation-state and the emergence of a more Europeanized society. This opens up the charge of Eurocentrism, the complaint that such a perspective ignores, on the one side, anti-cosmopolitan trends within Europe and, on the other side, it ignores similar developments in other parts of the world (Delanty and He 2008).

These various positions to do not amount to an overall cosmopolitan interpretation and many claims or assumptions can be disputed or relativized. For instance, as in Habermas's writings, the intimation that European political modernity is somehow superior to that of other parts of the world because of the relative advancement of the constitutional nation-state and democratization. It is also not clear if cosmopolitanism is simply another term for transnational cooperation, internationalization, or for the blurring of borders and thus where the line separating a cosmopolitan polity and a supranational one is not clear. Is Europe a new normative power that has lessons to teach the rest of the world or is it a global power itself competing alongside other major players?

It would not be difficult to argue that as far as identities are concerned European identities – in the sense of the identities of individuals – are quite weak and can be related only to those who have benefited from European integration, a point made by Neil Fligstein (2008). However this is quite substantial and confirms a general hypothesis that support for EU, and generally support for European integration, is correlated with education and younger people rather than with nationality. This suggests that the clash of values is more likely to be generational than territorial.

But not all are so sanguine about the prospects of a European identity. Adrian Favell (2008) has argued that Europeans who travel within Europe and who would normally be considered to be the bearers of European identity lack belief in Europe where they did not find the new freedoms they were looking for or found that they came at a considerable cost. The implication of Favell's thesis is that identity, in particular anything like a common identity, cannot be easily built out of freedom of movement.

The current situation today with major economic and financial crisis suggests that European solidarity and identity is limited. The project of European integration was after all built on the basis of economic recovery and growth. It was this prosperity that made possible political integration. The current crisis – post-September 11 2001 and post-2008 – has occurred just as cultural integration gained a new momentum. It is likely to be severely abated. Systemic forms of integration – the basis of the Europe project – do not generate social integration, which is a prerequisite for the formation of political community and the expansion of cosmopolitan identities. However understood, identities need some affective bonds of commonality. When put to the test, as in referenda, the trend has been towards popular questioning if not outright rejection of the EU, as in the initial Danish rejection of the Maastricht Treaty in 1992, the initial Irish rejection of Lisbon in 2008 and the French and Dutch no votes in 2005.

For those in search of a European cosmopolitan identity there may not be much to find comfort in. But it should be considered that all kinds of identity find themselves in much the same predicament: the bonds of commonality are weak in a globalized and crisis ridden world. This is true too of national identities, which are also embattled and now more defensive than forward looking. However in any case most national identities have been considerably Europeanized, one of the paradoxes of European integration. So the kinds of national identity in existence today are not always to be reduced to atavistic nationalism. What then can be claimed for a cosmopolitan interpretation of Europe? In what sense can it be reasonably argued that Europe is cosmopolitan?

A critical cosmopolitan perspective

As used here, cosmopolitanism is primarily a critical term and refers to a number of characteristics which are variously present in contemporary societies. A critical cosmopolitan approach emphasizes the inherently critical undertaking in a cosmopolitanism analysis; it is focused on the identification of how normative principles are interpreted and appropriated by social actors and the processes and mechanisms by which these enter into institutional forms. Much of the project of European integration is imbued with the language of cosmopolitanism, but this does not make Europe cosmopolitan, since cosmopolitan norms are often not realized in practice or are partially realized and, moreover, they are interpreted differently by various social actors. This is easily illustrated by the example of human rights. Today we live in age of rights and of democracy, but not everyone understands rights and democracy in the same way.

Critical cosmopolitanism is also about the identification of the transformative potentials within the present. Cosmopolitanism itself is a transformative condition that seeks the transformation of the present in light of universalistic ideas or principles of inclusion by which the horizons of the political community are broadened. In this respect it is possible to associate support for Europe – and more generally support for European identification – with cosmopolitan values, understood as a general support for human rights and the extension of solidarity beyond the nation-state.

Cosmopolitanism is based on an imaginary, in much the same way that nations are based on imaginary communities. However in the case of a cosmopolitan form of life the imaginary would be based on the imagined reflexive counterfactual principle of cosmopolitanism. The cosmopolitan imagination is not unreal, but is part of the self-understanding of contemporary society and of many social actors. What needs to be understood is how this imaginary becomes part of the cognitive structures of contemporary society and how, as a consequence, it enters into the self-understanding of social actors.

Two mechanisms by which this might be understood are learning and interaction. As a learning process, cosmopolitanism is expressed in cognitive shifts, for instance in seeing the world in abstract terms or reflexively from the perspective of others. In this sense it is possible that the cosmopolitan ethic of, what Habermas (2006: 76) has called, a 'solidarity among strangers' becomes a reality. So here the reality in question is more cognitive than symbolic or juridical and it is to be found in modes of communication. A second mechanism is through processes of interaction.

One of the most important characteristics that can be called cosmopolitan are those that arise from the interactions or encounters between culturally different groups who interpret themselves in a new light as a result of the encounter. The assumption for cosmopolitanism is that a process of learning occurs as a result of one group encountering another. Without this it is meaningless to speak of cosmopolitanism. Cosmopolitanism is thus not a matter of multi-cultural co-existence, but of the mutual interaction and learning from cultural diversity. However, it is not only a question of the interaction of diverse cultures, but relevant too are other groups that are not specifically culturally defined, such as corporations, governments, activists and various kinds of international organizations.

To speak of European identity as cosmopolitan must therefore involve a shift in self-understanding and not simply identification with a transnational order. It is undoubtedly the case that in the course of European history the project of European integration was a major case of societal learning insofar as it was a project to bring about lasting peace within Europe and in moving beyond a politics based exclusively on the national interest. It is possible that its capacity for sustained learning has reached its limits and that as a consequence there is now the real possibility of blockages leading to regression. If this is correct, then, a cosmopolitan European politics will have to find alternative forms of expression beyond the current institutional channels.

An additional characteristic of cosmopolitanism is its transformative potential and the creation of alternative spaces. These need not be always in opposition to the nation-state or in the service of transnational orders. Indeed, they may be quite local and nationally specific. It needs also to be considered that not all aspects of Europeanization are cosmopolitan and that national politics may often be more cosmopolitan.

Critical cosmopolitanism as a political imaginary is best seen as a critique of both nationalism and of globalization: it rejects the limits of nationalism without embracing the capitalist vision of a globalized world. Unfortunately, for now, it would appear that the main opposition to globalization is not coming from the bearers of cosmopolitan values, but from the defenders of nation-states. The result is the false comfort of the nation-state.

Cosmopolitanism is a process, not an end state. So the question is not whether Europe is cosmopolitan or not but of the degree to which it is. This can be answered only by reference to concrete instances and will require a differentiated analysis, for it is possible that cosmopolitanism is more in evidence in a particular sphere (for example, in legislation on rights or in education) than in an entire society.

An adequate view of Europe as cosmopolitan will have to go beyond an internal European cosmopolitanism to a consideration of the external aspect. Most discussions of Europe and cosmopolitanism consider only the internal erosion of borders within the EU and the order of governance it has created. Rarely if ever is attention given to its relation with the external world. There is much to suggest that while borders are being eroded within the EU there is a new frontier being established between the EU and the rest of the world.

The question what is Europe today is not easily answered by reference to the political project of European integration. This project itself is currently at a turning point in its some 50-year history. Many of its older objectives have now been achieved and it is unlikely the transnationalization of the European nation-state will continue its course. The present situation is one of uncertainty. The reality of Europe is not simply a post-national polity, but a more complex field of practices, memories, narratives, forms of symbolic representation, imaginaries; it is a field of exchange and of dialogue, as it is too of contestation. The result is that Europe is open up for new definitions. Cosmopolitan trends are part of this multiplicity as is nationalism, but one should not draw the conclusion that the project of European integration leads inexorably to cosmopolitanism. As argued, it may indeed be the case that the EU has fostered anti-cosmopolitanism more than cosmopolitanism.

A critical cosmopolitan approach does not assert that Europe is cosmopolitan, but offers a critical angle on how Europe may or may not be cosmopolitanism. In this view, cosmopolitanism emerges in contexts of interaction and of learning from cultural interaction through the reflexive application of normative ideas and new cognitive frameworks. A cosmopolitan approach thus seeks to identify such spaces and sites of both self and societal transformation. The critical cosmopolitan approach thus distinguishes itself from the post-national position in that it is not primarily about the transnationalization of the nation-state or the creation of a new kind of polity. It does not seek the completion of a project of integration, but the exploration of exchange, dialogue and the space of the encounter. It may be the case that a deeper level of democracy is at stake in this venture which is about the transformation of the meaning of the political. Democracy, after all, is based on the space of relations between citizens and as such it is the logic of the encounter that defines the space of the political. This has been the basic insight in much of modern political philosophy, as in specifically the writings of Hannah Arendt and more recently in approaches as different as those of Bonnie Honnig (2001) and Claude Lefort (1989).

A broader perspective of the project of European integration should view it as part of the wider transformation of the political of which the transnationalization of Europe's 27 states is only one part. The wider context is the 193 states that comprise the United Nations. The future of democracy will not be settled within Europe alone, but will require dialogue on an international level rather than a simple transfer of sovereignty from the national to the European. Just as national domestic politics fails to deliver democratic outcomes, it is now apparent that EU level domestic politics needs to be expanded in a more cosmopolitan direction. The global economic crisis since 2008, which has been particularly damaging for Europe, is evidence of the need for a new direction beyond the existing model of statist integration. The stakes in this are as much about democracy as about capitalism.

13

Age of Austerity: Contradictions of Capitalism and Democracy

The project of European integration has been marked by many shifts in its more than five decade history. This history can of course be viewed as having a much longer span since the foundation of the EU. The general dominant tendency both in academic discussion and in popular opinion has been to see in that project a progressive movement towards unity and alongside this an emphasis on continuity over discontinuity. The EU has certainly become embedded in its member states, which have been irreversibly transformed as a result of European integration, and the various enlargements of the EU can be seen as a continuation of a project of systemic integration that began in the post-Second World War period. The crisis that escalated in 2012, with the prospect of Greece's exit from the EU at least as a possible development, suggests a shift of a different nature and the possibility of a rupture that calls into question a narrative of continuity and one of progressive integration based upon the institutionalization of solidarity.

Any account of the European project today will have to consider the reality of a deep crisis, the possible failure of the project of European integration, and an emerging new political landscape marked by a certain fragmentation of Europe between what could be characterized as Old and New Europe, North and South, a two or multi-tier Europe, or a generational clash between Eurosceptics and Europhiles and different forms of political mobilization (see for example Habermas 2009, 2012; Fligstein 2008; Taras 2009). This chapter is an exploration of the extent to which it can be said that the European project has entered a new stage in which a more divided Europe is emerging in the context of an age of austerity.[1] The aim is to offer a framework to conceptualize the current situation of Europe, which can be variously described as divided along national lines or according to some other geopolitical or socio-cultural category such as creditor and debtor countries. Until the post-2008 context it could plausibly be argued that the popular opposition to the EU – such as that expressed in no votes on EU treaties, as in 2005, 2008 – was not decisive and an expression of the application of democratic legitimacy to something that previously was seen as lying outside the domain of democratic political community. However, the current situation suggests a deeper crisis – economic, political, cultural and social – at the heart of the European project as now embroiled in a more complex field in which national, European and global forces collide.

The argument is that there needs to be far greater attention to the balance between capitalism and democracy in the making of Europe and that this must be seen in terms of a European societal model. This is not something that can be reduced either to the EU or its member states, but is nonetheless a discernable reality and an expression of European political modernity. This view would suggest that the apparent failure of the EU to crystallize into a new polity is due to the recalcitrance of the European societal model, which does not take one form but many. Today the conflict between capitalism and democracy is all the more stark and the forms of identity that can be associated with the democratic ethic may be in tension with the capitalist spirit of the European project, which appears to have lost its relationship with solidarity as a basis for political community. The economic argument was once the basis of European integration, it is now becoming evident that the neglected fiscal planning of economic integration is leading to a situation in which the economic rationale has lost its force and in its place is a new concern with the political and the need for a social project.

The idea of a European societal model

A useful place to begin is to return to the argument made in Chapter 8 concerning European political modernity. What defines Europe is ultimately best answered by considering what is distinctive about Europe from other parts of the world and what might be said to define patterns of identification and claim-making (see Roche 2010; Therborn 1995). The specificity of Europe as a world historical region does not consist in democracy, human rights, republican government, liberty, freedom – all of which have been regarded as defining the core of European values – but in the ways in which these ideas have been taken up in social struggles as well as in the institutional forms that followed from such struggles. If there is a core European value it has been the assertion of social justice and has been expressed in the ways in which modernity has unfolded in Europe generally. Despite the huge variability in the social, political and cultural shape of modern Europe, something like a European societal model – as opposed to the EU institutional notion of a European model of society – has existed and is based on solidarity and the pursuit of social justice.

According to Claus Offe (2003: 442) if there is anything distinctive about a specifically European model of capitalism it is the prominence of state-defined and state-protected status categories, which set limits to the rule of markets and of voluntary transactions. Stressing the diversity of types of capitalism in Europe, Offe notes that viewed in a global perspective it is possible therefore to speak of a European model of social capitalism that underlies the diversity of these different national models. Although Offe is sceptical that this can be reproduced on the EU transnational level, he thinks it has been an integral part of the European national states.

From the perspective of a theory of European modernity such a conception of capitalism suggests that the form that political modernity has taken has been in a certain tension between state, economy and civil society whereby capitalism has always been constrained by civil society, which has also set limits to state power. The relation between these forces, which defines the matrix of political modernity, gives rise to a societal model that in turn offers a way for modernity to interpret itself and articulate an identity, or what is better characterized as a social imaginary. Solidarity and social justice are not concrete facts, but transcendental and cognitive ideas that make possible institutional arrangements and guide political practice. The concrete outcome has been a certain balance between capitalism and democracy. This has been variously reflected in the nation-states of modern Europe and is an important structural feature of modern Europe, as Karl Polanyi also recognized with the argument that a certain consensus was worked out between European socialism and conservatism. T. H. Marshall's famous account of the formation of modern social citizenship reflected in part this view of democratic citizenship as a counter-balance to the inequalities of capitalism (Marshall 1987). It is true that this perspective was limited by the absence of any sense of social struggles, seeing as he did the social contract as an achievement of the state and not as negotiated outcomes of political mobilization spear-headed by trade unionism, socialist movements, labour and various social democratic parties.

With the foundation of the EU, from 1958 onwards, this basic balance between capitalism and democracy has been a structural presupposition in the project of European integration. The contentious elements of this were mostly kept out of the European sphere as they were largely negotiated within the national state. The project of European integration from the early years after the Second World War was made on the basis of economic recovery and growth and underpinned by a firm belief in the need for state planning. While that project was primarily economic in its initial aim to link the economies of Germany and France, its political aspirations were to secure lasting peace in Europe through the stabilization of liberal democracy. The success of the early EEC and its gradual enlargement was due in no small measure to the fact that it operated within the confined space of the Cold War, post-war economic recovery and the values of liberal democracy and capitalism. Economic growth, wealth creation and the democratic constitutional state gave to that project its basic animus and support from both the right as well as the left, which increasingly came to take on the cause of European integration following an initial scepticism (often forgotten today the UK Conservative Party was pro Europe and the Labour Party anti). European integration can thus be situated within the horizons of European political modernity and a belief in the desirability in the pursuit of social goals. This can be characterized as the embedding of capitalism within democracy in the form of what has been often referred to as democratic capitalism (Streeck 2011). The two and a half decades of more or less uninterrupted economic growth, *Les trentes glorieuses*, which saw the emergence of the EU and the consolidation of democratic capitalism left a paradoxical legacy. On the one side, as Wolfgang Streeck has argued, this was not a period of normality. The series of crises that followed should rather be seen as representing the normal condition of democratic capitalism when it became more apparent that capitalism and democracy do not fit together so neatly. On the other side, in the subsequent decades despite the conflict between capitalist markets and democratic politics the project of European integration sought to achieve a balance between economic competitiveness and social cohesion. In the longer view of history, it may thus be the case that the present crisis is more normal and, as a result, state intervention is a necessary measure to ensure the delivery of social goals.

In the present day there has been an uncoupling of capitalism and democracy. This has now manifested itself not only on the national level, but also on the European level of governance. Despite the inflation crisis in the 1970s and the arrival of economic liberalism in the 1980s, European integration was broadly conceived within the terms of the European societal model. Indeed, in the early 1990s the notion of a European Social Model was articulated by the policy-makers within the European Commission as an alternative to a purely market-based model of European integration. Although this notion lacked substance and ultimately did not offer an alternative to national social models, it reflected a concern with social cohesion that was to become an increasingly important part of the project of European integration and supposedly a counter-balance to market competitiveness and growth (see also Pichierri 2013). The idea that capitalism had to be made compatible with democracy remained a strong influence on European integration. The European social model can be described as one which holds that political control of markets is a necessity in order to achieve a certain degree of social justice. There are of course different national models and the balance between capital and labour, capitalism and democracy, market forces and solidarity, Keynesianism and monetarism, has never been constant for long. The European welfare state and the aspiration for full employment were among the outcomes that were achieved despite the basic tension between capitalism and democracy. But, as Streeck (2011: 14) has argued, this balance became difficult to maintain and when inflation was finally defeated the result was a new period of crises in which unemployment became the problem and with this the increase in public debt, which became for a time the functional equivalent of inflation in securing social peace. In the early 2000s the solution found was private indebtedness through house prices, which fuelled relative wealth creation and temporarily solved the fiscal crisis of public indebtedness. Until 2008 it is possible to see European integration as broadly within this model, increasingly crisis prone to be sure, of European political modernity as a period of what Wagner (1994) has termed 'organized modernity' in which the state – responding to the demands of labour – seeks to manage the crises produced by capitalism, thus adverting what Habermas (1976) termed a 'legitimation crisis'. The Euro currency, launched in 2002 in 12 countries, was part of this general framework in which political steering of the economy was considered to be a viable basis for Europe.

Has something changed? The current situation suggests that something has indeed changed. The crisis of the financial markets that began in September 2008 marks a point at which capitalism has entered a new phase leading to the fragmentation of the European model of social capitalism and with it the wider European societal model. Crisis in the financial markets may be seen as yet another crisis generated by capitalism, which according to David Harvey (2010) is by its very nature crisis prone. As Streeck (2012) has also argued capitalism is dynamically unstable. The present situation is different in that the capacity of the state to reconcile capitalism and democracy has reached a point at which this may no longer be possible due to the global scale of the problems, the de-stabilizing consequences of crisis management, as well as to new kinds of mobilization (see also Deutschmann 2011). Until now the national state was able to secure the pact between labour and capital, market and democracy. The regulatory framework of the EU assisted in this. However this functional system is less equipped to deal with the scale of the problems produced by financial liberalization and the so-called 'privatized Keynesianism' adopted by several countries (in particular those that have experienced the most severe economic crisis). National states are no longer able to secure the balance between capitalism and democracy, as is evident today in the case especially of Iceland and Greece, but also Ireland and Portugal and increasingly Spain. The result is a pervasive crisis of confidence in institutions of governance. But this is also apparent in the case of the larger economies, such as the UK and Italy (both of which have huge internal regional divisions and in the case of Spain this is the now the basis of a revitalized Catalan nationalism drive for independence).

The current political and economic crisis – post-September 2001 and post-September 2008 – occurred in a period when the EU had embarked on both enhanced integration and enlargement, placing additional strain on its regulatory capacity. It is now apparent that the single currency without a sovereign state to back it up produces outcomes that undermine the very possibility of integration in any meaningful sense. Within the Eurozone the member states have lost the power to devaluate their currency, leading to an unsustainable economic and political situation of financial and political bankruptcy. This was a basic mistake in the fiscal design of the single currency that is now all too evident. Given the absence of an EU level public budget and the prevalence of so-called austerity measures in several countries along with more awareness of corporate corruption and the questionable morality of European banking, it is hardly surprising that Europeans are increasingly looking to other sources of solidarity leading to a potential governability crisis for the EU.

Social and system integration

The project of European integration is essentially driven by systemic forms of integration as opposed to social integration, to follow a distinction made originally by Lockwood (1964) and later Habermas (1984, 1987a) in his theory of communicative action. System integration is achieved via the state and economy through the media of power and money while social integration is culturally produced by social institutions and the life-world. Both are forms of institutionalization. Applied to European integration, it is evident that it has been essentially driven by systemic forms of integration and has not in any significant sense generated social integration, which is a prerequisite for the formation of political community. The nation-state is a welfare state, but the political form of the EU, where neoliberal tendencies are strong, lacks the integrative mechanisms of the national state. If we view the state as a system of guarantees and a sphere in which diverse interests are worked out, it must entail a capacity for social integration. This historically has been the basis of the nation-state and the forms of citizenship associated with it. To develop further the notion of integration, both social and system integration can be negative or positive, to borrow a distinction made variously by Claus Offe (2003) and others. Negative integration concerns the removal of obstacles while positive integration entails the creation of new structures.

The four mobilities – labour, capital, goods, services – that were the basis of the project of European integration were predominantly conceived of in terms of a model of negative integration. It is easier to remove obstacles than create new structures, thus making the basic aims of European integration more achievable than if they were to be a design for a new kind of state and society. Thus the general logic of European integration has been to remove national barriers to enhance competitiveness. The economic liberalism that lay behind this was constrained by statist tendencies, the result of which was that negative integration was complemented by positive integration thus checking the erosion of national autonomy. In the course of its history there had been indeed a shift to positive systemic modes of integration (e.g. the adoption of the Euro, the provisions of the Maastricht Treaty, the structural funds), but there has been little by way of social integration, which has been more or less entirely the domain of the nation-state. This is not to say the EU did not bring about or contribute to social integration. Anti-discriminatory legislation, labour rights and gender equality, 'European' citizenship, have been notable achievements and can be seen in terms of a model of social integration, though these have been predominantly limited to negative forms of integration, i.e. the removal of obstacles rather than the creation of new social forms. Indeed, much of this was the consequence of the more extensive

diffusion of systemic forms of integration. These have now been complemented by the adoption of neoliberalism by the EU and by many
countries, notably in Central and Eastern Europe where the attraction
of economic deregulation and privatization for the ex-communist
elites has proven to be irresistible (Supiot 2012: 35).

There is a limit to the extent to which system integration can
achieve social cohesion and solidarity. At most it can put in place some
of the institutional prerequisites needed, such as legislation and the
creation of policies designed to maximize economic and technological
development. Social integration requires more extensive and positive
steps, including social protection and welfare, that is social and economic citizenship. Such forms of citizenship have been underdeveloped at the European level and to the extent to which they exist,
it is only at the level of negative integration and on the level of what
Scharpf (1999) has referred to as 'input' legitimacy as opposed to
'output' legitimacy. This macro-economic balance between, on the one
side, public support rooted in democratic will formation and, on the
other side, pragmatic support based on efficiency as a system of trade-
offs runs into problems when there are major shifts in at least one of
the two types of legitimacy. Citizenship entails not only rights, but
also involves participation, responsibilities and solidarity. It is possible
to discern in the project of European integration a tension between solidarity and mobility, which reflects the conflict between social and
system integration. Much of the tension between the national and the
European levels can be explained in terms of the conflict between these
two forms of integration and the resulting lack of congruence between
them is the basis of the divisions within European societies. This is
now being fought out as a conflict between different types of legitimation. Solidarity figured increasingly in the EU's policies in the 1980s
and 1990s, but has been noticeably in decline in the past decade since
the eastern enlargement and the sovereign debt crisis. When Italy
invoked the principle of solidarity in March 2011 when faced with an
influx of Arab migrants from Tunisia in the aftermath of the Arab
Spring it was refused and the French government introduced border
controls leading to a disintegration in the Schengen system (Monar
2012). With the crisis in sovereign debt and the transformation of
Europe into creditor and debtor countries, the notion of solidarity has
been further tested by austerity measures.

The crisis in the Euro zone countries, which forms the core of the
EU, draws attention to an additional problem with the nature of
European integration, which was based on economic and political inte-

gration. Currency integration is a different matter than other kinds of trade or an entity that can be simply regulated since it cannot be given a stable value, and, for every country, the Euro is in effect an external currency (see Aglietta 2012). The attempt to fix exchange rates within a context of national banking systems with very different economies pre-supposed economic stability in Europe and worldwide, but when that stability ceased the result was catastrophic for both the banking and the public sector. The result is a shift from East and West to North and South, with the sharpest lines of division now between the Mediterranean South and Germany. Alongside this division is a further one between the 17 Eurozone and ten non-Eurozone countries, in particular the UK.

Viewing European integration in this light it is apparent then that there is not just one process at work, EU-led systemic integration – or some notion of political integration – but many and all of them are embroiled in a more complicated societal field that ultimately extends beyond the contours of the EU to include global processes. Indeed, from the national perspective, the EU is in part a globalizing force in that it is often viewed as having an impact on European societies similar to that associated with economic globalization. However, it is important to distinguish between globalization, in the sense of the expansion of global markets, and the dynamics of the European free trade area, given the regulated nature of the latter and the fact that it is deeply embedded in national economies. The complicated issue of whether the EU can resist globalization cannot be entirely separated from the question whether nation-states can resist globalization. The societal complexity of European integration also cannot be so easily disengaged from globalization given the multiple forms of integration, pluralization and differentiation involved: the national, European and global dimensions are all entangled in a complex political and economic field. For this reason European integration and the normative question of political resistance is best viewed in terms of a wider theory of political modernity.

European political modernity took shape around a conflict between capitalism and democracy whereby state, economy and civil society interacted in ways that led to the domestication of capitalism by forces emanating from civil society and the state. The result was a societal model built on solidarity and social justice as a generative force that was to form the basis in the making of political community. The European societal model can be seen as a generative process that provided the primary ideas of modern Europe influencing both left and right conceptions of social order and political community ranging from social democracy, Christian democracy to democratic socialism and other radical democratic movements. As with all such models it crystallized into different forms due to the ways in which it was taken up and transformed by different social actors. So in civil society claim-making and the broadening of the scope of democracy led to tensions between state and society, on the one side, and, on the other, between capitalism and democracy. What we are witnessing today is the re-activation of these generative and transformative processes, which are re-activating the field of European integration understood as a largely institutionalizing process. What is at stake is more than simply the assertion of social integration over systemic integration, but an emerging politics that is not so easily explained by recourse to notions of 'European identity' or 'European citizenship'.

In the longer perspective of modernity, the current situation in which crisis looms large might be best seen in terms of a major shift in the relation of economy and society. The assumptions of European integration are in question, but with uncertain outcomes. These assumptions can be summed up as follows:

The assumption that social justice can be taken care of by the nation-state and that EU integration is supplementary (i.e. entailing a balance of negative and positive mechanisms of integration).
The assumption that globalization can be resisted by the EU.
The assumption that there is a balance between capitalism and democracy.
The assumption that European societies are on a broadly similar trajectory and one which can be steered by the EU towards a common future.
The assumption that economic growth will provide the basis for a politics of solidarity.

These assumptions are now in question with the return of the economic question, a transformation in the nature of the state and with it new questions about social justice and the meaning of the political. Examples of a shift in the political landscape abound: the London Riots in 2011, the Occupy Wall Street movement and other anti-capitalist movement such as the 15th May Movement in Spain, the riots in Greece in 2011, the public protests against the cuts to public spending in the UK and in other European countries, an increase in homelessness and poverty. These seemingly unconnected examples as well as a growing scepticism about the EU amongst the European electorates, a crisis in public confidence in national institutions, and, too, the rise of nationalist and populist parties and movements suggest the ground is shifting in the direction of anti-systemic politics in an increasingly crisis prone Europe.

Four kinds of crisis should be distinguished to make sense of this situation: economic crisis, political crisis, social crisis and cultural crisis. There is firstly an economic crisis, with its origins in the financial system and driven by mounting sovereign debt, if the full implications are less clear. A political crisis has in part become evident in terms of the capacity of the state and the EU, as well as other global institutions, to manage the crisis and maintain political legitimacy. This has not yet reached the level of a governability crisis and as yet there is no evidence of any state, with the exception of Greece and Cyprus, collapsing. As previously mentioned, the management of crisis is the normal condition of capitalism. However, there are now signs of a growing political crisis in legitimation with widespread scepticism of the EU. There are also signs of an emerging social crisis in terms of the corrosive impact of the economic crisis on the social fabric of societies. While the current austerity measures adopted by many countries have had significant implications for citizenship and social wellbeing, there are as yet no signs of a new kind of austerity polity resulting and there is considerable room for a social project to appear. In addition, it is possible to speak of a cultural crisis in the collapse of a common normative system of values that provides the basic cultural orientations for the functioning of societies.

Anti-systemic politics and political crisis

The context in which to view current developments is a theory of political modernity that recognizes its various currents, such as generative, transformative and institutionalizing processes, which have led to a European societal model and a growing tension between social and system integration. Many of these tensions and processes play out in the conflict between democracy and capitalism where a new phase in political conflict is becoming manifest. The new politics of Europe can be seen as anti-systemic, challenging new sources of power. The rise of anti-systemic trends are not primarily directed against the EU and cannot also be entirely understood in terms of diversification or some vague notion of 'unity in diversity'. They are anti-elite and anti-mainstream and are in part an expression of a new wave of democratization, which has also spread to the Arab world. Not all can be characterized as progressive, as the example of the New Dawn nationalist movement in Greece suggests. However, in Europe a social movement whether of the right or of the left is not emerging and claims of a new age of riots and the 'rebirth of history' are premature (Badiou 2012). For the foreseeable future the challenge is not the end of capitalism, as Badiou claims, but its taming by democracy and the recovery of a social project.

As argued earlier, the paradox is that the EU may itself have formed the ground on which this has unfolded. From being an elite driven project, European integration is now a more pluralized framework and operates within a context of the structural weakness of the state and a more globalized capitalist system over which its regulatory order does not control. In this sense the EU is not unlike and over-stretched empire that has created the conditions for both opposition and for re-directions of its project.

The adoption of positive modes of system integration have possibly come too late or at least have not succeeded in securing social forms of integration. Indeed, many of its most progressive integrative processes – labour rights, anti-discriminatory legislation, environmental legislation – have politicized the wider political field and made possible increased political contestation. EU cultural policy-making, which has increasingly embraced diversity as opposed to cultural unity, had confirmed the broader trend towards pluralization (Sassatelli 2009). So what we witness today is a general expansion in claim-making and contentious politics on a European level. This is because the democratic state – and the EU is in part at least a democratic polity – is inseparable from civil society which has expanded the sphere of the political (Johnson 2011). The result is a perpetual challenge to democratic legitimation (Trenz and Eder 2004).

This is the context – the collision of different logics of integration – in which we should view the apparent collapse of consensus on the European project. If elites do not share a collective sense of purpose – and they are seemingly divided between the proponents of market liberalism and statism, let alone have a collective identity – it cannot credibly be expected that the citizenry will generate identification with a state perceived to be in crisis and whose capacity for action in the wake of the financial collapse of several member states has been severely tested. The current situation is one in which systemic integration – at the price of democracy and social integration – has been the means to save a project that has undermined its presuppositions and at the same time it has also increased the capacity for a politicization of the population. What in fact we are witnessing is a conflict between capitalism and democracy in the wake of the break-up of democratic capitalism as a model for European integration, which has become what Colin Crouch (2004) has called a 'post-democracy'. The major crises of the twentieth century – the Great Depression, the Second World War – all led to new solutions, such as the welfare state, the New Deal, the United Nations and the European Union. The present predicament, which has generally been recognized to be the most serious crisis since 1945, has not led to any new ideas other than the production of rescue packages that result in the pile of public debt rising to a level that can no longer be satisfied by austerity measures. This is the point at which a political crisis comes both a social and a cultural crisis.

To conceptualize this situation we need to locate the current crisis – in its economic, political and social dimensions – and a new wave of contentious politics in a broader framework of modernity of a shift in the relationship between capitalism and democracy. In this, Europe may be becoming more European in that conflicts around social justice appear to be returning and there is now a debate about capitalism on a national, European and wider global level. Indeed, all elections in recent years have been dominated by the global crisis of capitalism and the systemic failure of democratic institutions to alleviate the situation. The notion of 'European citizenship' will need to be reconceived beyond its current status as a right to mobility for EU nationals. The notion of citizenship needs to be connected to a political conception of society not as a normative ideal or one that can be formulated in the EU's own discourse, but one that can be linked to the European societal model.

The way forward is not simply the creation of a European federal super-state, but nor is a retreat to national unilateralism the way forward. With increasing differences between the economies of the European countries, it would take a powerful central federalized state acting over the heads of national governments to alleviate the current situation. The dilemma is a great one, for such a transfer of sovereignty upwards would come at the cost of democracy unless new political structures were created to safeguard what remains of popular sovereignty. It would go far beyond all hitherto understanding of the meaning of 'integration' and it is not for now a likely prospect.

To sum up, the main identity currents in Europe today are more likely to be oppositional and the background to which is the uncoupling of democracy and capitalism. Citizens, as taxpayers who now have to pay for the systemic failures of the banking system, are less likely to embrace the technocratic and elite driven project of European integration, which is becoming increasingly viewed as another face of globalization that leads to the de-nationalization of the state (Kriesi et al 2008). This however is ambivalent in that these democratic identities are in part products of the European project, which should be seen as the extension of the state rather than its negation. The overall consequence has been a fragmentation of European integration into a plurality of projects, many of which are anti-systemic while others may be carriers of new kinds of social integration which may involve a different model of solidarity to that which was sustained by democratic capitalism.

It is unlikely that the social pact on which this was based can be renewed in the same way as the economic presuppositions, which were those of industrial capitalism, as they no longer exist and the political context has changed, making class compromise, the basis of democratic capitalism, all the more difficult due to new demands. The possibility of economies based on full employment, which were a realistic objective in the post-Second World War decades, is no longer an option for the post-industrial societies today which have also witnessed the tremendous incorporation of women into the work force. This is possibly the greatest challenge for Europe in the future and a challenge that will have to be addressed in the context of a changing global economic order and environmental limits to growth. Satisfying social expectations along with the demands for democratic legitimacy without growth-driven economies will be the test of the Europe project for many decades to come.

14

The European Heritage as a Conflict of Interpretations

As is now only too apparent, the open horizon of the future that seemed to have been signalled by 1989 considerably faded by the early 1990s when the European past re-asserted itself in the form of numerous nationalist conflicts and the revival of memory. Prior to 1989 it was possible to speak of European unity only at the cost of excluding Central and Eastern Europe. The unity of Europe was the unity of the West and a unity that could with some plausibility be described as a political project underpinned by certain assumptions, such as liberal democracy, capitalism and Christianity. While 1989 opened up new opportunities for the project of European integration, leading to the enlargement process and the movement towards a quasi-constitutional structure, it has paradoxically led to greater uncertainty as to the identity of Europe and its values. It is not an exaggeration to speak of a crisis of European identity since about 1991. On the one side, the movement towards enhanced unity that came with the Maastricht Treaty, which led to widespread debate on a post-national future for Europe and, on the other side, the stark reality of a divided Europe that was most vividly characterized by the ethnic-nationalist conflict that followed in the wake of the break-up of Yugoslavia. This final chapter examines this crisis with respect to the question of how we should understand the European heritage today in light of the issues opened up by 1989. The challenge for the present is whether it is possible or meaningful to speak of a common European tradition or heritage. In what sense should we understand the idea of 'unity' or commonality today as a feature of the European heritage? Is it meaningful to speak of common values in post-modern times? The argument of the chapter, in essence, is that instead of a conception of culture as a system of common values it is best seen in terms of a field of conflicting interpretations.[1] No conception of cultural commonality can exclude the dimension of critique and reflexivity that has been a feature of modernity. Consequently what should be resisted is a view of the European heritage as one that is somehow prior to modernity. Instead, what is needed is a new narrative of European modernity that is attuned to the positive features of modern Europe and sensitive to the catastrophes of its recent history. But this will demand a step beyond a conception of heritage defined only in terms of memory.

It would be tempting to conclude that a large-scale multi-national entity such as the European Union cannot be based on a shared value system and that therefore there is no possibility for Europe to exist outside the domain of ideology and politics. Despite the apparent obstacles it is possible to conceptualize commonality in ways that are appropriate to the present day. Before looking at this in more detail, I would like to offer two refutations of the possibility of a European identity that one often hears and which derive from two quite different positions. The first is the thesis that a European political identity either does not exist or can be only a weak identity in contrast to allegedly durable national identities. The second is the view, often associated with post-colonialism, that philosophically the European heritage is necessarily Eurocentric and inseparable from colonialism or is beset by internal divisions to a point that no unity is possible or even desirable.

Regarding the first argument, the current situation is less one of the absence of a political identity than one of competing visions of the future of the crisis-ridden project of European integration. This element of competition is more important than is immediately apparent since it does not mean the impossibility of identity or community. Such competition can be seen as productive of new realities which are generated in contexts of debate. The dominant force is undoubtedly the idea of a democratic Europe based on the sovereign national constitutional state, with the EU as a regulatory regime concerned largely with economic pursuits around market regulation. Against this largely inter-governmental vision of Europe rooted in notions of sovereignty and national autonomy, there are various post-national visions that stand for a post-sovereign Europe in which the nation-state has reduced significance. For the moment it would appear that the latter trend has been weakened, due both to the consequences of the enlargement of the EU and the global financial crisis, which has revealed a limited capacity of the EU to act as an integrated body. However, whatever shape the EU will take in the future, it will not entirely escape from the post-sovereign course it has embarked on and its political identity will doubtlessly be contested. But, then, too most expressions of national identity are also contested.

The absence of a straightforward European political identity does not foreclose the possibility of a European political community based on values other than technocratic ones relating to market integration. The fact that these values may be contested does not mean that there can be no community or warrant the conclusion that it can only be a 'thin' kind of commonality in contrast to an allegedly 'thick' national identity. Collective identities of all kinds are variously both thin and thick and increasingly take more discursive forms than they did in the past and they are open to more and more interpretations. Indeed, it has often been noted that people's identity is often too ambivalent to amount to a coherent fully formed collective identity. This lack of coherence is particularly apparent when it comes to considerations of Europe and the question of a European post-national identity. Post-national identity should be distinguished from supranationalism in that it refers not to a layer of identity that is above and beyond national identity. It is rather a condition shaped by a reflexive relation whereby both the national and the European act on each other. This means that nations are variously 'Europeanized'. As argued in Chapter 12, European identity is best conceived of as an Europeanization of identities, that is an internal transformation of national identities. This is not unlike how national identity emerged out of a process of the nationalization of regional identities or in some cases of other collective or societal identities. The identity of many countries has been greatly transformed due to European integration leading to a change in the national self-understanding. This is also why the argument that only small nations can achieve strong collective identities is wrong: where this might once have been true is now only possible through the suppression of difference. The current obsession with the alleged failure of multi-culturalism is such an example. The absence of a coherent and dominant national identity does not signal the impossibility of political community. However, this will require us to see political community in terms of difference, conflict and self-problematization as opposed to seeing it as a coherent and underpinned by a fixed set of cultural reference points. This is a challenge for all kinds of political community, whether they are large nation-states, such as the UK, Germany or France or larger polities, such as the European Union.

A second argument is addressed to a wider conception of Europe beyond the political. An objection frequently made against the notion of a European identity or the viability of an alternative reading of the European heritage is that the very idea of the European past is inseparable from Europe's legacy of colonialism. The main consideration to highlight in this context is that this position does not address what is an essential precondition for any debate on the European heritage, namely the recognition of the critical and post-universalistic strand within European culture over the past 200 years. An interpretation of the European heritage that takes this into account is what is needed. One core tradition within the European heritage, with its origins in humanism is the on-going interrogation of the past and the genesis of a post-traditional conception of culture. This can be associated with the notion of modernity understood as a site of conflicting interpretations of the world rather than a legislating authority. This notion of modernity has been variously suggested by Zygmunt Bauman (1987), Cornelius Castoriadis (1987), Jürgen Habermas (1987a) and Alain Touraine (1995) as a tension between different orientations. Habermas has argued for a conception of culture based on collective learning processes in which communicative modes of reason gain increased salience. Post-universalistic conceptions of truth and identity have been widely recognized in almost every aspect of late twentieth-century thought. The various philosophies of Deleuze, Derrida and Foucault have also argued for the absence of a constitutive subject and oppose representational conceptions of culture with more transformative ones. Derrida has specifically taken up the implications of deconstruction for the possibility of European identity (Derrida 1992). History contains no inherent pattern of meaning and cannot be viewed in holistic terms as constitutive of an overall unity or the expression of a subject. The importance of these ideas for theorizing the European heritage should not be underestimated. What they point to is an anti-essentialistic view of culture that has lost its capacity to legitimate and which exists only as a mode of communication in which the past is interrogated. In short, what is required is a theory of cultural heritage that is sensitive to dialogic concepts of rationality, self-problematization and critique.

This perspective places the experience of crisis and the exercise of critique as central to Europe's cultural heritage. It suggests the need to arrive at a conception of culture that is capable of capturing its diverse currents and moments of self-transformation. To discuss culture – in the sense of cultural identity or heritage or European or national values or ethnicity – unavoidably requires recourse to the symbolic level of meanings but it also requires recognition of the fact that all of culture is today fragmented, fluid and there is no form of life that is not contested and divisive. Culture moreover has a cognitive dimension in that it involves ways of thinking and an imaginary component that is irreducible to the symbolic level and offers societies with a resource of renewal (Strydom 2012). Rather than choose one of these options or abandon the notion of culture altogether it makes more sense to find a more general definition of culture that makes possible an accommodation of these divergent approaches. Many of the problems reside in the reduction of culture to a particular subject. The question of a European cultural heritage needs to be posed in a way that does not reduce heritage to a specific subject to which a particular form of life can be related. Rather what is more pertinent is to specify the ways by which European societies interpret themselves and their collective goals and aspirations. This is best termed a cultural model, which includes normative content, cognitive forms, and imaginary significations.

The notion of a cultural model, introduced by Alain Touraine (1977), refers to a society's capacity for self-interpretation. As used here it is also influenced by Habermas's notion of culture as a domain of critique and reflection and Castoriadis's (1987) notion of imaginary significations. The cultural model of society includes its normative orientations and self-understanding. It is not reducible to a cultural or political identity or a collective identity, since it does not relate directly to a specific collectivity and nor is it an objective cultural system of meaning or value framework. The cultural model of society is a more general level of cognition, reflection, and creativity (Touraine speaks of an 'image of creativity' that allows a society to give political direction). The concept of a cultural model has the advantage of solving a basic problem in the concept of culture, namely a view of culture as a whole way of life and culture as divided and contested.

The notion of a cultural model has particular relevance to something as broad as Europe, though arguably the same applies to the analysis of a national society given the highly differentiated and diverse nature of all societies today. The notion of a cultural model offers a way to conceive of public culture as non-essentialistic. Notions of culture as either 'thick' or 'thin' frequently lurk in the background of many approaches to post-national culture, which is generally regarded as a thin version of national culture. The argument put forward in this chapter is that we need to avoid the dualism of thin *versus* thick conceptions of culture and also the notion that political identity must be underpinned by a cultural identity understood as a whole form of life. The contention, then, is that the notion of a European cultural heritage should be best seen in terms of a cultural model by which societies interpret themselves. Viewed in these terms we can reconcile the contested conception of culture with a more general view in that a cultural model can constitute itself a site of conflicting interpretations of the world, but in which there are possibilities for acts of signification. This essentially communicative concept of culture also opens up the cosmopolitan possibility for a reflexive relation between cultures.

Beyond the grand narratives: The pluralization of the European heritage

The question of the European heritage should be seen in terms of not one grand narrative, but rather in terms of several competing ones. In short, to follow Lyotard's (1984) characterization, we are in the age of the break-up of grand narratives. However the idea of a European heritage should still be seen as a narrative, but of a different kind. Narratives offer new interpretations of the present; they are ways of experiencing and interpreting time and situate the present in relation to the past and future (see Eder 2009). They are also ways in which societies or collective actors articulate a self-understanding. As Wagner has argued (2009, 2012), the self-understanding of contemporary societies has been irreversibly shaped by the predicament of modernity and therefore such self-understandings are necessarily open in terms of their solutions to the problems modern society face.

Unlike earlier histories, which generally contained a 'grand narrative', new histories of Europe are entirely devoid of any attempt to discern a meaningful pattern. Norman Davies (1996) in his history of Europe does not tell the story of Europe in terms of anything that could be the basis of a self-understanding for the present. G. A. Pocock has denied the existence of such things as European history, claiming that there are only different constructions of Europe which means many different things to many different people (Pocock 1997, 2002). In his history of post-war Europe, Tony Judt (2005) went further with a general conclusion on the legacy of history: the European achievement was in the end the overcoming of the divisions and violence of the past and creating the basis for a new beginning, which does not reside solely in the emergence of the EU. This is a good point of departure, since it avoids the contradictory conclusions that, on the one side, there is persistence of history and, on the other side, there is nothing in European history to offer the present other than the overcoming of history. It is not implausible to argue that a narrative can be found to express a different account of European self-understanding.

The aim of this book has been to develop a perspective on the course of European history that avoids recourse to either grand narratives or a purely historical analysis and also resists a conception of the European heritage that reduces it to the politics of memory. The teleological arguments with their characteristic Eurocentric assumptions are now discredited while historical research does not offer an alternative since it avoids normative assessments and is generally circumscribed within narrow temporal domains whose significance for the present is generally left unexplored. Memories too are a poor guide to the past and are contested, as Judt (2005) has argued, and until they have been laid to rest a mature approach to the past will not be possible. What is needed is an approach than can place the past in a broader framework of analysis and which can provide both a normative reference point and a narrative that can connect the past and present. But this will involve going beyond memory-driven approaches to history. It may now be the time for such a new narrative to emerge.

It is possible to see four main narratives of the European heritage at work today: heritage as a shared political tradition, heritage as a unity in diversity, heritage as trauma, and a cosmopolitan heritage. These are not purely speculative positions or merely academic constructions, but are variously present and debated in discourses about Europe. A brief discussion of these is in place before final conclusions can be drawn.

Heritage as a shared political tradition

The first and most obvious way to define the European heritage is to relate it to a political tradition as opposed to a wider cultural characteristic of European civilization. Against, for instance, a definition of Europe as Christian or a definition that posits a universalistic value such as freedom, a narrower political conception of the specificity of Europe offers an alternative to the grand narratives that posit the progressive unfolding of an idea becoming embodied in a political form. In this regard, one can find within European history a value orientation that might be the defining characteristic of its political heritage for the present day. Whatever this will be will partly depend on what might be taken as the most important development or direction Europe is undergoing. If we take the trend towards a post-sovereign order, on the one side, and on the other the contemporary concern with democracy and citizenship, we get quite different understandings of history. Thus, the post-sovereign trend will highlight alternatives to the state tradition, while a concern with democracy and citizenship will draw attention to civil society.

To take the latter case of the centrality of democracy and citizenship, it has been argued that the political tradition that most captures the European heritage is republicanism (Van Gelderen and Skinner 2002; see Chapter 6). The republican tradition, or to be more specific the civic republican tradition, with its concern with civil society and the notion of a self-governing political community based on autonomous individuals is indeed a distinctive feature of the European political tradition. While it can plausibly be argued that it offers a shared heritage for much of Europe, it is possibly not as widely shared as is often assumed. For instance, its applicability to Central and Eastern Europe is not evident and it has not always led to democracy, as is illustrated by the example of seventeenth-century English republicanism; indeed it has often been autocratic. It is also not evident why republicanism is more central than, for instance, liberalism, which has arguably provided the foundations for European democracy and the modern state.

The most plausible case that can be made for a conception of the European heritage based on republicanism is the Kantian vision of a Europe based on a narrative of peace and constitutionalism. This vision, which has been invoked by Habermas (2001b), extends the republican idea from the national level to the wider international context in a way that has some resonances in the current trend towards a post-sovereign European political order. However, this interpretation does not go unchallenged, since an alternative reading of European political liberalism will posit less the transformation of the state than the assertion of individual rights as the salient factor.

The problem, in essence, is that the European political heritage does not consist of just one tradition, but several. The tension between liberalism and republicanism – between an emphasis on individual rights and on a self-governing political community – is one illustration of this wider tension within democracy. But more than this, it can also be argued that the defining feature of the European political heritage is neither liberty nor democracy as such, but the concern with social justice. As argued in the previous chapter, when one looks at Europe from a global perspective, it is the struggle for social justice that stands out as the most prominent feature of Europe's political heritage and a key characteristic of the formation of modernity. Modernity evolved in Europe, unlike in other parts of the world, in a way that capitalism and state formation were constrained by the taming influences of civil society, including social movements concerned with social justice. The result of the interaction of state, capitalism and civil society in modern Europe was the triumph of social justice. However, rather than conclude that democratic socialism was more important than liberalism or republicanism, one should rather draw the conclusion that the European political tradition did not lead to one overall outcome. Instead, what is more important is a plurality of political traditions leading to a plurality of interpretations of heritage (see Wagner 2009). This perspective is a necessary corrective to the emphasis on the 'dark side' of European history and to approaches that see in the European past only the legacy of colonialism (for example Mignolo 2011). While no approach to the European past can neglect these dimensions, it is important that an interpretation of the European heritage is sufficiently broad to be able to grasp the different and frequently contrary currents within it.

An alternative approach to the Kantian one, would be to locate the political roots of the European republican heritage in the tradition of resistance to tyranny that lay at the root of both Greek republicanism and the Judaeo-Christian concepts of civic solidarity and brotherly solidarity (see Chapter 2 and Brunkhorst 2005). The progressive transformation of these traditions of solidarity by modernity would bring the European political imagination in the direction of a global or cosmopolitan ethic. It may be objected that this characterization of the European heritage based on resistance to tyranny is not specifically European and in its most potent forms it was resistance to European tyranny that formed the political heritage of many parts of the world, in particular in the Americas. However, to say that a particular political trend has been a formative factor in history is not to say that it has not been equally present in other parts of the world. But it can be plausibly argued that a particularly pronounced feature of European modernity has been the relatively advanced degree to which a social project was forged against both the state and capitalism, leading to a strong tradition of social democracy and civil society.

Heritage as a unity in diversity

The search for a political tradition that defines the specificity of the European political heritage as a shared tradition runs into the problem of multiple political traditions. An alternative narrative that has considerable relevance today and is influential in EU cultural policy is the idea of unity in diversity. In this perspective, a narrative of becoming overshadows the idea of a past shared or one that is derived from an historical origin, such as an authentic original identity that was lost in the course of history. Europe is not yet a unity, but out of its diversity a political unity based on national cooperation and understanding is possible.

In this narrative, which runs the risk of becoming teleological – seeing in the present the signs of the future – European history is represented as one in which difference has been a factor that cannot be ignored or regarded as an inconvenient obstacle to unity, which can only be a political project. The idea of unity in diversity has increasingly come to the fore in European cultural policy, which shifted the earlier emphasis on unity to one of regional diversity (Sassatelli 2009). The earlier cultural policies were dominated by a vision of the essential unity of Europe as a cultural basis from which political unity might be possible. The trend in recent years has been a move in the direction of the recognition of cultural plurality. As stated in the Maastricht Treaty in 1992: 'The Community shall contribute to the flowering of the cultures of the Member States, while respecting their national and regional diversity and at the same time bringing the common cultural heritage to the fore.' But exactly what this might consist of is at best vague and open to interpretation. It certainly suggests that there is not a prior unity and that diversity is not an obstacle to a common Europeaness. The nature of that common Europeanism may in the end reside only in the condition of diversity. This is clearly an unsatisfactory place to end since plurality makes sense only in relation to a notion of commonality that it qualifies.

Despite these drawbacks, the notion of unity in diversity serves a critical function in highlighting problems with the older conceptions of Europe that fail to interrogate the notion of unity. Unlike the previously discussed narrative of a common republican heritage, the idea of unity in diversity suggests a conception of the European heritage that is not defined in the terms of what might be called 'Old Europe', namely a Western European-oriented definition of the European heritage or one based on a narrow interpretation of republicanism. With the enlargement of the EU, and generally a more pluralized conception of Europe, there is clearly a need for a wider definition of the European heritage to include the various historical regions of Europe.

Heritage as trauma

A different reading of the European heritage would take the unity and diversity theme to its limit and claim that the history of Europe has been inseparable from suffering. In this narrative it is more than a question of diversity; it is a matter of divisions and the inclusion of diversities other than national and regional ones, such as those of marginal and persecuted groups. There are no common memories, only divided ones. For instance, any account of the Christian nature of European civilization must consider that this heritage divided as well as united Europe. Christianity, like Europe itself, did not lead to a single church, but a diversity of religious traditions and different interpretations as to the meaning of secularism (see Taylor 2007).

The concern with divisions in European history has recently been overshadowed by a stronger notion of trauma and collective memories shaped by trauma. The notion that the only adequate account of the European heritage is one based on the recognition of trauma has gained increased currency in recent years (see Alexander et al 2004). This narrative is reflected in accounts of the European heritage that highlight the Holocaust, as in Christian Meier's (2005) *From Athens to Auschwitz*. He argues that the problem of history is the centrality of Auschwitz, as the symbolic term to refer to the Holocaust as a whole. Auschwitz was the 'definitive end' of European history and must be taken into account in any assessment of the European heritage. In this case, for Meier there is no doubt that Europe begins in Athens as its primary origin.

It is certainly correct that the past is becoming increasingly difficult to commemorate. The more voices that are included in the political community the greater will be the number of voices and memories. Nation-states have generally succeeded in commemorating the past around a heroic narrative of liberation from an imperial power or wars against neighbouring countries. But for Europe as a whole, unlike most nation-states, there is no European people as such and consequently commemoration can only take a very general acknowledgement of the traumas that have been integral to the memories of many groups and whole societies. For this reason, it is often held that for post-amnesiac Europe the idea of trauma may be a more appropriate way to articulate its historical self-understanding. The proposal for the Holocaust to be recognized as a European commemorative event is one such example of the entry of trauma into the very idea of the European heritage. This is not without problems, since it raises the issue of which traumas should figure in such a reading of the European heritage or whether, as has been argued, the Holocaust is the collective symbol of all traumas. Since 1989 there has been a proliferation of discourses of victimhood, many of which are products of communist oppression in Central and Eastern Europe and cannot be easily reduced to a single or dominant position of victimhood. Indeed, in such discourses the line separating victim and perpetrator is a thin one, and often, as also in the case of Vichy, the category of victims includes a very large part of the population, if not its entirety. There is also the problem discussed above that the European past cannot only be portrayed in terms of just one narrative, such as one of colonialism and violence against minorities. Yet, it is evident that today after the fall of the grand narratives of European mastery and progress that the experience of suffering has entered into almost every attempt to express the European heritage in a manner that is not unlike the ways in which national commemoration has also become increasingly more and more about the experiences of the vanquished than the victors. The theme of trauma as the content of a European narrative unavoidably runs into the problem of memory as a reliable basis for societies to construct a durable heritage; it is a necessary step, but it cannot be the basis for the future which requires positive modes of identification.

Cosmopolitan heritage

The historical heritage, including the conventional reference points, can be interpreted in different ways. The received interpretation is to see Europe as based on a singular civilization, with difference overshadowed by unity. A challenge to this is suggested by cosmopolitanism. What would be a cosmopolitan conception of the European heritage? The answer to this will partly depend on a theory of cosmopolitanism, since the different theoretical approaches emphasize either the cultural or political expressions of cosmopolitanism and also take up different positions on the question of globalization and its relation to the nation-state. Three broad directions are: (a) deriving from Alexander von Humboldt's vision of the unity of the world, a concern with commonality, and dialogue between different cultural traditions (b) the Kantian tradition of cosmopolitanism reflected in the work of Habermas and Benhabib with its characteristic emphasis on 'solidarity among strangers' and based on an developing post-national normative framework in which an ethic of hospitality and rights becomes embedded in all societies (c) an emphasis on transnational processes, such as the de-nationalization of societies and growing impact of globality, including global civil society and more generally a view of Europe as part of a wider global context in which borders are becoming blurred (Balibar 2003; Rumford 2007, 2008).

Rather than search for patterns of unity or diversity, a cosmopolitan interpretation of the European heritage would therefore begin by identifying those aspects of European history and society that give expression to interaction and dialogue. While diversity and especially the recognition of the civilizational plurality of Europe would be part of this, it is not the essential feature of a cosmopolitan perspective. Of greater importance is the inter-relation of the different historical traditions, including too the relation between Europe and non-Europe. The latter is important not least due to the fact that Europe from the beginning was itself formed through the constant incorporation of non-Europe. More generally, a view of Europe as shaped by the wider global context would be an essential dimension of a cosmopolitan approach. This does not mean that all aspects of European history should be reinterpreted in this light, or that the interaction of societies produces cosmopolitan outcomes such as dialogue. This kind of naïve cosmopolitanism is plainly absurd. The point would rather be to identify those cases where interaction has led to dialogue and the enlargement of the communicative space – whether by design or by unintended consequences – and to take such instances as the foundation to build a different European tradition. The conception of cosmopolitanism reflected in the Kantian tradition, which is more overtly normative, has considerable relevance in evaluating the place of institutional change in European societies, especially since the end of the Second World War when a demonstrable shift occurred in the commitment to create the conditions for lasting peace within Europe. While some cosmopolitan theorists, such as Ulrich Beck, believe that Europe has become increasingly cosmopolitan and that nation-states are relics of the past, another view is that the cosmopolitan current is one of many in the formation of European societies.

The debate around cosmopolitanism is generally a debate about the degree of cosmopolitanism and the claims that can be made for it. Some more than others make larger claims about the impact of globalization or the transnationalization of Europe. It is also contentious whether such processes are to be equated with cosmopolitanism, which can also be seen as a critical response to globalization. Obviously the issue here lies in the understanding of globalization. Cosmopolitanism, which should not be reduced to globalization, is more concerned with the normative potentials of the present – which include both the global and the local – and is unavoidably found in social struggles, which are located in an increasingly complex political context that cannot be so easily reduced to any one level, be it national or global.

One contemporary illustration of a cosmopolitan approach to the European heritage is in museums and exhibitions. In recent years there has been a shift in the nature of the representation of the past towards a concern with the representation of exchange and dialogue. A challenge for museums is the representation of accounts of the past that were ignored in the formative period of the modern nation-state when national museums sought to narrate the grandeur and prestige of the national heritage. Post-national conceptions of history have recently become the focus of attention for museums and exhibitions seeking to offer alternative accounts of history. Of particular importance are accounts of the past that seek to highlight the role of cross-cultural dialogue and other expressions of global history, such as those reflected in cross-cultural trade, communication and the arts. There have been some notable attempts to give expression to cultural encounters between Europe and Asia that preceded the imperial age as well as projects aimed at giving greater attention to the representation of transnationalism.[2]

The conflict of interpretations

These four narratives are all present in different ways in debates about the European heritage and in that sense they are real, for the European imaginary is discursively produced in debates and in communication about Europe. In this sociologically-oriented approach to the European heritage the objective is not to try to define it in ways that are derived from a reading of European history, since all such aims can easily be contested with rival interpretations. The aim is rather to see how in the present day, or in a specific period, the past has been interpreted by the present. As I have argued, heritage is neither the memory of a subject nor the past as documented by historians; it is rather – as suggested by Paul Ricoeur (2004) – an evaluation by the present of the past and as such involves self-reflection. I have characterized the European heritage in terms of a cultural model composed of a plurality of narratives. The age of the singular western grand narrative has passed not only because of the plurality of narratives, but because all of these, different though they are, do not tell a story of the triumph of the West, but are responses to the European predicament since 1989. The European heritage has become an unavoidable a site of conflicting interpretations of the past.

In this chapter I have sought to explore some of the considerations that are at stake in the debate on the European heritage. The period since 1989 has been marked by a break-up of the grand narratives of the past. Their place has been filled by a plethora of memories, of which the memory of the Holocaust stands out as the singular event that has defined European consciousness in the twentieth century. But a new narrative that could overcome the vicissitudes of memory and be the basis of the European heritage has not yet emerged.

New narratives are indeed emerging in the vastly growing discursive space of Europe. Looking at four major narratives, it can be concluded that there is in fact no underlying European self or constitutive subject. To claim otherwise is to ignore some of the most important debates and developments in European thought over the past few decades that call into question the notion of a primary subject or an authentic core of values. It is also not possible to claim that the European heritage has been always defined by reference to an external other, since much of the concern with otherness has been the European past itself. In sum, there is neither a clearly defined self nor other and much of the European heritage has been the endless re-interpretation of its own past. The notion that there is a past that can be recovered and made meaningful for the present has been seriously undermined by philosophical and historiographical scholarship. Yet, this does not mean the past cannot be of service to the present. But rather than providing the present with a comfortable illusion of a unity that transcends its divisions, new and emerging narratives of the European heritage offer interpretations that are more in tune with the changing nature of European self-understanding in an increasingly post-European age.

At the moment there is no single narrative in ascendance. Europe taken as a whole is in an uncertain position with regards to its relation to the past. While many nations have increasingly come to terms with the past, others are discovering the legacy of divided histories, making all the more difficult a European memory or a shared political heritage, which has been further undermined by the current political and economic crisis of the EU. I have argued that the most promising option for European self-understanding is the re-invention of the cosmopolitan current in the European past in order to find a model of solidarity with which Europe can come to terms with its own cultural and political diversity. However, this will need to be as much future oriented as past, since the past does not always offer the present the means to renew itself. The time may therefore be ripe for Europe to move beyond the past.

Conclusion: Europe – A Defence

The idea of Europe has now become a reality in a number of very specific senses and which are a challenge to some of the conventional conceptions of the meaning of Europe. The traditional view is that the primary reality is the nation-state and that Europe is nothing much more than an aggregation of largely separate nations. This is also one of the most common ways the history of Europe has been written: an aggregation of national histories. To the extent to which it has any meaning Europe is generally regarded as synonymous with the idea of the West and a vague notion of civilization. With the rise of European Union, Europe has acquired a new political meaning as a geopolitical entity. However, the general tendency is also to see this embodiment of the idea of Europe as epiphenomenal with nations as constituting the primary reality. Although this view is becoming increasingly challenged by those who see the project of European integration as contesting many of the older assumptions about national autonomy, such perspectives are limited by a narrow focus on the institutional form of the EU. The argument developed in this book is rather that Europe can itself be seen as having a structural form as opposed to being a derivative of nations or an external dimension. In this view, a long-run historical consideration of Europe is needed in order to discern the nature of its specificity, which is neither to be found in national trajectories nor in the project of European integration. This means, too, that any notion of the 'crisis of Europe' must be placed in a broader historical context than that of the recent past.

There have been surprisingly few attempts to do this and those that have sought to provide an interpretation of the course of European history have generally operated within the confines of a narrative history of Europe. As argued in the Introduction, such endeavours are beset with epistemological and methodological challenges, due to the problem of identifying independent variables for long periods of time and the fact that almost every reference point has changed considerably in the course of history. For these reasons, Europe cannot be used to explain itself. Purely constructivist approaches are inadequate, for while the idea of Europe has been a historically variable discursive construction as opposed to being a natural entity, historical specificity remains unexplained. Such attempts to de-naturalize Europe serve a useful function, but fall short of a macro-sociological analysis of how enduring forms take shape. The method adopted in this book is to approach the problem of the significance of Europe from the perspective of a macro-sociological theory of modernity, for only by adopting a broader framework of analysis is it possible to make sense of a long-run historical process in which virtually all the elements changed considerably over time. The fact that the constitutive elements did not all change at the same time made possible the relative objectivity of what can be designated Europe. A backward glance suggests that the object of analysis is in fact not Europe, but a structure-forming process to which we give the name Europe. This has two main dimensions to it, a cultural and a social one. I have characterized these in terms of a cultural model and a societal model. Both of these have given form to modernity and define the particular path of European modernity. The sources of modernity are civilizational and can be found in the various civilizations that constitute, what I have called, the European inter-civilizational constellation. However, the formation of Europe took shape from processes that ultimately go beyond the civilizational background. For this reason a different framework is needed than one confined to the civilizational context. A conception of modernity offers a more comprehensive way to make sense of the various structure-forming processes that emerged from the civilizational context and which give Europe a certain specificity. I have characterized these processes, as generative, transformational and institutional. An adequate account of the formation of modernity must take into consideration all three processes. In this view, the current emphasis on plurality and the multiple forms of Europe needs to be corrected to take into account the structures that make plurality possible and the outcomes, since any account of variation presupposes a more general framework.

I have argued, furthermore, that any account of the formation of Europe must take appropriate account of the global context, for many of the formative developments were the result of encounters with the non-European world. This affirms the importance of a relational view of Europe as shaped in relation to the rest of the world. However, a relational perspective does not only entail a consideration of dichotomous relations, as is often the case in much of the literature, such as friends and enemies, but also needs to take account of how structures are formed from relations with a multiplicity of reference points, including a relation to new conceptions of the world. Indeed, the idea of Europe developed alongside the very notion of the world and thus entails not just immanent or internal, logics of development, but also ones that can be termed transcendental.

The emergence of a cultural structure that constitutes the European cultural model includes within it a certain reflexivity, since the resulting form is not an unchanging structure, but a form that makes possible self-interpretation. The cultural model that formed over many centuries was in part shaped out of a relation to transcendental or, following Strydom (2011a), 'meta-cognitive ideas' – freedom, autonomy, solidarity, equality, social justice – that took on an increased salience with modernity and gave to modernity its characteristic openness and transformative impact. This cultural model guided reflexively the construction of social and political projects ranging from the constitutional state and nation-state to the welfare state and to the post-Second World War project of European integration as well as many other and earlier societal models that have defined the course of European history as one of shifts in modernity.

The process by which cultural and social models develop is not easily summed up. A general conclusion is that cultural models tend to crystallize producing new visions of social and political order. I have stressed how generative and transformative processes lead to the translation of these new ideas into new political and institutional forms. In this view, there is a certain tension between cultural models and societal models, as in the tension between democracy and social justice, on the one side, and on the other capitalism. I stressed this tension as constituting the core of European modernity. Viewed in such terms, the current situation with Europe widely perceived to be in crisis should be assessed from this wider context of modernity. The form of modernity in Europe offers the present with resources for addressing the future. It may be the case that the solutions to the present predicament lie in part in a re-interpretation of the past, that is both in modernity and in Europe's inter-civilizational sources.

The current predicament has three main dimensions to it. The first is a deep malaise in the coping with diversity, as expressed in increased xenophobia and racism. This is a social crisis rooted in fear driven by insecurity and uncertainty. But it is also symptomatic of a wider cultural crisis in the values on which Europe is based. The second concerns problems in democratic legitimacy and in the political design of the EU with the growth of unaccounted for powers at both national and EU levels of governance. The third, a relatively recent one, concerns the economic crisis of Europe and the prospect of a model of capitalism emerging that is no longer embedded in the normative structures of what I have called the European societal model. These are of course related: the so-called crisis of capitalism – which I characterized in terms of a crisis in systemic integration – is bound up with the crisis of democracy and takes the form of a crisis in governability and this in turns provides the context for a breakdown in solidarity leading to intolerance and anti-cosmopolitan trends. However rather than see in the present predicament the signs only of societal regression, a broader perspective is necessary.

The broad historical sketch outlined in this book draws attention to the plural and hybrid nature of Europe and challenges a conception of society that erases such differences in favour of a notion of unity. The argument has been that notions of unity must be predicated on the basis of diversity and variation within a civilizational matrix that took shape through multiple levels of encounters and reflexivity. The rediscovery of such diversity and unity should be part of the European heritage. The conception of modernity proposed builds on this interpretation which affirms the potential cosmopolitan currents to the European heritage. The idea of Europe has for much of its history been linked to a counter-factual future orientation. This needs to be recovered and placed on a new level in order to move beyond the current situation. So what is at stake in the question whether Europe can be defended is precisely a matter of re-invigorating its cultural model and potentiality for new institutional possibilities.

In the second half of the twentieth century the main challenge for those who took up the idea of Europe was to overcome fascism and the legacy of totalitarianism. This began in 1945 but was not complete until 1989 when Central and Eastern Europe emerged from the vestiges of totalitarianism. In the course of these decades European countries also made the uncertain transition from colonialism to becoming post-imperial nations within a post-national polity. The idea of Europe has remained opaque with respect to the past and to the future. It has always been more allied to the right than the left. Today it is a more contested discourse and open to new visions of political community. It has been the purpose of this book to seek a new narrative that may be the basis of European self-understanding as the old grand narratives lose their conviction and the vicissitudes of memory fade with the passing of the century that for many was one of nightmares. The danger today is that a politics of fear will take the place of the older narratives and that social fragmentation will erode the capacity for social and political renewal. To defend Europe in this climate of uncertainty is to defend the social against the destructive forces of globalization and the dismantling of the institutions and structures of political community and solidarity that have been an integral part of European modernity. The best chances, then, for the idea of Europe to gain a revitalized significance for the present lie in the revival of its social dimensions rather than in the search for a supranational state or in the pursuit of exclusionary politics. However it is evident that nation-states cannot achieve this alone, and much of globalization has been a product of the actions of states. The transnational dimension of European integration is essential to the viability of political community, which needs to expand in a cosmopolitan direction.

Notes

Introduction: A Theoretical Framework

1 Delanty and Rumford (2005), Therborn (1995), and Roche (2010) are examples that move in this direction.
2 See Anderson (2007), Brague (2002), Morin (1987), Stråth (2000, 2002), Wagner (2009, 2012). See also Fontana (1995) and on the idea of Europe, Pagden (2002).
3 One such example is the tendency to reduce cultural forms, such as Europe, to identity. The concept of identity when applied to such large-scale entities is considerably more complicated than when used with respect to social actors, whether individuals or groups.
4 See Adams et al (2005) and Delanty and Isin (2003) for general accounts of trends in the literature. Sewell (2005) and Tilly (1984) are good examples of major sociologically-based studies on problems in historical analysis.
5 In an earlier book, *Inventing Europe* (Delanty 1995a), the objective was a critique of the grand narratives.
6 See McLennan (2000, 2003).
7 'A product of modern European civilization, studying any problem of universal history, is bound to ask himself to what combination of circumstances the fact should be attributed that in Western Civilization, and in Western Civilization only, cultural phenomena have appeared which (as we like to think) lie in a line of development having universal significance and value' (Weber 1978: 13).
8 See Delanty (2006) for an expanded discussion of the relation between Europe and Asia that questions the validity of both the orientalist critique as well as the notion of a clash of civilizations.
9 See Bayly (2004), Frank (1998), Hobson (2004), Armitage and Subrahmanyam (2010), Pomeranz (2000).
10 This is a perspective that has been developed by Johann Arnason (2003). See also Burke (2010) and Dallmayr (1996).
11 See for example Sewell (2005).
12 This perspective informs the idea of the European Union as a new kind of empire (see Beck and Grande 2007; Zielonka 2006).
13 However, arguments for hybridity are important insofar as they have a de-masking function, demonstrating how taken for granted entities are composed of diverse components.
14 A full account of the notion of structure is not possible in the present context. See Giddens (1984) for an influential theory of structure and its relation to agency. See also for a discussion of the concept of structure in relation to agency, social change, and culture, Chapter 5 of Sewell (2005).
15 I am following Klooger's interpretation of Castoriadis here: 'We must learn to think the unity of society without conflating it with homogeneity; we

must learn to imagine a form of unity within which heterogeneity is essential' (Klooger 2013: 503).

16 On the problem of geographical conceptions of continents, see Lewis and Wigen (1997).

17 In the case of Weber the basic animus was the problem of the explanation of human suffering and in the case of Marx the class struggle arising from the experience of injustice.

18 For an exception, see North et al (2009).

19 For an application, see O'Mahony and Delanty (1998).

20 See Habermas (1979) and the debate on collective learning processes by Eder (1999) and Strydom (1987, 1993).

21 This is a perspective variously present in the work of Castoriadis, Eisenstadt and Habermas.

22 This model has been developed in Delanty (2012a). See also Strydom (2012).

23 This can be broken into two, selection from variety and consequent cultural and societal transformation.

24 I agree with Strydom (2011b) that properly speaking they are essentially part of the meta-cognitive order, but are realized within specific cultural models.

25 See Delanty (2010).

26 For some time this was a typical characterization of post-modernity, but is now seen as a feature of modernity and that the post-modern is a part of the project of modernity rather than something that succeeds it (Delanty 2000a).

27 On the methodology of a reconstructive critical theory, see Strydom (2011a) and Delanty (2011b).

28 I have developed this in Delanty (2009a, 2012b). See also Delanty (2012a).

Chapter 1   The European Inter-Civilizational Constellation

1 See Lewis and Wigen (1997) for a critique of what they call 'metageography'.

2 In Chapter 12, I argue that Europe is now 'post-western'.

3 I have explored further the theme of cultural encounters in Delanty (2011a).

4 My understanding of civilizations is influenced by the work of Arnason. See in particular Arnason (2003).

5 The notion of a 'constellation' is suggested in the present context by T. W. Adorno, who borrowed the term from Walter Benjamin, to mean a juxtaposed structure of contradictory elements that is not underpinned by a common foundation and does not have a core.

6 This follows a distinction made by Paul Ricoeur in his work on memory (Ricoeur 2004). Some of this discussion draws on Delanty (2009b).

Chapter 2   The Greco-Roman and Judaic Legacies

1 The debate goes back to Bernal's controversial 'Black Athena' thesis of the African roots of Greek culture (Bernal 1987).

Chapter 3   Christianity in the Making of Europe

1   On Ottoman practices of 'the gift of law', see Isin and Lefebvre (2005).
2   Some of the following draws from Chapter 9 of Delanty (2009a).

Chapter 5   The Islamic World and Islam in Europe

1   For a nuanced recent interpretation, see Brague (2009).

Chapter 6   The Renaissance and the Rise of the West Revisited

1   There were clearly national variations of a more general trend, such as the thesis of the special case of the origins of English individualism (MacFarlane 1978). For a discussion of the wider literature on the Renaissance and the emergence of the individual, see Martin (1997).

Chapter 7   Unity and Divisions in Early Modern European History: The Emergence of a Westernized Europe

1   See O'Mahony and Delanty (1998) and Hechter (1975).

Chapter 8   The Enlightenment and European Modernity: The Rise of the Idea of Europe

1   On its global dimension, see Hunt (2010).
2   Eder (1999, 2009), Habermas (1979), Strydom (1987, 1993).
3   See for example Eisenstadt (2000, 2003), Gaonkar (2001), Jameson (2003), Taylor (1999), Taylor (2004), Wagner (2004, 2009, 2011).

Chapter 9   The Rise of the Nation-State and the Allure of Empire: Between Nationalism and Cosmopolitanism

1   See Magubane (2005). This perspective over-states the causal impact of empire on state formation, since the basic structure of the European state system was in place by the end of the seventeenth century.

Chapter 10   The Historical Regions of Europe: Civilizational Backgrounds and Multiple Routes to Modernity

1   I am grateful to Johann Arnason for comments on an earlier version of this chapter.

2 Arguably a case could be made for the inclusion of Judaism as a separate civilization (in Eisenstadt's (1992) terms, a diasporic civilization).
3 There may be an argument for Scandinavia to be considered part of a distinct Nordic region. For present purposes, given the model of modernity that evolved there it is considered part of the wider North Western region (see Arnason and Wittrock 2012).
4 This section draws in part on Vidmar-Horvat and Delanty (2005).

Chapter 11   Europe in the Short Twentieth Century: Conflicting Projects of Modernity

1 For an interpretation of the relevance of Nietzsche for contemporary Europe, see Elbe (2003).
2 See Delanty (1995b).
3 This almost certainly did not apply in the case of Spain, where economic liberalism was a later development following economic degeneration. In contrast, in Germany and Italy fascist economic and social policies had some early results.
4 Arguably international crises, such as the Korean War, had potential implications for a conflict within Europe between the USSR and NATO. However, this was generally contained and there was no serious prospect of war.

Chapter 12   Europe since 1989: Nationalism, Cosmopolitanism and Globalization

1 Some of the following is based on a section of Blokker and Delanty (2010). The notion of a 'post-western Europe' was originally formulated in Delanty (2003).
2 See Habermas's interpretation of the problem of sovereignty (Habermas 2012: 13ff).

Chapter 13   Age of Austerity: Contradictions of Capitalism and Democracy

1 An earlier version of this chapter appeared in *International Critical Thought* 2(4): 445–55.

Chapter 14   The European Heritage as a Conflict of Interpretations

1 This chapter is based in part on Delanty (2010) 'The European Heritage from a Critical Cosmopolitan Perspective, LSE "Europe in Question"' *Discussion Paper Series* No. 19.
2 For example, the Victoria and Albert Museum's *Encounters: The Meeting of Asia and Europe 1500–1800* in 2004.

Bibliography

Abu-Lughod, J. (1963) *The Arab Discovery of Europe: A Study in Cultural Encounters*. Princeton: Princeton University Press.

Abu-Lughod, J. (1989) *Before European-Hegemony: The World-System AD 1250–1350*. Oxford: Oxford University Press.

Abulafa, D. (2000) *Mediterranean Encounters Economic, Religious, Political, 1100–1550*. Aldershot: Ashgate.

Adams, J., Clemens, E. and Orloff, A. S. (eds) (2005) *Remaking Modernity: Politics, History and Sociology*. Durham, NC: Duke University Press.

Adorno, T. W. (1998) 'The Meaning of Working Through the Past?' in *Critical Models: Interpretations and Catchwords*. New York: Columbia University Press.

Adorno, T. W. and Horkheimer, M. (1979) *Dialectic of Enlightenment*. London: Verso.

Agadjanian, A. and Roudemetof, V. (2006) 'Introduction: Eastern Orthodoxy in a Global Age' in Roudemetof, V., Agadjanian, A. and Pankhurst, J. (eds) *Eastern Orthodoxy in a Global Age*. New York: Rowman & Littlefield.

Aglietta, M. (2012) 'The European Vortex' *New Left Review* 75, May–June: 15–36.

Alexander, J., Eyermann, R., Giesen, B., Smelser, N. and Sztompka, P. (2004) *Cultural Trauma and Collective Identity*. Berkeley: University of California Press.

Alsayyad, N. and Castells, M. (eds) (2002) *Muslim Europe or Euro-Islam: Political Culture and Citizenship in the Age of Globalization*. Plymouth: Lexington Books.

Alting von Gerusau, F. (1975) *European Perspectives on World Order*. Leyden: Sijthoff.

Amin, S. (1989) *Eurocentrism*. New York: Monthly Review Press.

Anderson, B. (1983) *Imagined Communities: Reflections of the Origin and Spread of Nationalism*. London: Verso.

Anderson, P. (1974) *Lineages of the Absolute State*. London: Verso.

Anderson, P. (1997) 'Under the Sign of the Interim' in Gowan, P. and Anderson, P. (eds) *The Question of Europe*. London: Verso.

Anderson, P. (2007) *The New World Order*. London: Verso.

Antonsich, M. (2008) 'Europe between "National" and "Postnational" Views' *European Journal of Social Theory* 11(4): 505–22.

Arendt, H. (1958) *The Human Condition*. Chicago: University of Chicago Press.

Arendt, H. (1963) *Eichmann in Jerusalem: A Report on the Banality of Evil*. London: Penguin.

Arjomand, S. and Tiryakian, E. (eds) (2004) *Rethinking Civilizational Analysis*. London: Sage.

Armitage, D. and Subrahmanyam, S. (eds) (2010) *The Age of Revolutions in Global Context, c.1760–1840*. London: Palgrave.

Arnason, J. (1991) 'Modernity as a Project and a Field of Tensions' in Honneth, A. and Joas, H. (eds) *Communicative Action*. Cambridge: Polity Press.

Arnason, J. (1993) *The Future that Failed: Origins and Destinies of the Soviet Model*. London: Routledge.

Arnason, J. (2000a) 'Approaching Byzantium: Identity, Predicament and Afterlife' *Thesis Eleven* 62(1): 39–69.

Arnason, J. (2000b) 'Communism and Modernity' *Daedalus* 129(1): 61–90.

Arnason, J. (2003) *Civilizations in Dispute: Historical Questions and Theoretical Traditions*. Leiden: Brill.

Arnason, J. (ed.) (2005a) 'East Central European Perspectives', Special Issue of the *European Journal of Social Theory* 8(4): 387–400.

Arnason, J. (2005b) 'Alternating Modernities: The Case of Czechoslovakia' *European Journal of Social Theory* 8(4): 435–51.

Arnason, J. (2006) 'Contested Divergence: Rethinking the "Rise of the West"' in Delanty, G. (ed.) *Europe and Asia Beyond East and West*. London: Routledge.

Arnason, J. and Doyle, N. (eds) (2010) *Domains and Divisions of European History*. Liverpool: University of Liverpool Press.

Arnason, J. and Raaflaub, K. (eds) (2011) *The Roman Empire in Context: Historical and Comparative Perspectives*. Oxford: Blackwell.

Arnason, J., Raaflaub, K. and Wagner, P. (eds) (2013) *The Greek Polis and the Invention of Democracy*. Oxford: Wiley-Blackwell.

Arnason, J. and Wittrock, B. (eds) (2012) *Nordic Paths to Modernity*. Oxford: Berghahn Books.

Asad, T. (2003) *Formations of the Secular: Christianity, Islam, Modernity*. Stanford: Stanford University Press.

Ascherson, N. (1995) *Black Sea: The Birth Place of Civilization and Barbarism*. London: Cape.

Assmann, J. (1987) *Moses the Egyptian: The Memory of Egypt in Western Monotheism*. Cambridge, MA: Harvard University Press.

Assmann, J. (2011) *Cultural Memory and Early Civilizations: Writing, Remembrance and Political Imagination*. Cambridge: Cambridge University Press.

Baban, F. and Keyman, F. (2008) 'Turkey and Postnational Europe: Challenges for Community' *European Journal of Social Theory* 11(1): 107–24.

Badiou, A. (2007) *The Century*. Cambridge: Polity.

Badiou, A. (2012) *The Rebirth of History: Times of Riots and Uprisings*. London: Verso.

Bala, A. (2006) *The Dialogue of Civilizations in the Birth of Modernity*. London: Palgrave.

Balibar, E. (2003) *We are the Europeans: Reflections of Transnational Politics*. Princeton: Princeton University Press.

Bang, P. (2011) 'The King of Kings: Universal Hegemony, Imperial Power, and a New Comparative History of Rome' in Arnason, J. and Raaflaub, K. (eds) *The Roman Empire in Context: Historical and Comparative Perspectives*. Oxford: Blackwell.

Barraclough, G. (1963) *European Unity in Thought and Practice*. Oxford: Blackwell.

Bartlett, R. (1993) *The Making of Europe: Conquest, Colonization and Cultural Change, 950–1350*. London: Allen Lane.

Bassin, M. (1991) 'Russia between Europe and Asia: The Ideological Construction of Geographical Space' *Slavic Review* 50: 1–17.

Bauman, Z. (1987) *Legislators and Interpreters: On Modernity, Postmodernity and Intellectuals*. Cambridge: Polity Press.

Bauman, Z. (1989) *Modernity and the Holocaust*. Cambridge: Polity Press.

Bayly, C. A. (2004) *The Birth of the Modern World, 1780–1914*. Oxford: Blackwell.

Beck, U. (2006) *The Cosmopolitan Outlook*. Cambridge: Polity Press.

Beck, U. and Grande, E. (2007) *Cosmopolitan Europe*. Cambridge: Polity Press.

Beevor, A. (2006) *The Battle for Spain: The Spanish Civil War, 1936–1939*. London: Phoenix.

Benevolo, L. (1993) *The European City*. Oxford: Blackwell.

Benhabib, S. (2008) *Another Cosmopolitanism*. Oxford: Oxford University Press.

Benhabib, S. (2011) *Dignity in Adversity: Human Rights in Troubled Times*. Cambridge: Polity Press.

Benjamin, W. (1969[1940]) *Illuminations: Essays and Reflections*. New York: Schocken.

Bentley, J. (1993) *Old World Encounters: Cross-Cultural Contacts and Exchanges in Premodern Times*. Oxford: Oxford University Press.

Berend, I. (2005) 'What is Central and Eastern Europe?' *European Journal of Social Theory* 8(4): 401–16.

Bernal, M. (1987) *Black Athena: The Afro-Asiatic Roots of Classical Civilization*. New Brunswick: Rutgers University Press.

Bhambra, G. (2007) *Rethinking Modernity: Postcolonialism and the Sociological Imagination*. London: Palgrave.

Bhambra, G. (2009) 'Postcolonial Europe, or Understanding Europe in Times of the Postcolonial' in Rumford, C. (ed.) *Handbook of European Studies*. London: Routledge.

Biebuyck, W. and Rumford, C. (2012) 'Many Europes: Rethinking Multiplicity' *European Journal of Social Theory* 15(1): 3–20.

Biedenkopf, K., Geremek, B. and Michalski, K. (2004) *The Spiritual and Cultural Dimension of Europe*. Vienna: Institute for the Human Sciences.

Billington, J. H. (2004) *Russia in Search of Itself*. Baltimore: John Hopkins University Press.

Birchwood, M. and Dimmock, M. (eds) (2005) *Cultural Encounters Between East and West: 1453–1699*. Cambridge: Scholar's Press.

Bisaha, N. (2004) *Creating East and West: Renaissance Humanists and the Ottoman Turks*. Philadelphia: University of Pennsylvania Press.

Bitterli, U. (1986) *Cultures in Conflict: Encounters between European and Non-European Cultures, 1492–1800*. Stanford: Stanford University Press.

Blaut, J. M. (1993) *The Colonizer's Model of the World: Geographical Diffusion and Eurocentric History*. New York: Guilford Press.

Bloch, M. (1961) *Feudal Society*. Vol. 1. London: Routledge & Kegan Paul.

Blok, A. (1998) 'The Narcissism of Minor Differences' *European Journal of Social Theory* 1(1): 33–56.

Blokker, P. (2005) 'The Post-Communist Modernization, Transition Studies, and Diversity in Europe' *European Journal of Social Theory* 8(2): 503–25.

Blokker, P. (2008) 'Europe "United in Diversity": From a Central European Identity to Post-Nationality' *European Journal of Social Theory* 11(2): 257–74.

Blokker, P. (2010) 'Romania at the Intersection of Different Europes: Implications of a Pluri-Civilizational Encounter' in Arnason, J. and Doyle, N. (eds) *Domains and Divisions of European History*. Liverpool: University of Liverpool Press.

Blokker, P. and Delanty, G. (2010) 'European Identity, Post-Western Europe, and Complex Cultural Diversity' in Browning, C. and Lehti, M. (eds) *The Struggle for the West: A Divided and Contested Legacy*. London: Routledge.

Böröcz, J. (2010) *The European Union and Global Social Change*. London: Routledge.

Bova, R. (ed.) (2003) *Russia and Western Civilization: Cultural and Historical Encounters*. New York: M. E. Sharpe.

Brague, R. (2002) *Eccentric Culture: A Theory of Western Civilization*. South Bend, IN: St. Augustine's Press.

Brague, R. (2009) *The Legend of the Middle Ages: Philosophical Explorations of Medieval Christianity, Judaism, and Islam*. Chicago: Chicago University Press.

Braudel, F. (1990/1987) *The Mediterranean and the Mediterranean World in the Age of Philip II*, vols 1 and 2. London: Fontana.

Braudel, F. (1994) *A History of Civilizations*. London: Penguin.

Breuilly, J. (1982) *Nationalism and the State*. Chicago: Chicago University Press.

Bronner, S. E. (2004) *Reclaiming the Enlightenment: Toward a Politics of Radical Engagement*. New York: Columbia University Press.

Brottom, J. (1997) *Trading Territories: Mapping the Early Modern World*. London: Reaktion Books.

Brottom, J. (2002) *The Renaissance Bazaar: From the Silk Road to Michelangelo*. Oxford: Oxford University Press.

Brugmans, H. (1966) *L'ideé Europeéne, 1918–1965*. Bruges: De Tempel.

Brugmans, H. (ed.) (1987) *Europe: Réve-Aventure-Réalité*. Brussels: Elsevier.

Brunkhorst, H. (2005) *Solidarity: From Civic Friendship to a Global Legal Community*. Cambridge, MA: MIT Press.

Bruter, M. (2005) *Citizens of Europe? The Emergence of a Mass European Identity*. London: Palgrave.

Buck-Morss, S. (2009) *Hegel, Haiti and Universal History*. Pittsburgh: Pittsburgh University Press.

Bulliet, R. (2004) *The Case for Islam-Christian Civilization*. New York: Columbia University Press.

Burke, P. (1998) *The European Renaissance*. Oxford: Blackwell.

Burke, P. (2010) *Hybridity*. Cambridge: Polity Press.

Burkert, W. (1995) *The Orientalizing Revolution: The Near Eastern Influences on Greek Culture in the Early Archaic Age*. Cambridge, MA: Harvard University Press.

Burns, R. (1984) *Muslims, Christians, and Jews in the Crusader Kingdom of Valencia*. Cambridge: Cambridge University Press.

Buruma, I. and Margalit, A. (2004) *Occidentalism: The West in the Eyes of its Enemies*. London: Penguin.

Buss, A. (2003) *The Russian Orthodox Tradition and Modernity*. London: Brill.

Cahnman, W. (1952) 'Frontiers between East and West' *Geographical Review* 49: 605–24.

Calhoun, C. (ed.) (1994) *Social Theory and the Politics of Identity*. Oxford: Blackwell.

Cameron, A. (2006) *The Byzantines*. Oxford: Blackwell.

Cannadine, D. (2001) *Ornamentalism: How the British Made Their Empire*. Oxford: Oxford University Press.

Carrithers, M., Collins, S. and Lukes, S. (1985) (eds) *The Category of the Person: Anthropology, Philosophy, History*. Cambridge: Cambridge University Press.

Casanova, J. (2000) 'Civil Wars, Revolutions and Counterrevolutions in Finland, Spain, and Greece (1981–1949): A Comparative Analysis' *International Journal of Politics, Culture and Society* 13(3): 515–37.

Castells, M. (1996) *The Rise of the Network State*. Oxford: Blackwell.

Castoriadis, C. (1987) *The Imaginary Institution of Society*. Cambridge: Polity Press.

Centeno, M. (2002) *Blood and Debt: War and the Nation-State in Latin America*. University Park, Penn: Pennsylvania State University Press.

Cerutti, C. (ed.) (2001) *A Soul for Europe: Vol. 1 A Reader*. Leuven: Peeters.

Chadwick, O. (1993) *The Secularization of the European Mind in the Nineteenth Century*. Cambridge: Cambridge University Press.

Chakrabarty, D. (2000) *Provincializing Europe: Postcolonial Thought and Historical Difference*. Princeton: Princeton University Press.

Chambers, I. (2008) *The Mediterranean Crossings: Politics of an Interrupted Modernity*. Durham, NC: Duke University Press.

Checkel, J. and Katzenstein, P. (eds) (2009) *European Identity*. Cambridge: Cambridge University Press.

Clarke, J. J. (1997) *Oriental Enlightenment: The Encounter between Asian and Western Thought*. London: Routledge.

Cohen, N. (1993) *Europe's Inner Demons: The Demonization of Christians in Medieval Christendom*. London: Pimlico.

Crankshaw, E. (1982) *Bismark*. London: Macmillan.

Crouch, C. (2004) *Post-Democracy*. Cambridge: Polity Press.

Curtin, P. (1984) *Cross-Cultural Trade in the Modern World*. Cambridge: Cambridge University Press.

Dainotto, R. (2007) *Europe (in Theory)*. Durham, NC: Duke University Press.

Dallmayr, F. (1996) *Beyond Orientalism: Essays on Cross-Cultural Encounter*. Notre Dame: Notre Dame University Press.

Dann, O. and Dinwiddy, J. J. (eds) *Nationalism and the French Revolution*. London: Hambledon Press.

Darwin, J. (2009) *After Tamerland: The Rise and Fall of Global Empires, 1400–2000*. London: Penguin.

Davies, N. (1996) *Europe – A History*. Oxford: Oxford University Press.

Davies, N. (2006) *Europe East and West*. London: Jonathan Cape.

Dawson, C. (1932) *The Making of Europe: An Introduction to the History of European Unity*. London: Sheed and Ward.

De Rougement, D. (1965) *The Meaning of Europe*. London: Sidgwick & Jackson.

De Rougement, D. (1966) *The Idea of Europe*. London: Macmillan.

de Tocqueville, A. (1948) *Democracy in America*, vols 1 and 2. New York: Knopf.

Delanty, G. (1995a) *Inventing Europe: Idea, Identity, Reality*. London: Macmillan.

Delanty, G. (1995b) 'The Limits and Possibility of a European Identity: A Critique of Cultural Essentialism' *Philosophy and Social Criticism* 21(4): 15–36.

Delanty, G. (1999) *Social Theory in a Changing World: Conceptions of Modernity*. Cambridge: Polity Press.

Delanty, G. (2000a) *Modernity and Postmodernity: Knowledge, Power, the Self*. London: Sage.

Delanty, G. (2000b) *Citizenship in the Global Age: Culture, Society and Politics*. Buckingham: Open University Press.

Delanty, G. (2003) 'The Making of a Post-Western Europe: A Civilizational Analysis' *Thesis Eleven* 72: 8–24.

Delanty, G. (ed.) (2006) *Europe and Asia Beyond East and West*. London: Routledge.

Delany, G. (2007) 'The European Civilizational Constellation: A Historical Sociology' in *Encyclopaedia of Life Support Systems*. UNESCO.

Delany, G. (2009a) *The Cosmopolitan Imagination: The Renewal of Critical Social Theory*. Cambridge: Cambridge University Press.

Delany, G. (2009b) 'The European Heritage: History, Memory and Time' in Rumford, C. (ed.) *Handbook of European Studies*. London: Sage.

Delany, G. (2010) 'Civilizational Analysis and Critical Theory' *Thesis Eleven* 100: 46–52.

Delany, G. (2011a) 'Cultural Diversity, Democracy and the Prospects of Cosmopolitanism: A Theory of Cultural Encounters' *British Journal of Sociology* 62(4): 633–56.

Delany, G. (2011b) 'Varieties of Critique in Sociological Theory and Their Methodological Implications for Social Research' *Irish Journal of Sociology* 19(1): 68–92.

Delany, G. (2012a) 'A Cosmopolitan Approach to the Explanation of Social Change' *Sociological Review* 62(2): 333–54.

Delany, G. (ed.) (2012b) *Handbook of Cosmopolitanism Studies*. London: Routledge.

Delany, G. and He, B. (2008) 'Comparative Perspectives on Cosmopolitanism: Assessing European and Asian Perspectives' *International Sociology* 23(3): 323–44.

Delany, G. and Isin, E. (eds) (2003) *Handbook of Historical Sociology*. London: Sage.

Delany, G. and O'Mahony, P. (2002) *Nationalism and Social Theory*. London: Sage.

Delany, G. and Rumford, C. (2005) *Rethinking Europe: Social Theory and the Implications of Europeanization*. London: Routledge.

Derrida, J. (1992) *The Other Heading: Reflections on Today's Europe*. Bloomington, IN: Indiana University Press.

Deutschmann, C. (2011) 'Limits to Financialization: Sociological Analyses of the Financial Crisis' *European Journal of Sociology* 52(3): 347–98.

Diez Medrano, J. (2003) *Framing Europe: Attitudes toward European Integration in Germany, Spain and the United Kingdom*. Princeton: Princeton University Press.

Diment, G. and Slezkine, Y. (eds) (1993) *Between Heaven and Hell: The Myth of Siberia in Russian Culture*. New York: St Martin's Press.

Dinan, M. (2006) *Origins and Evolution of the European Union*. Oxford: Oxford University Press.

Diner, D. (2008) *Cataclysms: A History of the Twentieth Century from Europe's Edge*. Madison, WI: University of Wisconsin Press.

Dobson, J. (2004) *The Eastern Origins of European Civilization*. Cambridge: Cambridge University Press.

Domingues, J. (2011) 'Beyond the Centre: The Third Phase of Modernity in a Globally Compared Perspective' *European Journal of Social Theory* 14(4): 517–35.

Dudley, D. (1995) *Roman Society*. London: Penguin Books.

Dumont, L. (1986) *Essays on Individualism: Modern Ideology in Anthropological Perspective*. Chicago: University of Chicago Press.

Durkheim, E. (1960[1893]) *The Division of Labour in Society*. Glencoe, Ill: Free Press.

Duroselle, J.-B. (1990) *Europe – A History of its Peoples*. London: Viking.

Eder, K. (1999) 'Societies Learn and Yet the World is Hard to Change' *European Journal of Social Theory* 2(2): 195–215.

Eder, K. (2006a) 'The European Public Sphere' in Delanty, G. (ed.) *Handbook of Contemporary European Social Theory*. London: Routledge.

Eder, K. (2006b) 'The Narrative Construction of the Boundaries of Europe' *European Journal of Social Theory* 9(2): 255–71.

Eder, K. (2009) 'A Theory of Collective Identity: Making Sense of the Debate on a "European Identity"' *European Journal of Social Theory* 12(4): 427–47.

Eder, K. and Giesen, B. (eds) (2001) *European Citizenship: National Legacies and Transnational Projects*. Oxford: Oxford University Press.

Eder, K. and Spohn, W. (eds) (2005) *Collective Memory and European Identity*. Aldershot: Ashgate.

Eisenstadt, S. N. (ed.) (1986) *The Origin and Diversity of Axial Age Civilizations*. New York: SUNY Press.

Eisenstadt, S. N. (1992) *Jewish Civilization: The Jewish Historical Experience in Historical Perspective*. Albany: SUNY Press.

Eisenstadt, S. N. (2000) Special Issue on 'Multiple Modernities' *Daedalus* 129(1).

Eisenstadt, S. N. (2003) *Comparative Civilizations and Multiple Modernities*. Vols 1 and 2. Leiden: Brill.

Eisenstadt, S. N. and Schluchter, W. (eds) (1998) Special Issue on 'Early Modernities' *Daedalus* 127(3).

Eisenstein, E. (1993) *The Printing Press in Early Modern Europe*. Cambridge: Cambridge University Press.

Elbe, S. (2003) *Europe: A Nietzschean Perspective*. London: Routledge.

Elias, N. (1982) *The Civilizing Process, Vol. 2: State Formation and Civilization*. Oxford: Blackwell.

Eriksen, E. O. (2005) *Making the European Polity: Reflexive Integration in the EU*. London: Routledge.

Eriksen, E. O. (2009) 'Reflexive Integration: A Perspective on the Transformation of Europe' in Delanty, G. and Turner, S. (eds) *Routledge International Handbook of Social and Political Theory*. London: Routledge.

Ertman, T. (1997) *Birth of the Leviathan: Building States and Empires in Medieval and Early Modern Europe*. Cambridge: Cambridge University Press.

Evtuhov, C. and Kotkin, S. (eds) (2003) *The Cultural Gradient: The Transmission of Ideas in Europe, 1789–1991*. New York: Rowman & Littlefield.

Favell, A. (2008) *Eurostars and Eurocities: Free Movement and Mobility in an Integrating Europe*. Oxford: Blackwell.

Favell, A. and Guiraudon, V. (eds) (2011) *Sociology of the European Union*. London: Palgrave.

Featherstone, K. and Kazamias, G. (2001) (eds) *Europeanization and the Southern Periphery*. London: Frank Cass.

Featherstone, M., Lash, S. and Robertson, R. (1995) (eds) *Global Modernities*. London: Sage.

Feher, F. (1987) 'Eastern Europe's Long Revolution against Yalta' *East European Politics and Societies* 2(1): 1–34.

Feher, F., Heller, A. and Markus, G. (1983) *Dictatorship over Needs*. Oxford: Blackwell.

Fisher, H. A. L. (1935) *History of Europe*, 3 vols. London: Eyre & Spottiswoode, Ltd.

Fligstein, N. (2008) *Euroclash: The EU, European Identity, and the Future of Europe*. Oxford: Oxford University Press.

Fontana, J. (1995) *The Distorted Past: A Reinterpretation of European History*. Oxford: Blackwell.

Forst, R. (2002) *Contexts of Justice: Political Theory Beyond Liberalism and Communitarianism*. Berkeley: University of California Press.

Fossum, J-E. and Schlesinger, P. (2007) *The EU and the Public Sphere*. London: Routledge.

Fowden, G. (2011) 'Contextualizing Late Antiquity' in Arnason, J. and Raaflaub, K. (eds) *The Roman Empire in Context: Historical and Comparative Perspectives*. Oxford: Blackwell.

Frank, A. G. (1998) *Re-Orient: Global Economy in the Asian Age*. Berkeley: University of California Press.

Friedmann, M. (1981) *The Monstrous Races in Medieval Art and Thought*. Cambridge, MA: Harvard University Press.

Friese, H. (2006) 'Europe's Otherness. Cosmopolitanism and the Construction of Cultural Unities' in Delanty, G. (ed.) *Europe Beyond East and West*. London: Routledge.

Friese, H. and Wagner, P. (2002) 'The Nascent Political Philosophy of the European Polity' *The Journal of Political Philosophy* 10(3): 342–64.

Furet, F. (1999) *The Passing of an Illusion: The Idea of Communism in the Twentieth Century*. Chicago: The University of Chicago Press.

Gadamer, H.-G. (1992) 'The Diversity of Europe: Inheritance and Future' in Misgeld, D. and Nicholson, G. (eds) *Applied Hermeneutics*. NY: SUNY.

Gallant, T. (2006) 'Europe and the Mediterranean' in Delanty, G. (ed.) *Europe and Asia Beyond East and West*. London: Routledge.

Gaonkar, D. P. (ed.) (2001) *Alternative Modernities*. Durham, NC: Duke University Press.

Garner, R. (1990) 'Jacob Burkhardt as a Theorist of Modernity: Reading *The Civilization of the Renaissance in Italy*' *Sociological Theory* 8(1): 48–57.

Garton Ash, T. (1993) *The Magic Lantern: The Revolutions of '89 Witnessed in Warsaw, Berlin, and Prague*. London: Vintage.

Gellner, E. (1983) *Nations and Nationalism*. Oxford: Blackwell.

Gellner, E. (1998) *Language and Solitude: Wittgenstein, Malinowski, and the Habsburg Dilemma*. Cambridge: Cambridge University Press.

Gentile, E. (2003) *The Struggle for Modernity: Nationalism, Futurism, and Fascism*. London: Praeger.

Giddens, A. (1984) *The Constitution of Society: Outline of a Theory of Structuration*. Cambridge: Polity Press.

Giddens, T. (1985) *The Nation-State and Violence*. Cambridge: Polity Press.

Gilroy, P. (2005) *Postcolonial Melancholia*. New York: Columbia University Press.

Goffman, D. (2002) *The Ottoman Empire and Early Modern Europe*. Cambridge: Cambridge University Press.

Goldberg, D. T. (2006) 'Racial Europeanization' *Ethnic and Racial Studies* 29(2): 331–64.

Goldstone, J. (2008) *Why Europe? The Rise of the West in Global Context, 1500–1850*. New York: McGraw-Hill.

Göle, N. (2004) 'The Making and Unmaking of Europe in its Encounter with Islam' in Karangiannis, N. and Wagner, P. (eds) *Varieties of World-Making: Beyond Globalization*. Liverpool: Liverpool University Press.

Goody, J. (1986) *The Logic of Writing and the Organization of Society*. Cambridge: Cambridge University Press.

Goody, J. (2004) *Islam in Europe*. Cambridge: Polity Press.

Goody, J. (2010) *Renaissances: The One or the Many*. Cambridge: Polity Press.

Goody, J., Watt, I. and Gough, K. (eds) (1968) *Literacy in Traditional Societies*. Cambridge: Cambridge University Press.

Gouldner, A. (1973) 'Romanticism and Classicism: Deep Structures in Social Science' in *For Sociology: Renewal and Critique in Sociology Today*. London: Allen Lane.

Greenblatt, S. (2005) *Renaissance Self-Fashioning*. Chicago: University of Chicago Press.

Greenblatt, S. (2010) *Cultural Mobility*. Cambridge: Cambridge University Press.

Gregory, D. (1994) *Geographical Imaginations*. Oxford: Blackwell.

Griffin, R. (2009) *Modernism and Fascism: The Sense of a New Beginning under Mussolini and Hitler*. London: Palgrave.

Gruen, E. (2011) *Rethinking the Other in Antiquity*. Princeton: Princeton University Press.

Gunn, G. (2003) *First Globalization: The Eurasian Exchange, 1500–1800*. Lanham, MD: Rowman & Littlefield.

Gurevich, A. (1995) *The Origins of European Individualism*. Oxford: Blackwell.

Habermas, J. (1976) *Legitimation Crisis*. London: Heinemann.

Habermas, J. (1979) *Communication and the Evolution of Society*. London: Heinemann.

Habermas, J. (1984) *The Theory of Communicative Action*, vol. 1. Cambridge: Polity Press.

Habermas, J. (1987a) *The Philosophical Discourse of Modernity*. Cambridge: Polity Press.

Habermas, J. (1987b) *The Theory of Communicative Action*, vol. 2. Cambridge: Polity Press.

Habermas, J. (1989) 'On the Public Use of History' in *The New Conservatism: Cultural Criticism and the Historians's Debate*. Cambridge, MA: MIT Press.

Habermas, J. (2001a) 'Why European Needs a Constitution?' *New Left Review* 11(Sept–Oct): 5–26.

Habermas, J. (2001b) *The Postnational Constellation*. Cambridge: Polity Press.

Habermas, J. (2003) 'Towards a Cosmopolitan Europe' *Journal of Democracy* 14(4): 1–25.

Habermas, J. (2006) 'Is There Development of a European Identity Necessary, and Is It Possible?' in *The Divided West*. Cambridge: Polity Press.

Habermas, J. (2009) *Europe – The Faltering Project*. Cambridge: Polity Press.

Habermas, J. (2012) *The Crisis of the European Union: A Response*. Cambridge: Polity Press.

Habermas, J. and Ratzinger, J. (2005) *Dialektik der Säkularisierung: Über Vernuft und Religion*. Freiburg: Verlag Herder.

Halbfass, W. (1988) *India in Europe: An Essay in Understanding*. New York: State University of New York Press.

Hale, J. (1993) 'The Renaissance Idea of Europe' in Garcia, S. (ed.) *European Identity and the Search for Legitimacy*. London: Pinter.

Halecki, O. (1950) *The Limits and Divisions of European History*. New York: Sheed and Ward.

Halecki, O. (1953) *Borderlands of Western Civilization: A History of East Central Europe*. New York: Ronald Press.

Hall, J. (1996) *Powers and Liberties: The Causes and Consequences of the Rise of the West*. Oxford: Blackwell.

Hall, S. (ed.) (1992) *Formations of Modernity*. Buckingham: Open University Press.

Halperin, S. (2007) 'Re-Envisioning Global Development: Conceptual and Methodological Issues' *Globalizations* 4(4): 547–88.

Hampson, N. (1984) *The Enlightenment*. London: Penguin.

Hansen, P. (2002) 'European Integration, European Identity and the Colonial Connection' *European Journal of Social Theory* 5(4): 483–98.

Harrington, A. (2004) 'Ernst Troeltsch's Concept of Europe' *European Journal of Social Theory* 7(4): 479–98.

Harrington, A. (2012) 'Weimar Social Theory and the Fragmentation of the European World Picture' *Thesis Eleven* 111(1): 60–8.

Harris, W. (ed.) (2006) *Rethinking the Mediterranean*. Oxford: Oxford University Press.

Hartz, L. (1964) *The Foundation of New Societies*. New York: Harcourt and Brace.

Harvey, D. (2010) *The Enigma of Capital and the Crises of Capitalism*. Oxford: Oxford University Press.

Hauner, M. (1990) *What is Asia to Us?* Boston: Unwin Hyman.

Hay, D. (1957) *Europe: The Emergence of an Idea*. Edinburgh: Edinburgh University Press.

Hazard, P. (1953) *The European Mind: The Critical Years, 1680–1715*. New Haven: Yale University Press.

Headley, J. M. (2008) *The Europeanization of the World: On the Origins of Human Rights and Democracy*. Princeton: Princeton University Press.

Hechter, M. (1975) *Internal Colonialism: The Celtic Fringe in British National Development*. Berkeley: University of California Press.

Heller, A. (1984) *Renaissance Man*. London: Routledge.

Heller, A. (2006) 'European Master Narratives of Freedom' in Delanty, G. (ed.) *Handbook of Contemporary European Social Theory*. London: Routledge.

Herf, J. (1986) *Reactionary Modernism: Technology, Culture and Politics in Weimar and the Third Reich*. Cambridge: Cambridge University Press.

Herlihy, D. (1997) *The Black Death and the Transformation of the World*. Cambridge, MA: Harvard University Press.

Herrin, J. (1987) *The Formation of Christendom*. Princeton: Princeton University Press.

Herrmann, R. K., Risse, T. and Brewer, M. B. (eds) (2004) *Transnational Identities: Becoming European in the EU*. Lanham, MD: Rowman & Littlefield.

Hess, A. (1978) *The Forgotten Frontier: A History of the Sixteenth-Century Ibero-African Frontier*. Chicago: Chicago University Press.

Hobsbawm, E. (1990) *Nations and Nationalism since 1780*. Cambridge: Cambridge University Press.

Hobsbawm, E. (1994) *Age of Extremes: The Short Twentieth Century, 1914–1991*. London: Michael Joseph.

Hobsbawm, E. and Ranger, T. (1983) (eds) *The Invention of Tradition*. Cambridge: Cambridge University Press.

Hobson, J. (2004) *The Eastern Origins of Western Civilization*. Cambridge: Cambridge.

Hobson, J. (2006) 'Revealing the Cosmopolitan Side of Oriental Europe' in Delanty, G. (ed.) *Europe and Asia Beyond East and West*. London: Routledge.

Hochstramer, T. (2000) *Natural Law Theory in the Early Enlightenment*. Cambridge: Cambridge University Press.

Hodgson, M. (1974) *The Venture of Islam: Conscience and History in a World Civilization*, 3 vols. Chicago: University of Chicago Press.

Hodgson, M. (1993) *Rethinking World History. Essays on Europe, Islam and the World*. Cambridge: Cambridge University Press.

Holmes, D. (2006) 'Nationalism-Integralism-Supra Nationalism: A Schemata for the 21st Century' in Delanty, G. and Kumar, K. (eds) *Handbook of Nations and Nationalism*. London: Sage.

Honneth, A. (2011) *Das Recht Der Freiheit*. Frankfurt: Suhrkamp.

Honnig, B. (2001) *Democracy and the Foreigner*. Princeton: Princeton University Press.

Hopkins, A. G. (ed.) (2002) *Globalization in World History*. New York: Norton.

Horden, P. and Purcell, N. (2000) *The Corrupting Sea: A Study of Mediterranean History*. Oxford: Blackwell.

Hughes, S. H. (2002[1958]) *Consciousness and Society: The Reorientation of European Social Thought 1890–1930*. New York: Transaction Publishers.

Hunt, L. (2010) 'The French Revolution in Global Context' in Armitage, D. and Subrahmanyam, S. (eds) *The Age of Revolutions in Global Context, c.1760–1840*. London: Palgrave.

Inglis, D. and Robertson, R. (2005) 'The Ecumenical Analytic: "Globalization", Reflexivity and the Revolution in Greek Historiography' *European Journal of Social Theory* 8(2): 99–122.

Inglis, D. and Robertson, R. (2006) 'Discovering the World: Cosmopolitanism and Globality in the "Eurasian" Renaissance' in Delanty, G. (ed.) *Europe and Asia Beyond East and West*. London: Routledge.

Inglis, D. and Robertson, R. (2008) 'The Elementary Forms of Globality: Durkheim and the Emergence of and Nature of Global Life' *Journal of Classical Sociology* 8(1): 5–25.

Isin, E. and Lefebvre, A. (2005) 'The Gift of Law: Greek Euergetism and the Ottoman Waqf' *European Journal of Social Theory* 8(1): 5–23.

Jackson, A. and Jaffer, A. (eds) (2004) *Encounters: The Meeting of Asia and Europe 1500–1800*. London: Victoria and Albert Museum.

James, C. L. R. (1980) *The Black Jacobins*. London: Allison & Busby.

Jameson, F. (2003) *A Singular History: Essays on the Ontology of the Present*. London: Verso.

Jardine, L. and Brottom, J. (2000) *Global Interests: Renaissance Art between East and West*. London: Reaktion Books.

Jaspers, K. (1948) *The European Spirit*. London: SCM Press.

Jenkins, R. (1996) *Social Identity*. London: Routledge.

Joas, H. and Wiegandt, K. (eds) (2007) *Europe's Cultural Values*. Liverpool: Liverpool University Press.

Johnson, H. (2011) *States and Social Movements*. Cambridge: Polity Press.

Jones, E. (1987) *The European Miracle: Environments, Economies and Geopolitics in the History of Europe and Asia*. Cambridge: Cambridge University Press.

322 *Bibliography*

Jones, P. (2011) *The Sociology of Architecture*. Liverpool: Liverpool University Press.
Jones, W. R. (1971) 'The Image of the Barbarian in Medieval Europe' *Comparative Studies in Society and History* 13(1): 376–407.
Judt, T. (2005) *PostWar: A History of Europe since 1945*. London: William Heinemann.
Judt, T. (2008) *Reappraisals: Reflections on the Forgotten Twentieth Century*. London: Penguin.
Judt, T. (2010) *Ill Fares the Land*. London: Penguin.
Judt, T. (2012) *Thinking the Twentieth Century*. London: Penguin.
Kaelble, H. (1989) *A Social History of Western Europe, 1880–1980*. Dublin: Gill and Macmillan.
Kaldor, M. (1990) *The Imaginary War: Understanding the East-West Conflict*. Oxford: Blackwell.
Kaldor, M. (1991) 'After the Cold War' in Kaldor, M. (ed.) *Europe from Below: An East-West Dialogue*. London: Verso.
Kant, I. (1991[1795]) *Perpetual Peace: Political Writing*. Cambridge: Cambridge University Press.
Kantner, C. (2006) 'Collective Identity as Shared Ethical Self-Understanding: The Case of an Emerging European Identity' *European Journal of Social Theory* 9(4): 501–23.
Karangiannis, N. (ed.) (2007) *European Solidarity*. Liverpool: Liverpool University Press.
Karangiannis, N. and Wagner, P. (eds) (2007) *Varieties of World-Making: Beyond Globalization*. Liverpool: Liverpool University Press.
Katzenstein, P. (ed.) (2012) *Anglo-America and its Discontents*. London: Routledge.
Kennedy, H. (1996) *Muslim Spain and Portugal: A Political History of al-Andalus*. London: Longman.
Kennedy, P. (1987) *The Rise and Fall of the Great Powers*. London: Vintage Books.
Keyman, F. (2006) 'Turkey between Europe and Asia' in Delanty, G. (ed.) *Europe and Asia Beyond East and West*. London: Routledge.
Kharkhordin, O. (1999) *The Collective and the Individual in Russia: A Study of Practices*. Berkeley: University of California Press.
Kirkpatrick, R. (2002) *The European Renaissance, 1400–1600*. Harlow: Longman.
Kleingeld, P. (2008) 'Novalis's Romantic Cosmopolitanism: "Christianity or Europe"' *Journal of the History of Philosophy* 46(2): 269–84.
Klooger, J. (2013) 'Plurality and Indeterminacy: Reviewing Castoriadis's Overly Homogeneous Conception of Society' *European Journal of Social Theory* 15(4): 488–504.
Kolakowski, L. (1990) *Modernity on Endless Trial*. Chicago: University of Chicago Press.
Konrad, G. (1984) *Antipolitics: An Essay*. London: Quartet Books.
Koselleck, R. (1988) *Crisis and Critique: The Enlightenment and the Pathogenesis of Modern Society*. Cambridge, MA: MIT Press.
Kozlarek, O. (2011) *Moderne asls Weltbewustein: Ideen für eine humanistische Sozialtheorie in der globalen Moderne*. Bielefeld: Transcript.
Kriesi, H-P., Grande, E., Lackat, R., Dolezol, M. and Bornshier, S. (2008) *Western European Politics in an Age of Globalization*. Cambridge: Cambridge University Press.

Kristeva, J. (2000) *Crisis of the European Subject*. New York: Other Press.

Kumar, K. (1991) *Utopianism*. Milton Keynes: Open University Press.

Kumar, K. (2009) 'Empire and Imperialism' in Delanty, G. and Turner, S. (eds) *International Handbook of Contemporary Social and Political Theory*. London: Routledge.

Kundera, M. (1984) 'The Tragedy of Central Europe' *New York Review of Books* 26(April): 33–8.

Laitin, D. 2002 'Culture and National Identity: "The East" and European Integration' *West European Politics* 25(2): 55–80.

Larsen, S. E. (2006) 'The Lisbon Earthquake and the Scientific Turn in Kant's Philosophy' *European Review* 14(3): 359–67.

Latour, B. (1993) *We Have Never Been Modern*. Hemel Hempstead: Harvester Wheatsheaf.

Le Goff, J. (2006) *The Birth of Europe*. Oxford: Blackwell.

Lefort, C. (1989) *Democracy and Political Theory*. Cambridge: Polity Press.

Lemberg, H. (1985) 'Zur Entstehung des Osteuropabegriffs im Jahrhundert vom "Norden" zum "Oste" Europas' *Jahrbuch für Osteuropas* 33: 48–9.

Levy, D., Pensky, M. and Torpey, J. (eds) (2005) *Old Europe, New Europe, Core Europe: Transatlantic Relations after the Iraq War*. London: Verso.

Lewis, B. (1982) *The Muslim Discovery of Europe*. New York: Norton.

Lewis, M. and Wigen, K. (1997) *The Myth of Continents: A Critique of Metageography*. Cambridge: Cambridge University Press.

Lichtheim, G. (1972, 1999 new edition) *Europe in the Twentieth Century*. London: Weidenfeld and Nicolson.

Livi-Bacci, M. (2000) *The Population of Europe*. Oxford: Blackwell.

Lockwood, D. (1964) 'Social Integration and System Integration' in Zollschan, G. and Hirsch, W. (eds) *Explorations in Social Change*. London: Routledge.

Luebbert, G. (1991) *Liberalism, Fascism, or Social Democracy*. Oxford: Oxford University Press.

Luhmann, N. (1995) *Social Systems*. Stanford: Stanford University Press.

Lyotard, J.-F. (1984) *The Postmodern Condition*. Manchester: Manchester University Press.

Machiavelli, N. (2009[1513]) *The Prince*. London: Oneworld Classics.

MacFarlane, A. (1978) *The Origins of English Individualism*. Oxford: Blackwell.

MacLean, G. (ed.) (2005) *Re-Orienting the Renaissance: Cultural Exchange with the East*. London: Palgrave.

Magris, C. (2001) *Danube*. New York: Random House.

Magubane, Z. (2005) 'Overlapping Territories and Intertwined Histories: Historical Sociology's Global Imagination' in Adams, J., Clemens, E. and Orloff, A. (eds) *Remaking Modernity: Politics, History, and Sociology*. Durham, NC: Duke University Press.

Malette, K. (2010) *European Modernity and the Arab Mediterranean: Towards a New Philology and Counter-Orientalism*. Philadelphia: University of Pennsylvania Press.

Malmorg, M. and Stråth, B. (eds) (2002) *The Meaning of Europe*. Oxford: Berg.

Mann, M. (1993) *The Sources of Social Power: The Rise of Classes and Nation-States, 1760–1914*. Cambridge: Cambridge University Press.

Mann, M. (2006) *The Dark Side of Democracy*. Cambridge: Cambridge University Press.

Mantana, K. (2000) *Alibis of Empire: Henry Maine and the End of Liberal Imperialism.* Princeton: Princeton University Press.

Marshall, T. H. (1987) *Citizenship and Social Class.* London: Pluto.

Martin, J. (1997) 'Inventing Sincerity, Refashioning Prudence: The Discovery of the Individual on Renaissance Europe' *The American Historical Review* 102(5): 1309–42.

Marx, K. and Engels, F. (2004[1848]) *The Communist Manifesto.* London: Penguin.

Masaryk, T. (1918) *The New Europe.* London: Eyre & Spottiswoode, Ltd.

Massis, H. (1928) *Defence of the West.* New York: Harcourt, Brace & Co.

Matlock, J. (2003) 'Russia, Europe, and "Western Civilization"' in Evtuhov, C. and Kotkin, S. (eds) *The Cultural Gradient: The Transmission of Ideas in Europe, 1789–1991.* New York: Rowman & Littlefield.

Mayer, A. (1981) *The Persistence of the Old Regime.* London: Croom Helm.

Mazower, M. (2000) *Dark Continent: Europe's Twentieth Century.* New York: Vintage.

McLennan, G. (2000) 'Sociology's Eurocentrism and the "Rise of the West" Revisited' *European Journal of Social Theory* 3(3): 275–91.

McLennan, G. (2003) 'Sociology, Eurocentrism and Postcolonial Theory' *European Journal of Social Theory* 6(1): 69–86.

McNeill, W. (1963) *The Rise of the West: A History of Human Community.* Chicago: Chicago University Press.

McNeill, W. (1964) *Europe's Steppe Frontier.* Chicago: University of Chicago Press.

McNeill, W. (1974) *The Shape of European History.* Oxford: Oxford University Press.

Meier, C. (2005) *From Athens to Auschwitz: The Uses of History.* Cambridge, MA: Harvard University Press.

Meinecke, F. (1970) *Cosmopolitanism and the National State.* Princeton: Princeton University Press.

Melucci, A. (1996) *Challenging Codes: Collective Identity in the Information Age.* Cambridge: Cambridge University Press.

Metlitzki, D. (1977) *The Matter of Araby in Medieval England.* New Haven: Yale University Press.

Meyerson, M. and English, E. (eds) (2000) *Christians, Muslims and Jews in Medieval and Early Modern Spain: Interaction and Cultural Change.* Notre Dame, IN: Notre Dame University Press.

Mignolo, W. (1995) *The Dark Side of the Renaissance: Literacy, Territoriality, and Colonization.* Ann Arbor: University of Michigan Press.

Mignolo, W. (2006) *The Idea of Latin America.* Oxford: Blackwell.

Mignolo, W. (2011) *The Dark Side of Western Modernity.* Durham, NC: Duke University Press.

Mikkeli, H. (1998) *Europe as an Idea and Identity.* London: Macmillan.

Miller, M. and Urry, S. (2012) 'Dangerous Liaisons: Jews and Cosmopolitanism in Modern Times' in Delanty, G. (ed.) *Handbook of Cosmopolitanism Studies.* London: Routledge.

Milward, A. (1982/2000 2nd edition) *The European Rescue of the Nation-State.* London: Routledge.

Minehan, P. (2006) *Civil War and World War in Europe: Spain, Yugoslavia, and Greece, 1936–1949.* London: Palgrave.

Mishkova, D. (2008) 'Symbolic Geographies and Vision of Identity: A Balkan Perspective' *European Journal of Social Theory* 11(2): 237–56.

Mollat du Jourdin, M. (1993) *Europe and the Sea*. Oxford: Blackwell.

Monar, J. (2012) 'The EU in Crisis: Testing the Limits and Potential' *Euroscope Newsletter* (Spring) No. 48: 1–2.

Moore, R. I. (1987) *The Formation of a Persecuting Society: Power and Deviance in Western Europe, 950–1250*. Oxford: Blackwell.

Moore, R. I. (2000) *The First European Revolution, c.970–1215*. Oxford: Blackwell.

Morin, E. (1987) *Penser l'Europe*. Paris: Gallimard.

Morris, C. (1972) *The Discovery of the Individual, 1050–1200*. London: SPCK.

Mosse, G. (1961, 3rd edition 1988) *The Culture of Western Europe*. Boulder, CO: Westview.

Mota, A. (2012) 'Sobre Metamorfoses e Transformações: uma perspectiva sociológico-histórica a respeito do liberalismo constitucional atenuado latino-americano', PhD Thesis: IESP/UERJ, Rio de Janeiro.

Mudimbe, V. Y. (1994) *The Idea of Africa*. Bloomington, IN: Indiana University Press.

Müller, M. (2001) 'Southern Europe as a Historical Meso-Region' *European Review of History* 10(2): 393–408.

Müller, M. (2010) 'Where and When Was (East) Central Europe? in Arnason, J. and Doyle, N. (eds) *Domains and Divisions of European History*. Liverpool: University of Liverpool Press.

Murray, P. (2009) 'Uses and Abuses of the Concept of Integration' in Rumford, C. (ed.) *Handbook of European Studies*. London: Routledge.

Muthu, S. (2003) *Enlightenment Against Empire*. Princeton: Princeton University Press.

Nauert, C. G. (2006) *Humanism and the Culture of the Renaissance in Europe*. Cambridge: Cambridge University Press.

Naumann, F. (1915) *Mitteleuropa*. Berlin: Reimer.

Nelson, B. (1976) 'Orient and Occident in Max Weber' *Social Research* 43(1): 114–29.

Nelson, B. (1981) *On the Road to Modernity*. Totowa, NJ: Rowman and Littlefield.

Neumann, I. (1996) *Russia and the Idea of Europe*. London: Routledge.

Nielsen, J. (1999) *Towards a European Islam*. London: Palgrave.

Nietzsche, F. (1973) *Beyond Good and Evil*. London: Penguin.

Nietzsche, F. (1979) *Ecco Homo*. London: Penguin.

Norris, P. and Inglehart, R. (2004) *Sacred and Secular: Religion and Politics Worldwide*. Cambridge: Cambridge University Press.

North, D. C., Wallis, J. J. and Weingast, B. (2009) *Violence and Social Orders: A Conceptual Framework for Interpreting Recorded Human History*. Cambridge: Cambridge University Press.

O'Mahony, P. and Delanty, G. (1998) *Rethinking Irish History*. London: Palgrave Macmillan.

O'Malley, J. (2004) *Four Cultures of the West*. Cambridge, MA: Harvard University Press.

Offe, C. (1997) *Varieties of Transition: The East European and East German Experience*. Cambridge, MA: MIT Press.

Offe, C. (2003) Can the European Model of "Social Capitalism" Survive European Integration?' *The Journal of Political Philosophy* 11(4): 437–69.

Ortega y Gasset, J. (1932/1972) *The Revolt of the Masses*. London: Unwin.

Ossewarde, M. (2007) 'The Dialectic between Romanticism and Classicism in Europe' *European Journal of Social Theory* 10(4): 523–42.

Osterhammel, J. (1998) *Die Entzauberung Asiens*. Munich: Beck.

Outhwaite, W. (2006) *The Future of Society*. Oxford: Blackwell.

Outhwaite, W. (2008) *European Society*. Cambridge: Polity Press.

Outhwaite, W. (2012) *Critical Theory and Contemporary Society*. New York: Continuum.

Outhwaite, W. (2013) 'Towards a European Society. What Can European Sociology Tell Us?' in Koniordos, S. and Andreas Kyrtsis, A. (eds) *The Handbook of European Sociology*. London: Routledge.

Outhwaite, W. and Ray, L. (2005) *Social Theory and PostCommunism*. Oxford: Blackwell.

Pace, M. (2004) *The Politics of Regional Identity: Meddling with the Mediterranean*. London: Routledge.

Pagden, A. (1995) *Lords of All the World: Ideologies of Empire in Spain, Britain, and France c.1500–c.1800*. New Haven: Yale University Press.

Pagden, A. (2001) *Peoples and Empires*. London: Penguin.

Pagden, A. (ed.) (2002) *The Idea of Europe: From Antiquity to the European Union*. Cambridge: Cambridge University Press.

Parker, C. (2010) *Global Interaction in the Early Modern Age, 1400–1800*. Cambridge: Cambridge University Press.

Parker, M. and Strath, B. (eds) (2010) *A European Memory? Contested Histories and Politics of Commemoration*. Oxford: Berghahn.

Parsons, T. (1971) *The System of Modern Society*. Englewood Cliffs, NJ: Prentice-Hall.

Patocka, J. (2002) *Plato and Europe*. Stanford: Stanford University Press.

Personen, P. (1991) 'The Image of Europe in Russian Literature and Culture' *History of European Ideas* 13(4): 399–409.

Pichierri, A. (2013) 'Social Cohesion and Economic Competitiveness: Tools for Analysing the European Model' *European Journal of Social Theory* 15(3).

Pichler, F. (2008) 'How Real is Cosmopolitanism in Europe?' *Sociology* 42(6): 1107–26.

Pico della Mirandola, P. (2012[1498]) *Oration on the Dignity of Man*. Cambridge: Cambridge University Press.

Pillorget, R. (1988) 'The European Tradition of Movements of Insurrection' in Baechler, J. (ed.) *Europe and the Rise of Capitalism*. Oxford: Blackwell.

Pirenne, H. (2001) *Mohammed and Charlemagne*. London: Dover.

Pocock, J. G. A. (1997) 'Deconstructing Europe' in Gowan, P. and Anderson, P. (eds) *The Question of Europe*. London: Verso.

Pocock, J. G. A. (2002) 'Some Europes in Their History' in Pagden, A. (ed.) *The Idea of Europe: From Antiquity to the European Union*. Cambridge: Cambridge University Press.

Poe, M. (2003) *The Russian Moment in World History*. Princeton: Princeton University Press.

Polanyi, K. (1944) *The Great Transformation*. New York: Rinehart.

Pomeranz, K. (2000) *The Great Divergence: China, Europe and the Making of the World Economy*. Princeton: Princeton University Press.

Porter, R. and Teich, M. (eds) (1981) *The Enlightenment in National Context*. Cambridge: Cambridge University Press.

Rabb, T. K. (1975) *The Struggle for Stability in Early Modern Europe*. Oxford: Oxford University Press.

Rabb, T. K. (2006) *The Last Days of the Renaissance and the March to Modernity*. New York: Basic Books.

Ragan, C. (1987) *The Comparative Method*. London: Sage.

Remer, G. (1996) *Humanism and the Rhetoric of Tolerance*. University Park: Penn State Press.

Renfrew, C. (1987) *Archaeology and Language: The Puzzle of Indo-European Origins*. London: Pimlico.

Riasanovsky, N. (1972) 'Asia Through Russian Eyes' in Vucinich, W. (ed.) *Russia and Asia*. Stanford: Hoover Institution Press.

Ricoeur, P. (2004) *Memory, History, Forgetting*. Chicago: University of Chicago Press.

Riley, D. (2010) *The Civic Foundations of Fascism in Europe: Italy, Spain and Romania, 1870–1945*. Baltimore: Johns Hopkins University Press.

Ringer, F. (1990) *The Decline of the German Mandarins: The German Academic Community, 1890–1933*. Middletown, CT: Wesleyan University Press.

Risse, T. (2010) *A Community of European? Transnational Identities and Public Spheres*. Ithaca, NY: Cornell University Press.

Robertson, R. (1992) *Globalization: Social Theory and Global Culture*. London: Sage.

Robertson, R. and Krossa, S. (eds) (2012) *European Cosmopolitanism in Question*. London: Palgrave.

Robinson, C. (2011) 'The First Islamic Empire' in Arnason, J. and Raaflaub, K. (eds) *The Roman Empire in Context: Historical and Comparative Perspectives*. Oxford: Blackwell.

Roche, M. (2000) *Mega-Events and Modernity: Olympics and Expos in the Growth of Global Culture*. London: Routledge.

Roche, M. (2010) *Exploring the Sociology of Europe*. London: Sage.

Roseman, M. (2011) 'National Socialism and the End of Modernity' *The American Historical Review* 116(3): 688–701.

Roudemetof, V. (2005) 'Transnationalism, Cosmopolitanism and Glocalization' *Current Sociology* 53(1): 113–15.

Rumford, C. (ed.) (2007) *Europe and Cosmopolitanism*. Liverpool: Liverpool University Press.

Rumford, C. (2008) *Cosmopolitan Spaces: Europe, Globalization, Theory*. London: Routledge.

Said, E. (1979) *Orientalism*. New York: Vintage.

Said, E. (1994) *Culture and Imperialism*. New York: Vintage.

Sakwa, R. (2006) 'Russia as Eurasia: An Innate Cosmopolitanism' in Delanty, G. (ed.) *Europe and Asia Beyond East and West*. London: Routledge.

Sarkisyanz, E. (1954) 'Russian Attitudes toward Asia' *Russian Review* 13: 245–54.

Sassatelli, M. (2009) *Becoming Europeans: Cultural Identity and Cultural Politics*. London: Palgrave.

Sassen, S. (2008) *Territory, Authority, Rights: From Medieval to Global Assemblages*. Princeton, NJ: Princeton University Press.

Sassen, S. (2009) 'The Limits of Power and the Complexity of Powerlessness' in Delanty, G. and Turner, S. (eds) *Routledge International Handbook of Social and Political Theory*. London: Routledge.

Sasson, D. (2006) *The Culture of the Europeans: From 1800 to the Present*. New York: HarperPress.

Sayyid, S. (2003) *A Fundamental Fear: Eurocentrism and the Emergence of Islamism*. London: Zed Books.

Scharpf, F. (1999) *Governing in Europe: Effective and Democratic*. Oxford: Oxford University Press.

Schlereth, T. (1977) *The Cosmopolitan Ideal in Enlightenment Thought*. South Bend: The University of Notre Dame Press.

Schmidt, H. D. (1966) 'The Establishment of "Europe" as a Political Expression' *Historical Journal* 9: 172–8.

Schmitt, C. (2006) *The Nomos of the Earth in the International Law of the Jus Publicum Europaeum*. New York: Telos Press.

Schrag, C. (2013) *The Struggle for EU Legitimacy: Public Contestation, 1950–2005*. London: Palgrave.

Schulen, E. (1985) 'European Expansion in Early Modern Times: Changing Views on Colonial History' *History of European Ideas* 6(3): 253–65.

Schwab, R. (1984[1950]) *The Oriental Renaissance: Europe's Rediscovery of India and the East, 1680–1880*. New York: Columbia University Press.

Sewell, W. (2005) *Logics of History: Social Theory and Social Transformation*. Chicago: Chicago University Press.

Shore, C. (2000) *Building Europe: The Cultural Politics of European Integration*. London: Routledge.

Southern, R. W. (1962) *Western Views on Islam in the Middle Ages*. Cambridge, MA: Harvard University Press.

Springborn, P. (1992) *Western Republicanism and the Oriental Prince*. Austin: University of Texas Press.

Stoeckl, K. (2011) 'European Integration Theory and Russian Orthodoxy: Two Multiple Modernities Perspectives' *European Journal of Social Theory* 14(2): 217–33.

Stoeckl, R. (2010) 'Modern Trajectories in Eastern European Orthodoxy' in Arnason, J. and Doyle, N. (eds) *Domains and Divisions of European History*. Liverpool: University of Liverpool Press.

Stråth, B. (ed.) (2000) *Europe and the Other and Europe as the Other*. Brussels: Peter Lang.

Stråth, B. (2002) 'A European Identity: To the Historical Limits of the Concept' *European Journal of Social Theory* 5(4): 387–401.

Streeck, W. (2011) 'The Crisis of Democratic Capitalism' *New Left Review* 71(Sept/Oct): 5–25.

Streeck, W. (2012) 'How to Study Capitalism' *European Journal of Sociology* 53(1): 1–28.

Strydom, P. (1987) 'Collective Learning: Habermas's Concessions and Their Theoretical Implications' *Philosophy and Social Criticism* 13(3): 265–81.

Strydom, P. (1993) 'Sociocultural Evolution or the Social Evolution of Practical Reason? Eder's Critique of Habermas' *Praxis International* 13(3): 304–22.

Strydom, P. (2000) *Discourse and Knowledge: The Making of Enlightenment Sociology*. Liverpool: Liverpool University Press.

Strydom, P. (2011a) *The Methodology of Contemporary Critical Theory*. London: Routledge.

Strydom, P. (2011b) 'The Cognitive and MetaCognitive Dimensions of Contemporary Social and Political Theory' in Delanty, G. and Turner, S. (eds) *International Handbook of Contemporary Social and Political Theory*. London: Routledge.

Strydom, P. (2012) 'Modernity and Cosmopolitanism: From a Critical Social Theory Perspective' in Delanty, G. (ed.) *Handbook of Cosmopolitanism Studies*. London: Routledge.

Subrahmanyam, S. (2011) *Three Ways to be Alien: Travails and Encounters in the Early Modern World*. Waltham, MA: Brandeis University Press.

Supiot, A. (2012) 'Under Eastern Eyes' *New Left Review* 73(Jan/Feb): 29–36.

Szamuely, T. (1988) *The Russian Tradition*. London: Fontana.

Szporluk, R. (1991) 'The Soviet West – or Far Eastern Europe?' *East European Politics & Societies* 5(3): 466–82.

Szücs, J. (1988) 'Three Historical Regions of Europe' in Keane, J. (ed.) *Civil Society and the State*. London: Verso.

Tanner, M. (1993) *The Last Descendants Aeneas: The Hapsburgs and the Mythic Image of the Emperor*. New Haven: Yale University Press.

Taras, R. (2009) *Europe Old and New: Transnationalism, Belonging, Xenophobia*. Lanham, MD: Rowman & Littlefield.

Taylor, A. J. P. (1942) *The Habsburg Empire 1815–1918*. London: Hamish Hamilton.

Taylor, A. J. P. (1988) *The Course of German History*. London: Routledge.

Taylor, C. (1989) *Sources of the Self: The Making of Modern Identity*. Cambridge, MA: Harvard University Press.

Taylor, C. (2004) *Modern Social Imaginaries*. Durham, NC: Duke University Press.

Taylor, C. (2007) *A Secular Age*. Cambridge, MA: Harvard University Press.

Taylor, P. (1999) *Modernities: A Geopolitical Interpretation*. Cambridge: Polity Press.

Thaden, E. C. (1984) *Russia's Western Borderlands, 1710–1870*. Princeton: Princeton University Press.

Therborn, G. (1995) *European Modernity and Beyond: The Trajectory of European Societies* 1945–2000. London: Sage.

Therborn, G. (2002) 'The World's Trader, the World's Lawyer: Europe and Global Processes' *European Journal of Social Theory* 5(4): 403–17.

Therborn, G. (2003) 'Entangled Modernities' *European Journal of Social Theory* 6(3): 293–305.

Thompson, E. P. (1982) *Exterminism and the Cold War*. London: New Left Review.

Tilly, C. (1984) *Big Structures, Large Processes, Huge Comparisons*. New York: Russell Sage Foundation.

Tilly, C. (1990) *Coercion, Capital, and European States, AD 990–1990*. Oxford: Blackwell.

Tilly, C. (1993) *European Revolutions 1892–1992*. Oxford: Blackwell.

Todorova, M. (1997) *Imagining the Balkans*. Oxford: Oxford University Press.

Tolz, V. (2001) *Russia: Inventing the Nation*. London: Arnold.

Torpey, J. (1999) *The Invention of the Passport: Surveillance, Citizenship and the State*. Cambridge: Cambridge University Press.

Toulmin, S. (1990) *Cosmopolis: The Hidden Agenda of Modernity*. Chicago: University of Chicago Press.

Touraine, A. (1977) *The Self-Production of Society*. Chicago: University of Chicago Press.

Touraine, A. (1995) *Critique of Modernity*. Oxford: Blackwell.

Toynbee, A. (1934–63) *A Study in History*, 12 vols. Oxford: Oxford University Press.

Tracy, J. (ed.) (1993) *The Rise of Merchant Empires: Long Distance Trade in the Early Modern World 1350–1750*. Cambridge: Cambridge University Press.

Trenz, H. J. and Eder, K. (2004) 'The Democratizing Dynamics of a European Public Sphere: Towards a Theory of Democratic Functionalism' *European Journal of Social Theory* 7(1): 5–25.

Troebst, S. (2003) '"Intermarium" and "Wedding to the Sea": Politics of History and Mental Mapping of East Central Europe' *European Review of History* 10(2): 293–21.

Ullmann, W. (1969) *The Carolingian Renaissance and the Idea of Kingship*. London: Methuen.

Van Gelderen, M. and Skinner, Q. (eds) (2002) *Republicanism: A Shared European Heritage*. Vols 1 and 2. Cambridge: Cambridge University Press.

Vidmar-Horvat, K. and Delanty, G. (2005) 'Mitteleuropa and the European Heritage' *European Journal of Social Theory* 11(2): 203–18.

von Humboldt, A. (2011[1856]) *Political Essay on the Island of Cuba*. Chicago: University of Chicago Press.

Wagner, P. (1994) *A Sociology of Modernity: Liberty and Discipline*. London: Routledge.

Wagner, P. (2004) *Theorizing Modernity*. London: Sage.

Wagner, P. (2009) *Modernity as Experience and Interpretation: A New Sociology of Modernity*. Cambridge: Polity Press.

Wagner, P. (2011) 'From Interpretation to Civilization – and Back: Analyzing the Trajectories of Non-European Modernities' *European Journal of Social Theory* 14(1): 89–106.

Wagner, P. (2012) *Modernity: Understanding the Present*. Cambridge: Polity Press.

Wallerstein, I. (1974) *The Modern World System, Vol. 1: Capitalist Agriculture and the Origins of the European World Economy in the Sixteenth Century*. New York: Academic Press.

Walls, D. L. (2009) *The Passage to Cosmos: Alexander von Humboldt and the Shaping of America*. Chicago: University of Chicago Press.

Watkins, S. C. (1991) *From Provinces into Nations: Demographic Integration in Western Europe*. Princeton: Princeton University Press.

Webb, W. P. (1952) *The Great Frontier*. Boston: Houghton Mifflin.

Weber, E. (1971) *A Modern History of Europe: Men, Cultures, and Societies from the Renaissance to the Present*. New York: Norton.

Weber, E. (1976) *From Peasants into Frenchmen: The Modernization of Rural France, 1870–1914*. Stanford: Stanford University Press.

Weber, M. (1952) *Ancient Judaism*. New York: The Free Press.

Weber, M. (1978) *The Protestant Ethic and the Spirit of Capitalism*. London: Allen & Unwin.

Weingrow, D. (2010) *What Makes Civilization? The Ancient Near East and the Future of Civilization*. Oxford: Oxford University Press.

Whittaker, C. R. (1994) *Frontiers of the Roman Empire: A Social and Economic Study*. Baltimore: Johns Hopkins University Press.

Wieczynski, J. L. (1976) *The Russian Frontier: The Impact of Borderlands upon the Course of Early Russian History*. Charlottesville: University Press of Virginia.

Wiener, A. and Diez, T. (eds) (2004) *European Integration Theory*. Oxford: Oxford University Press.

Wilde, P. and Trenz, H.-J. (2013) 'Denouncing European Integration: Eurosceptism as Polity Contestation' *European Journal of Social Theory* 15(4): 537–54.

Wimmer, A. (2002) *Nationalism Exclusion and Ethnic Conflict*. Cambridge: Cambridge University Press.

Wittfogel, K. A. (1957) *Oriental Despotism*. New Haven: Yale University Press.

Wittram, R. (1973) *Russia and Europe*. London: Thames and Hudson.

Wolf, E. (1982/1997) *Europe and the People Without History*. Berkeley: University of California Press.

Wolff, L. (1994) *Inventing Eastern Europe: The Map of Civilization of the Mind of the Enlightenment*. Stanford: Stanford University Press.

Woodward, K. (ed.) (1997) *Identity and Difference*. London: Sage.

Yapp, M. E. (1992) 'Europe in the Turkish Mirror' *Past and Present* 137: 134–55.

Yates, F. (1975) *Astrae: The Imperial Theme in the Sixteenth Century*. London: Routledge.

Zielonka, J. (2006) *Europe as Empire: The Nature of the Enlarged European Union*. Oxford: Oxford University Press.

Zimmermann, A. and Favell, A. (2011) 'Governmentality, Political Field or Public Sphere? Theoretical Alternatives in the Political Sociology of Europe' *European Journal of Social Theory* 14(4): 489–515.

Index

Afghanistan, 190
Africa, 5, 25, 54, 62, 101, 104, 188,
    189, 191
Albania, 106, 173, 202, 221, 209
Algeria, 189, 191, 193, 202, 222, 237
Antiquity (Greek and Roman), 50
Asia, 33, 34, 53, 90, 91, 126

Balibar, E., 186, 245
Balkans, 92, 106, 209
Bartlett, R., 71, 72, 73, 140, 312
Blake, W., 155
Brazil, 33, 125, 135, 136, 245
Britain, 102, 146, 188, 189, 192, 193,
    222, 223, 227, 230, 232, 237, 238,
    240
    Churchill, W., 227
    Great Fire of London (1666), 169
Buddhism, 26, 50
Burckhardt, J., 114, 118
Byzantine, 83

Capitalism
capitalism, conflict with democracy,
    274
    capitalism, era of organized, 225
    Capitalism, transition to, 213
    free market, 143, 240, 241
Caribbean, the, 135
Celts, the, 47, 53, 58, 143
Chakrabarty, D., 7, 315
China, 33, 38, 90, 91, 100, 126, 165,
    190, 228, 245
Christianity, 67
    New Testament, 68
    Old Testament, 64
    Orthodox Church, 78, 81, 92, 94, 95
    Orthodox Greek, 90 see also Greece
    secularization, 79
    theology, 75, 124
civilization, 23
    anti-essentialist, notion of, 36 see
        also essentialism

Axial Age, 38
    crisis of, 218
    civilizational constellation, 40
    'civilizational process' see Elias, N.
    Greek civilization, 51–56, 58 see
        also Greece
    Hellenic civilization, 51–52
    inter-Civilizational, 33
    inter-civilizational constellation
        29–31, 41
    Jewish civilization, 51–54, 63
    Muslim civilization, 103 see also
        Islam
    Roman civilization, 46–51, 58
colonialism, 5, 36, 72–73, 123,
    188–190, 192, 222, 241, 288, 290,
    295, 298
    Colonialism, transition from, 305
    Haiti revolution, 194
communism, 66, 81, 94, 205, 225,
    230, 260, 280, 367
Confucianism, 38
constitutionalization, 245, 251, 254,
    262
constructionism, 8 see also
    constructivist approaches
cosmopolitanism, 26–27, 181–182,
    258, 269, 270, 271, 298, 299
    Critical cosmopolitanism 256–259,
        268
    Cosmopolitan heritage, 286–288,
        298 see also Heritage
    Cosmopolitanism and
        nationalism, 170, 262
    Cosmopolitanism, political
        community, 167–170, 179
    Cosmopolitanism, possibility of,
        14–16, 26
Crimea, the, 211
Crisis
    crisis, political, 271–272, 283
    Europe, 'crisis of', 302 see also
        Europe

Culture
cultural commonality, 288
cultural gradient, 95
cultural model of Europe, 144–145,
156
cultural model of modernity,
149–153, 161 *see also*
Modernity
cultural model of society, 291

Davies, N., 1, 97, 292, 315
democracy
democracy, Western liberal,
209–213, 221
democratization, 74, 116, 173,
180, 186, 187, 199, 200,
213, 219, 224, 250, 253,
267, 283
Denmark, 81, 173, 188, 240
Derrida, J., 290, 316
Descartes, R., 117, 119
dissent, 12, 16, 77, 78, 123, 145, 146,
229
Durkheim, E., 184, 185, 220, 316

East and West
binary, 98
collapse of distinction, 248
cultural encounters, 111–117, 118
see also Culture
Economy
Asian world economy, 146
economic crisis, 261
economic crisis since 2008, 272
economics, Keynesian, 212–213,
224
Egypt, 52, 61, 64, 158, 189, 202, 222,
223, 237, 312
Eisenstadt, S., 14, 15, 20, 21, 23, 38,
39, 63, 73, 161, 308, 309, 310,
317
Elias, N., 141, 317
Empire 176–181, 188
Byzantine Empire, 62, 73, 83–86,
89, 95, 202
Empire, German, 70, 139
Empire, Ottoman, 61, 84, 87, 88,
90, 93, 100, 106, 107, 108,
127

Empire, Roman, 58, 59, 60, 61
decline of, 62, 68–9
emergence of Europe, 201
expansion of, 121–125, 133
Enlightenment, 46, 48, 80, 104, 147,
149–153, 167, 218
post-Enlightenment, 154
romantics, the 141–144
European Union (EU), 2, 5, 4, 9, 107,
139, 202, 250, 266, 288
EU and nations, relationship,
239–246, 251
Europe
Black Death, the, 144, 320
cultural model of, 25, 28, 113,
156, 160 *see also* Culture
constructivist approaches, 303
Early Modern unity and divisions,
119–121, 130
Europe, idea of, 214
Europe and Islam, relationship, 99
Europe, federal 239
Europe, 'Oceanic' and
'Continental', 136
Europe, political construct, 158
Europe, post-Western, 234–237, 246
Europe, reunification of, 248
Internal accounts versus external
accounts, 3–4, 15
internal homogenization, 133
politics of fear, 306
transformation, 187
transnationalization, 236, 238, 249,
255, 267 *see also* nation-state
Eurasia, 34, 42, 88, 91, 129
Euro, the, 108, 202, 238, 253, 264,
277, 279, 280, 281, 311
Eurocentric, 4, 5, 7, 15, 26, 87, 288
Eurocentrism, 5, 6, 10, 36, 152,
267, 311
European citizenship, 285
European consciousness, 33, 65, 84,
102, 127, 131, 148, 192, 207, 301
European cosmopolitanism, prospects
for 254–256, 266 *see also*
cosmopolitanism
European Economic Community
(EEC), 199, 222–223, 238,
239–240, 276

European heritage, 290
European identity, 263
European imperialism *see* Empire
European integration, 235, 238, 252,
    254, 267, 273, 276–277, 279, 281,
    282, 286, 288, 302, 306
European integration,
    assumptions of, 282
European integration, negative
    integration, 279
European integration, realist and
    neo-functionalist schools, 239
European integration, social and
    system 266–271, 278
European integration,
    transnational dimension, 306
Maastricht Treaty, 239, 279
European Islam, 93–97, 105 *see also*
    Islam
European model of statehood, 194
European race, 46, 191, 192
European society, development of, 184
Europeanization, 3, 242, 250, 252,
    256–258, 265
Euroscepticism, 251
Eurozone, 278, 281
democracy, influence of, 129

Fascism, 230
authoritarian populist, 231
Foucault, 8, 9, 12, 25, 77, 119, 291
freedom, age of, 170
French Revolution, 80, 146, 150,
    154, 158, 168, 172, 175

Gellner, E., 172 *see also* Nationalism
Germany, 154, 159, 173, 215, 228 *see*
    also Hitler, Second World War
Holocaust, the, 222, 285, 289 *see*
    also Fascism, War
Nazism, 156, 219, 230, 231
Unification (1981), 245
globality, 27, 28, 124, 149, 154–156,
    166, 167, 168, 179, 298
globalization, 27, 40, 41, 129, 168,
    179, 242, 249, 250, 257, 270, 281,
    286, 298, 299, 306
Goody, J., 38, 52, 104, 108, 109, 113,
    319

Grand Narrative(s), 4, 5, 10, 39, 83,
    113, 130, 131, 166, 218
Greece, 54, 81, 87, 201, 209, 225,
    273, 282

Habermas, J., 11, 18, 19, 26, 48, 80,
    162, 163, 253, 266, 267, 269, 273,
    277, 279, 290, 291, 294, 298, 308,
    321, 309, 310, 319
Halecki, O., 54, 196, 205, 213 *see also*
    homogenization and plurality
Hay, D., 54, 99, 147
Hegel, 19, 35, 155, 159, 314
Heritage *see* memory
Heritage as a shared political
    tradition, 281–283, 393
Heritage as a unity in diversity,
    283–284, 295
Heritage as trauma, 284–286, 296
Hinduism, 38
Hippocrates, 54
Hitler, A., 219–220, 221 *see also* Fascism
Hobsbawm, E. J., 1, 17, 44, 174, 215,
    222, 232
Holocaust *see* Germany
Judaism, 51, 52, 56 *see also* Fascism,
    War
homogenization, 12, 51, 62, 72,
    132–134, 139, 140, 141–144, 175,
    176, 179, 222
Hong Kong, 189
Humanism, 14, 20, 76, 113, 115, 117,
    146
Humboldt, 6, 26, 34, 91, 153, 298
Hungary, 203, 205–208, 216, 229
hybridity, 10, 307

Ideology
'end of ideology', 242
ideological bond, 177 *see also*
    Nationalism
interactionism
relational, 10
Introduction into Central and Eastern
    Europe (sub of State Socialism),
    228
Iraq, 99, 223 *see also* war
Ireland, 81, 140, 188
Battle of the Boyne, 159

Islam, 88–109, 114, 131, 209, 247
  Koran, the, 101
  Muhammad, 99, 101
Italy, 122, 150, 200, 278, 280
  Mussolini, B., 230–233, 319 *see
    also* Fascism

Judaism, 38, 52, 63, 64, 67, 68, 98,
    103, 108, 310, 314
Judt, T., 1, 2, 3, 215, 237, 292, 293

Kant, E., 26, 80, 122, 150, 151, 152,
    153, 160, 169, 180

Le Goff, J., 23, 71
Lichtheim, G., 3
Lyotard, J. F., 292 *see also* Grand
  Narratives

Machiavelli, N., 101, 120, 121
Malta, 103, 107, 202
Marshall, T. H., 15, 164, 224, 225, 275
Marx, K. 82, 169, 174, 209, 215 *see
    also* Communism
Mauss, M., 35, 118
memory, 43
Middle Ages, the, 7, 37, 71, 103, 114,
    141
Modernity
  crisis of, 205–209, 217
  homogenizing logic, of, 182
  modernity and the holocaust, 234
    see also Fascism
  political modernity, 19, 71, 115,
    122, 146, 170, 180, 229, 274
  post-modernism, 15, 163, 241, 287,
    308
  routes to, 185–202
    Central Europe, 191–193, 203
    East Central Europe, 193–197, 205
    Mediterranean Europe, 189–191,
      201
    North Eastern Europe 199–201,
      211
    North Western Europe 186–188,
      198
    South Eastern Europe, 197–199,
      209
  societal model, 153–154, 165

Mongol, 89, 90, 105, 134
Montaigne, M., 117
Morris, C., 75–77
myth, 10, 56, 64, 89, 92, 102, 122,
    124, 191, 237

Napoleon, B., 70, 80, 93, 151, 158,
    159, 227
narratives, 5, 292, 280–281
nation-state
  national imaginary, 255
  national minority, 163 *see also*
    minorities, racism
  post-national identity, 289
nationalism
  extreme nationalist movements,
    259
  liberal nationalism, 173
  nationalism and cosmopolitanism,
    262
  nationalism post-1989, 246–251,
    258
  nationalism, imperial 222 *see also*
    Western Liberal
  nationalism, revival of, 245
  nationalism, rise of 159–166, 171
  populist nationalist parties, 259
  post-national, 11, 242, 245, 250,
    254, 255, 258, 262, 264, 266,
    267, 271, 287, 388, 289, 291,
    298, 305
nationhood, 74, 82, 124, 125,
    174–176, 200, 235
  nationhood, models of, 79
Nelson, B., 38, 40
neoliberalism, 224, 245, 280
Netherlands, 81, 185, 261
New World, 119, 134, 136, 137, 141,
    311 *Compare* Old World
Nietzsche, F., 218, 219, 310
Norway, 81, 173, 188, 211, 240, 251

Occident, the, 16, 55, 62, 67, 104
Offe, C., 166, 245, 275, 279
Old World, 133, 136 *Compare* New
  World
Orthodox, 13, 28, 42, 59, 78–79, 81,
    83, 86–90, 92, 94–95, 106, 209,
    314 *see also* Orthodox Church

Other, 4, 6, 14, 23, 25, 27, 37, 46, 48, 76, 95, 98, 99–101, 104, 123, 131, 141, 152, 155, 157, 167, 175, 184, 205, 211, 219, 230, 240, 247, 248, 316

paganism, 14, 50, 59, 69, 74
Parsons, T., 185
Patocka, J., 57, 118
Persia, 51, 54, 55, 98, 99, 102, 104, 152, 190
Plato, 57, 76, 118, 119, 120, 219
Poland, 92–94, 138, 173, 203, 205, 220, 213, 223, 229
Polanyi, K., 200, 275
Portugal, 221, 225
    Lisbon earthquake (1755), 169
post-colonial, 8, 194, 241
Protestant, 5, 13, 73, 74, 79, 87, 92, 116, 147, 159 *see also* Christianity

Race
    racial superiority, 191–192
    see also colonialism
Renaissance, 14, 113–114, 117, 123–125, 127–128, 149 *see also* Enlightenment and the Self
    'dark side', the, 5, 117, 216, 221, 295
    Galileo, G., 116
republicanism, 28, 101, 115, 119, 120–123, 146, 150–151, 171, 173, 181, 182, 294–296
Romania, 83, 88, 138, 173, 208, 209, 210, 212
Russia, 88–90, 92–95, 109, 136, 210, 213, 215, 228, 235
    Moscow, 64, 89
    October Revolution, 43, 131, 226
    Russia, hybrid civilization, 95
    Russian Revolution, 216, 218, 225
        see also communism
    Soviet occupation, 208
    Soviet Union, 83, 184, 200–201, 212 *see also* plural forms of Modernity
    State socialism, 225, 226, 228
    St Petersburg 'window to Europe', 90, 92, 94

Said, E., 5–7, 101, 102, 188, 191
Schmitt, C., 57, 74, 219, 232
secularization *see* Enlightnment
Self
    modern self, emergence of *see also* Renaissance
    national Self, 175
    self-determination, 121, 145, 146, 151, 163, 165, 171–173, 181
    self-examination, 76 *see also* Christianity
    self-image, 25 *see under* Europe
    self-problematization, 289
slavery, 48, 72, 136–137, 153, 192–194
Slavic, 42, 47, 91, 95, 96 108, 206, 207, 210, 249
social movements, 8, 18, 48, 133, 142, 294
Spain, 103, 118, 128, 134, 189, 233, 278
    Franco, F., 69, 193, 200, 215, 225, 230–235
    War of the Spanish Succession, 147
subjectivity, 103, 182, 208 *see also* Self
Szücs, J., 126, 138, 145, 196, 205, 206

Taylorism, 224
Tocqueville, A., 93, 160, 191, 232
Touraine, A., 278, 279 *see also* Culture
Turkey, 42, 98, 106–108, 165, 190, 202, 210, 237

Ukraine, the, 33, 84, 91, 210, 212, 213
United Nations, 236, 272, 285
United States of America (USA), the, 93, 136, 152, 159, 165, 167, 173, 188, 218, 223, 227, 238, 247, 248
unity, 10
    geopolitical unity, 145
utopian thought, 120

Versailles Treaty (1919), 227, 231

Wagner, P., 6, 7, 150, 153, 211, 280
    see also modernity

war, 147, 178, 185, 202, 215, 229, 234, 234–237
   civil war, 193, 202, 230
   Cold War, the, 34, 200, 212, 215, 216, 228, 229, 236, 242, 247, 276 *see also* East and West
   First World War, 217, 221–222, 233

Herero War, 189
   Second World War, 44, 131, 184, 215, 223, 227, 249, 259, 273, 276, 285, 299, 304
Weber, M., 2, 3, 23, 107
Westphalia, 13, 78
   post-Westphalian state system, 180

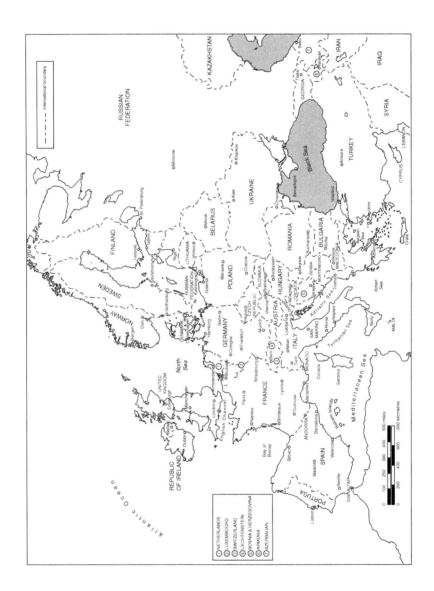

Lightning Source UK Ltd.